In Quest of a Vital Protestant Center

In Quest of a Vital Protestant Center

An Ecumenical Evangelical Perspective

GEORGE DEMETRION

Foreword by
WILLIS E. ELLIOTT

WIPF & STOCK · Eugene, Oregon

IN QUEST OF A VITAL PROTESTANT CENTER
An Ecumenical Evangelical Perspective

Copyright © 2014 George Demetrion. All rights reserved. Except for brief quotations in critical publications or reviews, no part of this book may be reproduced in any manner without prior written permission from the publisher. Write: Permissions. Wipf and Stock Publishers, 199 W. 8th Ave., Suite 3, Eugene, OR 97401.

All Scripture quotations, unless otherwise indicated, are taken from the New International Version, NIV Study Bible (fully revised). Copyright, 1985, 1995, 2002. Zondervan.

Wipf and Stock
An Imprint of Wipf and Stock Publishers
199 W. 8th Ave., Suite 3
Eugene, OR 97401

www.wipfandstock.com

ISBN 13: 978-1-62564-048-2

Manufactured in the U.S.A.   10/16/2014

I dedicate this book to you, Sue, my most precious wife, for your love and support in our shared life of these past thirty-five years. I'm grateful for our many quiet evenings, the friends we have made together, especially through our Sunday evening study group, and the life we share with those are closest to us, Audrey and Cyndy, Jennifer and Amy, and of course, the boys, Cameron and Chase. I'm grateful that you are my soul mate as we journey together in life. I'm grateful for our daily reading of Scripture, devotional books, and studies on Christian thought and life through such authors as Charles Stanley, Chuck Swindoll, and Dallas Willard, which have mutually enriched our life of faith in the daily living of our lives. I appreciate the time you gave me to write this book, even as it took up time that I would have rather shared with you. I am grateful for what we been graced to have together. I cannot imagine life without you.

In memory of Dr. Willis E. Elliott, 1918–2014

Contents

Foreword by Willis E. Elliott | ix
Acknowledgments | xi
List of Abbreviations | xiii

1   In Search of a Vital Protestant Center | 1
2   Theological, Historical, and Autobiographical Explorations of Twentieth-Century Protestant Thought and Culture | 18
3   Defending the Fundamentals of Historical Evangelicalism: J. I. Packer and the Written Word of God | 54
4   The Mediating Theology of Donald Bloesch: Catholic, Reformed, Evangelical | 81
5   Restoring the Center: Gabriel Fackre's Evangelical Ecumenism | 115
6   Reading Walter Brueggemann through a Fluidly Canonical Lens: Texts That Linger in a Fragile World | 167
7   Re-Envisioning the Neo-Orthodox Legacy | 219
8   Postliberal Dialectical and Evangelical Narrative Theology in Critical Juxtaposition | 268

Bibliography | 293
Author Index | 305
Subject Index | 308

Foreword

An unfamiliar book has only three minutes to continue holding my interest. A minute to tell me who wrote it. A minute to tell me why. And a minute to tell me why it should interest me.

Who wrote this book? George Demetrion, who studied US history at the PhD level at the University of Connecticut from 1979–1983, after which he entered the field of adult education, where he still works some thirty years later as an adjunct instructor in adult education and program coordinator in support of homeless adults in San Diego, California. With no formal academic training in the field of adult education, Demetrion launched and managed adult literacy programs in the Hartford, Connecticut, area, published a dozen academic articles, and in 2005, completed a major monograph of wide scope titled, *Conflicting Paradigms in Adult Literacy Education: In Quest of a U.S. Democratic Politics of Literacy.*

While at the height of his academic career in adult education, in 2006, Demetrion shifted gears to follow his true vocation as a self-educated Christian scholar. I initially met George online as a prolific participant on the United Church of Christ–based Confessing Christ listserv where I first encountered the depth and scope of his theological insights. The day I met him at a Craigville Theological Colloquy on Cape Cod, he handed me the earliest chapters of the project, which has now come to fruition as this book.

Why did he write it? After he became a Christian forty-two years ago, at age twenty-four, his brilliant mind began to absorb the work of dozens of Christian theologians with the intention of asking their help, as though in a round-table, on what he came to consider the most urgent questions the gospel is asking of the present and the future. That searching continues to this day and has given shape to the underlying architecture of his book in which his personal odyssey of faith and his formal theological probing are indelibly linked.

Why should it interest you? Your time, our time, is history's most questioning time—old answers being more questioned, new questions being asked. Key issues in George's book center on the ever complex relationship between Christ and culture in contemporary Protestant religious culture, the role of Scripture, and the enduring legacy of the great divide between fundamentalism and modernism in the theology and religious culture of contemporary US Protestantism. His probing insights into these pivotal themes are unique, fresh, liberating, hopeful. If you are alive to these and related concerns, the forty-two-year-long theological pilgrimage of Demetrion, which is encapsulated in this book, should interest you. In these seventy-five years since my ordination, I have never met another so competent self-trained lay theologian. Wherever you stand, particularly on the evangelical/mainline axis within contemporary Protestant thought and culture, George's study just might help you, on your pilgrimage, to hear the Voice that says, "Behold! I make all things new."

Willis E. Elliott, ThD, PhD
Former Dean of Exploratory Programs
New York Theological Seminary

Acknowledgments

This book is the result of the contribution of many. I extend my foremost thanks to Gabriel Fackre, Samuel Abbot Professor of Christian Theology, Emeritus, at Andover Newton Theological School, whose centrist Protestant vision sparked this book and whose encouragement and guidance, especially in the first few years of the development of this project, provided the essential support and direction I needed to persevere in the hard work of writing the early drafts. Gabe, looking back at the convoluted prose of that initial effort, I marvel even more at your willingness to work through those many pages in providing the constructive support that gave me the fortitude to persist. You have been a mentor and a friend, whom I cherish very much.

I owe a great debt of gratitude as well to the participants of the United Church of Christ–based Confessing Christ discussion list, where I was able to explore, with esteemed colleagues, many of the core issues on theology, biblical interpretation, and contemporary Protestant culture that I have incorporated in this book. In addition to Gabe, Willis Elliott and Herb Davis have read and commented on, with much discernment, various chapters of this book in its the several draft forms. The participants of the Confessing Christ discussion list have provided a source of continuous insight on the significant issues of faith in our time, including much perceptiveness on the relationship between Protestant mainline and evangelical theology and the central role of Karl Barth as a mediating figure. I extend my thanks, also, to two additional discussion list participants, Chris Anderson, who has generously reviewed and commented on the almost complete version of this book, and Scott Paeth, who encouraged me to contact Wipf & Stock at a point in time when I came close to abandoning the project. All of these, and other contributors to the Confessing Christ discussion listserv, made important contributions to the development of this book.

I thank John Lillis for bringing to my attention the prospect of auditing courses at Bethel Seminary in San Diego, where he served as dean for thirteen years and is currently serving as vice president of academic affairs at Grace College and Seminary in Indiana. The several courses that I have audited at the seminary have considerably expanded my understanding of the complexity and range of evangelical theology and biblical theology and biblical studies, which I have sought to incorporate into this book. John also referred me to Phil Corr, who brought to my attention various problems in my prose that masked gaps in content mastery that I needed to address. Phil's close reading of each of the eight chapters provided the insight I needed to substantially revise the book. It is not an exaggeration to say that, without the critical editing that Phil provided in 2013, this book would not have been published. I am also appreciative of the review of chapter 3 on J. I. Packer that Bethel Seminary professor of theology, Glen Scorgie, provided, as well as his review of the first few pages of chapter 1, which, at the time Glen read it, served as the book's preface. I took to heart Glen's important comment to make sure that the centrist thesis that I proposed became infused throughout the book. The result was a re-crafting of the preface into what became the first chapter and a re-writing of portions of all of the chapters, with an eye to Glen's concern.

I'm very grateful, also, for Audrey Lapointe's excellent grammatical editing of the book's final draft. Audrey has saved me from many errors that would otherwise have marred the text. I marvel at her technical grasp of the structure of the English language. Of course, I am responsible for omissions and errors.

My thanks to our weekly Sunday evening study group at Clark and JoEllyn Short's hospitable home. My wife and I are grateful that we belong to this dedicated group, where, over the past two years, we have studied important texts with a sharp focus on Christian spirituality.

I extend my appreciation to the visionaries at Wipf & Stock who have filled an important gap in enabling many significant books to come fruition. Thanks to Christian Amondson, my first editor, for accepting this book and providing supportive guidance and understanding as I needed to extend the projected deadline several time. I also extend thanks to my second editor, Matthew Wimer, for his timely and generous support.

Abbreviations

JETS Journal of Evangelical Theology Society
KJV   King James Version
NRSV New Revised Standard Version

1

In Search of a Vital Protestant Center

A new theological coalition is developing that confesses Jesus Christ and the core biblical framework of salvation history as the norm for the Christian life. Instead of conforming the confession of Christ to American culture or to Enlightenment epistemology, this coalition insists that Jesus Christ is not subject to some higher authority. These theologians confess that Jesus Christ is primary and all other reality needs to be construed in relation to him. What is at issue here is our identity as Christians. To acknowledge Jesus as the Truth in "whom are hidden all the treasures of wisdom and knowledge" (Col 2:3) means that he alone is our norm and judges every other aspect of reality. Either Christ confronts us with his exclusive claim as Lord overall, or he does not confront us at all.[1]

In their concern to keep orthodox doctrine at the heart of the church, harbingers of the new center must orient themselves around the grand consensus of the church throughout the ages and take care that they avoid dogmatizing points of doctrine beyond the consensus. But even in upholding the grand consensus, yet a more overtly expressed generous spirit must reign. This generosity of spirit emerges out of certain theological considerations.[2]

---

1. Phillips and Okholm, *Nature of Confession*, 11.
2. Grenz, *Renewing the Center*, 342.

INTRODUCTION

Throughout the course of the forty-two years since my conversion to Christianity, I have studied many academic and lay-oriented religious texts on a wide assortment of themes. Much of this reading has played out at the critical intersection between a sharply attuned critical evangelical and a more open-ended mainline Protestant identity, largely within various Assemblies of God, American Baptist, United Church of Christ, and United Methodist Church settings. It is within these denominational contexts—in the realm of church affiliation, personal faith formation, small group study, or in my stint as a campus ministry associate as a graduate student in a state college—that I have placed theological exploration and searching biblical discernment at the center of an ongoing faith formation process. This book represents an imaginative integration of this process in search of an invigorating theological center.[3]

3. I have placed some of my reflections on the Connecticut Conference United Church of Christ website, *TheoTalk*. It was on the *TheoTalk* listserv that I met Gabe Fackre almost a decade ago, who encouraged me to participate in the *Confessing Christ* listserv. The *Confessing Christ* website is subtitled "Joyful and Serious Theological Reflection within the United Church of Christ." It includes a statement of principles, blogs, core documents, and a listserv. The Confessing Christ network within the UCC is a call for the denomination to embrace the creedal position of the Reformation tradition. Specifically, "*Confessing Christ* is committed to listen for God's Word in the Holy Scriptures of the Old and New Testaments and in our rich theological heritage. Central to the United Church of Christ, which baptizes in the name of the Father, Son and Holy Spirit, is its faith in Jesus Christ as Lord and Savior. This faith is grounded in the authority of Scripture and is expressed in the ecumenical creeds, in the confessions and covenants of our Reformation traditions, in the Preamble of its Constitution, and in the prayers, worship and public witness of the Church." See "Confessing Christ, Statement of Principles," http://confessingchrist.net. See third bullet. From the outset, Gabe served as a most gracious and generous mentor with whom I share a deep congruence with his centrist "evangelical ecumenical" vision. My Christian journey was rooted in a conversion experience which has remained formative for my understanding of faith even when I overtly rejected the significance of an evangelical identity that characterized my faith walk throughout the 1970s. Over a period of several years in the first half of the last decade, I shifted back from various postmodern, process, and death of God theological perspectives to an overt evangelical sensibility. I did so in a way that enabled me to absorb what I learned about the culture and myself during the 1980s and 1990s while enrolled in a PhD program in US history, in my career in adult education, and my engagement with various "secular" pursuits within the culture and in the realm of the intellectual life. While there remains a sharp edge to my current evangelical identity, I experience greater fluidity in relating to the secular realm than was the case in the 1970s. In Fackre's lexicon, I now view myself as an "ecumenical evangelical," hence, the subtitle of my book. For a summary of my religious journey in Christianity, see the *TheoTalk* archived speech I gave at my church titled, "This Is My Story." For my return to an ecumenical evangelical identity, see my similarly archived essay, "Small Still Shadow Voice of Secular Modernity." For Fackre's discussion of evangelical ecumenical

In Search of a Vital Protestant Center: An Ecumenical Evangelical Perspective probes the relationship between Scripture and culture in US Protestant theology and biblical studies, mostly during the past fifty years. It points to the necessity of turning to what neo-orthodox theologian Karl Barth has referred to as "the strange new world within the Bible"[4] for any revitalization of mainline Protestantism on its own foundational premises in critical dialogue with serious evangelical theology.

The book addresses two consequential issues facing contemporary US Protestantism: acceptance of the Bible in its canonical integration as the primary source of Christian revelation and the viability of creating a durable centrist position between moderate evangelical and moderate mainline theological perspectives. The convergence I seek is based on a common acceptance of the historic Reformation tradition on the sovereignty of God, the incarnation, the Trinity, the atonement, and scriptural revelation.[5] My aim in this book is "the recovery of a centrist position standing thoroughly in the tradition of orthodoxy but not averse to articulating the faith in new ways that relate creatively to the contemporary situation."[6] The challenge of doing so is underlined by the persistence of the modernist/fundamentalist divide on the interpretation and role of the Bible—an issue that came to symbolic climax with the Scopes Trial of 1925. Mediating theologies in both evangelical and mainline camps have moved well beyond the intense polarization unleashed on both sides of this crucial divide. Still, its enduring

---

and ecumenical evangelical perspectives, see Fackre, *Ecumenical Faith in Evangelical Perspective*, iv.

4. Gleghorn, "Karl Barth's Early Hermeneutics." Gleghorn dates the "Strange New World within the Bible" address as February 6, 1917. The theme of the strange new world of the Bible reverberates in Walter Brueggemann's postmodern Old Testament reflections through what he refers to as the third world of evangelical imagination, a distinctively countercultural construction to contemporary secular and traditionally religious worldviews. See Brueggemann, "Third World of Evangelical Imagination." In their various ways all of the primary authors addressed in this book play off of the imagery of the strange new world in its juxtaposition to the contemporary US culture, even J. I. Packer who is least favorable to Barth.

5. Bloesch and others refer to the "Great Tradition," which, in addition to classical Protestant theology, includes the early church reflections from the Catholic and Eastern Orthodox traditions. Packer, Bloesch, and Fackre identify this founding bedrock as the basis for the shaping of a contemporary orthodox faith. With somewhat different nuances, they acknowledge that new light does break out in new historical circumstances in ways that may require responses from the Christian community that could not have been anticipated by the New Testament writers or the early church. Their predominant orthodoxy is reflected on the epistemological priority they grant to Scripture, church tradition, and the historical context, in that order, in the shaping of their theological perspectives.

6. Bloesch, *Theology of Word and Spirit*, 31.

influence persists into the current era as a continuous strain adversely impacting more comprehensive efforts toward the construction of a vital theological center.

This book builds on the current dialogue between evangelical and postliberal theology as depicted in the collection of essays titled *The Nature of Confession*.[7] By incorporating the neo-orthodox perspective, it provides an additional resource in the construction of a centrist theological project that builds on the triple pillars of canonical scriptural integrity, theological acuity, and ecumenical comprehensiveness. The book is written in the spirit of two short books by Andover Newton Professor emeritus, Gabriel Fackre,[8] and is resonant in content with Fackre's more extensive theological work, as discussed in chapter 5.

In constructing my argument on both Bloesch's and Fackre's centrist vision, *In Search of a Vital Protestant Center* provides an in-depth overview of some key theologians and biblical scholars who are broadly ecumenical within the context of their particular spheres of influence. Given their respective impact across the theological landscape of contemporary Protestant thought and culture and the relative dearth of secondary work on the four main writers I focus on—J. I. Packer, Donald Bloesch, Gabriel Fackre,

---

7. See the various essays in Philips and Okholm, *Nature of Confession*. Critically attuned evangelical theologians acknowledge the insights of the liberal academic scholarship on biblical and historical interpretation of the last 150 years, but do not accept its findings as determinate of faith. Alister McGrath expresses such a perspective in "An Evangelical Evaluation of Postliberalism," 23–44. Barthian scholar George Hunsinger presents the postliberal perspective in "What Can Evangelicals and Postliberals Learn from Each Other?," 134–50. Postliberal theology refers to the discursive power of the biblical text to redescribe reality on its own narrative terms in which, in the semiotic logic of its most extreme expression, there is nothing beyond the text, including ontological truth claims about the reality of God or the incarnation of Christ. In this account, the reader engages the biblical world through the revelatory power intrinsic in the text to evoke the imagination in which its narrative resonance becomes sufficiently credible to evoke ultimate commitments to its plot lines. For a nuanced discussion of postliberal discourse, see Volf, "Theology, Meaning, and Power," 45–66, esp. 52–61. Old Testament scholar Walter Brueggemann is the preeminent narrative postliberal theologian who reads the Bible through the lens of a postmodern, dialectical, and moderate liberationist sensibility. Fackre is also a narrative theologian who traverses the space between a critical evangelical and postliberal sensibility. Unlike Brueggemann, he interprets Scripture through a broad canonical lens, in which the trajectory of the entire biblical story is both revelatory and makes unequivocal ontological truth claims on the reality of the God revealed in the Scripture. Fackre maintains that this is the case even as our knowledge (our epistemological competency) remains fragile, finite, and flawed. As discussed in chapters 5 and 6, while Fackre and Brueggemann are narrative theologians and influenced by the postliberal perspective, their biblical and theological interpretations take them in significantly different directions.

8. *Ecumenical Faith in Evangelical Perspective* and *Restoring the Center*.

and Walter Brueggemann—the profiles in themselves help fill an important gap.[9] Placing their work on an evangelical to postliberal mainline continuum provides critical insight for drawing out and working through the prospects and the challenges of establishing a centrist Protestant culture through a comprehensive Protestant sensibility on the centrality of the Bible in its critical role of encountering the culture. In linking evangelical, postliberal, and neo-orthodox theology to a common search for a vital Protestant center, this book is intended to move this effort forward by facilitating fruitful dialogue among divergent schools of Protestant thought both in seminary circles and among theologically discerning clergy and lay practitioners.

CHAPTER OVERVIEW

Chapter 2 provides a historical overview underlying this pivotal challenge, particularly the persisting influence of the great divide between fundamentalism and modernism within Protestant theology and religious culture during the past century. I examine this split during three consequential time periods (1875–1925, 1940–1965, and 1970–present) in order to illustrate something of its enduring impact within the past century's collective consciousness and cultural experience. Chapter 2 includes an autobiographical section based on Lesslie Newbigin's influential book *The Gospel in a Pluralistic Age* as I encountered it in the late 1990s. Newbigin argues that the New Testament offers its own metanarrative truth claim to counteract the reigning ideology of cultural pluralism. His thesis evoked an imaginative chord within my consciousness. It opened up the possibility that I could reengage the evangelical tradition that had formed my adult Christian identity, but had since become distanced. That encounter did not lead to a direct evangelical return. Yet it remained an undercurrent in my awareness throughout the several-year transition that ultimately led to a return to a distinctive evangelical identity. I conclude chapter 2 with a formal discussion of Newbigin's theology. I focus on his rejection of dominant "plausibility structure(s)"

---

9. Important secondary works on Packer include Payne, *Theology of the Christian Life in J. I. Packer's Thought*, McGrath, *J. I. Packer*, and the collection of essays by George, *J. I. Packer and the Evangelical Future*. For Bloesch, the most notable work is the collection of essays edited by Elmer Colyer, *Evangelical Theology in Transition*. Colyer also has an extensive essay on Bloesch titled "Theology of Word and Spirit." For Fackre, see the edited collection by Gibson, *Story Lines*. Timothy Beal and Todd Linafelt have edited a collection of essays on Brueggemann titled *God in the Fray*. Patrick Miller has written substantive introductions to several of Brueggemann's collection of essays. Perdue has a chapter in *Collapse of History* titled "From History to Imagination" that includes a section on Brueggemann, 285–98.

of contemporary Western culture and the case he makes for the "enterprise of trying to understand modern thought in light of the biblical story."[10] I contrast this effort with the theological project of Bishop John Shelby Spong, whose anti-theistic rhetoric draws out the logical assumptions of liberal Protestant theology to its more extreme, but latent, conclusions.[11] I end chapter 2 with the contention that the mainline denominations have two choices. One of them is to continue the trajectory of liberal thought and orthopraxy, with the prospect of moving toward Spong's new Christianity. The other is that of embracing a scholarly informed, ecumenically oriented Christian orthodoxy in which the core precepts of the New Testament revelation becomes the basis for interpreting and engaging the culture. *In Search of a Vital Protestant Center* is premised on the second alternative.

In the next few chapters, I explore four representative twentieth-century Protestant writers that span in range from the influential evangelical theology of J. I. Packer in chapter 3 to the postliberal narrative theology of Old Testament scholar Walter Brueggemann in chapter 6. In their respective impact on evangelical and mainline Protestant thought and practice, Packer and Brueggemann represent the boundaries of the theological circumference that I explore in this book—Packer as a classical evangelical theologian and Brueggemann as a postliberal biblical scholar with strong dialectical sensibilities. During different time periods, these two authors have influenced my faith journey in highly formative ways. Brueggemann's stimulating collection of essays linking pivotal Old Testament scenarios to contemporary political, social, cultural, and religious experience opened a deep chord in my own imagination in the 1990s in a manner that enabled me to reengage with the Bible in a fresh way. My absorption of his work became a catalyst to my ultimate shift from a broad-based liberal theological

---

10. Newbigin, *Gospel in a Pluralistic Age*, 8, 95.

11. Spong, *New Christianity for a New World*. The New Age impetus seems clear in Spong's discussion following his initial critique of theism, which he claims "put a pious face on human fear and made the threat of nonbeing and the trauma of self-consciousness manageable. That has been the major agenda by theistic religious systems throughout human history." Ibid., 51. "If theism dies, is atheism the only alternative? Is it not a possibility worth pursuing that our very self-consciousness might be the means by which our lives could be opened to nontheistic dimensions of our existence, even nontheistic dimensions of God?. . .Could we not begin to envision a transcendence that enters our life but also calls us beyond the limits of our humanity, not toward an external being but toward the Ground of All Being including our own, a transcendence that calls us to a new humanity?" Ibid., 54. "The time has surely come when human beings must begin a new exploration into the divine, must sketch out a vision of the holy that is beyond theism but not beyond the reality for which the word *God* was created to point." Ibid., 55, original italics. (Unless otherwise noted, emphasis throughout is original to the source being quoted.)

perspective toward a centrist evangelical identity—a process that took about a decade. I encountered Packer in 2006 after making this shift. I appreciated the evangelical eloquence of his theological reasoning, his commitment to the Bible, and his theologically grounded spirituality evident within virtually all of his writing. His books played an important role in strengthening my reemerging evangelical identity at the level of orthopraxy and formal theological understanding.

In the two chapters on these authors, I address the autobiographical influence to the extent that it has had direct bearing on my analysis of their theological visions, more so with Brueggemann than with Packer. I focus on each of their interpretations of the Bible and theology of God as discerned from their principal texts. I discuss major themes in their work for readers who would be naturally inclined to read either of these authors. I also seek to make each of the authors accessible to those who, by theological inclination, would not naturally gravitate to one or the other of these writers. I encourage mainline Protestant readers to consider Packer's work in order to attain a better understanding of the depth and range of serious evangelical theology. I also encourage mainline Protestant readers to draw on Packer's biblical insights to inform their own faith journeys, however much they may reject his socio-political conservatism and limited engagement with non-evangelical biblical scholarship and theological analysis.

I address major themes in Brueggemann's biblical theology with the intent of providing an in-depth assessment of his major ideas for mainline Protestants who would likely be drawn toward to his insights. I also seek to open up to evangelical readers the value of Brueggemann's many insights into both the Old Testament and contemporary culture. His perspective is profoundly dialectical with the intent of being faithful to the text and to the context. The persistence by which Brueggemann pursues this aspiration is one of his major strengths.

Greater clarity is warranted on whether it is the biblical text that drives his interpretation of contemporary experience or whether it is the context (including the direction of contemporary liberal and mainline theology and biblical studies) that shapes his biblical perspective. Evangelical readers will point out that Brueggemann's analogizing of Old Testament scenarios to the exigencies of contemporary culture is overstated, even as they might appreciate the "wonderful insights"[12] in his retelling of the many Old Testament stories that infuse his essays. Such readers will challenge Brueggemann on

---

12. Carson, *Gagging of God*, 170. See 169–72 for Carson's overview of Brueggemann's theology. Carson notes that it is not "truth in any enduring sense" that underlies Brueggemann's Old Testament theology, but "a kind of theologically flavored liberationism." Ibid., 171.

his reluctance to embrace the biblical canon as an ultimately unified text, notwithstanding their appreciation of the many insights he provides on concrete biblical passages. Brueggemann's stimulating work on the theology of imagination provides additional resources for discerning evangelicals to draw upon, even as they would press him to more thoroughly connect his biblical theology with the historical Reformation theological tradition.[13] In short, there are important insights in Brueggemann's work on the Old Testament and contemporary culture for evangelical readers to draw on, despite their concern over some of the claims and implications embodied in his theological reflections.

In chapters 4 and 5, I review the theological perspectives of Donald Bloesch and Gabriel Fackre, who, along with Brueggemann, have had a primary association with the United Church of Christ (UCC). Bloesch, who played an instrumental role in the formation of the Biblical Witness Fellowship, represents the most conservative perspective of the three. Fackre (former Abbot Professor of Christian Theology at Andover Newton Theological School) identifies with the theological center. Brueggemann's influence is with the moderate liberal wing of the denomination. All three have been inspired by Barth and the broader neo-orthodox movement. Each has embraced some form of dialectical theology. Bloesch presses hardest on the dogmatist strain in Barth's theology while seeking to engage the contemporary secular culture primarily through a comprehensive Christian critique. With Bloesch, Fackre stresses the importance of foundational Christian truths claims based on the incarnation, atonement, and resurrection of Christ. He takes a more fluid approach than Bloesch in allowing scope for secular influences to draw out themes in Christianity and the Bible that would not otherwise come to the fore. Brueggemann is the most dialectical of the three in stressing the formative impact of culture and history in shaping Jewish and Christian identity. He argues that context shaping is indicative of the biblical narrative itself as well as within contemporary Protestant faith communities.

In chapter 4, I focus on Bloesch's seven-volume *Christian Foundation* series in which he seeks to lay out a comprehensive and consensus building centrist approach based on the major themes of the orthodox Christian tradition: theology, Scripture, Christology, God, the Holy Spirit, the Church, and eschatology. In doing so, he builds on his earlier work in evangelical theology[14] by drawing widely on resources from Catholic, Eastern Orthodox, and Protestant traditions in his latter project. Bloesch is less interested

---

13. Childs, *Biblical Theology of the Old and New Testaments*, 72–73.
14. See Bloesch's *Essentials of Evangelical Theology*.

in facilitating dialogue with the contemporary culture on its own terms than that of illuminating the ways in which theologians have grappled with religious and cultural forces in maintaining an orthodox position through an almost two thousand–year history, including the contemporary period.

Bloesch's interpretation of Scripture is a case in point. With traditional evangelicals, he embraces the entirety of Scripture as revealed by God to the initial writers and to readers across the centuries. He has sought to do this through a mediating theology that is unequivocally orthodox, while shorn of any vestige of biblical literalism or adherence to the doctrine of scriptural inerrancy. He rejects what he views as the rationalistic excesses that buttress these emphases within traditional evangelical theology. In drawing out what he interprets as a more profound grappling of the mystery of revelation illuminated by the Holy Spirit *through* the Bible, he is skeptical of the attention placed on propositional truth statements based on scriptural warrants reflective of certain streams of classical evangelical theology. In this Barthian move, Bloesch is critiqued by theological conservatives for not relying sufficiently on the Bible and by theological liberals for his overly cautious dogmatic adherence to orthodoxy and consequently, of not taking into account the breaking in of new light through a fuller attention to the mediational role of culture.

Bloesch acknowledges the canonical integrity of Scripture, both as witness and as the repository of God's revealing Word to humankind. He recognizes that, without the biblical text, there can be no reasonably accurate understanding of God in Christ and the ways in which people are called to respond through the discerning work of the Holy Spirit. He acknowledges that Scripture is "related to real history," while accepting Barth's depiction of biblical history as saga, which is "not accessible to historical investigation."[15] Bloesch draws on the centrality of paradox, mystery, and analogical language as primary forms through which revelation becomes illuminated within human experience. God's intervention takes place within actual historical experience, but the story revealed is "superhistorical, not simply historical." Stated otherwise, the narrative "has a historical setting but a theological focus,"[16] not necessarily susceptible to empirical investigation. Bloesch also draws on the term "*mythopoetic*" to characterize the more figurative aspects of the Bible rather than on Bultman's term myth, or what traditional evangelicals might describe as history.[17] In his biblical theology,

15. Bloesch, *Holy Scripture*, 256.
16. Ibid.
17. Ibid., 259. Bloesch argues that Christian "faith is based on mythical symbolization of universal truth rather than divine disclosure in real historical events." Ibid., 258. Though this is a position that moves beyond what Packer can embrace—as discussed

Bloesch presents an interpretation of Scripture intended to span a wide theological arc, even as his effort has engendered a good deal of criticism from the theological right and left.

Ecumenical dialogue across the range of the orthodox Protestant tradition is at the core of Fackre's centrist theological vision, a topic discussed in chapter 5. Fackre draws broadly from Reformed and Lutheran as well as Catholic and Eastern Orthodox theological resources in his quest for an ecumenical center. He has also given much attention to the prospects opened up by recent postliberal-evangelical dialogue in contemporary Protestant thought and practice.[18] As he states: "The possibilities are there, right now, for a moment of mutual conversation and consolation: mutual conversations about perils to a classical Christianity, and mutual consolation of comrades in a church struggle for theological integrity."[19] Fackre envisions such dialogue taking place through a dialectic of affirmation and admonition. By affirmation, Fackre means all that can be mutually embraced on the essentials of faith. By admonition he does not imply rejection, but "mutual correction."[20] By this he means "the willingness of each to affirm the *differences* as well as the similarities" in the "charism(s)" of the other for the edification of the body of Christ.[21]

The revelation of Christ as the incarnation of God is the centerpiece of Fackre's theology. He offers a hierarchical model for accessing this revelation. The Bible is its primary source. The primary resource is the two-thousand-year legacy of church tradition and theological development. The historical and cultural context is the setting in which the revelation of God in Christ is enacted in time and place. Fackre is aware that the interactions of the Bible, church tradition, and the context are more dynamic than what might be evident in such a structured framework. This ranking of priorities (Bible, tradition, and setting, in that order) serves for him as a working model. It provides a way of holding together balance and complexity within the context of his overarching evangelical ecumenical vision. His stratified methodology is built into his construction of a "combinationist" and

---

in the opening pages in chapter 4—there is much commonality between Packer's and Bloesch's overarching theological perspectives. Bloesch's embrace of Barth is a clear difference.

18. Fackre, "Wither Evangelicalism," 119–22, and "Narrative Evangelical, Postliberal Ecumenical," 123–33.

19. Fackre, "Wither Evangelicalism," 122.

20. Fackre, "An Alter Call for Evangelicals," 118.

21. Fackre, "New Ecumenism," 124.

"contextual" mode of biblical interpretation that he links to a set of "internal" and "external hermeneutics."[22]

In his discussion of internal hermeneutics Fackre highlights the importance of the "common sense," "critical sense," and "canonical sense" interpretation of Scripture. He associates a common-sense reading to both the "plain meaning" of the text and to twentieth-century appropriations of taken-for-granted meanings opened up through various "historicist, existential, and communitarian" theological perspectives.[23] By critical sense, Fackre refers to the higher criticism of contemporary biblical scholarship. He acknowledges the value of "historical-literary criticism" but challenges its "ideological accompaniments"[24] and historicist presuppositions. In his discussion of the canonical sense, Fackre argues that a surer source for the revelation of Christ is available when interpreted through the arc of the entire biblical narrative than what may be accessible through a more fragmented hermeneutics as exhibited, for example, in Brueggemann's postmodern inclinations.[25]

By external hermeneutics, Fackre refers to the *significance* of the text as determined by various interpreters of the Bible, including those at the margins as well as more centrist voices. He believes that perception is invariably shaped by historical contingency, in which one aspect or another of the biblical revelation is emphasized over others in any given historical context. In Fackre's view, "historical awareness is an outworking of the assumptions of human finitude"[26] through which new light from God has the capacity to break through to illuminate aspects of the biblical text that otherwise might be marginalized or not attended to at all.

I draw on Fackre's *Doctrine of Revelation: A Narrative Interpretation* in the second part of chapter 5. Fackre assimilates the insights of four key twentieth-century theologians—Tillich, Barth, Henry, and Rahner—into his vision of revelation. He draws on each of these luminaries to highlight pivotal storylines within the arc of the Grand Narrative of the biblical trajectory, from creation to consummation. Fackre borrows from Tillich's theology of culture to discuss the importance of general revelation as reflected in the Noachic Covenant of world preservation. He selects Barth for his discussion of the centrality of Jesus Christ within the Christian story. He turns

---

22. Fackre, *Christian Story*, 2:94–124.

23. Ibid., 157–70.

24. Ibid., 172. See ibid., 170–76, for Fackre's extended discussion of the critical sense interpretation of Scripture.

25. Ibid., 176–94.

26. Ibid., 214. See 211–53 for Fackre's discussion of external hermeneutics.

to Carl Henry to showcase the affinities and differences that he shares with this major evangelical theologian on the role and authority of Scripture. Key matters include the importance of language which, for Fackre, includes paradox and mystery as well as propositional truth claims. Fackre's final interlocutor is Catholic theologian Karl Rahner, through whom he highlights ecclesial illumination.

The chapter on Fackre concludes with a hopeful but cautionary assessment of his centrist project. I am less hopeful than is he that the quest for the restoration of the center is going to bring the type of faithful unity to mainline theology and ecclesial practice that he so ardently desires. I do, however, envision the prospect that such efforts can buttress confessional movements within mainline denominations. As evident in the many in-depth discussions on the *Confessing Christ* listserv, these movements are prime vehicles for establishing creative linkages with moderate evangelical perspectives.

Chapter 7 explores the prospect of reclaiming the neo-orthodox legacy as a mediating resource in bringing evangelical and postliberal theology into an increasingly discerning dialogue on the core issues of theology, faith, and religious culture. Following along the lines of Douglas J. Hall's *Remembered Voices*, chapter 7 highlights pivotal movements in neo-orthodox history. With Hall, I find that the neo-orthodox tradition contains an abundance of resources to mediate in the present theological context "the revelatory Christological basis of the gospel; the indispensability of the study of scriptures; keen and informed historical consciousness; [and] an internalized and nuanced interpretation of the Reformation traditions."[27] I seek to illustrate this mediational influence by highlighting key themes and texts in classical neo-orthodox history.[28]

The discussion hones in on the Barth/Bultmann debate on the role of culture and history in shaping human experience, specifically on

---

27. Hall, *Remembered Voices*, 144–45.

28. Hall declares that the neo-orthodox legacy "define(s)" for him not only "of what 'excellence' in theology would have to mean—more importantly—the meaning of Christ's discipleship." He argues that, in the failure to embrace the teachings of neo-orthodox theologians, "a rich legacy has not been adequately appropriated." He further contends "that the future of Protestantism in North America depends upon whether, and to what extent, that heritage is laid hold of, both by Christian scholars and the churches, in the years and decades ahead." Ibid., preface. Most evangelical theologians would challenge Hall on the assertion that the neo-orthodox legacy holds the central degree of influence that he attributes to it. This does not discount the significance of neo-orthodoxy within certain streams of evangelical thought. Neither does Hall's possible exaggeration of its significance discount its role as a mediating resource between centrist evangelical and postliberal perspectives.

Bultmann's call to de-mythologize, in order to re-mythologize the Bible in making Christianity relevant to pervasive twentieth-century historical, scientific, and philosophical modes of thought and cultural formation. Barth acknowledged the impossibility of avoiding historical constructivism. Yet he assiduously sought to avert its absolutizing tendency, as reflected in the scholarly literature within nineteenth and early twentieth-century biblical criticism. Barth's response was an imaginative leap, embracing the "objectivism" of the ontology of God, which can only be grasped in the "actualist" moment of revelation.[29]

I also discuss Tillich's critique and Barth's response. While tightly poised on the boundary between faith and doubt, Tillich's inclination was to perceive God's indwelling within and through the cultural matrix, typically more so than in the church, even as he never denied the dynamic potentiality of the latter to mediate God's grace in contemporary experience. Tillich's most searing critique of Barth was that, in his shift from dialectical theology to dogmatics, Barth had become distinctively undialectical.

One of the key differences is Tillich's "substantialistic"[30] ontology, in contrast to Barth's relational ontology. From the outset, Barth drew on the Hebraic perspective of covenantal bonding and the corresponding capacity for right and wrong action and thought, in response to the presence of the unfathomable God as revealed through Scripture. In direct contradistinction to his counterpart's point of departure in starting from human need and finding the response in "the conceptualization of symbols" that have the capacity to convey "the Christian message"[31] within a given historical context, Barth came to a radically different set of presuppositions by embracing biblical revelation as foremost reality.

I next offer a more churchly depiction of Bonhoeffer than reflected in the secular theologians of the 1960s, who were attracted principally to his "worldly" Christianity. My interpretation of Bonhoeffer is also worldly in the sense of drawing primarily on his ethics, noting as well that, with Barth, he adheres to a vision of Christ-the-center in his incarnated fullness. With Barth, Bonhoeffer was utterly theistic in his theology, but placed more emphasis than his mentor on right action, buttressed by right thought in the midst of the maelstrom of living history. Through Scripture, church

---

29. Hunsinger provides an overview of the six "motifs" that underlie Barth's theology in *How to Read Karl Barth*, 3–64. Hunsinger summarizes Barth's meaning of actualism as an occurrence in the human "relationship to God . . . continuously established anew by the ongoing activity of grace" in which the sovereignty (objectivism) of God is presupposed. Ibid., 31.

30. Hall, *Thinking the Faith*, 359.

31. Tillich, *Systematic Theology*, 2:140.

tradition, the discernment of the gathered community, and the Holy Spirit, an abundance of resources are available from Bonhoeffer's theology, in which the challenges of a costly faith become subject to careful, yet risky, appropriation in the stream of living history. I conclude the section on Bonhoeffer by discussing the four principle areas of application of his ethics: "labor, marriage, government, and the Church."[32]

I pick up this theme in the next section in making a case that the United States from the 1930s to the 1950s provided a more normative milieu for the realization of Bonhoeffer's public theology than the extremity of Nazi Germany. I argue that the broad affinity between his work and Reinhold Niebuhr's work on Christian ethics provides an imaginative force field for such an exploration. I also note important differences between the two in terms of Bonhoeffer's uncompromisingly theistic emphasis, compared to Niebuhr's apologetic focused Christian pragmatics.

At the core of Niebuhr's anthropological theology was a quest for proximate justice in a fallen world even as, in his interpretation, the unequivocal love of Christ provided the source for the ultimate meaning of existence as exhibited within and beyond history. With Niebuhr, there was an eschatological hopefulness as true myth, which provided an ultimate direction to ethics and to the very meaning of existence, even as its realization could, at best, be only partially realized in profoundly ambiguous and fragmentary ways. Niebuhr's insights have been discerningly appropriated across a wide theological stream. When placed in juxtaposition to Barth and Bonhoeffer, Niebuhr's interpretation of history, his commitment to culture, and his apologetic focus have a great deal to contribute toward the revitalization of contemporary Protestant thought and orthopraxy, even as problems with his work are duly noted.

I focus next on H. R. Niebuhr, whose concept of "centers of value" and his elevation of monotheism over lesser centers of value, as laid out in *Radical Monotheism and Western Culture*, is an underlying presupposition of my book. I conclude the section on H. R. Niebuhr with an extended discussion of his typological analysis in *Christ and Culture* on how the revelation of Christ gets played out in specific historical settings.

The overarching argument of chapter 7 is that the neo-orthodox legacy provides a valuable set of resources in constructing a centrist Protestant vision in the current setting. The neo-orthodox perspective has been influential in shaping the dialectical postliberal orientation of Brueggemann, Hall, and Christian historian Gary Dorrien. Barth, Reinhold Niebuhr, and Bonhoeffer have also influenced evangelicals, from the moderately conservative

---

32. Bonhoeffer, *Ethics*, 204.

perspectives of Bloesch to the post-conservative views of Stanley Grenz.[33] In underscoring iconic themes in the neo-orthodox theology, as they played out in the 1930s and 1940s, I suggest ways in which the reach of this movement continues to have salience in contemporary Protestant thought and culture.

I return to the contemporary period in chapter 8, in a comparative analysis of the postliberal dialectical theology of Douglas Hall and the evangelical narrative theology of Richard Lints. A central theme in Hall's work is the disestablishment of mainline Protestantism within the social and cultural setting of mainstream North American life. Hall insists that this unaccustomed "diaspora" holds theological significance for a renewal of the mainline denominations within context of the prophetic faith of the historical Protestant tradition. He argues that an intentional embrace by faithful Protestants of the declension in status has the capacity to break the stranglehold of the mid-twentieth-century "Constantinian" temptation of conflating the Christian faith with the American way of life, in which a deliberate relinquishment of power will come with much pain. He contends that a theology of the cross is required for any mainline renewal of authentic Christian faith at this time in history.

Lints identifies critical dialogue with postmodern theology a necessary task in contemporary evangelical theology. He argues that this is essential for *evangelical* theology if it is to move beyond its own particular enclaves in embrace of a broader ecumenical effort to critically evaluate culture from the grounding point of a generous orthodoxy. Lints seeks to be more persuasive than dialectical in his quest to open up to the postmodern reader the viability of a biblical world view. He shares a close similarity to Bloesch's theological project, in the desire to illuminate the New Testament revelation of God in Christ rather than to engage in critical dialogue with the postmodern theologians on their terms.[34] He is closely aligned with Fackre's narrative theology in his embrace of the progressive trajectory of the biblical story leading to the revelation of Christ and which comes to ultimate consummation in the eschaton. Lints's biblical theology holds potential for creative dialogue with postliberal theology on the centrality of the biblical narrative as the basis for shaping a Christian worldview. A difference is that Lints presses beyond the linguistic coherence of the biblical worldview and

---

33. Bloesch, *Theology of Word and Spirit*; Grenz, *Renewing the Center*.

34. In his critique of postmodern theology, Lints notes "that we have gradually abandoned the goal of attempting to establish an 'objective' reading of the Bible and have as a result stranded theology into a quagmire of a thousand different frameworks." *Fabric of Theology*, 194.

unequivocally asserts the New Testament revelation of God in Christ as a universal truth claim.[35]

Both Hall and Lints interpret Scripture as in some sense foundational. A prime difference is that Hall is unrelentingly dialectical in his analysis of the relationship between faith and culture, whereas Lints unequivocally presses the radical particularity of the Christian claim to truth as revealed in the Bible. With Lints, Hall identifies the Bible as a primary resource in revealing the Word of God, but associates "Truth" as "God in person, the living God . . . who transcends all description and expression."[36] For Hall, the fullness of this revelation cannot be captured in a book—even the Bible. While calling for a renewal of evangelical theology in a manner that accords more effectively with postmodern cultural reality, Lints ascribes to a traditional evangelical hermeneutics based on a unified canonical interpretation of the Bible. He argues that, in its language, narrative flow, and impact on attuned readers, the Bible provides primary access to knowledge of, and the will of, God.[37]

I complete my discussion of Hall and Lints in noting that they each have much to offer for mainline and evangelical readers seeking a more expansive theology within their respective traditions. There is much for advocates of Hall and Lints to draw from both of these authors. Evangelicals can benefit from Hall's emphasis on disestablishment, his dialectical theology, and his engagement with the full range of neo-orthodox theology, from Barth to Tillich. Mainline Protestant readers can derive much from Lints's extensive analysis of postmodern theology and the critique he brings to it, his redemptive historical biblical theology, and his in-depth knowledge and appreciation for the range and nuance of the evangelical theological tradition. Both Hall and Lints seek their ultimate grounding in the historic Protestant tradition that extends back to Luther and Calvin. Both seek to link this heritage to the challenges facing Protestant faith in the contemporary setting. They do so in ways that are complementary and divergent. In the depiction of their respective theologies, I argue that there is much to draw upon to construct a vital Protestant center for our times.

---

35. See Lindbeck, *Nature of Doctrine*, for the classical postliberal "cultural-linguistic" defense of the biblical worldview.

36. Hall, *Thinking the Faith*, 260.

37. Lints, *Fabric of Theology*, 74–77. Lints argues that "the Scriptures hold together because they have been delivered by a single author." Accordingly, "Our reading of the text ought to be guided by the inherent unity of the biblical text, and we ought to construct our theological framework in keeping with this kind of reading of the text." Ibid., 74.

I conclude with a general review of the key themes covered throughout the book. This includes the persisting divide between Scripture and culture in contemporary Protestant thought and practice, the potentiality of moving toward a more mediating ground through the collective work of the theologians and biblical scholars highlighted in the book, and the importance of positing dogmatics over dialectics in the midst of epistemological uncertainty. I also point to the significance of continuing dialogue between evangelical, postliberal, and neo-orthodox perspectives and to the importance of the Barthian turn to "the strange new world within the Bible" as the basis for grounding such discussion.

2

Theological, Historical, and Autobiographical Explorations of Twentieth-Century Protestant Thought and Culture

A great deal of contemporary theology attempts to . . . understand the biblical message in the light of modern thought. Yet, no believer can really be content with this since it assigns the final authority to what is called modern thought. What we are required to attempt is the much more difficult enterprise of trying to understand modern thought in the light of the biblical story.[1]

Therefore, since we are surrounded by such great a cloud of witnesses, let us throw off everything that hinders and the sin that so easily entangles, and let us run with perseverance the race marked out for us. Let us fix our eyes on Jesus, the author and perfecter of our faith, who for the joy set before him endured the cross, scorning its shame, and sat down at the throne of God. (Heb 12:1–2)

---

1. Newbigin, *Gospel in a Pluralistic Society*, 95.

Autobiographical Explorations of Twentieth-Century Protestant Thought   19

OVERVIEW

Through decades of study and personal experience, I have concluded that a powerful fissure exists between a sharply defined Christian identity and the basic assumptions of the contemporary era variously described as postmodern, post-industrial and post-Christendom. In summary form, the precepts of faith and those of the times in our secular age do not easily fit in with each other, nor can they be strictly correlated even by the most rigorous interpretative sensibility.[2] One cannot come to faith through the pathway of historical or scientific reasoning, but only through revelation, however interlaced with culture may be that still, small voice of God. This acknowledgment is not a denial of the role of reason, since Christians are called to seek God with all their minds, as well as their hearts and souls, and to persist at it, until a pathway is opened up for new life in Christ. It does, however, point to the limited capacity of even the most astute reasoning and cultural analysis in opening up the Christian experience to the inquiring mind. As a point of contrast, even a strong faith stance can seem woefully inadequate in dealing with the challenges of contemporary existence, particularly since the early decades of the twentieth-century, in which the notion of God has been evacuated from the intellectual history of the West and vast portions of its culture.[3] From this vantage point, the Bible, theological reflection, hymnology, Holy Communion, the preached word, and prayer can be perceived, even by the most devout Christian, as anachronistic or simply irrelevant to the main currents of contemporary life, however personally significant these forms of worship and resources for reflection may be to one's faith journey.

This schism is a major characteristic underlying the past century of Protestant thought and culture. It is expressed in its sharpest tones in the great divide between modernism and fundamentalism, which continues to have an indelible influence on the relationship between faith and Protestant culture in our time, particularly in the United States, the focal area of my study.[4] It is my contention that calls for a return to the tradition of the Protestant Reformers as a primary resource in revitalizing a twenty-first-century

---

2. The sharp contrast between a radical Christian worldview and the pluralistic values of the current era is not based simply on personal experience. It is also a common theme within contemporary Christian literature. In addition to *Gospel in a Pluralistic Society*, see Taylor, *Secular Age*, esp. 505–93.

3. In addition to the texts cited in n2, see also Hart, *Beauty of the Infinite*, 35–151.

4. For a comprehensive overview of the range of twentieth-century US Protestant thought and culture, see Grenz and Olson, *20th Century Theology*; Dorrien, *Soul in Society*, *Word as True Myth*, and *Remaking of Evangelical Theology*; Marsden, *Fundamentalism and American Culture* and *Understanding Fundamentalism and Evangelicalism*.

faith in the mainline denominations can come only by way of a substantial resolution of problems rooted in the conflicts that continue to give force to this great divide. I argue that any sustainable working resolution will require direct grappling with the crisis in faith that was evoked in the late nineteenth and early twentieth centuries—the problem opened up by modernity—which continues to have a profound impact on contemporary Protestant culture in its varying theological, denominational, ethical, and pietistic expressions.

The core tension running throughout contemporary US Protestant culture is exemplified by the more radical strands within this divide. Among conservative evangelicals, there is the pull toward rejecting large aspects of secular identity as defined by those outside the realm of faith in exchange for a firmly based, biblically grounded belief on the fundamentals of the faith. Among Protestant liberals, there is a corresponding tendency to mute a strong orthodox faith stance in order to achieve deep congruence with prevailing precepts of secular assumptions in the realms of personal and public identity.[5] Various "two-world" positions as advocated by sociologist

---

5. I am speaking in terms of theological tendencies, as exemplified in the work of D. A. Carson, Wayne Grudem, and David Wells from the conservative evangelical perspective, and those of Shubert Ogden, Mary Daly, and Bishop John Shelby Spong from the more radical liberal wing of contemporary Protestant thought and culture. An illuminating example of the tension can be discerned in John Frame's review of Ogden's core text *On Theology*. The following blog post by Frame speaks directly to the main tension I am here identifying:

> I suppose my biggest disappointment in the book was that Ogden rarely even seems aware of the most serious kinds of questions that can be raised against them. Of course the questions I have in mind come from the standpoint of orthodox theology, and it is plain that Ogden has so little sympathy with that standpoint that he is entirely out of touch with it. Like Bultmann, he seems to believe that the course of intellectual, cultural and technological history has made it impossible for twentieth century man to accept Christian orthodoxy without intellectual ignorance, stupidity or dishonesty. Well, that view has often been stated dogmatically, but the case has never been made with any cogency. Boiled down, it amounts to the view that one must never believe anything u*nfashionable*; a proposition at odds both with Scripture and with the great Socratic tradition of western rational thought.
>
> Frame, review of On Theology.

Ogden counters with the following:

> *Theology today has an all but impossible job in determining what is to count as the truth about human existence. My own belief is that the job can still*

Peter Berger are also plausible and require substantial "bracketing" between the secular and religious spheres of life, in which the twain only seldom meet.[6] Still, matters of ultimate value orientation are operative, even if only latently so, regarding whether faith or cultural identity is the primary source of identification, even in the acknowledgment that they are intertwined.

I argue that there is no alternative except to stand somewhere, ultimately as an article of faith, no matter how exacting, nuanced, or reasonable one's thinking. In H. R. Niebuhr's terms, "centers of value" cannot be avoided, even in the knowledge that such centers can only fall short of their desired objective.[7] This is so, even if one adheres to the postmodern credo that "metanarratives"—whether capitalism, democracy, or Christianity— need to be understood as historical constructs, and therefore contingently created, whatever their claims of truth may be in given historical contexts. Such historicism as the final vocabulary of the contemporary era has had a profound influence on Protestant thought and culture throughout the last century and into the current one, particularly on Protestant liberalism, but also on fundamentalism, a product of modernity in its own right.[8]

> be done—or reasonably attempted, at any rate—in so far as some understandings of the truth are at least more relatively more credible than others. But if there was ever a time when theologians could be excused for looking to some one theology or philosophy to provide such an understanding, it has long since passed. We today are without excuse for all our traditional provincialisms, and we must scrupulously avoid even a hint of dogmatism in our attempts to formulate existential truth.
>
> Doing Theology Today, 17.

There is a strong quest for more centrist ground among a broad theological spectrum, as exemplified in the current evangelical/postliberal dialogue, as well as in such venues as the Confessing Christ community within the UCC. The fleshing out of such middle ground represents the underlying intent of this book. Notwithstanding this mediating impetus, I am pointing to the persistence of the modernist/fundamentalist divide as an enduring strain within contemporary US Protestantism. Creatively grappling with this tension will require some considerable attenuation in order for a mainline-evangelical convergence grounded in the tradition of the Protestant Reformers to take substantial hold. While this strain is most clearly exemplified at the radical edges of the theological spectrum, it permeates almost the entirety of the contemporary US Protestant discourse.

6. See Berger, *Sacred Canopy*, preface, where he states that his discussion "never leaves . . . the frame of reference of the empirical discipline of sociology. Consequently, it must rigidly bracket throughout any questions of the ultimate truth or illusion of religious propositions about the world."

7. Niebuhr, "Center of Value," 100–113.

8. Lints defines historicism "as an attempt to reject moral and theological absolutes by suggesting that all people are fundamentally rooted in the particularity of their own

In grappling with the thorny issue of one's ultimate identity, the underlying concern remains not only the stance, but also the grounds upon which one's choices are based. The issue of where and upon what basis one locates this identification is of no minor significance and cannot, therefore, be slid under the gaze of postmodern relativism. Wherever one places what Tillich refers to as one's "ultimate concern,"[9] it is one of costly faith. To put it in the most radical of terms, and regardless of how analogical one's reasoning may be, the key question remains whether one's faith is based on the unswerving belief that Jesus the Christ is the way, the truth, and the life as God incarnate in human flesh, ultimately without equivocation (John 14:6). If not this incarnational Christology, however nuanced the theological expression of it may be, the issue becomes the determination of the narrative construct in which one places New Testament claims about Christ.

A related matter in the deconstruction of the radical particularity of the Christian credo is the interfaith vision in which all the great faiths of the world are viewed as various pathways leading to God (or the ineffable). The interfaith interpretation of the Christian "story" has had obvious appeal in different historical contexts, including our own. Viewed from this vantage point, any claims of ultimate religious truth based on the radical particularity of the Christian revelation, are not merely considered archaic, and therefore, naïve. They are also suffused with consequences, intended or otherwise, of cultural and political imperialism, as reflected throughout the last two centuries in the operative assumptions of at least certain depictions of Protestant missions.[10]

The issue, in brief, is whether the Barthian dictum of the "strange new world within the Bible" absorbs the world, however subtly, or whether the "world," that is, the culture, absorbs the Bible within the precepts of its various narrative construals. If there is a dialectical tension between the two in that neither stance is absolutely clear cut, the lurking questions remains on what and where ultimate identification resides. On this latter challenge, there is no escape: for to evade this matter is to choose sides even in the acknowledgment that much nuance is required in the hard work of coming to terms with the ways in which the revelation of God, as embodied within the Bible, is refracted within and through historical experience.[11]

---

historical circumstances, that there is no transcultural principles applying to all people in all times and places." *Fabric of Theology*, 314. I am using the term in the similarly broad sense as Lints.

9. Tillich, *Dynamics of Faith*, 1–4.

10. See Dilley, "World the Missionaries Made," 35–41, for a perspective that portrays the cultural sensitivity of nineteenth-century missions in a more enlightened manner.

11. Grenz and Olson provide a succinct overview on Barth that focuses on the

In my view, the challenge among those seeking to understand the faith within a broad-based ecumenical-evangelical sensibility requires acknowledging the centrality of a distinctively biblical worldview as the operative grounding point of Christian faith. Based on the centrist perspective that drives my argument, this includes drawing in as much as possible from the best insights across the theological spectrum, from conservative to liberal, for which I appropriate Brian McLaren's concept of a "generous orthodoxy"—a term he borrowed ultimately from postliberal theologian Hans Frei. I also draw into this phrase what Lewis refers to as "mere Christianity."[12]

Any substantial easing of the modernist/fundamentalist divide entails separating out as much as possible what is essential from what is secondary or outright dubious within US fundamentalist, evangelical, and liberal theologies. This would encompass a more discerning depiction of theological liberalism within evangelical theology. Such discernment would also include a deeper appreciation for the centrality of the Bible as the decisive, if not the primary source of revelation within the mainline sector. The current discourse between postliberal and evangelical theologians reflects the type of critical dialogue that I build on in this book.[13]

The judgment of the tipping points within US Protestant theology during the past century is obviously mine. However, my discernments are

---

centrality of faith and the revelation in "God's Word," first and foremost in Jesus Christ as "the primary form," Scripture as "privileged witness to divine revelation," the "second form" and "the church's proclamation of the gospel" as "the third mode." *20th Century Theology*, 71. For the authors' overview on Barth, see ibid., 65–77. It is "God's Word" in its various forms that Barth places in critical juxtaposition to the culture, a key perspective that undergirded the neo-orthodox movement in mid-twentieth-century European and US Protestant theology. In this book, I am drawing on Barth as "signifier" for the importance he places on the shift within Protestant thought and culture on "God's Word" as the basis for the Christian faith community to engage the culture. In chapter 7, I draw on the substance of the neo-orthodox tradition in contributing to a centrist theological network constructed along the lines of a broad-based Trinitarian, incarnational, and biblically-centered orthodoxy.

12. McLaren, *Generous Orthodoxy*, 28, 72–74; Lewis, *Mere Christianity*. What McLaren and Lewis share in common is a focus on beliefs that, in the words of Lewis, are "common to nearly all Christians at all times"—namely, the belief "that there is only one God and that Jesus Christ is his only Son." *Mere Christianity*, viii, ix. In summarizing the seven types of Christianity that give shape to his sense of generous orthodoxy, McLaren "acknowledge[s] that Christians of each tradition bring their distinctive and wonderful gifts to the table." *Generous Orthodoxy*, 74. I share the irenic spirit of McLaren and Lewis without necessarily accepting the entirety of their respective theological perspectives. In working through tensions in twentieth-century US Protestant thought and religious culture, I have a narrower, more articulated theological focus; one in common with Fackre's centrist vision, as articulated in *Ecumenical Faith in Evangelical Perspective*.

13. Philips and Okholm, *Nature of Confession*.

more than simply my opinion in a narrowly subjective sense. In the effort to move beyond mere subjectivism, I seek, through close historical, biblical, and theological analysis, to establish a solid grounding within the key discourses of contemporary Protestant thought and culture in a manner that moves toward what the philosopher Karl Popper refers to as "objective knowledge."[14] As Popper states:

> We can never rationally justify a theory—that is, a claim to know its truth—but we can, if we are lucky, rationally justify a preference for one theory out of a set of competing theories, for the time being; that is, with respect to the present state of the discussion. And our justification, though not a claim that the theory is true, can be the claim that there is every indication at this stage of the discussion that the theory is *a better approximation to the truth* than any competing theory so far proposed.[15]

It is with such a degree of what Popper refers to as "verisimilitude" that I seek to defend the view that a canonically comprehensive appreciation of the biblical text, in its various narrative and dogmatic articulations interpreted through a New Testament lens, can serve as a cogent and highly imaginative baseline for the potential revitalization of contemporary Protestant theology. The existential matter of meaning would serve in a ministerial role, and therefore, in service to the revelation of "the God who is there,"[16] as proclaimed in Scripture. Much theological discernment would be required to work through the competing sources of Protestant thought and popular religious culture that have given shape to the issues that divide in order to come to a reasonably satisfactory common ground for which I argue. Such a challenge is further complicated in the realization that any cognitive claim invariably overshoots its appropriation in that world-word interaction is more complex than what can be possibly described in words.[17]

Still, the crucial matter of "centers of values," pointing to the indisputability of ultimate vocabulary and identity is inescapable. I argue that it is on the bases laid out above that mainline Protestant theology has the capacity to come to terms with its most formative religious identification—rooted in

---

14. Popper, *Objective Knowledge*.
15. Ibid., 82.
16. Schaeffer, *God Who Is There*.
17. As Dulles states in his 1992 edition preface, "I may be called a 'continuist' insofar as I hold that revelation does not suppress but presupposes and perfects the perceptual and cognitive faculties of the recipient. But my approach allows for a certain discontinuity. I maintain, symbolic communication effects a profound conversion, carrying the subject across a logical gap and providing a new interpretative framework." *Modes of Revelation*, vii.

the tradition of the Protestant Reformers—that places a grounded biblical interpretation of culture in a central theological role. Without this focus, the specter of relativism and syncretism—more fundamentally, the ubiquity of history as ultimate discourse—can only continue to plague such denominations as the United Church of Christ (UCC) and the United Methodist Church (UMC), which are the ones that I know best. Based on such a mindset, faith claims can be contextualized only within the frame of their varying historical perspectives, rendering any notion of truth as a regulative ideal devoid of meaning. I do not argue that one can escape historical finitude. I do maintain that any privileging of historical interpretation over that of the authorial claims embedded throughout the New Testament on the central redemptive role of Christ as God incarnate in human flesh gives to the former a sense of epistemological absolutism that by definition requires attenuation of the latter.

To state it baldly, Protestant mainline denominations need to directly respond to the primary question of "who do you say I am" (Matt 16:15). This is my core thesis, for if any other name or title is given than the incarnate Jesus Christ, the author and finisher of our faith, then what is in jeopardy is Christianity itself as a sharply distinctive faith. There are schools of contemporary theology that move in this direction of other naming. I encourage those who seek to travel this pathway to continue to flesh out the logic of such assumptions, including the fruit thereof derived.[18] My objective is to lay out the implications of a most generous orthodoxy that is consistent with a fully-embodied theology of Scripture, in which the latter serves as the interpretive lens to define the parameters of the former, however much else remains unsettled.

Such work will need to go forth with consummate sensibility to other perspectives within Christianity. Human understanding remains incomplete. Nevertheless, ultimate identifications are still required—for any effort to escape the issue of the radical particularity of the Christian revelation is to posit an absolutism of some sort, even if it is that of "self-evident" acceptance of relativism and the underlying grounding in radical historicism as the foundational interpretive lens of human knowledge. In this revitalization effort, triumphalism (the temptation of fundamentalism) will need to be avoided. So, too will a too easy accommodation with what Hinkle refers to as "privatization, pluralization, and rationalization," the primary temptation of contemporary Protestant liberalism.[19]

---

18. See Spong, *New Christianity for a New World*.
19. Hinkle, "American Protestant Preaching," 97.

The argument that I lay out is grounded on the assumption that the most radical faithfulness to the religious tradition, founded on the revelation of Jesus the Christ, requires a thorough embrace of the Bible as a holistic canonical text. This necessitates a reading that is both generous and textually faithful to the core precepts of the biblical claims about God, Christ, and humankind for any serious mainline-evangelical encounter in the midst of the challenges posed by modernity, postmodernity, globalization, and the marginality of Christian identity in the contemporary setting.[20]

Any intentional shift in this direction will require some fundamental recasting of at least a few key assumptions of mainline and evangelical sectors, particularly those that fuel the persisting culture wars in contemporary Protestantism, which stem from the modernist/fundamental divisions of the early twentieth century. Many of the specific issues that shook Protestantism to its core in the earlier decades of the last century have seeped into the background. An enduring culture lag lingers as a continuing influence on the collective consciousness of both sectors in contemporary Protestantism. This will need to be substantially attenuated before denominations such as the UCC and the UMC will be able to embrace a twenty-first-century revitalization of its theology, ecclesial structure, and sense of core identity based on a hermeneutical retrieval of the legacy of the Protestant Reformation. Any such effort may be viewed as quixotic. I argue that it is worthy of the most intentional pursuit as a praxeological quest to expand the influence of the theological center.

As discussed in chapter 1, the heart of this book is a detailed examination of the theology of Scripture and a corresponding theology of God of four key contemporary expositors along the continuum from conservative to postliberal. This biographical approach provides one critical way to examine the various tensions within contemporary US Protestantism and to explore avenues for potential constructive work within the identified spectrum. For the remainder of this chapter, I provide a selective survey of key issues that have divided Protestant theology and culture over the last century. I conclude chapter 2 with a discussion of Lesslie Newbigin's *Gospel in a Pluralistic Society*, through which I present my centrist argument in more detail.

HISTORICAL OVERVIEW: 1875–1925

The literature on twentieth-century Protestantism in the United States is vast, in which major themes are reviewed and the tensions between

---

20. Hall, *Thinking the Faith*, 145–244.

fundamentalism, evangelicalism, and liberalism well covered.[21] My objective is not to retell that history, although I draw on critical elements of it throughout this book. In the following discussion, I focus on some of the key pointers that have given shape to, and have sustained, the great divide in twentieth-century US Protestantism—one that continues to have resonance in the current century.

For the early period (1875–1925), critical issues have pivoted around the impact of Darwinism, academic research on the "historical Jesus," the emergence of "progressive" theology, and the rise of the social gospel and its accompanying postmillennial eschatology in its conflation of the realm of God and the brotherhood of man. The result was the breakdown of the northern Congregationalist, Presbyterian, and Methodist evangelical synthesis of the mid-nineteenth century. Marsden subtly describes a series of tensions within evangelicalism throughout the later decades of the nineteenth century, especially the influence Darwin's theory of evolution. He also illustrates the pathways that led to the bifurcation of liberalism and fundamentalism from its core root in mid-nineteenth-century evangelicalism.[22]

By the second decade of the twentieth century, the tensions became transformed into irrevocable fissures between an increasingly humanist-centered, transcendent minimalist Christian liberalism and a correspondingly contentious fundamentalism at the populist level. This battle within the household of Protestantism was similarly played out in the development of a rigorous Calvinist theology on the one hand, and a progressive theology on the other, in which the leading seminaries of Princeton and Yale were pitted against each other in elemental conflict.

---

21. Marsden, *Understanding Fundamentalism and Evangelicalism* and *Fundamentalism and American Culture*; Dorrien, *Soul in Society* and *Word as True Myth*.

22. As Marsden succinctly summarizes it, "The vast cultural changes of the era from the 1870s to the 1920s created a major crisis within" the preceding evangelical movement, which he identified as a broad coalition of the Protestant denominations influenced by the revival movements of the eighteenth and nineteenth centuries. This evangelical coalition became sharply bifurcated. "On the one hand were theological liberals who in order to maintain better credibility in the modern age, were willing to modify some central evangelical doctrines, such as the reliability of the Bible or the necessity of salvation only through the atoning sacrifice of Christ. On the other hand were conservatives who continued to believe the traditionally essential evangelical doctrines." The result was that "by the 1920s, a militant wing of conservative emerged and took the name fundamentalist." Marsden, *Understanding Fundamentalism and Evangelicalism*, 3. See ibid., 9–61, and Marsden, *Fundamentalism and the American Culture*, 11–32, for a historical sketch of the theological and cultural tensions within American Protestantism during this time period. For more empathetic perspectives to the liberal tradition, see Hutchison, *Modernist Impulse in American Protestantism*, and Dorrien, *Soul in Society*, 21–75.

The symbolic culmination of this early period was encapsulated in the Scopes Trial in the rank defeat of a seemingly know-nothing fundamentalism as it has been commonly and, inaccurately, portrayed. This culture war within US Protestantism of the 1920s was played out at a more subtle, but still polarizing level in the contrasting polemics between the renowned liberal minister Harry Fosdick and his counterpart, conservative theologian Gresham Machen. The key texts in this quarrel were Fosdick's (1922) highly influential article, "Shall the Fundamentalists Win?," and Machem's (1923) rebuttal, *Christianity and Liberalism*.[23] This culture war resulted in a powerful rift in the iconography of the American religious imagination that continues to have much resonance.

Advocates of progressive theology sought to "reconstruct" the faith, bringing out what they deemed most essential, particularly social morality, through the ethical teaching of Jesus. They did so by focusing on his earthly vocation rather than on any robust Trinitarian understanding of God linked to a vigorously articulated "supernatural" theology. This liberal strain in American Protestantism resonated with modernistic sensibilities within the culture and in scholarship, particularly science, historical research, and literary analysis. This new scholarship challenged the "Baconian ideal" of the "common sense" Scottish philosophy that undergirded nineteenth-century evangelical and Princetonian theology of the late nineteenth and early twentieth centuries.[24] Conservative theologians and clergy worked diligently to preserve what they perceived as the essential truths of the faith that seemed to face immediate prospect of erosion through the corrosive force of Darwinism and "higher biblical criticism."

---

23. Fosdick, "Shall the Fundamentalists Win?," 716–22.

24. Marsden, *Fundamentalism and American Culture*, 55–62. The reference is to the seventeenth-century philosopher of science Francis Bacon whose inductive approach to reasoning became incorporated into the eighteenth-century philosophical Scottish School of Common Sense. Its impact on theological method resulted in an empirical approach in which the interpretive task was that of "taking the hard facts of Scripture, carefully arranging and classifying them, and thus discovering the clear patterns which Scripture revealed." Ibid., 56. Marsden further draws out the implications of this philosophical perspective on fundamentalist biblical and theological interpretation in *Understanding Fundamentalism and Evangelicalism*. As he states, "humans are capable of positive knowledge based on sure foundations. If rationally classified, such knowledge can yield a great deal of certainty. Combined with biblicism, such a view of knowledge leads to supreme confidence on religious questions. Despite the conspicuous subjectivism throughout evangelicalism and within fundamentalism itself, one side of the fundamentalist mentality is committed to inductive rationalism." Ibid., 117–18. See Dorrien, *Soul in Society*, 29–75, for an in-depth discussion of the progressive impetus in the early twentieth-century Protestant liberal tradition.

In substantive ways, US Protestant thought, in its mainline and evangelical trajectories in the latter decades of the twentieth and into the current century, has moved well beyond these early concerns. This modulation has included varying efforts of mediation within moderate and centrist streams within both mainline and evangelical theology and practice. Nonetheless, the archetypical conflict between modernism and fundamentalism on the relationship between the Bible and the culture, which came to a pinnacle in the 1920s, continues to play out in the current period, as persisting voices on each side of the great Protestant divide feel compelled to envision the other with the most acute anxiety.

This concern is not meant to negate the value of various efforts at grappling with these tensions, or the reality of the complexity of congregational life and the diverse perceptions that impinge on individual belief that can be found throughout the theological/ecclesial landscape of contemporary Protestant life. It is to argue that in very broad, but enduring ways, a divide of significant proportions, grounded in the conflicts within US Protestantism of the early twentieth century, continues to possess much defining influence. In its starkest polarity, the essential conflict is between those who look to the Bible first as an operative ideal to interpret the culture and those within the Christian fold whose religious identity is influenced much more by the basic assumptions of the contemporary secular culture. In summary, this early twentieth-century period was pivotal in giving shape to one of the sharpest-edged theological issues that has confronted American Protestantism within its almost four hundred–year history.

HISTORICAL OVERVIEW: 1940–1965

Neo-orthodox realism and the biblical theology movement (detailing the "mighty acts" of God)—both of which were pervasive in the period between 1940 and 1960—sought to bridge the gap through an embrace of the tradition of the Protestant Reformers in a manner that, in theory, could incorporate the major precepts of critical biblical scholarship.[25] Much exciting work in theology and biblical studies emerged in this mid-century period in Europe and the United States that relegitimized the biblical notion of God's transcendence and the broad-based unity of the Bible in a manner, which, in principle, if not always in practice, could be reconciled with higher biblical criticism. The neo-orthodox and biblical theology movements played a major role in modulating the centrality of theological liberalism within the

---

25. For neo-orthodoxy, see Dorrien, *Word as True Myth*, 73–127, and *Soul and Society*, 91–161. For the biblical theology movement, see Perdue, *Collapse of History*, 19–68.

mainline denominations and its impact in the broader religious culture of the nation during this two-decade period. Notwithstanding this mediating resurgence, the forces unleashed in the early twentieth century that fueled the modernist/fundamentalist divide, were still operative, and needed little force to break out into open conflagration in the post-1945 period.

The great divide was held at bay to some degree in this "consensus" period of US history, as depicted in such key texts as Richard Hofstadter's *American Political Tradition* and *Age of Reform* and Louis Hartz's often referenced *Liberal Tradition in America*. Yet, the enduring fissures between the biblical focus of even the neo-orthodox variety and modernism re-exploded in the later decades of the twentieth century, as this consensus period broke down in the "culture wars" unleashed by worldwide protest over the United States involvement in Vietnam. The result was that the most fundamental issues on the nature of Christian faith within the context of the modern world became encased in a highly contentious polemic, notwithstanding continuing mediating work to the contrary.[26]

A critical factor in the breakdown of any budding neo-orthodox synthesis was the emergence of a diffusive civil religion within the mainline churches in the early post–World War II period. This muted "civil" religion stood in stark juxtaposition to a rigorous biblical focus in the increasing merger of certain strands of fundamentalism and evangelicalism, as reflected in the formation of Fuller Seminary in 1947 and the Billy Graham crusades of the 1950s.[27] In this maelstrom, the theological insights of the neo-orthodox theologians became viewed with increasing irrelevance within the Protestant mainline, while Karl Barth's interpretation of biblical narratives as "sagas" and Reinhold Niebuhr's reconstruction of biblical orthodoxy as "myth" were rejected by a broad swath of scholarly evangelicals, which brooked no compromise over biblical inerrancy.[28]

Prospects for any broad-based consensus within Protestant theology were further eroded by directions taken on both sides of the fundamentalist/modernist divide from the 1960s to the present. Evangelicalism, in its many variants, grew exponentially through charismatic and Pentecostal revivals, the explosive growth of the "megachurch," and, with the onset of the Reagan presidency, the political flourishing of the religious right. There were many fissures, disputes, and disagreements within the evangelical

26. See Berger and Neuhaus, *Against the World*.

27. Marsden, *Reforming Fundamentalism*, 277–90; Dorrien, *Remaking of Evangelical Theology*, 114–23.

28. On civil religion, see Bellah, "Civil Religion in America," and Herberg, *Protestant-Catholic-Jew*. For a traditional evangelical critique of the biblical theology movement and neo-orthodoxy, see Packer, *Truth and Power*, 110–22.

sector, including a progressive minority, as reflected in the work of Jim Wallis and the formation of the monthly magazine *Sojourners*. Despite the differences and exceptions, common enough positions on abortion, gay rights, the role of women in society and in the church, and the toxic impact of the 1960s on traditional American values helped establish an evangelical distinctiveness sharply differentiated from mainline Protestantism. A literal and inerrant reading of the Bible undergirded a conservative social polity based on a vision articulated by the Christian Coalition of bringing America back to God—a force in its various guises that has been a major source of conservative political power for the past thirty years. Additional discussion of evangelical theology and religious culture—including my own relationship to it—is interspersed throughout this book beginning with the last two sections of this chapter.

For the remainder of this section, I focus on a few of the ways in which mainline and liberal theology were infused by a wide stream of fresh thinking broadly influenced by Harvey Cox's *Secular City*. In this key text, which became a byword of an era, the ethos of modern urbanity became the context in which Christianity—if it were to have force in the modern world—would have to find its voice. More radical were the writings of the "death of God" theologians who argued that the traditional notion of a supernatural, transcendent God was no longer a viable concept, at least for the residents of the secular city.[29] Any rebirth of Christianity could only emerge through an embrace of the faith's core symbol—the cross—within the context of secular experience and language. Traditional notions of "God-talk" were dismissed as obscurantist. In roundly repudiating this position, fundamentalists and evangelicals rejected the entire thrust of the secularization argument.

The death of God movement did not have a large following even within the mainline denominations. However, it represented the culmination of a half-century of existential theology extending from Rudolf Bultmann, Paul Tillich, and certain strands within Dietrich Bonhoeffer's thought, although the latter remained an uncompromising theist through the course of his short and heroic life.[30] As a major proponent of "process theology," Langdon Gilkey integrated both existentialism and neo-orthodoxy in his search for the articulation of God's immanence within the very fabric of "secular" history.[31] The searching for and living out of this ineffable presence was viewed

---

29. For a succinct overview of the major death of God theologians of the 1960s, see Genz and Olson, *20th Century Theology*, 156–69.

30. See chapter 7 for a discussion which emphasizes the "churchly" impetus in Bonhoeffer's theology.

31. For an extensive discussion of Gilkey's theology, see Dorrien, *Word as True Myth*, 155–86.

as the fundamental basis for any reconstruction of theological, biblical, and religious language, in which any vestige of spatial notions of God in heaven and humankind on earth impeded rather than facilitated the emergence of the Spirit's indwelling in the modern period.[32]

Notwithstanding its secularist appeal, the rarefied terminology of death of God and process theologians was too esoteric for direct appropriation in the mainline denominations. Through seminary training, these influences indelibly played into the religious formation of at least certain clergy. However, ministers would generally find these theological precepts exceedingly difficult to translate into inspiring pulpit sermons that could speak in any convincing idiom of a new theology of practice in the secular city. Given the theological abstruseness of such work—to say nothing of the radical nature of their implications for traditional understanding of the Christian faith—the gap between the seminary and the pew, more often than not, led to clerical avoidance rather than to rigorous embrace. Consequently, the hard work of theological exposition needed for any appropriation of its core insights at the congregational level was largely left waning for the religiously inclined laity hovering around the boundaries of the secular city.

One result was that mainline congregants typically lacked substantial reasons at the level of clear articulation for hard-won religious beliefs, even though rigorous thinking in the professional life of the middle class required a direct analysis of facts and operative constructs at the level where it counted in practical application.[33] Thus, a dichotomous view of the relationship between the church and the world was all too characteristic of mainline experience, in which neither the implications of existential nor traditional-based theologies held full sway. For adult male members of the mid-1960s of mainline denominations, in particular, a widening experiential gap between the reality-based perception of the world of work and a Sunday church experience could not be papered over by building projects and stewardship campaigns.

These various modes of existentialist theology spoke to broad currents in the post-1960 mainline religious culture. While certain key phrases about the need for "relevance" were appropriated into congregational life, little systematic work was accomplished in integrating death of God and process schools of theology within the context of the institutional life of the church. A more dynamic relationship between the seminary and the pew emerged in the 1970s in an appropriation of the "identity politics" of black and feminist theologies. This was a double-edged sword. Those who embraced

---

32. Robinson, *Honest to God*.
33. Drucker, *Practice of Management*.

these more recent streams of religious thought were better able to translate theology into practical action than the advocates of the death of God and process theology. However, this came only at the price of very sharp conflict between the advocates of the new political theologies and others of more moderate inclinations who remained less convinced, as well as among the overtly critical even within the mainline denominations.

As the 1970s dawned, the broad-based consensus of the early cold war era gave way to a polarizing tendency in US culture between conservative and progressive forces, fueled by radically conflicting stances on the Vietnam War. These countervailing worldviews had sharply defined gender, race, class, and theological components, which melded into conflicting ideological constructions, symbolized most fully in competing perspectives on interpretations of the "countercultural" decade of the 1960s. The following discussion focuses on the two central issues of race and gender. The broad themes that have given shape to theological liberalism from the late nineteenth century are subsumed and radicalized in the theologies of race and feminism in the post-civil rights era.

HISTORICAL OVERVIEW: 1965 TO THE PRESENT

Afro-Centrist Theology and the Civil Rights Movement

The civil rights movement of the early 1960s was a major galvanizing force among mainline theologians, clergy, and congregations. At the center was the poignant rhetoric of Martin Luther King Jr., capsulated most fully in his "I Have a Dream" speech of 1963. King's inspiring vision of radical equality built on the twin foundations of the Declaration of Independence and the New Testament vision that in Christ we are all God's children regardless of race and other pernicious distinctions that separate groups from one another as a result of hatred and fear. The civil rights movement under King's leadership embodied a rhetorical and cultural force of major proportions that continues to resonate with the highest of national ideals some forty-five years after his tragic assassination.

With King's death, the "new liberal consensus"—already shaky with race riots and protests over US involvement in Vietnam—no longer held sway, as what became referred to as "identity politics" came more and more to the fore in the 1970s.[34] With the advocates of black power, King, too,

---

34. Dorrien subtitles the fourth chapter in *Soul in Society* as "Disputing the 'New Liberal Consensus,'" 162–220. He does so by detailing the breakdown of the influence of Niebuhr's neo-orthodoxy, first through the work of John C. Bennett, whose "social ethic

accented the theme of economic justice, even as he remained unswervingly committed to nonresistance and the vision of a fully integrated society. The unquestionable reality of "de facto" segregation in the urban north, arguably ever much egregious as legal segregation in the south, drew stark attention to the enduring reality of black poverty and the long legacy of slavery which was far from overcome with the passage of the Civil Rights Act of 1965. The quest for racial equality has continued to permeate the mainline social conscience and corresponding sense of prophetic biblical justice.

As the initial enthusiasm of the early civil rights era faded, by the end of the twentieth century the sense of dynamic vision that the movement evoked in the mainline imagination in the early 1960s no longer possessed its original powerful force as a galvanizing source of congregational or theological direction. King's vision of racial equality continues to have strong resonance in mainline congregations. Nonetheless, the militant black theology of James Cone—however much it speaks "truth to power" from the symbolic voice of the racially "oppressed"—could not provide a platform that would galvanize primarily declining, aging, and mostly Caucasian suburban-based mainline denominations.[35]

There were more moderating black theological voices than that of Cone's in the conservative/progressive culture wars on race in the post-King era. However, Cone's voice had a potent symbolic power in sharpening issues and polarizing sides that severely tested any semblance of consensus upon which King sought to build. The logic of Cone's economic, racial, and theological analysis appealed to the more progressive sectors within the mainline denominations. It was much less favorably received by many others within the Protestant mainline churches, regardless of whether those less predisposed to the radical view on race would directly speak out against whatever liberal orthodoxies prevailed among their denominational leadership. As the conservative movement became increasingly visible by the 1980s, an articulated counter discourse arose that gave populist voice to

---

. . . closely resembled Niebuhr's realism without duplicating Niebuhr's exaggerations or his stigmatizing attacks on liberalism." Ibid., 164. In the next major section of the chapter, Dorrien traces the breakdown through a discussion of liberation theologies. Ibid., 181–89. He completes the chapter by narrating the rise of the theological right through the works of Michael Novak and John Newhaus. This includes their appropriation of Niebuhrian realism in support of a conservative social and political ethics. Ibid., 189–220. He extends his survey of the breakdown of the "new liberal consensus" in the next chapter, which he titles "De-Centering Voices: Pluralization and the Liberationist Revolutions." Ibid., 221–81.

35. For a brief overview of Cone's black liberationist's theology, see Grenz and Olson, *20th Century Theology*, 206–10, and Dorrien, *Soul in Society*, 235–52.

such hot button topics as busing, affirmative action, quotas, and welfare reform against the professed claims of black "victimology."

Even if the shaper tones of this conservative discourse only modestly seeped into the mainline denominations, it nonetheless provided a language through which a formal opposition was mounted against the politics, culture, and "relativism" of the progressive 60s. By the end of the twentieth century within much of American Protestantism—evangelical as well as mainline—a practical consensus stabilized around King's vision on the importance of character. The crowning achievement of this consensus was the widespread acceptance of the inviolability of formal equality as an unequivocal birthright of a democratic political culture and the plain teachings of Christian social ethics. Of significance also, was a broad understanding of the persistence of urban poverty and the acknowledgment that the destructive legacy of slavery continues to have persisting negative impact on the lives of millions of lower class African Americans. The degree to which this continuing influence is still pervasive, and therefore relevant, has generated much debate, as reflected, for example, over the contentious issue of reparations for the injustice and inhumanity of slavery. Both conservative and progressive Protestants recognize that there is additional work to do and a broad range of practical steps that can be taken through various service projects and longer-range missions work in the inner city. Nonetheless, ideology remains a sticking point, in which for mainline progressive Christians, King's "I Have Dream" speech was a starting point, whereas for conservatives it was the consummation and crowning achievement of the civil rights movement.

On the conservative interpretation, slavery was viewed "a mistake." It was a singular blight that the nation corrected in the inevitable progress of the growth of American democracy, as expressed in the evocative language of Lincolnian rhetoric as "the last best hope for mankind." This vision was undergirded by a continuous messianic strand, ironically referred to as "American exceptionalism" in the academic literature and favorably re-appropriated in contemporary conservative rhetoric. This vision had its origins in the Puritan vision of a City on a Hill that became embodied in eighteenth- and nineteenth-century democratic and Protestant culture that interpreted America as a Christian nation called to fulfill its destiny in bringing not only liberty, but God's own light to a needy world.[36] In its

---

36. The historical roots of the imagery of American exceptionalism are examined in much depth in Sacvan Bercovitch's *Puritan Origins of the American Self, American Jeremiad*, and *Rites of Assent*. For an earlier study, Perry Miller's classic, *Life of the Mind in America*, 3–95, and his collection of essays, *Errand into the Wilderness*, 184–239, are indispensable for tracing the Puritan influence on the nineteenth-century American

various religious and secular forms, the imagery of American exceptionalism continues to reverberate within the contemporary US cultural imagination and has had particularly potent salience in the conservative political culture from the period of Goldwater to the present. Viewed from the vantage point of conservative historiography and cultural interpretation, with the correction course in place in the abolition of slavery and the end of legal segregation, African Americans can join the mainstream of American life where they too can embrace the upward trajectory of the American Dream and concentrate on the core values of moral rectitude, the entrepreneurial spirit, and individual salvation.

In focusing more on the pressing reality of institutional racism, various advocates of a more progressive vein viewed things in a considerably different light. Such issues as teenage pregnancy, drugs, illiteracy, excessively high school dropout rates, crime, and gang violence were not the result of a dysfunctional family, as sometimes claimed by conservative commentators. Rather, as argued by liberals and progressives, these problems need to be viewed as symptoms of a broader structural factors rooted in urban poverty and the persisting endurance of de facto segregation.[37] At issue is the availability of resources so that equal opportunity can become a live option, in which government is viewed as a major, but far from only source of support. Interpreted in this way, the federal budget is a major source of power that telegraphs the true heart of the nation's commitment to the poor and oppressed. Advocacy in such areas as equal education, adequate housing, and job training represented more than simply "leftist" political polemics, as conservatives charge. Rather, progressive Christians view such commitment to the poor, through the deployment of governmental resources, as a core biblical mandate—a faithful application of the prophetic tradition in the contemporary setting.[38]

From this interpretation, it follows that substantial social problems can never be resolved by voluntary associations, however important they are as an echo of the nation's conscious and as a contributing resource, in conjunction with more stabilizing institutional sources of influence. In this respect, there is clear lineage between contemporary political theology

---

cultural imagination.

37. O'Conner, *Poverty Knowledge*, 259–82.

38. In chapter 6 of *Soul in Society*, subtitled, "Economic Democracy and the Economics of Nature," Dorrien examines a range of proposals for working out a contemporary Christian progressive approach in coming to terms with the critical issue of economic justice (see 282–335).

of the mainline denominations and the social gospel heritage of the early twentieth century.[39]

In the quest for relevance, mainline denominations often downplay the biblical and theological significance of the social justice theme, which makes it difficult for them to distinguish their objectives from those of other social and religious groups. Inter-group and inter-religious collaboration on the critical issues of the day is both essential and desirable in a pluralistic society. It is an act of humility—to say nothing of civility and common sense—to draw support from a wide variety of sources in the challenging work of enhancing the social capital of the more marginalized sectors of the society. It is equally important for mainline Protestants to sharply articulate the biblical and theological rationale that grounds their social missions, at the least in terms of what Walter Brueggemann refers to as "behind the wall" conversation—that is, within the life of the church itself—and arguably in the broader public square, as well.[40]

This is essential for the purpose of establishing a strong and coherent Christian identity within the mainline denominations among the membership itself, and for articulating, fully and without apology, the theological basis upon which mainline social ethic is grounded. Justice is not an add-on to a strongly grounded biblical faith—it is, as Jim Wallis ably argues, a core component.[41] This is a case that needs to be made within the context of a fully embodied biblical theology as a reflection of evangelical intent as well as missions—a position that mainline denominations should not shy away from, both in terms of addressing their own house, as well as speaking in an avowedly prophetic voice to the wider culture.

Given its crucial importance within the history of the United States, a biblically based political theology that substantially addresses the issue of race can serve as a powerful organizing center to ground a broad range of social and political issues related to poverty, oppression, gender inequality, and the marginality of the socially outcast. Such work requires high Christologies from "above" based on the logos theology of John, as well as those from "below," as reflected, particularly in Luke, in the earthly ministry of Jesus to the poor, the oppressed, the marginalized, and the maimed. It is in the Trinitarian nexus that the Suffering Servant knows and takes on our pain within the pressing realities of our daily lives. It is this God

39. Throughout *Soul in Society*, Dorrien explores the relationship between the early twentieth-century social gospel movement and its various evolutionary tributaries throughout the century.

40. Brueggemann, "Legitimacy of a Sectarian Hermeneutic," 41–68.

41. This theme is a constant refrain in *Sojourners*, the monthly journal edited by Wallis (http://sojo.net/magazine).

that participates in the struggle for social justice (Luke 4:18–19) in a world turned upside down by the liberating values of the reign of God. With God's grace, a biblical theology that unequivocally addresses the challenging topic of race could be an important instrument in helping to unify an evangelical quest for the realm of God in which "the whole creation groans and labors with birth pangs" (Rom 8:22) for its fulfillment. To the extent that it is acted upon as an imaginative and potent theo-political vision with consequences in the real world, "justice [will] roll on like a river, righteousness like a never-failing stream" (Amos 5:24).

Such a vision will not come easily and may be fraught with considerable controversy. But if well-constructed on solid biblical and theological principles, it could provide the mainline denominations with a degree of authenticity and authority at a more extensive level than it currently possesses. Any such revitalization would require a great degree of theological acumen as well as political courage. Yet, it is one that could bring together the fundamental tenets of the social gospel and the traditional biblical faith in God transcendent and richly immanent. It is a vision of a God who participates in the joys and struggles of the daily existence of the marginalized and all who struggle with and for a view of reality based on the realm of God. It is one that provides hope within and also beyond history in the pressing forth and the waiting for the coming of God in all of the facets of personal and public life.

Feminist Theology and the Protestant Mainline

The topic of race has stimulated more than its share of controversy between progressive and conservative Protestants. For a variety of reasons, gender has proven to be an even more explosive issue. For one thing, while race has affected the mainline denominations more by way of indirection, gender concerns are more directly raised within the immediacy of the suburban pews as well as in the seminary lecture halls. Even more to the point, the nature of gender critique against traditional theology and the emergence of a distinctive feminist theology have challenged the very core of traditional biblical beliefs. That has been less the case on matters of race in which bigotry against African Americans can be directly analogized to the biblical story of an exodus people escaping slavery in the search for freedom in the promised land.[42] As summarized by Grenz and Olson, feminist theology

---

42. As summarized by Grenz and Olson: "Black theology was not concerned with the intellectual problems of secularized culture; its concern lay instead with the realities of the experiences of Blacks in America. As a result, Black theologians did not debate

"has allowed principles from outside" the Christian "heritage to become the controlling norms of what is truly 'Christian.'"[43]

In a similar vein, Dorrien points out that, in contrast to "other kinds of liberationist religion, white feminist theology inevitably raises the question whether its fundamental impulse is inimical to Christianity itself,"[44] particularly any notion of Jesus the Christ as the incarnate Son of God, the Father. For such language cannot be easily dispensed with if the biblical text is to be taken as the single most bedrock source of Christian revelation.

The title alone of Mary Daly's *Beyond God the Father* telegraphs the challenges posed by feminist theology and the inherent problematic of traditional Protestant theology, even in its contemporary variants, as holding any prospect of a liberationist potential to committed feminists. Daly's most epigraphic argument is that in defining the biblical deity primarily through male terminology, half the human race is ruled out as made in the image of God.[45] Moreover, while the father metaphor may have conveyed a vision of the holy in an ancient patriarchal society, the core challenge for contemporary Christian spirituality is that of authentically conveying "the relationship between the divine and the human that no [singular] model can encompass."[46] More radically put, if too much insisted upon, God the father imagery becomes a form of idolatry in conflating a product of the human imagination with the creator of the universe.[47]

Sallie McFague does not rule out traditional imagery of God, but places greater emphasis on positing alternative "models," including the more horizontal metaphor of God as friend. She acknowledges that "an immanental, exclusively feminist perspective [cannot] be absorbed into the

---

the question of how the idea of God could be made palatable to the modern mindset, for this was not an issue among their people. They sought rather to harness the biblical imagery for the goal of the advancement of the Back community." *20th Century Theology*, 202.

43. Ibid., 235.

44. Dorrien, *Soul in Society*, 257.

45. For an elaboration of this theme, consider the following from Daly: "Paul Tillich described himself as working 'on the boundary' between philosophy and theology. The work of this book is not merely on the boundary *between* these (male-created) disciplines, but on the boundary of both, because it speaks out of the experience of that half of the human species which has been represented in neither discipline." Ibid., 6.

46. McFague, *Metaphorical Theology*, 146.

47. This is a major theme in McFague's last chapter in *Metaphorical Theology*, "God the Father: Model or Idol?" McFague maintains that "the root-metaphor of Christianity is not God the father but the kingdom or rule of God." Ibid., 146. This opens up a range of "models" to depict the relationship between humankind and God that includes both "maternal imagery," and "shepherd" imagery of God providing "comfort, physical nurture, care, guidance, compassion." Ibid., 135.

Christian paradigm."[48] However, she points to this alternative imagery for "the genuine insights it offers for needed reform in that paradigm."[49] Such a depiction, critics fear, is one that may come at the cost of marginalizing the transcendent, as embodied in the master metaphor of God the Father inherent in the historical Protestant tradition that simultaneously preserves the personal and immanent aspects of God as reflected in Trinitarian and creational theology.[50]

McFague maintains that feminist theologians dispute the notion that God the Father conveys the imagery of a healthy relationship, at least to many women, in which the long reach of patriarchy has had a deleterious influence. A general theme in feminist theology is that the toxic effects of a patriarchal God extend beyond its impact on women to many facets of Western culture, particularly its penchant for violence, competitiveness, and related forms of oppression against the hated "other."[51]

McFague pushes well beyond the boundaries of traditional Protestant thought in her "reformist perspective" in which a child might conceivably "pray to a Mother in Heaven."[52] In this, she resonates with Rosemary Ruether who seeks to "deepen and transform Christianity's liberating-prophetic tradition" in a manner, in Ruether's words, "to include what was not included: women."[53] Sharing a mutual perspective with McFague, Ruether does not identify gender oppression as a master narrative within which all other forms are subsumed, but one, nonetheless, of central importance as reflected in traditional orthodox theologies. Similarly, McFague and Ruether place great weight on a theology rooted in lived experience and an embrace of nature as the incarnational space in which God as mother, father, and, for McFague, friend may be found. A passionate quest for a redeemed society underlies their theology in which the oppressed are liberated from the powers and principalities that keep them in bondage.

48. Ibid., 155.

49. Ibid., 156.

50. Moltmann, whose work may be viewed as a bridge between the dialelctical theology of Barth and the liberationist and ecological theologies of the contemporary period, maintains God the Father imagery in *The Trinity and the Kingdom* and *God in Creation*, though clearly in the mode of the crucified God.

51. Schüssler Fiorenza, *Power of the Word*, 217. Schüssler Fiorenza argues that a major problem of depicting God through a monotheistic lens is "the price that is to be paid when collective identity is imagined under a single principle, be it G*d or nationalism which necessitates violence against others and defines religious identity as exclusive identity." Ibid.

52. McFague, *Metaphorical Theology*, 160, 161.

53. Dorrien, *Soul in Society*, 267. Dorrien cited reference is from Ruether, *Sexism and God Talk*, 32.

Daly takes a more radical stance on the need for women to exorcise "the demonic destructiveness of the super-phallic society [internalized] in our own being."[54] Daly's root and branch anti-biblical stance includes a repudiation of the Genesis story of the fall, particularly the characterization of Eve as the human temptress, and much of the biblical narrative which, on her reading, builds upon oppressive imagery of women.[55] Dorrien characterizes "radical feminism" as "a revolt against every male produced religion and ideology" in which, as Daly characterizes it, "women are the dreaded anomie" of man's alienation and apprehension.[56] In her embrace of goddess language, Gnosticism, and even the occult, Daly pushes well beyond any prospect of reforming orthodox biblical theology, which she views as hopelessly mired in a patriarchal mindset. Any notion of God the Father is also stuck in an outdated notion of a transcendent "'Supreme Being' as an entity distinct from this world but controlling it according to plan and keeping human beings in a state of infantile subjection."[57]

Elizabeth Schüssler Fiorenza calls for a "hermeneutics of suspicion"[58] to challenge claims that identify dominant scriptural interpretations underlying biblical and theological orthodoxy as the primary source of authentic revelation of God's holy light. Rather, the Bible needs to be interrogated in its positing of a radical dualism between the redeemed and the rest of humanity. This includes the radical dualism between monotheism and polytheism and the underlying biblical association of monotheism with acts of violence against the practitioners of other religions, as described especially throughout the Old Testament. She argues that, as the result of such dualism, "Christian identity" has developed historically in violent opposition to the "Other." At the very least, dualistic assumptions built into the Old and New Testaments and reinforced through dominant theological interpretation should be interrogated through a rigorous hermeneutics of suspicion. Schüssler Fiorenza rejects radical exclusivism of any type, however biblically justified.

As Dorrien summarizes her stance as it relates to women, "rather than claim a biblical warrant for feminism on liberationist grounds, Schüssler Fiorenza begins with a feminist commitment that needs no support from

---

54. Daly, *Beyond God the Father*, 10.

55. Ibid., 44–68.

56. Dorrien, *Soul in Society*, 260. The Daly citation that is from the same page in Dorrien is from *Gyn/Ecology*, 39.

57. Daly, *Beyond God the Father*, 18.

58. Schüssler Fiorenza, *Power of the Word*, 218.

biblical religion."⁵⁹ It is this position to which she adheres in her decision to remain within the church for the purpose of radically reconstructing its fundamental precepts on the grounds for which she advocates.⁶⁰

For Schüssler Fiorenza, any viable reconstruction of Christianity would include a rejection of the prevailing "kyriocentric [i.e., domineering] rhetoric of scripture" for a more life healing "the*logy" based on "the open house of Wisdom [which] engages in critical questioning and debate in order to be able to arrive at a deliberate judgment about the bible's contribution to the 'good life,' to democratic self-determination and self-esteem."⁶¹ Part of Schüssler Fiorenza's task is one of historical reconstruction in searching out aspects of a largely repressed early Christianity where women played a significant role, as indicated in portions of Acts, some of the Pauline letters, and in the marginalized non-canonical literature of the early Christian period. The call, in short, is for a more inclusive canon through dialogue and "radical democratic thinking, which requires a particular quality of vision and civic imagination."⁶²

Feminist theology includes a wide range of perspectives, the breadth of which I have obviously not covered in this section.⁶³ My purpose in focusing on these four highly influential leaders is historical in highlighting some of the foremost tensions within Protestant thought and culture in the later decades of the twentieth century. The result is that I have emphasized the more contentious aspects of the work of these formative authors rather than placing the accent on the more constructive aspects of their theology. Underlying their various reflections is a common belief in the need to provide women with a much more extensive legitimacy at the very foundation of religious life. Core themes in their work include; an emphasis on social justice for all oppressed and marginalized groups; an immanent view of revelation; an embrace of the earth as a central focus of an ecologically

---

59. Dorrien, *Soul in Society*, 270.

60. Dorrien notes that Schüssler Fiorenza assumes that "feminists can fight the power of Christian patriarchy more effectively within the church than by renouncing their ties to the church." Ibid.

61. Schüssler Fiorenza, *Power of the Word*, 64, 263. In addition to such terms as kyriarchy, Schüssler Fiorenza references the neologism, "the*logy" throughout *The Power of the Word*. Her use of this term parallels her repudiation of "the orthodox Jewish writing of G-d . . . to the spelling of G*d with an asterisk, which seeks to avoid the conservative malestream [sic] association which the writing of G-d has for Jewish feminists." Ibid., 1n6. For a fuller discussion of historical and current trends in feminist theology, see Hunt and Neu, *New Feminist Christianity*, which includes a chapter by Schüssler Fiorenza, "Christian Feminist Biblical Studies," 86–96.

62. Schüssler Fiorenza, *Power of the Word*, 263.

63. See Hunt and Neu, *New Feminist Christianity*.

informed theology, and a relentless critique of resident forms of patriarchy grounded in biblical imagery and traditional theological commentary. These themes hold potential for incorporation into an ecumenically rich orthodox theology, but will require much careful work.[64] My concern is that a widespread appropriation of the views of these four luminaries, as currently articulated, would effectively deconstruct some of the most foundational presuppositions of Protestant theology as reflected in its nearly five hundred-year history.

To summarize this section, I acknowledge that there is much subtlety in feminist theology that I have not addressed. I also contend that placing the Bible in its fully orbed depth and narrative range in less than a central canonical role comes at a profound cost of marginalizing Christianity as a distinctive religion, with a consequent loss of its most potent rhetoric. The critical embrace of a comprehensive biblical vision has much to offer a revitalized mainline Protestant theology and religious culture, including a coherent theological rationale to ground its social ethic. A pathway toward this realization, including a substantial rethinking of the Word-World relationship and a corresponding modulation of the modernist-fundamentalist great divide, represents the quest, if not the realization of this book. The critique of feminist theology presented above is meant to be understood within this broader context of theological refashioning in placing the Word as the centerpiece for interpreting the World.

THE GOSPEL IN A PLURALISTIC SOCIETY: A PERSONAL REFLECTION

The title of this section comes from Leslie Newbigin's *Gospel in a Pluralistic Age*. I first came across this book while teaching an adult Sunday school class at the United Church of Christ in Bayberry located in Liverpool, New York, during the academic year of 1997–1998. The pastor, Mark Lawson, is a biblical scholar and a master Bible teacher of adults who would often draw in twenty or more participants in the many sessions that he led. Through Mark's leadership, serious, systematic, and informed Bible study became a major part of the adult education curriculum at Bayberry.[65]

When Mark asked me to teach a Sunday morning class for adults, I told him that my interests were rather specialized and that I was not the best

---

64. Fackre, in *Christian Story*, 2:103–24, makes an effort at doing so without eschewing criticism. I further address Fackre's commentary on feminist theology in chapter 5.

65. See Lawson, *Cracking the Book*, for an introduction to the Bible, with special appeal for the mainline Protestant community.

person for what he needed. I recommended a parishioner who I thought would do well in teaching a course, and who also had the capacity to connect effectively with a greater range of people than would I. Mark, in fact, asked that person, who did an exemplary job. Still, he did not let me off the hook. While I told him I was not likely to draw eight into my class, he asked me if I could attract four. I thought that was feasible. Moreover, I appreciated the fact that he thought I had something of value to offer. I organized the course on twentieth-century US theology and drew on Grenz and Olson's *20th Century Theology* as the key text for my preparation and planning.

Through the various courses that Mark taught, I was encountering a renewed appreciation for the Bible and drew imaginatively on a somewhat latent evangelical-Pentecostal mindset stemming from a "born-again" experience in 1972 which, though it had receded from the central focus it had in my life, had never gone dormant. While at Bayberry, I was reading the Bible meditatively on my own, with much emphasis on the book of Psalms. The Psalms have served for me, as for countless others over the centuries, as an essential prayer book through which I experienced a fresh connection with God, which sometimes only biblical language can open up. At the same time, I experienced this revitalized Christian faith as a supplemental counter-narrative to an identity that was primarily shaped by what might be described as a non-foundational, postmodern sensibility in which the prevailing secular culture set much of the context for my engagement with the biblical word. Throughout much of the 1980s and 1990s, this evangelical counter-narrative acted as a persisting minority refrain to the "logic" and compulsion of a secularly shaped identity that had much existential force for me. It was in this dualistic mindset that I taught the course and appropriated the Grenz and Olson text, which I interpreted as a solidly balanced survey written by highly educated moderate evangelicals who had the capacity to empathize with other theological perspectives, while raising critical concerns from their own theological stance.

I drew on the central transcendent/immanent tension, the underlying focus of *20th Century Theology*, to organize the topics of the course, which I sifted through the various typologies discussed in H. R. Niebuhr's classic, *Christ and Culture*. The latter text, which I discuss in some detail in chapter 7, points to the ineradicable influence of history in shaping the context in which the indwelling of Christ is experienced, in any and every given time and place. Niebuhr was exemplary in fleshing out the transcendent/immanent tensions between the universality of God's revelation in Christ and the ever present reality of human interpretation in shaping the relationship between faith and culture in given historical contexts. These tensions pointed to the consequent inescapability of the finitude of human experience in coming to terms with the transcendence of God, a topic Niebuhr also takes up in *Radical Monotheism and Western Culture*.

While having some desire to more fully embrace the transcendent and universal aspects of faith, in this course I remained more focused on the historical and immanent, with the culture providing the key context for interpreting the Word. We considered the various positions of Water Rauschenbusch, Harry Fosdick, and the Niebuhr brothers. Following H. R. Niebuhr in *Christ and Culture*, but emphasizing the liberal dimension of modern theology more than he, I adopted a hermeneutical perspective in which the culture—particularly contemporary historical, philosophical, literary, and anthropological scholarship—served as the primary context to interpret the Word. At the same time, my evangelical sensibility was provoked by Newbigin's *Gospel in a Pluralist Society*, a text that provided an important counterweight to my historicist interpretive framework. A scientist—whose daughter attended church school—was the most skeptical of our group in terms of accepting the validity of the Christian revelation, as depicted in the New Testament. I brought to his attention Newbigin's argument that one could credibly start with the Word, which had considerably different consequences on the relationship between faith and culture than if beginning with the operative assumptions of the culture.

I sought to impress upon him, as a point of informed consideration, that Newbigin's approach was an eminently rational one. If its biblically based premises were accepted, I reasoned, it provided a pathway to faith and a corresponding life reorientation. I was intrigued by what Newbigin opened up, yet remained uncertain about the extent to which his premise was something I could embrace, even as there was something within me that desired very much the sense of clarity that this pathway seemed to offer. My intent may have been more in the realm of self-persuasion than that of convincing my friend. Still, I did seek to press the logic of Newbigin's argument upon him—one which I was confident that he had not previously encountered. In this, I sought to appeal to my colleague's capacity for reasoned judgment by opening up the world of faith that Newbigin's argument evoked. Drawing also on Tillich's notion of "ultimate concern," I surmised from Newbigin's argument that a Word-first approach was a potentially viable one that individuals of substantial intelligence and educational background have followed and could do so with integrity.[66]

66. Newbigin speaks to "a difference between two ways of interpreting the data which are (potentially) available to all. The Christian believer is using the same faculty of reason as his unbelieving neighbor and he is using it to deal with the same realities, which are those which every human being has to deal. But he is seeing them in a new light, in a new perspective. They fall for him in a different pattern. He cannot justify

Quick on the uptake, my friend telegraphed his thoughts through a knowing smile when I told him, on his query, that Newbigin was a missionary. He quipped that such a narrow vocational focus misses a great deal of what is interesting in contemporary life. This deserved a response, namely, a question back on what difference the background of the writer makes since the issue is the nature of the argument, regardless as to authorship. In terms of the narrowness of focus, the missing out of a great deal is—to draw on New Testament imagery—just as plausibly the consequence of refusing to sell all that one owns for that one precious pearl upon which new life in the realm of God may just depend (Matt 13:45–46).

Viewing Newbigin's thesis as eminently plausible, yet not being thoroughly persuaded myself, these seemingly offhanded comments pierced me, so that doubts which were never far from present, once provoked, again flooded into my consciousness, challenging any notion that a consistent evangelical resolution to religious identity could be a viable option for me. The class broke up in March 1998 as my wife and I headed back to Connecticut. As a parting gift I gave this probing scientist my copy of *20th Century Theology* which he accepted with genuine thanks. As both his and my searching on the relationship between Christ and culture remained very much in process, I would like to think that both he and I were mutually enriched by our joint encounter.[67] Other things began to crowd into my consciousness. I dropped for a time a focused attention on Newbigin's argument and returned to my more "historicist" interpretation of Christian faith.

THE GOSPEL IN A PLURALISTIC SOCIETY: ANALYSIS AND IMPLICATIONS

When I had initially read through *The Gospel in a Pluralistic Society* in the late 1990s, I was not in a position to give Newbigin's argument the sustained

---

the new pattern in terms of the old; he can only say to his unbelieving neighbor, stand here with me and see if you don't see the same pattern I see." *Gospel in a Pluralistic Society*, 11. Elsewhere, Newbigin argues for the necessity to "affirm the gospel as truth, universal truth, truth for all peoples and for all times, the truth which creates the possibility of freedom." He maintains that "we negate the gospel if we deny the freedom in which alone it can be truly believed." Ibid., 10. It was something along these lines, but through a less formal mode of argument, that I sought to bring to my friend's attention.

67. Rev. Lawson informed me that a couple of years after this encounter, this person joined the church and became a committed Christian. More specifically, "while he continues to bring some healthy skepticism to particular biblical texts, he affirms the basic confessions of Christian faith and deeply enjoys Christian worship." Personal email from Mark Lawson, April 4, 2013.

Autobiographical Explorations of Twentieth-Century Protestant Thought 47

attention that it merits. I view it now for the pivotal role it can play, along with Barth's biblical reorientation of the Christ/culture relationship (see chapter 7), toward a revitalization of mainline Protestant theology in discerningly placing the Word at the interpretive apex of assessing the culture. What has moved me in this direction is the fuller realization that regardless of what stance one takes on any number of positions, the faith dimension that gives shape to what becomes viewed as relevant knowledge is based on a given set of values and worldview. These considerations point to the inescapable relationship between the "facts" of a given investigation and the supportive "beliefs" and "values" that undergird them.[68] That is a partial explanation.

The other facet is a more personal one: continued interface with contemporary secular thought and culture as a primary value orientation, and finding that wanting in substantial ways. In stating this, I do not deny the possibility of some dissimulation on my part in taking a leap of faith based on an earlier conversion experience that I may have, at some level, tendentiously sought to appropriate as a way of smoothing over tension points that may well have required closer examination. I cannot categorically deny that. Neither would I want to overly stress its possibility in that the various streams of motivation are typically more complex than we can readily fathom. Whatever conscious and unconscious influences went into this shift back into an intentional Christian identity, I would like to think that the still, small voice of God's Holy Spirit was in the midst of my probing, however invariably mixed with the peculiarities of my own idiosyncratic searching.[69] With this clearer mindset in place—a re-echoing of an earlier evangelical worldview from a more extensive field of knowledge and experience—I have become better able to appropriate Newbigin's challenging re-description of reality in my own faith walk. I am also more appreciative of the important role that this Barthian-like turn to faith as foremost vocabulary could play in revitalizing mainline Protestantism on its own foundational faith claims.

Lesslie Newbigin (1909–1998) was no fundamentalist. As a twentieth-century British missionary, Newbigin was keenly appreciative of the

---

68. Newbigin, *Gospel in a Pluralistic Society*, 14–18. The quoted words are highlighted as such by Newbigin. Ibid., 15, 17. See 19–26 for Newbigin's discussion on the intrinsic relationship of facts, values, and beliefs and the centrality of interpretation that gives shape to what becomes defined as true. In Newbigin's words: "When I say 'I believe,' I am not merely describing an inward feeling or experience: I am affirming what I believe to be true, and therefore what is true for everyone." Ibid., 22. For Newbigin, Christians "are not claiming to know everything. They are claiming to be on the way, and inviting others to join them as they press forward toward the fullness of truth, toward the day when we shall know as we have been known." Ibid., 12.

69. I describe this shift in the online *TheoTalk* article, "Small Still Prompting."

intellectual diversity of European culture and the importance of interfaith dialogue. He was well attuned to the underlying pluralistic worldview of Western culture and the prevailing incongruity of any claims to a faith based on the unique revelation of Christ as the incarnate Son of God. Newbigin states that he was tempted by what he referred to as "reasonable Christianity," "one that could be defended on the terms of my whole intellectual foundation as an Englishman." He became persuaded that this adaptation led to "domesticating the gospel."[70] This recognition spoke to a consequent need for a reorientation of his theological perspective. These observations led to a rejection of the dominant "plausibility structures" of the prevailing secular worldview which included dismissal of any religion claims as inherently truth bearing.[71] This led him to argue that

> no coherent thought is possible without presuppositions. What is required for honest thinking is that one should be as explicit as possible about what these presuppositions are. The presupposition of all valid and coherent Christianity is that God has acted to reveal and effect his purpose for the world in a manner made known in the Bible. Of course it is open to anyone to ask, "Why choose this staring point rather than another"...But then one has to ask the questioner about the assumptions from which he starts, and which perhaps have not been examined.[72]

Newbigin acknowledges that there is no direct relationship between the pursuit knowledge and the attainment of truth. Rather, while "we are led toward the truth" through disciplined investigation and sustained commitment to the directive path opened up, "there is a true sense in which we are—with others—seekers after the truth."[73] All knowledge claims, including those grounded in science, reason, common, or critical sense, have an irreducibly faith-based component, which require acceptance in order to enter more fully into the pathway of what they reveal about human experience. This fallibilistic stance is an irreducible component of all knowledge, one to which Newbigin adheres.

Whether on the side of science or religion, absolute certainty is beyond the purview of the human grasp, although one can, and actually must, make absolute truth claims from an inescapable epistemological finitude and test

---

70. Ibid., 3.

71. Drawing on sociologist Peter Berger, Newbigin defines "plausibility structures" as "patterns of belief and practice accepted within a given society which determine which beliefs are plausible to its members and which are not." Ibid., 8.

72. Ibid.

73. Ibid., 12.

them within the frame of reference opened up by a given field of study.⁷⁴ As Newbigin states, the "power of the human mind to think rationally is only developed in a tradition which itself depends on the experience of previous generations." Signs and "evidence of things unseen" (Heb 11:1 KJV) are what is available for science and religion alike. "Within an intellectual tradition dominated by the methods of natural science it will appear unreasonable to understand and explain things in terms of personal will and purpose. But if God exists and he is capable of revealing his purpose to human beings, then human reason will be summoned to understand and respond to this revelation and relate it to all other experience."⁷⁵ It is this presupposition upon which Newbigin grounds his theological argument.

To state this in more formal theological terms, for orthodox Christianity, the lack of absolute certainty on the grounds of *knowledge* is the result of our residence between the "not yet" symbolized in the second coming of Christ, in which faith will be turned into sight, and "the already" of the first coming, as a foretaste of greater things to come. The tensions between these distinctive biblical ages are enduring, even as what Christians refer to as the Holy Spirit mediates God's grace in the here and now. The capacity for effective reasoning remains important, even as questions and gaps persist, but the movement, as in science or any other inquiry, is faith in search of an ever surer basis in knowledge. In this respect, commitment to the Christian revelation is no different than adherence to the scientific method or to the belief in the equal validity of all religions. What drives the specific commitment and the logic therein is the starting place of any narrative construction upon which a given truth claim is made.

Newbigin challenges the reader to come to terms with "the gospel as truth, truth which is not to be domesticated within the assumptions of modern thought but which challenges these assumptions and calls for their revision."⁷⁶ This requires a deliberate reason-based faith stance as the frame of reference to challenge the dominant plausibility structures of the prevailing cultural or scientific thinking that would reduce religious claims to a mere belief. Such explanations of truth seeking in the mode of fallibilistic inquiry, as described by Popper and Peirce, could open up the intellectual plausibility of faith in idioms those outside of its boundaries might consider.⁷⁷ Internal justification through the efficacy of the Holy Spirit, as an

---

74. Peirce, "Scientific Attitude and Fallibilism," 42–59; Popper, "Truth, Rationality and the Growth of Scientific Knowledge," 291–338.

75. Newbigin, *Gospel in a Pluralistic Society*, 9.

76. Ibid., 5.

77. In addition to Popper, who provides a theory of scientific inquiry on critical rational grounds, and Peirce, who does so through the perspective of philosophical

ultimate source of revelation needs to be linked to more external sources, such as the authorial claims intrinsic within the biblical text and theological "modifications which must be submitted to the judgment of the Christian community as a whole, and which may be subject to debate and dispute for many years."[78]

However valid a truth claim may be within a given tradition, the "logic" therein would not necessarily prove convincing or relevant to those outside its given framework. Such "evidence" offered, therefore, within a given plausibility structure may not necessarily "demand a verdict"[79] among those who remain outside its operative assumptions, however valid it may or may not be (e.g., proof offered for the physical resurrection of Jesus of Nazareth) for a given community of inquiring believers. Thus, beyond the apologetic function, there is an irreducible dogmatic core to the Christian faith, as there is with science, conveyed through its own inherent presuppositions that remain reasonably durable over time, which can accommodate scope for modification within a given paradigmatic range.

For Protestant Christianity, the core claims of the New Testament, canonically interpreted through the prism of the entire Bible, remain the primary source of belief. Theology emerges as a secondary and necessary source of illumination, which fleshes out aspects and conclusions of the primary text within the context of historical and cultural unfolding over time. Disputes about many specific aspects of contemporary or ancient Christian theology may or may not fall within the purview of what might be considered an ecumenically generous Christian orthodoxy. That is a matter of public discernment within the household of faith, in which disagreements over matters of much signification are likely to persist. However, to posit any other claim than the revelation of the incarnate Son of the living God as revealed first and foremost through the New Testament is to put faith in nothing less than another gospel.[80]

---

pragmatism, see also La Montagne, *Barth and Rationality*, for a theologically grounded fallibilistic, truth-claiming mode of inquiry based on the philosophical tenets of critical realism. While there are significant differences in these modes of inquiry, what they share in common is an acceptance of truth as a regulative ideal, which grounded inquiry progressively discloses, even as the gap between the quest and attainment remains unfathomable in scope.

78. Newbigin, *Gospel in a Pluralistic Society*, 50.

79. See the various books by McDowell following from his first apologetic text, *Evidence That Demands a Verdict*.

80. Newbigin argues that the Christian faith is best understood in narrative terms, as "a story which is not yet finished, a story in which we are still awaiting the end when all becomes clear." *Gospel in a Pluralistic Society*, 12. This is not a free-floating story, but one rooted in history, "not just in the sense that it depends on the historical

In the current era, the Christian faith can be easily absorbed within an ideology of pluralism, premised on the assumption that the various world religions provide equally valid pathways to right relationship with the living God. On this interpretation, Christianity represents one pathway to the holy. As a self-acknowledged de-centered Christian whose primary plausibility structure resided within the realm of the secular, this embrace of pluralism, in which Christianity represented one claim among others, was a position for which I had once argued with considerable tenacity. Against this (the stance maintained throughout this book) is the foundational point upon which orthodox Christianity may well stand or fall—namely, the radical particularity of Christ revealed as the very Son of the living God, the "High Priest" (Heb 8:1–6), in whom all the "fullness [of God, the father] dwell[s]" (Col 1:19). This primary belief in Jesus the Christ as the Son, and the very embodiment of God in human flesh, has been the prevailing source of orthodox Christian doctrinal stabilization for almost nineteen hundred years.

It is this "scandalous" vision which modern liberal Protestantism has considerably muted that provoked Newbigin's counter-response. From his point of view—as well as the one agued in this book—to accept the predominant premises of modern liberal Protestantism is to effectively uproot the very basis of the Christian revelation that God in human flesh is embodied in no name than that of Jesus the Christ. In the pluralist vision, which has so attracted modern liberal Protestantism, Christianity would survive as one of the great world religions. However, it would be shorn of its radical specificity, even as the Christ narrative as mythos "beyond incarnation" would be given credibility as, perhaps, a beautiful story possessing a certain appeal and revealing a certain metaphorical truth to a given community of believers.[81] In this light, Bishop Spong rejects any call of a Great Commission as an undesirable residue of an earlier era. Moreover, in his rendition, such core theological concepts as theism, the incarnation, and original sin would be eliminated or radically re-fashioned in the "new Christianity."[82]

This depiction of Spong might be seen as a caricature of liberal Protestantism—the complexity of which is far from cut from the same prefabricated

---

record" of interpreted facts, "but also in the sense that it is essentially an interpretation of universal history." Ibid., 13. Newbigin identifies the truth of Christian revelation, as mediated in the foremost manner in the Bible, as best expressed in a narrative mode. This includes scope for metaphor, paradox, overstatement, irony and mystery, as well as propositional truth statements. Newbigin shares a close affinity with Fackre's narrative theology which I discuss in chapter 5 and with Lints's redemptive-historical biblical theology which I discuss in chapter 8.

81. Spong, *New Christianity for a New World*, 129–46.

82. Ibid. See 171–85 for his critique of evangelical and world missions and 147–70 for his rejection of original sin as a viable theological concept in the "new Christianity."

cloth. My objective, at this point, is not to enter into the subtleties of liberal theology, with roots extending back at least to Schleiermacher.[83] I focus on Spong because in his "new Christianity for a new world" he logically carries out some of the most radical impulses of modern Protestant liberalism. In so doing, he places into sharp relief the core orthodox claim that Christ is "the way, the truth, and the life" (John 14:6) without equivocation and remainder, however much subtlety, explication, and humility is needed to effectively argue such, and however limited may be the understanding of particular expositors. Much hangs in the balance; namely, the legitimacy of Christianity as a distinctively unique religion with its own particular claims.

The question, as posed in mid-twentieth-century theological terms, is where one places one's "ultimate concern" or primary "center of value," and the role of the reigning plausibility structures of the modern secular era in giving shape to the response.[84] Newbigin takes contemporary thought with considerable seriousness. Nonetheless, he posits the "more difficult"—and, as argued throughout his book and mine—the ultimately more satisfying "enterprise of trying to understand modern thought in light of the biblical story."[85] This requires much subtle theological probing and apologetic explication in which any semblance of caricature is rejected as un-Christian. Such efforts are likely to be highly partial, although I argue for the importance of grappling diligently with truth claims, even as they remain beyond the realm of epistemological certainty. What is critical is the trajectory, namely a reversal of a century's theological tendency, by placing the biblical revelation as a central mainline Protestant concern in a manner that thoroughly comes to terms with modern critical scholarship. In this ambition, I am drawing on Newbigin as well as Barth for critical support in drawing on the Bible's central truth claims as the basis for contemporary Protestants to engage the culture.

For all intents and purposes there are two alternatives. The first is the direction posited by Spong, in which the core tenets of orthodoxy are gutted in order to preserve something of the essence of the Christian mythos in a pluralistic world. The second is the direction of a canonically grounded, scholarly informed ecumenically rich orthodoxy, in which the fundamental precepts of the New Testament revelation becomes the basis for interpreting and engaging the culture. With Newbigin and Barth I posit the latter, clearly through a position of faith in search of greater knowledge and with

83. See Dorrien, *Word as True Myth*, 10–72, and *Soul in Society*, 1–90, for substantial overviews of twentieth-century American liberal Protestant history.

84. See Tillich, *Dynamics of Faith*, 1–29, on ultimate concern and H. R. Niebuhr, "Center of Value," 100–113.

85. Newbigin, *Gospel in a Pluralistic Society*, 95.

the acknowledgment that the questions stemming from the culture have much penultimate signification. This presupposition cannot be proven by human reason, evidence, or logic, even as reason, logic and evidence "of what we do not see" (Heb 11:1) can and will be given.

In the next four chapters I seek to do so by exploring ways in which Packer, Bloesch, Fackre, and Brueggemann probe into the relationship between faith and culture, with a particular focus on their theology of Scripture and theology of God. In so doing I am unfolding the historical discussion of the impact of the fundamentalist/modernist divide into the theological work of these four, in search of a mediating centrist perspective, with the acknowledgment that my reach invariably exceeds my grasp. My effort is primarily irenic in that I am seeking to tease out theological resources for strengthening an orthodox Protestant center in a manner that places the Bible in the privileged relationship to that of the culture. Chapter 7, which focuses on the neo-orthodox legacy, continues along this vein. That three of the four protagonists in my book—Bloesch, Fackre, and Brueggemann—have drawn deeply from the neo-orthodox theology, and even Packer is supportive of the Barthian turn to the Bible, is a consideration of no minor importance for incorporating this perspective into the argument. The theological depth and range of Barth's vision also underlies the dialectical and postliberal theology of Douglas J. Hall and Gary Dorrien whose work richly informs my understanding of neo-orthodoxy. Chapter 8 brings the discussion back to the contemporary era through a comparative discussion of postliberal dialectical and evangelical narrative theology in the respective theologies of Hall and Lints, the latter of whose work shares many similarities with Newbigin and Fackre. In seeking to counteract the enduring influence of the fundamentalist/modernist divide in contemporary US Protestant thought and culture, my effort does not stand alone.[86]

---

86. In addition to Fackre, *Ecumenical Faith in Evangelical Perspective* and *Restoring the Center*, and Phillips and Okholm, *Nature of Confession*, see Grenz, *Renewing the Center*; Lindbeck, *Nature of Doctrine*; Murphy, *Beyond Liberalism and Fundamentalism*; and Placher, *Unapologetic Theology*, which seek to establish centrist ground in contemporary Protestant thought and culture.

3

Defending the Fundamentals of Historical Evangelicalism

J. I. Packer and the Written Word of God

When Christians debate whether Christ's authority attaches to what the church teaches or to what individuals think or to what the Bible says, they are not suggesting that these three never coincide or that two of them have no authority at all. What they are trying to decide is which of these three is *decisive*. This giving of decisive direction is what authority is all about.[1]

Knowing God involves, first, listening to God's Word and receiving it as the Holy Spirit interprets it, in application to itself; second, noting God's nature and character, as his Word and work reveal it; third; accepting his invitations and doing what he commands; fourth, recognizing and rejoicing in the love that he has shown in thus approaching you and drawing you into his divine fellowship.[2]

All your words are true; all your righteous laws are eternal (Ps 119:160).

---

1. Packer, *Truth and* Power, 16.
2. Packer, *Knowing God*, 37.

OVERVIEW

We begin our survey of contemporary biblical scholars and theologians with the highly influential J. I. Packer. My selection of former Anglican, British born J. I. Packer as the representative non-Barthian evangelical voice is based on influence rather than geographical location.[3] Given Packer's engagement with the American evangelical tradition, including his subtle grappling with fundamentalism and the broad receptivity of his work amongst evangelicals in the United States, Packer became for me a logical choice.

Packer captures the heart pulse of the piety and intellectual rigor of the twentieth-century US evangelical movement in a way that honors its fundamentalist influences in its unwavering repudiation of privileging the cultural assumptions of secular modernity. At the same time, he rejects the anti-intellectual tendencies and the spirit of tendentiousness sometimes fostered within fundamentalism in the various "battles for the Bible" that keep the faith once for all delivered to the saints in a much more insular status than necessary.[4]

He is well known for his popular writing, as attested by his "over one million sold" *Knowing God*.[5] As evident in Packer's first book, *"Fundamentalism" and the Word of God*, his hermeneutical and theological acuity are more complex than what may be initially perceived from his better selling works, which are directed toward bridging the gap between formal theo-

---

3. Due to its support of same-sex marriage, Packer broke with the Anglican Diocese of New Westminster in 2002. See his Christianity Today article titled, "Why I Walked." For Packer's assessment of Barth, see *Truth and Power*, 115–18.

4. Packer, *"Fundamentalism" and the Word of God*, 9–40. In this early publication (1958) Packer recommended foregoing the term fundamentalism as a theological label. "The word is prejudicial, ambiguous, explosive and in every way unhelpful to discussion. It does not clarify; it merely confuses. It is only in use today because its critics have dragged it up." Ibid., 40. In this early publication, Packer also called for a tactical rejection of the term, but not the concept of biblical inerrancy. See *Truth and Power*, 101. In his more recent writings, Packer has embraced the doctrine of inerrancy as long as it is "circumscribed by precise hermeneutical guidelines" based on "the meaning that can be read out of the [biblical] text in its own context" rather than "any imposed sense, any meaning that can be read into the words when they are placed in a different context." Packer's meaning is that Scripture has decisive authoritative standing "as a sure rule for faith and life." Ibid., 102. It is this authoritative Scripture, so defined, Packer argues, that represents the underlying spirit of fundamentalism and biblical inerrancy, whether or not those specific terms are used. See *"Fundamentalism" and the Word of God*, 41–74, for Packer's discussion on the authoritative finality of Scripture as the spoken Word of God, which as he regularly notes, can only be discerned through the efficacy of the Holy Spirit.

5. The citation is on the back cover of the 20th-anniversary paperback edition of *Knowing God*.

logical studies and the pastoral and pietistic needs of practicing clergy and the educated laity. In his popular texts, Packer shares a similar theological perspective with his fellow British colleagues John Stott, author of *Basic Christianity*, and C. S. Lewis, author of the highly influential *Mere Christianity*. Both of these classics in contemporary evangelical studies were published approximately at the same time (the early 1970s) as Packer's *Knowing God*. Packer's more technical writings in theology, biblical hermeneutics, apologetics, and religious culture illuminate the scholarly depth that underlies his more popular work, a connection that can be missed without a solid knowledge of the range of his work and attention to the diverse audiences that he has addressed throughout his lengthy career.

It is on the breadth of his influence and the depth of his biblical theology within the evangelical tradition that I draw on Packer as a valuable conversation partner in the development of an ecumenical Bible centered theological vision rooted within the core doctrines of the historical Reformation tradition. These "key features of Christianity—the divine triunity; human fallenness; incarnation; reconciliation; new creation; faith, hope, love—are found to be unambiguously plain and have, in fact, have been found so for centuries."[6] On these core tenets, Packer's reflections provide a wealth of insight that evangelical and mainline readers alike, who seek a substantial engagement with the Bible and the classical Protestant theological tradition, can appropriate from his many books.

One may disagree with certain aspects of Packer's biblical methodology, theology, analysis of the neo-orthodox, or his critique of the liberal Protestant tradition.[7] Even so, it is difficult to discount the depth of his biblical reflections that constitute the core of his work, along with his capacity to speak with much discernment to theologians, the ordained clergy, and

---

6. Packer, *Truth and Power*, 110.

7. Bloesch and Fackre are more empathetic to the neo-orthodox tradition—specially to Barth, Bonhoeffer, and Reinhold Niebuhr—than is Packer. With Packer, Fackre identifies the canonical Bible as the primary source of revelation. Yet, Fackre is more inclined than Packer to engage liberal Protestant theologians on their own terms, while maintaining a critical stance. The contemporary dialectical postliberal scholars Douglas J. Hall and Gary Dorrien, whose work I draw on in chapters 7 and 8, also take issue with Packer's critique of neo-orthodoxy and Christian liberalism. They are critical of Packer's emphasis on biblical inerrancy, infallibility, canonical harmonization, and refusal to "deny, disregard, or arbitrarily relativize, anything that the biblical writers teach." Packer, "Encountering Present-Day Views of Scripture," 16. For Packer's depiction of inerrancy, neo-orthodoxy, and Christian liberalism, see ibid., 15–18, 10–13, and 7–10. The differences between Packer and the cited authors are significant. Nonetheless, the common thread is a profound appreciation for the significance of the tradition of the Protestant Reformers, including a call to embrace the Bible as a primary source of Christian revelation and Protestant renewal.

the educated laity, largely within the evangelical community. A powerful orthopraxy flows through his writing, a studied passion for the realm of Christ that has resulted in Packer's broad influence within evangelicalism across the Anglo-American landscape over the last fifty years.[8] Any confessional mainline theology that seeks close dialogue with serious evangelical scholarship in placing the Bible in a central interpretive role of Christian meaning and praxis would do well to give close scrutiny Packer's proposal.[9]

PACKER'S CRITIQUE OF THE ENLIGHTENMENT PROJECT

Packer's theology of Scripture represents a fundamental challenge to the precepts of modern intellectual life and culture, particularly against the Enlightenment project which he seeks to turn on its head in what he refers to as "God's Freedom Trail." Freedom, liberty, and authority are the key topics Packer addresses in the first chapter of *Truth and Power: The Place of Scripture in the Christian Life*.[10] He contends that a substantial grounding in the biblical revelation through the Word and Spirit is the surest basis for the realization of human liberation which he contrasts to the Enlightenment's pathway "in [its] dreams of the perfectability of man."[11] Packer maintains that such visions became transformed in the nineteenth and early twentieth centuries into an unrelenting pursuit of progress through the elusive quest for the gradual control and organization of nature, society, and the self. It is this illusory quest that Packer views as an utter disaster for humankind. In the search for truth Packer acknowledges an innate human drive to identify legitimate sources of epistemological authority. Advocates of the Enlightenment place ultimate authority on human reason. Packer values reason as a penultimate good based on solid biblical precepts bestowed by the Creator, governed by the direction of the Holy Spirit.[12]

---

8. For a discussion on how Packer's theology informs his spirituality, see "Introduction to Systematic Spirituality," 194–209, and "Evangelical Foundations for Spirituality," 227–43. The cited texts include Alister McGrath's excellent introductions to each essay contained in an edited work by him, *J. I. Packer Collection*, which chronologically organizes Packer key essays. Packer's integration of theology and spirituality is also highlighted in the two most extensive profiles of Packer, McGrath, *J. I. Packer*, and Payne, *Theology of the Christian Life*.

9. See Fackre, *Ecumenical Faith in Evangelical Perspective*, for one such effort to engage evangelical scholarship from a centrist mainline theological sensibility.

10. Packer, *Truth and Power*, 11–55.

11. Ibid., 12.

12. Packer, *Fundamentalism and the Word of God*, 126–45.

According to Packer, an underlying belief in human reason represents the primary source of authority in both the academic disciplines and the broader cultural matrix of contemporary society. This overly optimistic view has been subject to a searing critique through various forms of postmodern philosophy and trends within contemporary pragmatism that focus on irony and social and intellectual complexity.[13] Whether through an Enlightenment or post-Enlightenment vantage point, religious faith is perceived as a historical construct that, by definition, cannot be interpreted on its own intrinsic grounds—theology.[14] Twentieth-century and twenty-first-century Western liberal theologians do not reject the religious as an authentic dimension of human experience. They have, however largely accepted the academic canons of history, science, and cultural anthropology as primary tools in interpreting the Bible and religious experience.[15]

Packer has labored diligently to counter the modern secular paradigm through the development of a highly cogent Reformed angle of vision. In this Reformed sensibility he shares a close affinity with Donald Bloesch and Gabriel Fackre who merge an evangelical worldview with a neo-orthodox theological perspective.[16] Like Bloesch and Fackre, Packer appreciates the influence of Barth's impact on the trajectory of twentieth-century theology in turning to the Bible. However, he is critical of Barth's refusal to embrace an inerrant view of Scripture.[17] While their styles and sensibilities are different, Packer's concerns are similar to those of Douglas J. Hall, as the latter presented them some forty years later. As Hall writes:

> (1) The Christian community must be occupied with the biblical and doctrinal substance of its faith because this is its window on the world, the intellectual-spiritual perspective from which it "discerns the signs of the times" (Luke 12:56). (2) This professional contemplation of the word when it is serious (and therefore not just "professional") *thrusts* the discipline community into *active engagement* with the world; that is, far from providing a once-remove from history, the right profession of the faith

---

13. On postmodern deconstructionism, see Foucault, *Archeology of Knowledge and the Discourse on Language*, and Lyotard, *Post-Modern Condition*, as representative works. Bernstein, *Pragmatic Turn* and Rorty, *Consequences of Pragmatism*, are well known examples of postmodern philosophical studies written in the philosophical pragmatic tradition.

14. Holly, review of *Religion and Rationality*.

15. Ogden, *On Theology*, 3–19, 154–68.

16. Compare this chapter with chapters 4 and 5 for a discussion of commonalities and differences between Packer, Bloesch, and Fackre.

17. Packer, *Truth and Power*, 115–18.

Defending the Fundamentals of Historical Evangelicalism

already serves, on the contrary, to push the no doubt reluctant church ever more insistently into the actual life of the world. (3) In particular such contemplation creates in the discipline community a vigilance for *whatever threatens its world's life*.[18]

In their mutual embrace of the tradition of the Protestant Reformers, Hall and Packer share a close affinity, despite their different biblical hermeneutics and interpretation of contemporary history.[19]

FUNDAMENTALISM, EVANGELICAL THEOLOGY, AND THE BIBLE AS THE WORD OF GOD

Packer has rejected anti-intellectual and self-righteous tendencies in fundamentalism, while remaining firmly anchored in the Reformed and evangelical traditions.[20] He appreciates the doctrinal soundness of fundamentalism

---

18. Hall, *Confessing the Faith*, 12. I address Hall's work in some depth in chapters 7 and 8.

19. See chapter 8 for an extensive discussion of Hall's theology and the similarities and differences between his perspective and that of evangelical theologian Richard Lints, whose biblical theology and analysis of contemporary secular culture shares strong affinities with that of Packer.

20. Packer contends that "'Fundamentalism' is just a twentieth-century name for historic Evangelicalism," though he disputes the usefulness of the label. *"Fundamentalism" and the Word of God*, 19. He identifies the term historically with the challenges posed to orthodox biblical Christianity by late nineteenth-century liberalism. Ibid., 24–29. In this objective, Packer associates himself with the theological intent of defending the fundamentals of the historical biblical faith. Nonetheless, he is critical of the "pronounced anti-intellectual bias" of the twentieth century fundamentalist movement, its "distrustfulness of scholarship," its "skeptical" attitude "to the value of reasoning in matters of religion and [its] truculent . . . attitude toward the argument of its opponents." Ibid., 32. Packer's objective in this early publication was to defend the underlying intent of the twentieth-century fundamentalist movement by associating the most important aspects of its claims and its critique of Protestant liberalism with the historic Reformed tradition. It is from this latter theological location that Packer refashioned the fundamentals of the faith, first and foremost, against the liberal, and secondarily, against what he took as the neo-orthodox challenge to historic Protestant biblical orthodoxy. In its theology, biblical hermeneutics, and critique of Protestant liberalism, *"Fundamentalism" and the Word of God* is characterized by a highly focused reasoned argumentation through which Packer seeks to defend the historic evangelical faith in a manner that can hold up against the best scholarship of Protestant liberalism and neo-orthodoxy. This book merits being taken seriously among theologians who are more or less in accord with Packer, as well as among those who veer toward a more liberal perspective. It contains the core themes for which Packer has advocated throughout his lengthy career. It remains an excellent distillation of traditional evangelical hermeneutics, theology, and analysis of mid-twentieth century liberal theology that Packer has updated in his more recent writings.

in its unequivocal repudiation of nineteenth- and twentieth-century Protestant theological liberalism. Yet, he is concerned with the negative connotations that have surrounded the term "fundamentalism" due, in part, to its argumentative excesses, as well as the result of polemical attacks from liberal theologians and the media that depend more on stereotype than substantive analysis. For these reasons, Packer initially advocated eliminating the term in order to focus on the resources and wealth of the historical biblically based evangelical theology that he associates with true Christianity.[21]

In his broad-based focus on historical evangelicalism, Packer notes that "the inerrancy debate about whether we should treat all Bible teaching as true and right is really about how far we can regard Scripture as authoritative."[22] Neither the concept of infallibility nor inerrancy, which Packer views "as substantially synonymous,"[23] are "essential for stating the evangelical view," even as the underlying intent of such language is indispensable for honoring and preserving a robust theology of the triune God. What Packer means by infallibility is the Bible's "wholly trustworthy and reliable" nature. What he means by inerrant is "wholly true." In this conjoint definition, Packer draws on these terms to express the conviction that the entirety of the Bible is the utterance of God "'who cannot lie,' whose word, once spoken, abides forever, and therefore, it may be trusted implicitly."[24]

As Packer further argues, "God's Word" is "infallible because God Himself is infallible." Further, "the infallibility of Scripture is simply the infallibility of God speaking." Packer's claim of biblical infallibility is based on what Scripture is designed to address; "all things necessary to salvation," but not to matters related to science, history, or grammar.[25] These topics are not unimportant. However, they need to be sifted through a careful process of biblical hermeneutics in light of the best available contemporary scholarship. They are subject to ongoing investigation. For Packer, what is not open ended is the sufficiency "of biblical language" in communicating God's will as related to "our life of faith and obedience" to Christ. However limited that knowledge, what we know of "Jesus Christ is adequate to bring us to God." In the same manner, "Holy Scripture is adequate to bring us to Jesus Christ."[26]

---

21. Packer, *"Fundamentalism" and the Word of God*, 40. See n4 in this chapter.
22. Packer, *Truth and Power*, 14.
23. Packer, "Adequacy of Human Language," 36.
24. Packer *"Fundamentalism" and the Word of God*, 95.
25. Ibid., 96.
26. Packer, "Adequacy of Human Language," 37.

Packer's argument in favor of biblical inerrancy and infallibility has less to do with reason, logic, or theological exactness. Its purpose, rather, is "soteriological, obediental, doxological, and devotional."[27] In receiving a Bible that we "can trust absolutely,"[28] we can rest with full assurance into the mystery of the revelation of God in Christ reconciling us and the world to him. Without this guarantee we are thrown back on the paltriness of our own resources, however much we may claim allegiance to the Christian faith.[29] It is these claims for which Packer contends against those of Protestant liberalism, neo-orthodoxy, and even evangelical perspectives that do not rely absolutely on the assurance of the Bible in its capacity to convey the very mind and will of God when interpreted appropriately.

Packer's overarching claim is "that Scripture sets before us the factual and moral nature of things" about the human condition. In its most ultimate intent, "God's law" corresponds to "created human nature, so that in fulfilling his requirements we fulfill ourselves." According to Packer, "not a touch of authoritarianism enters into his exercise of authority over us."[30] That is because in fulfilling our relationship with God we attain the very purpose of life, which to miss is to lose a great deal. Packer argues that there is no surer pathway to this realization than through a thorough appreciation of the Bible as the place where God most completely and unequivocally speaks.

He also argues that the precepts of faith, as disclosed in and through the Bible, "are not in themselves unreasonable, but they are above reason; they terminate in mysteries which the human mind can express only as paradoxes." As he further explains:

> Reasoning may prepare the mind for faith in these truths, by showing their meaning and biblical basis, their congruity with the total biblical outlook and the known facts of life, and the weaknesses of objectives made to them; but reasoning alone cannot produce faith, for faith goes further than reason could take it. Reasoning at best could only suggest probability, but the nature of faith is to be certain. Any measure of doubt or

---

27. Ibid.
28. Ibid., 36–37.
29. Packer avers that "Scripture, though human, is divine." In the Bible, "we have a divine reality that has in it more than we can understand, like the mystery of the Trinity or incarnation." Packer, "Inerrancy and the Divinity and Humanity of the Bible," 155. For Packer, absolute assurance in the Bible is understood within the mystery of God's revelation. It is not a possession. As Packer sees it, the Bible is a "divine" text—the Word of God given to humankind—"an integral element in the doctrine of revelation." Ibid., 157. For this reason, the Bible can be relied on absolutely in the very process of working out our faith in full assurance.
30. Packer, *Truth and Power*, 15.

uncertainty is not a degree of faith, but an assault upon it. Faith, therefore, must rest on something more sure than an inference of probability.[31]

That something more is trust through faith bestowed by grace that the highest truth of God available to humankind is revealed in and through the Bible. The validity of such faith cannot "be demonstratively proved; for such proof is only possible in principle on the basis of an exhaustive understanding of its object."[32]

The negative corollary is that once

> you give up the New Testament view of biblical inspiration—there is no limit on how far you will go in rejecting or relativizing biblical assertions. There is no limit apart from your own arbitrary will. Protestantism's current confusion is largely due to the way its teachers have fanned out at this point producing as many sub-biblical theologies as there have been thinkers to devise them.[33]

Packer contends that once the Bible is interpreted as anything less than the revealed word of God, every single tenet of faith—including God's theocentric reality—is open to radical revision, deconstruction, and re-mythologization. The Bible is far from exhaustive in its revelation of God. Nonetheless, Packer maintains that it is the most substantial bulwark available in sustaining a foundational Christian stance. This is based on the twin claim that Scripture is both a source of direct divine revelation of God's Word and the potency of its revelatory persuasiveness among receptive readers against the many intruding forces to the contrary when "sound doctrine" (2 Tim 4:3) is replaced with other teachings. As created beings, we neither need nor can expect to have complete knowledge of God. The quest for such is to be like God; the fundamental sin of Adam and Eve. Nonetheless, Packer holds that Scripture is absolutely reliable for that which it is relevant; the salvation of our souls and the reconciliation of the world. As he states:

> If we ask what knowledge about God biblical language communicates, the answer is not exhaustive knowledge of himself and of all things in relation to him—the knowledge that is distinctively his—but only such knowledge of those matters as he sees to be adequate (i.e., sufficient) for our life of faith and obedience.

---

31. Packer, *"Fundamentalism" and the Word of God*, 117.
32. Ibid., 116.
33. Packer, *Truth and Power*, 48.

"The secret things belong to the Lord our God, but the things revealed belong to us and our children forever, that we may follow all the words of the Lord" (Deut 29:29). This, in concrete terms, is the adequacy of biblical language: it suffices, not indeed to make us omniscient in any area, but as a "lamp to [our] feet and a light [for] our path" in discipleship (Ps 119:105).[34]

Biblical revelation proceeds on the basis of faith preceding knowledge. The illumination that God provides can seem like foolishness to the world (1 Cor 1:27). There is no moving outside the circularity and even the scandal of the revelatory claims of Scripture because the depths of "sound doctrine" are ever unfathomable in the riches of "the mystery that has been hidden for ages and generations, but is now disclosed to the saints" (Col 1:26). It is this gospel and this gospel only to which we are to "be prepared in season and out of season" (2 Tim:4:2) to proclaim. These statements reflect the core and substance of Packer's highly nuanced theology of Scripture.

THE BIBLE AS THE DECISIVE WORD OF GOD

Packer maintains that within Christianity there are three alternatives in the mediation of God's revelation to humankind:

1. The church as authority.
2. The individual as authority.
3. The Bible as authority.[35]

Packer does not suggest "that these three never coincide or that two of them have no authority at all."[36] His point is not that the Bible is the only source of revelation, but that of pinpointing Scripture as the decisive source of authority among the three. In practice there is much blending among these sources. Yet, the ideal of blending begs the question of determining where priorities lie in which subtle discernment is needed. Such judgment is both unavoidable and crucial, without which irresolvable confusion resulting in more ambiguity than what may be warranted. On Packer's reading (which I share), the result of such skirting can only be that progress toward theological clarity—an aspiration to be striven toward even in the midst of the unfathomable mystery of God—can only remain impeded. False closure has its own problems that Packer seeks to assiduously avoid. Nonetheless, perpetual openness is also fraught with far from positive consequences for

---

34. Packer, "Adequacy of Human Language," 37.
35. Packer, *Truth and Power*, 30, 31.
36. Ibid., 16.

the church and for countless individuals seeking reasonable resolution in stabilizing a vital Christian identity in a manner that integrates sound doctrine, personal understanding, and central biblical claims.

In placing the Bible in the determinative position, Packer acknowledges that absolute truth is beyond our grasp since "all doctrines terminate in mystery." In this, we can only bow to the reality that now "'we know in part' and only in part," even though—as faith has it—we shall ultimately see clearly (1 Cor 13:12). Whether about ourselves or the world (as it is the case for any type of knowledge) we only have partial information. This is especially so of our knowledge about God where "incompleteness is the essence of theological knowledge," which "of itself" is not "a valid criticism of what we say."[37] In Packer's view, what is required is that the grounds for any articulated position be as firmly based and as comprehensively worked out as possible in ways that include comparison with and critical analysis of competing viewpoints.

I contend (which I believe Packer does also) that the quest for absolute surety comes very close to an innate human drive and will not be denied even in the absolutist stance that all knowledge is relative. Evaluation can only take place within the inevitable given of human incompleteness, a point of agreement that Packer shares with the advocates of Protestant liberalism. The difference is his unequivocal embrace of the Bible as the revealed Word of God, a position that he fleshes out with much specificity and subtlety based on the core suppositions of a most studious and pietistic driven evangelical theology.

Packer's View of the Church as Authority

It is a core assumption of Catholic and Eastern Orthodox theology that the New Testament canon was a product of the fourth-century church.[38] Packer argues that the early church did not create the canon, but came to recognize "and set the limits of a class of books whose authoritative character had never been in doubt." The collection of texts that gained sacred status by the end of the first century included the four gospels, Acts, the letters of Paul, 1 John, and 1 Peter. The fully articulated New Testament canon emerged

---

37. Packer, *"Fundamentalism" and the Word of God*, 76.

38. Packer notes that the Catholic Church does not deny that "the Bible is God-given and therefore authoritative; but it insists that Scripture is neither *sufficient* nor *perspicuous*, neither as self-contained nor self-interpreting, as an account of God's revelation." For this reason the Church "supplies what is lacking in Scripture; it augments its (alleged) meaning." Ibid., 49.

Defending the Fundamentals of Historical Evangelicalism 65

over an extended period of time. Nonetheless, the criteria that the earliest writers and readers of the cited texts relied upon—"apostolic authorship or an equivalent apostolic sanction" and the corresponding belief that these texts were divinely inspired—became the theological basis for the selection of the final canon.[39]

Packer further contends that the existence of a God inspired Jewish canon by the end of the first century required a corresponding Christian text as God's "final, crowning revelation to be recorded in writing." The impetus for the canon, therefore, did not come from the theological challenges of the third- and fourth-century church, but from the "inner logic of Christianity" that "required an apostolic New Testament as a God given complement to the Old."[40] Packer acknowledges that the first-century church leadership did not have a fully articulated argument for a formalized New Testament canon; however, he contends that its core elements—God inspired writings, apostolic sanction, and the example of the Jewish canon—were in place by the end of the century.[41]

Packer's View of the Individual as Authority

Packer's second option—which is more of my focus here—is based on the assumption that the Bible, however divinely inspired, is essentially a human document through which one's understanding of God can be mediated by appropriating the testimony of the original writers' witness into one's own understanding of faith. As Packer characterizes this position, "God was with its authors. They were inspired to write, and what they wrote is inspiring to read. But their inspiration was not of such a kind to guarantee the full truth of their writings, or to make them all the word of God."[42]

What is determinative from this essentially liberal Protestant perspective is the shaping of the text and its interpretation by history, religious tradition, critical academic theory, and the ideological context of the contemporary milieu. Within any given context, any or all of these interpretive resources "help us to make up our own minds" about what can and cannot be accepted in the Bible. In this view, the Bible is best understood as a library collection of texts written over one thousand years. It is far from "infallible" and "include[s] both chaff and as well as wheat" that must be sifted by the discerning reader. Reason, imagination, and conscience are the ultimate

39. Ibid., 66.
40. Ibid., 67.
41. Ibid., 65–68.
42. Ibid., 50.

arbiters of authority, in conjunction with the Holy Spirit. The interpretive "task is to sort out what seems lastingly valid" in the Bible "and express that in contemporary terms."[43] As summarized by Packer:

> If the essential biblical message is to mean anything to modern man, it must be divorced from its obsolete trappings, re-formulated in light of modern knowledge and re-stated in terms drawn from the thought-world of today. Reason and conscience must judge Scripture and tradition picking out the wheat from the chaff and re-fashioning the whole to bring it in line with the accepted philosophy of the time . . . According to subjectivism, therefore, the proper ground for believing a thing is not that the Bible or tradition contains it, but that reason and conscience commend it; from which it seems to follow that faith is essentially a matter of being loyal to such religious convictions as one has.[44]

Interpreted through the contemporary socio-cultural milieu, the self becomes the source of its own deification in which both the Bible and the church are potential resources in the work of ultimately developing a more authentic Christian identity.[45] In principle, no ultimate source can reside beyond the socially interpreted self through which to assess the legitimacy of the individual's interpretation of the Bible. In practice, the result may be more subtle, in which matters of ultimate authority are not so clearly articulated, even as they are inescapable, on Packer's account and mine. By definition, the placing of final authority on consciousness instead of the Bible deconstructs any notion of "Scripture as the Revealed Word of God, true and trustworthy because of its divine source"; the Word that is "able to give us the basic certainties in life and death that we need."[46] As Packer sees it, the evangelical counter-narrative represents the scandalous truth that Protestant liberal and secular modern scholarship have sought to deconstruct.

Packer's View of the Bible as Authority

Packer identifies Christianity as a revealed religion in which its truths are most fully encapsulated in the Bible. He holds that "the infallible rule of

---

43. Packer, *Truth and Power*, 31.

44. Packer, *"Fundamentalism" and the Word of God*, 50–51.

45. A common sentiment from his perspective is the sense of one becoming a Christian rather than that of embodying a durable Christian identity that remains relatively stable over time.

46. Packer, *Truth and Power*, 128.

Defending the Fundamentals of Historical Evangelicalism 67

scripture is the scripture itself," in which "the full and true sense of any scripture . . . must be searched and known by other places [in the biblical text] that speak more clearly."[47] Revelation comes from "the inward voice of the Holy Spirit," without which personal experience of God cannot be perceived. The primary role of the Holy Spirit is to illuminate the words of the Bible to the believing reader.[48] The Holy Spirit is not only the indispensable guide for the reception of biblical truths by believers. Without denying one iota of the humanity and autonomy of its authors, Packer contends that through the Holy Spirit God conveyed his thoughts directly to the writers of the Bible. It is this revelation that underscores the thematic unity of Scripture, notwithstanding the diversity of genres and writers that comprise the biblical canon.

As Packer sees it, the Bible illuminates the character of God and describes his relationship to his people and his world, regardless of whether particular individuals internalize its message. That is the Bible's *authorial* value. Through attentive, discerning, and prayerful reading, the Bible provides the expectant believer many sources of help and direction in living in covenant relationship with God. This is the Bible's *receptive* value. In sum, the Bible is

> a record and explanation of divine revelation which is both complete (sufficient) and comprehensible (perspicuous); that is to say, it contains all that the Church needs to know in this world for guidance in the way of salvation and service, and it contains the principles for its own interpretation within itself. Furthermore, the Holy Spirit, who caused it to be written, has been given to the Church to cause believers to recognize it for the Word that it is, and to enable them to interpret it rightly and understand its meaning . . . Christians must therefore seek to be helped and taught by the Spirit when they study the Scripture, and must regard all their understanding of it, no less than the book itself, a the gift of God.[49]

According to Packer, any other reading is a misreading and a denial of what the Bible, as a unified text, was, and is meant to convey: namely, life everlasting in God the almighty through the mediation of Christ as the son of God.[50] Because the Bible embodies the most comprehensive life

---

47. Ibid., 106.
48. Packer, *Concise Theology*, 13.
49. Packer, *"Fundamentalism" and the Word of God*, 47.
50. Packer contends that the entirety of "Scripture is a real *unity*." In its most significant meaning, it is a God breathed text, "a single book with a single author—God the

affirming message available concerning God's covenantal relationship to humankind, "we are to bow to. . .[its] authority at every point, confessing that here we have both truth and wisdom."[51] The proof of Packer's claims is less the intrinsic logic of this explanation—which may not convince the skeptical reader, even as Packer seeks to demonstrate the reasonableness of biblical faith—than the persuasive power of the scriptural claims and the "harmonistic" integration of the canon as attested by the still, small voice of the Holy Spirit and conveyed from believer to believer.[52]

On Packer's account, Scripture does not provide an all-encompassing depiction of the reality of God. Since full disclosure of God's will remains perpetually beyond the human capacity to grasp, neither does the belief in the Bible's absolute trustworthiness resolve all exegetical problems or those of application. Packer contends that what the Bible does reveal is sufficient "as the final authority for all matters of Christian faith and practice."[53] To accept anything less than the total trustworthiness of the Bible as God's unique revelation to humankind is to relativize not only the Bible. It is to put into jeopardy the fundamental precepts of faith: namely, the sovereignty of God, the incarnation, the Trinity, and a penal substitutionary view of the atonement. Without the firm foundation of these core doctrines, the entire framework of historical evangelicalism and the almost five hundred year theology of the Reformation tradition can only falter. Packer cites the past hundred years of liberal Protestantism as *prima facie* confirmation that this is a valid, and far from fanciful, concern.[54]

Spirit—and a single theme—God the Son, and the Father's saving purposes, which all revolve around Him." Ibid., 84.

51. Packer, *Truth and Power*, 193. Packer maintains that the "inerrancy debate about whether we should treat all Bible teaching as true and right is really about how far we can regards Scripture as authoritative." Ibid., 14.

52. Packer, *"Fundamentalism" and the Word of God*, 109.

53. Ibid., 75. As Packer also states, "Christians are bound to receive the Bible as God's Word written on the authority of Christ, not because they can prove it such by independent enquiry, but because as disciples they trust their divine Teacher" who came to fulfill Scripture rather than to abolish it. Packer agrees that the veracity of Christian faith is beyond "full rational demonstration" given that "all the great biblical doctrines . . . are partly mysterious, and raise problems for our minds that are at present are insoluble." Ibid., 108. He maintains that the persistence of gaps in our understanding should not block our capacity to rest our complete reliance on the authority of Scripture as the foundation of our faith in the God revealed in the Bible.

54. This concern is a major theme in *"Fundamentalism" and the Word of God*, esp. 146–67, and *Truth and Power*, 9–125. In contrast to neo-orthodoxy and Protestant liberalism, Packer premises his biblical hermeneutics on "the analogy of Scripture." From this explanatory frame, Scripture is interpreted by its own intrinsic principles in which problematic, "secondary, incidental, and obscure" passages "should be viewed in light

PACKER'S THEOLOGY OF GOD

Packer emphasizes personal knowledge of and commitment to God over merely doctrinal belief, however soundly orthodox. In his view, "orthodoxy" without commitment of heart and will through the power of the Spirit's revelation is nothing short of idolatry—a daunting charge that calls all of us up short in the perpetual need for renewal and repentance. As Packer states, "If we pursue theological knowledge for its own sake, it is bound to go bad on us."[55] The participatory challenge that Packer presents is that of knowing *of* God rather than just *about* God; for the substance of what he expresses in *Knowing God* has relevance to the extent that readers are able to *experience* something of God's presence in the very process of grappling with the biblical text, in his case, through a range of highly orthodox Reformed, Puritan, and evangelical prisms.[56]

Packer's desire for total fidelity to God is, as he knows, beyond our capacity to fully achieve or embody. It is a passion for the eternal that yearns with a longing for the most steadfast confidence in God's loving faithfulness in the midst of our own faithfulness and faithlessness. This practical impetus—the genuine testing of our faith (1 Pet 1:7)—is based on the belief in the ontological certainty of God's reality and its central significance for our

---

of what appears to be primary, central, and plain." While some passages are difficult to understand, and even seem to contradict other biblical claims, through the "analogy of Scripture" Packer argues for the ultimate harmonistic integration of the Bible as a unified, coherent canonical text. See Payne, "J. I. Packer's Theological Method," 59 (Payne cites Packer, "Infallible Scripture and the Role of Hermeneutics," in Carson and Woodbridge, *Scripture and Truth*, 350). As Packer further explains: this "scriptural approach to Scripture is thus to regard it as God's testimony to Himself. When we call the Bible the Word of God, we mean, or we should mean, that its message constitutes a single utterance of which God is its author. What Scripture says, he says. When we hear or read Scripture, that which impinges on our mind (whether we realize it or not) is the speech of God Himself." Packer further notes that there can be "no such thing as an exhaustive exegesis of any passage" since the Holy Spirit illuminates additional "facets of revealed truth not seen before." Packer, *"Fundamentalism" and the Word of God*, 89. The broader point remains that the Bible, in all of its simplicity and complexity, is the single most trustworthy resource we have in knowing and understanding Gods heart, mind, and will. Moreover, the word of God is sufficiently revelatory to provide those seeking to be faithful to the Christian pathway with an absolutely trustworthy resource to guide and to structure their lives together as the body of Christ.

55. Packer, *Knowing God*, 21.

56. For Packer's opening discussion of the difference between knowing of God and knowing about God, see ibid., 24–27. While the primacy of an unmistakably Protestant sensibility would be difficult to miss, Packer's ecumenical outreach to traditional Catholicism, which caused much consternation in conservative evangelical circles, is duly noted. See Packer, "Why I Signed It," *Christianity Today*, December 12, 1994.

lives. The foremost purpose of *Knowing God* is that of stimulating the reader to link right knowledge *about* God with the passionate desire to know *of* God in the intimate depths of the soul. It is the tantalizing possibility of such orthopraxy that opens *Knowing God* to evangelical and mainline readers alike, potentially across a wide theological span.

Packer knows that the Bible does not encompass the entirety of God's reality. Yet, it provides sufficient insight into God's character and direction to lead humankind into a faithful relationship with him. The basic biblical plot line consists of God's embedded history in Israel and his incarnation in the life, death, and resurrection of Christ as described in the gospels. Through these narratives, and in various ways through the entirety of Scripture, God conveys to humankind essential information and insight of his truth, righteousness, and saving power in the light of enduring sin and evil. As illuminated by the Holy Spirit, Scripture provides enough direction for knowing what living a righteous life requires within the reign of God. However incomplete biblical revelation may be, without the central role of the Bible illuminated by the light of the Holy Spirit our knowledge of God would only remain general, abstract, uninformed, confused, and likely undifferentiated from the creation itself.

In the early sections of *Concise Theology*, Packer presents the core characteristics of the biblically revealed creator God as self-referent, self-existent, transcendent, omniscient, sovereign, and almighty. These characteristics underlie God's holiness, the purity of which cannot tolerate any form of sin (Hab 1:13). This emphasis on purity reinforces the depiction of God's transcendence as radically separate from the creation, however much God remains invested in its well-being; a holiness that "calls sinners to constant self-abasement in his presence (Isa 6:5)."[57]

God's immutable nature "guarantees his adherence to the words he has spoken in Scripture and the plans he has made."[58] This self-existent, omnipotent God discloses what he chooses of both his character and his plans to those whom he has called in covenant relationship—the people of Israel under the Mosaic covenant and those called to Christ in the new covenant fulfillment of the Abrahamic promise of Israel's God becoming a great blessing for all the world—to Jews and Gentiles alike. The depiction of God that Packer presents in *Concise Theology* and *Knowing God* represents the main contours of Christian orthodoxy within a Reformed sensibility.[59]

---

57. Packer, *Concise Theology*, 19–61; 43 for the quote.
58. Ibid., 29.
59. Packer, *Knowing God*, 43–98.

Packer suffuses the simple prose of *Concise Theology* and *Knowing God* with an abundance of scriptural references. His purpose in doing so is not simply to illustrate the biblical basis of his theology, but to encourage readers to meditatively work through the Bible, ideally by looking up every passage he cites. In both books, Packer provides a coherent theological overview of "right knowledge." His deeper objective always remains pietistic. Throughout his writing, Packer seeks to evoke the ineffable presence of the Holy Spirit in engendering a sense of majestic awe, as the reader on his or her own prompting encounters the living God. By such a pietistic exercise, Packer hopes the reader will come to an existential appreciation illuminated by the Holy Spirit that God's wisdom surpasses all human understanding and is worthy of infinite praise.

God's personal relationship with human beings is a key theme Packer develops in *Knowing God*. He explains that "the God with whom we have to do is not a mere cosmic principle, impersonal and indifferent, but a living Person, thinking, feeling, active approving of good, disapproving of evil, interested in his creatures all the time."[60] While in no way minimizing the quality of his majesty, the God of the Bible does not remain too far off "in heaven" or "beyond the sea." Rather, through his word he "is very near you, in your mouth and in your heart" (Deut 30:1–14) even as the "secret things" of God remain unfathomable (Deut 29:29). Packer contends that the unveiling itself is always God's work and not humankind's. Yet, what is revealed in covenant relationship between God and humankind is not so mysterious that it cannot be grasped by faith at the level that God seeks to convey it to the individual believer and collectively to the body of Christ.[61]

Packer contends that to trust "in the Lord with all. . .[our] heart and [to] lean not on [our] own understanding" is a foundational precept of the Bible in both testaments. In placing God as sovereign over one's own consciousness we "acknowledge him" in all our ways (Prov 3:5–6).[62] It is this radical yielding—which, in Packer's view, is a gift of God—that provides the faith that God shall direct our paths in which there can be no superior source of direction. Such faith is essential, even if the pathway leads to the cross, which in some fundamental sense it invariably does in a serious and sustained Christian commitment over a life time. Packer places grace at

---

60. Packer, *Concise Theology*, 84.

61. Packer maintains that *"knowing God is a matter of personal dealing."* Further, "it is a matter of dealing with him as he opens up to you, and being dealt with him as he takes knowledge of you." *Knowing God*, 39.

62. For a representative passage, consider the following: "Do I look habitually to the person and work of the Lord Jesus Christ as showing me the final truth about the nature and grace of God? Do I see all the purposes of God as centered upon him?" Ibid., 50.

the center of God's unrelenting commitment to human restoration. This is mediated to us through the power of the Holy Spirit as it works within us in radicalizing our own commitment to God. Such grace, in turn, propels our striving to live fully within the grace of God's light, despite our incapacity to fully realize what we seek. In the final analysis it is not us; rather, it is God working within us "in order to fulfill his good purpose" that is at work (Phil 2:12–13).

Packer maintains that the God revealed in the Bible is an enduring presence, "a God whose presence and scrutiny [if] I could evade would be a small and trivial deity."[63] It is this God who has "searched me and know[n] me" who is "familiar with all my ways," who "discern[s] my going out and my lying down" (Ps 139:1, 2, 3). It is this God who stays with me closer than a brother who is "great and terrible, just because he is always with me and his eye is always upon me." It is this God who humans seek to embrace and to flee in the "real[ization] that . . . [one] spends every moment of. . .[one's] life in the sight and the company of an omniscient, omnipotent Creator."[64] To sum up Packer's thoughts in the preceding paragraphs, the covenant is based on a relationship upheld by a committed God who acts in and through history, sometimes with us, often despite us, calling us to endure even the consciousness of our own sin for the sake of participating in his work of restoring humankind and the creation itself to his intended purpose.

The struggle with, at times, seemingly overwhelming unbelief is an ever present temptation. Against this enticement, Packer encourages readers to "wait upon the Lord" in faith "till we find our strength renewed through the writings of these things"—the revealed Word of God—"upon our heart."[65] One waits for a God who cares, who is with us to the point of his own crucifixion, yet who is other than us, who in the most fundamental sense is an enduring presence even amidst the profound silences that mark the chasm of who we are and who he is. Packer maintains that such claims are not only central in buttressing a devout and holy Christian life. The biblical revelation of the holy God passionately committed to reconciling the world to himself (2 Cor 5:19) reflects the true need about the human condition in a manner incomparable to any other source of worldly wisdom or knowledge: God reconciling *us* to himself in Christ, through whom, by his unblemished sacrifice, we ourselves enter into "the Most Holy Place" (Heb 10:19).

In the exuberance that marks his profession of faith, the emphasis Packer places on repentance—on what he refers to as "growing downward"

63. Ibid., 86.
64. Ibid.
65. Ibid., 89.

in order to "grow up"—may sometimes be missed.[66] Such repentance is a critical aspect in his orthopraxy of knowing God that Packer learned most fully from the English Puritans and those most directly influenced by that tradition. In his concern for what he views as the impoverished condition of much mainline and evangelical religious consciousness, Packer longs for a true quest for godliness in a manner that can be found in the incomparable writings of John Owen, Richard Baxter, John Bunyan, Jonathan Edwards, and Charles Spurgeon.[67]

GOD INCARNATE IN HUMAN FLESH

Packer identifies the incarnation of God in Jesus of Nazareth as the central story of the New Testament. It is also the basis from which the Bible as a whole—from promise to fulfillment—needs to be grasped.[68] In Packer's pithy expression, "Two mysteries [are revealed] for the price of one—the plurality of persons within the unity of God, and the union of Godhood and manhood in the person of Christ."[69] This high Christology is "a transcendent reality that confounds our finite mind" based on the God become man we are called to "acknowledge and adore."[70] However wide the chasm between the reality and our perception of it, this incarnational claim is a basic underpinning of orthodox Christianity that Packer embraces as foundational truth.

Packer explains that the intent of the church's early formulations of this core doctrine are less that of providing systematic explanation, in any fully satisfactory way, than "to safeguard this area of mystery" to which the incarnation refers; "namely, that a man named Jesus, a real human being, was truly and fully God, God the creator, God the Son."[71] On Packer's account, the purpose of the theological formulation is doxological and kerygmatic in the effort to give words to the mystery, one that is more intuited, and, in faith, hoped for than fully grasped. Packer's studied challenge has been to bring to bear the significance of both the incarnation and the Trinity within

---

66. Packer, *Passion for Holiness*, 119–56.

67. Packer, *Quest for Godliness*, 277–327.

68. Packer, *Knowing God*, 53–54. See also "Jesus Christ the Lord," 151–52. "The Christian consensus has been that, as Scripture is the proper source from which theology should flow, so Christology is the true hub around which the wheel of theology revolves." Ibid., 151.

69. Packer, *Knowing God*, 53.

70. Packer, "Jesus Christ the Lord," 162.

71. Ibid.

a late twentieth-century context against the core precepts of contemporary Protestant liberalism.[72] He is particularly critical of immanent leaning perspectives of Christ "from below" that give short shrift to the transcendence of God. By contrast, Packer defends a high view of the Trinity and the necessity of Christ's sacrificial atonement. The three interrelated doctrines of the incarnation, the Trinity, and the atonement account both for God's love of the world *and* the call to holiness, without which, Packer insists, we cannot enter into right relationship with the living God.

Packer forcefully argues that it is from such a perspective only—a biblically grounded, creedal-based orthodox faith—that Christ's teaching and earthly ministry can be accurately grasped in which the crucifixion and resurrection provide the central meaning for the entire recorded life of Jesus of Nazareth.[73] It is not simply that Jesus' life and teaching reflected the best of human idealism or that he was the most exemplary moral teacher the world has ever witnessed. Both of these are debatable assertions. Rather, on Packer's account, the attributes of his character, as well as the focal points of his mission and teaching, reflect the essence of his personhood and vocation—God revealed in human flesh: God incarnate who died and rose from the grave to make us free.[74]

Packer discusses the complex issue of whether the triune son of God in his earthly ministry had to abandon a portion of his deity to become truly human.[75] That Christ emptied himself on the cross is, on Packer's account, without dispute, a phenomenon prefigured in his temptations in the desert in which Satan left him for a time after Jesus of Nazareth resisted the quest for any semblance of self-aggrandizement. That is "until opportune time" (Luke 4:13) arose, namely at Gethsemane when in asking that the cup be removed said "not what I will but what you will" (Mark 14:36c) instead of an easier, but mission breaking "amen" that would have enabled him to live.[76] Packer asserts that, through the entirety of his earthly experience, Jesus of Nazareth maintained his full triune deity. While that would comprise the attributes of omniscience and omnipotence, Packer contends that the son's willingness to submit to the Father's will included that of being satisfied to know only what the Father wanted him to know and to experience.

As Packer hypothesizes, the "impression of Jesus which the Gospels give is not that he was wholly bereft of divine knowledge and power, but that

72. Ibid., 162–66.
73. Packer, *Taking God Seriously*, 33–49.
74. Packer, "Jesus Christ the Lord," 157.
75. Packer, *Knowing God*, 59–63.
76. Packer, *Concise Theology*, 192.

Defending the Fundamentals of Historical Evangelicalism 75

he drew on both intermittingly, while being content for much of the time not to do so. The impression, in other words, is not so much one of deity reduced as of divine capacities restrained."[77] Packer's broader point is that the humanity of Jesus "is adjectival to the person . . . who lives for ever in the consciousness of his identity as God's son."[78]

Packer's interpretation of the atonement is an organic complement to the doctrines of the incarnation and Trinity. The doctrine of penal substitution—which he develops with much theological subtlety—incorporates both the wrath and the love of God for a fallen humanity created in the divine image.[79] Packer insists that there is nothing capricious in God's wrath, maintaining that it is a holy response to Adam's sin in its cumulative effect upon a fallen humanity. By his sacrifice on the cross, Christ atones or "propitiates" God's wrath, which the purity of God demands, by taking the burden of sin upon himself. Through this divine exchange those who embrace the way of Christ have acquired a meritless righteousness with God. This is not through their own doing, but of God's through Christ, by fulfilling the demands of divine justice through an imputed righteousness, justifying "those who have faith in Jesus" (Rom 3:26). The result is reconciliation with God "through our Lord Jesus Christ, through whom we have gained access by faith into the grace in which we now stand" (Rom 5:2).

Packer maintains this traditional Protestant doctrine against its various critics through a comprehensive view of penal substitution that is "both descriptive of what all who have held this view had had in common, and also prescriptive of how the term should be understood in any future discussion."[80] He presents his integrative interpretation of the atonement as a biblical mystery (the full meaning of which is hidden within the unsearchable depths of God's being) and a theological model with substantial hypothetical standing. He rejects rationalistic explanations characteristic of post-Reformation scholasticism and posits a perspective that is "declaratory," "doxological and kerygmatic."[81] On Packer's account, the mystery of God reconciling the world to himself through the propitiation of Christ is "a reality we acknowledge as actual without knowing how it is possible, and which we therefore describe as incomprehensible."[82] He identifies this sense

---

77. Packer, *Knowing God*, 61–62.
78. Packer, "Jesus Christ the Lord," 167.
79. Packer, "What Did the Cross Achieve?," 98–136.
80. Ibid., 116.
81. Ibid., 100.
82. Ibid., 101.

of mystery with the light of the unfathomable breadth of God's love that knowledge can never surpass.[83]

Packer borrows a note from Aulen's *Christus Victor* atonement "motif" in his depiction of penal substitution as "dramatic" in the sense that it needs to be understood "kerygmatically," within the overarching mystery of God's revelation to humankind—something we cannot fully comprehend.[84] He accepts Aulen's claim that Christ will ultimately reign—thus, Christus Victor—but rejects the notion that the primary purpose of the atonement was that of defeating the power of Satan rather than that of saving humanity from its indwelling sin.

Packer places his most critical attention against the moral influence theory of the atonement that depicts Christ as the representative exemplar in modeling the ideal relationship between humankind and God. On this account, the effect of the cross is "entirely on men, whether by revealing God's love to us,...or by setting us a supreme example of godliness,...or by involving mankind in his representative obedience that the life of God now flows into us."[85] Packer acknowledges the significance of the imitation of Christ in the inspiration it evokes in the ardent believer. Yet he is critical of the reductionist nature of the moral influence theory that focuses the work of the atonement exclusively or even primarily upon the human response.[86]

Packer views the penal substitution model in its "eclectic exposition" as encompassing all that is of value in the other perspectives, while more fully accounting for the totality of the biblical depiction of God's relationship to humankind through the life, teaching, crucifixion, resurrection, and early church account of Christ.[87] Its central focus is the enduring problem of sin and the human need to re-establish a right relationship with the living God after the fall that the other atonement models do not address directly. For this central problem, "Christ's death had its effect first on God, who was hereby propitiated . . . and only because it had this effect did it become an overthrowing of the powers of darkness and a revealing of God's seeking and saving love."[88] Packer completes his portrayal of the atonement by linking his model with five interrelated biblical themes: God's need for retribution as a function of his holiness, Christ's solidarity with the human plight,

83. Ibid. Packer cites Eph 3:19.
84. Aulen, *Christus Victor*, 4; Packer, "What Did the Cross Achieve?," 116, 121–22.
85. Packer, "What Did the Cross Achieve?," 110.
86. For an overview of current theories of the atonement, see Calke et al., *Atonement Debate*.
87. Packer, "What Did the Cross Achieve?," 116.
88. Ibid., 111.

the overarching mystery of God, the central role of salvation, and God's enduring love.[89] He offers a dramatic summary of the "wonderful exchange" through various biblical imagery; namely "ransom, redemption, reconciliation, sacrifice, and victory."[90]

In his effort to counter the impact of the previous century of Protestant liberalism, Packer seeks through his atonement model to bring to the fore an appreciation of the "objective fact of Christ, the mystery that is 'there' whether we grasp it or not."[91] While God can be known only in part, the Bible testifies to, and reveals, the central attributes and directives of the God who actually exists and who we can come to know in a manner sufficient for life and faith. In his view of Scripture as an absolute trustworthy source of a living knowledge of the God who is there, Packer's penal substation model of the atonement serves as an indispensable facet of his broader biblical hermeneutics.

CONCLUDING REFLECTIONS

J. I. Packer has fleshed out a thoroughly developed evangelical theology that is apologetically poised for critical engagement with theological liberalism over the soul of contemporary Protestantism. He provides the receptive reader with a rich compendium of insights for deepening one's relationship with God for those who are able to embrace a fully articulated triune Christology and a high view of Scripture. He can be read with profit as well among those who cannot completely agree with the entirety of his nuanced concept of biblical inerrancy and his equally subtle discussion of the vicarious sacrifice of Christ's penal substitution theology of the atonement.[92] Packer's pointed question on whether the church, human experience, or the Bible is the definitive source of Christian authority provides clarifying focus in grappling with the implications of these alternatives.[93]

89. Ibid., 118–27

90. Ibid., 124.

91. Ibid., 120.

92. For a succinct overview on a range of evangelical perspectives on biblical inerrancy and infallibility, see Fackre, *Ecumenical Faith in Evangelical Perspective*, 4–19. Packer spans the bridge between what Fackre describes as moderate inerrancy and moderate infallibility. See ibid., 8–15. Fackre's irenic appreciation of the evangelical theologian Carl Henry has inspired a similar reading of my own of Packer. See ibid., 171–97.

93. Fackre also shapes his theological framework on this basis in defining the Bible as the primary source of revelation, ecclesial tradition as the resource, and the sociocultural context as the setting through which God's revelation takes place. See *Christian*

Regardless of whether the reality is more complex than what Packer presents in his model, he maintains that not to prioritize among the alternatives is to decide for an eclectic resolution. For reasons both intrinsic to the text as well as to what he views as the limitations of the alternative sources of authority, Packer places his absolute faith in the truth of the canonical Bible for all matters related to Christian faith and life. He has advocated this stance for a half-century in his scholarly and more popular work. Packer's biblical hermeneutics and his broader theological and pastoral insights offer much for those seeking to advance discussion between evangelical and postliberal perspectives, the focus of this book.[94]

Along with countless evangelicals, I have profited much from Packer's various discussions and by meditating upon the many biblical passages that he has cited in his books and articles. In an interpretation of Packer that has been largely appreciative, I have linked such passages, however fallibly so, to the voice and direction of the living God. On Packer's account, and in line with the "great tradition of Christian faith and life,"[95] the foundational source of revelation is the very word of God disclosed *in* the Scripture revealed via the Holy Spirit to the fallible, but God-inspired writers of the sacred text and to receptive readers. I concur with Packer that the scriptural basis for revelation is a timeless deposit of truth, without which there can be no objective basis for faith, even as the context needs to be taken with much penultimate significance. Schaeffer similarly refers to the God who is there as an ontological presence that does not depend on human experience for validity.[96] The "God hypothesis" (my phrase) is the axiomatic given of faith. In acknowledging this, Packer has frequently noted that it is only through the intuitive voice of the Holy Spirit that the foundational biblical texts have the capacity to connect to fallible readers in ways that transcend time, culture, and geography, even as historical contingency invariably influences how the revelation is received by contemporary readers.

Packer identifies reason as a key resource in knowing God, even as he grants that an infinite gulf separates what human beings can know through their own capacity and the indwelling Spirit of God that is given by grace and received in faith. This is because "man's mental 'eyes' are blind through sin and he can discern no part of God's truth till the Spirit opens them." In short, "inner illumination, leading directly as it does to a deep

---

Story, 2, 36–41.

94. As an example, compare Fackre's discussion of biblical hermeneutics in *Ecumenical Faith in Evangelical Perspective*, 37–70 (esp. 50–58) to Packer's discussion in *Engaging the Written Word of God*, 3–42, 127–59.

95. Packer, "On from Orr," 247.

96. Schaeffer, *God Who Is There*.

Defending the Fundamentals of Historical Evangelicalism 79

and inescapable conviction, is thus fundamental to the Spirit's work as a teacher"[97] in opening up Scripture as the revealed word of God to individual hearers.

These summary statements are central tenets of evangelical theology that Packer acknowledges cannot be proven through human reason, even as reason, evidence, critical argumentation, and theory construction are essential to any sound hermeneutics. As Packer explains, the task is to:

> *Display the rational coherence of historic mainstream Christian beliefs, both as a crystallizing of the doctrinal content of the Bible and also as a full-scale, comprehensive, and satisfying philosophy of life; one that embraces all the facts of human experience, good and bad; that ennobles human existence; and that makes better sense than any known alternative.*[98]

The ultimate revelation is through faith, itself a gift of the Holy Spirit by which the biblical texts of the scriptural writers are recognized as the word of God.[99]

As an evangelical centrist, I see much to ponder in the totality of Packer's work. His strengths are his biblical hermeneutics, his contemporary articulation of classical evangelical theology, his Puritan derived "systematic spirituality,"[100] and his capacity to address both the specialized theological issues of the seminary and the pastoral needs of the clergy and the educated laity. In drawing this chapter to a close, the following extended passage represents an apt summary of Packer's theological vision that he has expounded throughout the five decades in England, Canada, or the United States:

> Do evangelical principles inhibit the freedom of reason? On the contrary, they establish it. Freedom is no merely negative conception; anarchy is not freedom, either on the moral or intellectual level. True freedom is something positive; to possess it is to fulfill one's human destiny. Such freedom is to be found only in subjection to God and His truth; and the more subject, the more free—this is the biblical paradox of Christian liberty. Man

---

97. Packer, *"Fundamentalism" and the Word of God*, 118.

98. Packer, "On from Orr," 255.

99. Packer, *"Fundamentalism" and the Word of God*, 118. Packer sums up these points in the following: "Having disclosed Himself objectively in history, in His incarnate Son, and in His written, scriptural Word, God now enlightens men subjectively in experience, so that they apprehend His self-disclosure for what it is. Thus, He causes them to know Him and His end in revelation is achieved." Ibid.

100. Packer, "Introduction to Systematic Spirituality," 197–209.

becomes free only in bondservice to Jesus Christ; otherwise he is captive to sin. Man's mind becomes free only when its thoughts are brought into captivity to Christ and His Word; till then it is at the mercy of sinful prejudice and dishonest mental habits within, and of popular opinion, organized propaganda, and unquestioned commonplaces from without. Tossed about every wind of intellectual fashion and carried to and fro by cross-currents of reaction, man without God is not free for truth; he is forever mastered by the things he takes for granted, the vain victim of a hopeless and hapless relativism. Only as his thoughts are searched, challenged, and corrected by God through His Word may man hope to rise to a way of looking at things which, instead of reflecting merely passing phases of human thought, reflects God's eternal truth. This is the only road to intellectual freedom, and its sole safeguard is the principle of absolute subjection to Scripture. If, as our critics say, Evangelicals at present are not entering into this heritage, that does not mean it is not theirs to enter into. The truth is that, in principle, it is theirs and no one else's; for they alone treat the idea of biblical authority seriously enough to secure and preserve this freedom.[101]

While not without caricature, Packer's sustained evangelical critique against neo-orthodoxy, liberal theology, and less so, narrative and postliberal theology, offers pointed criticism that merits a response across a broad theological range.[102] Any student of Scripture who seeks a revitalization of the Bible as the revealed word of God has much to gain by delving into Packer's biography and his key works.

---

101. Packer, *Fundamentalism and the Word of God*, 143.

102. See Packer, "Contemporary Views of Revelation," 57–71, for an especially astute analysis of mid-twentieth-century Protestant liberalism and its variants.

4

The Mediating Theology of Donald Bloesch

Catholic, Reformed, Evangelical

Scripture in itself is the *written* Word of God, comprising by virtue of its divine inspiration a reliable witness to the truth revealed by God in Jesus Christ. But it becomes the *living* Word when it actually communicates to us the truth and power of the cross of Christ through the illumination of the Spirit.[1]

The sacramental model understands revelation as God in action, God revealing the depth of his love and the mystery of his will to the eyes of faith. Revelation has a personal, a propositional and an experiential pole. What is revealed is a personal presence in conjunction with a spoken or human witness and received by a believing heart. This view also holds that God is hidden in his revelation, that the truth of God is not directly available to human perception or conception. God can be known only as he gives himself to be known (Barth). Or as Augustine said, the truth can be apprehended by the mind only if the will has been converted by the Spirit of God.[2]

God is neither completed actuality nor infinite potentiality but a dynamic

---

1. Bloesch, *Holy Scripture*, 25–26.
2. Ibid., 42.

actuality that is constantly coming to himself, reclaiming and experiencing anew what he already is.³

BLOESCH AND PACKER IN QUEST OF COMMON GROUND

Our change in focus from the qualified rational evangelicalism of J. I. Packer to the "fideistic revelationism"[4] of Donald Bloesch represents an important shift in the American evangelical imagination, even as Packer and Bloesch share much in common on core essentials, as disclosed by a careful reading of their work. As Bloesch notes, Packer, too, "seeks to distance himself from an evangelical 'self-reliant rationalism' that downplays the role of the Holy Spirit in biblical interpretation." A difference, as Bloesch notes, is that he "would probably be more open [than Packer] to historical-critical study as an aid in biblical exegesis."[5] Packer is not averse to historical research as a resource to enhance biblical scholarship. However, he is wary of theological premises that dilute the decisive word of God revealed in Scripture, such as the historicist presuppositions that intrude upon neo-orthodoxy, the biblical theology movement, and contemporary liberal theology.[6] Bloesch is cautious in his largely empathetic appropriation of Barth, particularly in wanting to avoid any sense of "actualism" that the Bible is a primary source of revelation that comes to life only when internalized within the existential experience of the believer.[7] In contrast to Bloesch, Packer responds to the

---

3. Bloesch, *God the Almighty*, 96.

4. Grenz, "Fideistic Revelationism," 36–60. See also Bloesch, *Theology of Word and Spirit*, 21. In drawing on this term, Bloesch contends that "the decision of faith is as important as the fact of revelation in giving us certainty of the truth of faith."

5. Bloesch, *Holy Scripture*, 335.

6. Packer, "Contemporary Views of Revelation," 57–71. Packer argues that these theological schools share a common acceptance of the hermeneutical premises of the critical biblical scholarship of the late nineteenth and early twentieth centuries. On Packer's account, the result is an inescapably subjective interpretative methodology that views the Bible as a product of human consciousness. Packer notes that there is scope for revelation in liberal Protestantism through faith, but the God hypothesis cannot serve as a legitimate scholarly resource in formal theological discourse. On Packer's view, this results in a dogmatic rejection of formal theological argumentation that God speaks directly to human beings in, and through, the Bible.

7. Bloesch, *Holy Scripture*, 100–103. Bloesch notes that "neo-orthodoxy moved beyond fundamentalism . . . in its sharp distinction between Scripture as a historical and literary document and divine revelation." Ibid., 101. On this account, the Bible "carries the mark of human imperfection but also the potential of being a vehicle of divine

modernist challenge by establishing a thoroughly developed evangelical scholarship on the bedrock of an inerrant hermeneutics with a deep reach into the Puritan theological vision.[8]

Despite these differences, both Packer and Bloesch construct a theology of Scripture based on a dynamic interaction between the Word and the Spirit, even as Packer gravitates more freely toward the inscripturated Word.[9] Of more importance for the purposes of this book is that both theologians prioritize "the strange new world within the Bible" as the basis for encountering the culture. In so doing, Bloesch builds on the neo-orthodox insights of Barth and Emil Bruner.[10] By contrast, Packer draws on the Princeton theology of Charles Hodge, Benjamin Warfield, and J. Greshem Machen, as well as the English Puritans, in support of his nuanced concept of biblical inerrancy. Like Packer, Bloesch relies on the absolute trustworthiness of the Bible for all matters related to faith and life. As Bloesh states, "We must never say that the Bible teaches theological or historical error, but

---

grace." Ibid., 101–2. Further, Barth maintains that "inspiration refers to the subjective disposition of the biblical writers who are acted on by the Spirit of God. The view of orthodoxy is that inspiration refers to the production of inspired writings." Bloesch notes that "Barth would not affirm that inspiration guarantees the entire truthfulness and trustworthiness of Scripture, but it does assure us of finding the truth in Scripture. For Barth, there are two moments in inspiration: the enlightenment of the writers and the illumination of the readers." Ibid., 102. Bloesch resonates with the notion of God speaking with authenticity *through* the text in the presence of the ever given historical moment. Yet, he remains too much of an evangelical to give up the idea of the Bible as "a trustworthy and reliable account of the divine action in past history" regardless as to whether such truth is accepted in the existential moment of living reality. Ibid., 103.

8. For Packer's most sophisticated hermeneutical statement, see chapters 1–12 and 15 in *Engaging the Written Word of God*. See *Quest for Godliness* for the Puritan influence on Packer. For Packer's assessment of Barth that is both critical and not without empathy, see "Contemporary Views of Revelation," 10–13. Packer repudiates Barth's rejection of inerrancy, which results in a "ruinous irrationality." As Packer notes, "There is no road to rational faith this way." Yet, Packer observes that "Barth's exegesis shows him ready in practice to treat the testimony of all texts as divine truth." Ibid., 12. He also gives Barth high marks for placing emphasis "on God's sovereign freedom and lordship in grace, on man's incapacity in his sin to feel after God and find him, on the reality of God's communion with us through the word that he speaks in the Scriptures in conveying to us the knowledge of Christ and of grace that they exhibit." Ibid., 11.

9. Packer defines "inscripturation" as God communicating directly in "caus[ing] a written record" in the Bible of his actions, teaching, will, and narrated history in the story of ancient Israel and the early church as well as appropriate modes of "celebration" and much more. "Inerrancy and the Humanity of the Bible," 157.

10. On Bloesch's theological influences, see Olson, "Locating Bloesch in the Evangelical Landscape," 18–34. Olson observes that "the Princeton theologians Charles Hodge and B. B. Warfield, the Scottish commonsense realist Thomas Reid and his heirs and twentieth-century evangelical rationalist thinker Gordon Clark" are "notably missing" as influences on Bloesch. Ibid., 23.

we need to recognize that not everything in the Bible may be in exact correspondence with historical and scientific fact as we know it today."[11] These differences—Bloesch's partial Barthian move and Packer's qualified support of a rationalistic interpretation of the Bible—represent an important difference in evangelical consciousness, even as both theologians have sought to confront modernity with what they view as the incomparable truth claims of the Bible.

DONALD G. BLOESCH: AN OVERVIEW

Donald Bloesch was an ordained minister in the United Church of Christ who obtained his PhD at the University of Chicago in 1953. There he encountered the "extreme liberal theology" that challenged the fundamental precepts of his pietistic upbringing in the Evangelical and Reformed Church which merged with the Congregational Christian Churches in 1957 to form the UCC. Bloesch rejected the prevailing Whiteheadian-influenced process theology emerging then at Chicago and turned to the neo-orthodox theologians of Barth, Brunner, Tillich and Bultmann. Influenced by his pietistic upbringing, he gravitated more toward the theocentric views of Barth and Brunner and less toward the immanent streams of neo-orthodoxy and the Protestant liberalism of the 1950s and 1960s.[12]

In Erickson's view, Bloesch's "partial Barthianism . . . does not represent a defection from a more traditional variety of evangelical theology."[13] It was a deliberate embrace of historical Reformed tradition, similar to Barth's turn to the Bible in response to the epistemological challenges of nineteenth and twentieth-century biblical scholarship, philosophy, and intellectual history. Bloesch is not completely satisfied with neo-orthodox theology. However, he prefers it to what he describes as "Thomas Oden's 'paleo-orthodox' [position]. . .as a too hasty return to the orthodoxy of the past."[14] In this, he seeks to steer a middle ground between what he views as a staid traditionalism not sufficiently attuned to the theological and pastoral challenges of contemporary life and a postmodern accommodation to certain contemporary secular assumptions that are not sufficiently anchored in the core presuppositions of the Christian faith. His wide-ranging *Christian Foundations*

---

11. Bloesch, *Holy Scripture*, 36–37.
12. Colyer, "Donald Bloesch and His Career," 13 and 12–14. For an overview of Bloesch's theological development in the 1950s and 1960s, see ibid., 12–14.
13. Erickson, "Donald Bloesch's Doctrine of Scripture," 93.
14. Bloesch, *Holy Scripture*, 14.

project, consisting of seven substantial volumes, covers the broad span of theological, cultural, and ecclesial concerns of contemporary Protestantism.

Throughout the *Christian Foundations* series, Bloesch seeks to expand upon the breadth and depth of twentieth-century conservative evangelical thought by infusing it with broadened theological streams through historical encounters with Augustine, Luther, Calvin, Peter Forsyth, and selective appropriation of Barth and Brunner's neo-orthodoxy.[15] As Bloesch previously expressed it in his *Essentials of Evangelical Theology*, "The need for evangelicalism to recover its identity and present a united witness to the church and the world is particularly acute in this time when a new modernism threatens to engulf mainline Christianity."[16] It is this enriched neo-orthodox infused evangelicalism—shorn of obscurantism and biblical literalism—through which Bloesch seeks to encounter excessively rationalist strains within evangelical theology and subjectivist, pluralistic, and secular strains within Protestant liberalism.[17] Any effort to reposition the culture-Bible axis of contemporary mainline Protestantism toward a biblical turn has much to gain by giving close attention to Donald Bloesch's *magnum opus*.

CRITICAL COMMENTARY FROM POSTLIBERAL AND EVANGELICAL PERSPECTIVES

In *The Remaking of Evangelical Theology*, Dorrien criticizes Bloesch's moderate "classical evangelical" theology from a postliberal dialectical perspective. Dorrien notes the Barthian influence upon him and the central role Bloesch attributes to the Holy Spirit in illuminating the biblical text, without which the textual word does not convey the living presence of the Holy God—hence Bloesch's sacramental reading in which "scripture is treated as

---

15. Bloesch, *Holy Scripture*, 12.

16. Bloesch, *Essentials of Theology*, 1:1.

17. Olson refers to Bloesch as "an ecumenical evangelical . . . more interested in building bridges between diverse strands of the evangelical spectrum than in identifying who is in and who is out of the movement." "Locating Bloesch in the Evangelical Landscape," 23. At the same time, Bloesch's "fideistic revelationism" is marked, in places, by a sharp polemical style. Bloesch's theology includes a strong preference for mystery, "paradox and dialectical reasoning." Grenz, "Fideistic Revelationism," 36. For Bloesch own discussion on these topics, see *Theology of Word and Spirit*, 70–81. In his quest to link the elements of mystery, paradox, and dialectics to an integrative evangelical theology, Bloesch sometimes relies on stereotypical thinking in depicting competing schools of evangelical theology—particularly in contrasting a rationalist biblical hermeneutic dependent on the doctrine of inerrancy to a postconservative evangelical theology that moves to the left of "the historic, classical, Protestant-Pietistic heritage." Olson, "Locating Bloesch in the Theological Landscape," 30.

'the divinely prepared medium or channel of divine revelation rather than revelation itself.'" Dorrien refers to the open-ended and "paradoxical" nature of Bloesch's theology in its dual quest of speaking compellingly to the challenges of the contemporary setting while remaining firmly grounded in the classical orthodoxies Reformed theology. He also acknowledges the breadth of Bloesch's theology that "more fully reflect[s] the heritage of catholic orthodoxy"[18] than the American evangelical tradition rooted in the "rationalism" of late nineteenth- and early twentieth-century Princeton theology or of the anti-intellectual tendencies of various pietistic traditions.

Notwithstanding these more expansive theological dimensions, Dorrien maintains that Bloesch still holds to a view of scriptural infallibility, not in terms of being error free, but in its revelatory truth when "the Holy Spirit speaks in and through" the biblical text.[19] As Bloesch describes it, he is "not comfortable with the term *inerrancy* when applied to Scripture" because of its co-optation "by a rationalistic, empiricist mentality that reduces truth to facticity." Nevertheless, he adheres to the broader intent of the term, namely, to "the abiding truthfulness and normativeness of the biblical witness."[20] It is on this more dynamic and "paradoxical" reading of the relationship between Word and Spirit that Dorrien chides Bloesch for his cautious orthodoxy in failing to take a more open approach to God's revelatory power by not venturing out into more progressive avenues as reflected in the postconservative evangelicalism of Stanley Grenz, Roger Olson, Rodney Clapp, and others.[21] While acknowledging a certain subtlety in his theology, Dorrien depicts Bloesch as

> a dogmatist in the older-style evangelical sense of the term [who]. . .assumes that scripture contains a stable core of doctrine, and that the purpose of theology is to explicate this normative doctrinal material. To determine what the Bible teaches on any matter of faith and practice is to find whatever it is that evangelicalism must teach on that subject. For him, evangelicalism remains a form of gospel faith that lives decidedly within the house of authority.[22]

Specifically, Dorrien takes Bloesch to task for not drawing on the opportunities the postmodern challenge to the universal assumptions of the

---

18. Dorrien, *Remaking of Evangelical Theology*, 189. Dorrien cites the embedded quote from Bloesch, *Holy Scripture*, 18.

19. Ibid., 192.

20. Bloesch, *Holy Scripture*, 27.

21. Dorrien, *Remaking of Evangelical Theology*, 194, 196–209.

22. Ibid., 193.

Enlightenment project offer in establishing a more dialectical relationship with critical themes in contemporary theology and the secular culture. He views Bloesch as overly cautious, not as thoroughly open as he could be to what a more Spirit centered approach might illuminate about the will of God within the contemporary setting, where traditional "orthodoxy" so often comes up short, even in the (partly) Barthian mode that characterizes Bloesch's theology. Dorrien's overarching message is less the eternal verities of the "faith that was once for all entrusted to the saints" (Jude 3) than the dialectical claim "that God still has more light and truth to break forth from his Word."[23] This novel breakthrough of the Spirit's witness is more often than not occluded in Bloesch's adherence to what Dorrien takes as an ultimately uncritical biblical norm.

On the other end of the theological spectrum, John D. Morrison critiques Bloesch for not giving sufficient attention to the Bible as the "inscripturated" word of God. In Morrison's terms, Scripture is not synonymous with "The Word of God," but as "Word of God" that should not be dualistically separated from the Holy Spirit's illumination of Christ as a primary source of revelation. For without this inscripturated word—of God's direct hand in the vey writing of the Scripture through the power of the Holy Spirit to illuminate the minds of the human authors—the very ground of the christocentric nature of faith becomes jeopardized. Morrison does not deny that the core revelation is not exactly synonymous with Scripture. He acknowledges that "the *logos* who is God and who became flesh in Jesus of Nazareth *is* the self-disclosure of God in an eternally unique, absolute, and preeminent way." It is this Jesus who is "*the ontological* Word of God." However, there is no need to deny "legitimacy in calling Scripture too as Word of God" in its function as "the primary witness to the Word/Christ." Noting that "Scripture is distinguished from Christ as 'witness' to Christ; and finally, that God's revelation is one because God is one, then we must avoid a flat, blank, undifferentiated identity between Jesus Christ and Scripture as being Word of God in the same sense."[24]

Drawing on the analogy of physics, Morrison speaks of different "levels" or "strata of knowledge" within a unitary system in which, "at some level Scripture-as Scripture *is* (ontologically) Word of God."[25] In Morrison's terms, Scripture is "'disclosive down' as the derivative/inspired Word of God to be heard and known here and now"[26] without which the Logos could

---

23. Ibid., 11.
24. Morrison, "Scripture as Word of God," 188.
25. Ibid., 189–99, 166.
26. Ibid., 190.

not be named, and therefore ultimately heard, however partially so through a mirror, dimly. Viewing Logos and Scripture part of the same revelation, Morrison emphasizes "the identity-in-difference" of the two sources of revelation rather than positing any semblance of radical separation between the two.[27] Therefore, the truth of Scripture "is not simply *in itself* but, as 'open up' unitarily in and under Christ by the Spirit, [in which] its truth is ultimately grounded in Christ the ontological Word, i.e., in the Logos, and so finally in the perichoretic relations of the triune God." In Morrison's physics model, lower "strata" knowledge (Scripture) must be "grounded" in the "'higher level' [the revelation of Christ as Logos] of logical unity" from whence it derives its significance. In this revelation Scripture becomes "Word of God."[28]

Morrison acknowledges that there could be something salutatory in Bloesch's discussion of Scripture if the differences between the Word and Spirit are viewed more as "useful points of distinction in seeking to understand God's self-disclosure"[29] than in the sharply dialectical manner that Morrison interprets him as positing. Instead, he accuses Bloesch of a "straw man" creation in "lumping ... Carl Henry, Millard Erickson, and J. I. Packer together as advocates of a 'rationalistic neo-fundamentalism'"[30] and thereby evading the nuances of a rich, non-Barthian evangelical biblical theology that actually exists.

Despite the acknowledgment of his obvious orthodoxy, Morrison's concern is that, in placing a dialectic-like polarity between Scripture and the Spirit, Bloesch surrenders more than perhaps he realizes to the operative assumptions of modern liberalism. Morrison rejects whatever diminishes the Bible as anything less than "Word of God," even in his acknowledgment of it as "disclosive down." Morrison's critique includes Bloesch's implicit "actualism," in which revelation comes *through* the Bible via the Holy Spirit within the immediacy of the revelatory moment.[31]

Each of the contributors in the festschrift edited by Elmer Colyer—appropriately titled *Evangelical Theology in Transition: Theologians in Dialogue with Donald Bloesch*—acknowledges the importance of Bloesch's mediating theology within the household of evangelicalism. The contributors also exhibit a more tempered critique than Dorrien and Morrison of Bloesch's theology. In a similar vein to Dorrien, Stanley Grenz is willing to "speak

27. Ibid., 189.
28. Ibid., 189, 190.
29. Ibid., 168.
30. Ibid., 167.
31. Hunsinger, *How to Read Karl Barth*, 30–32.

of culture as a source for theology," though not in a manner analogous to Tillich's correlation project, in which Scripture and culture enjoy equal dialectical status. Speaking from a postmodern evangelical sensibility, Grenz argues that, in light of their doctrinal certainties based on one version or another of biblical foundationalism, evangelicals too easily push aside inescapably present cultural assumptions.

Grenz views Bloesch as more receptive than many evangelicals to the realm of culture in the latter's desire to relate the gospel to the contemporary context. Yet Grenz would like to see Bloesch move farther than his traditional evangelical sensibilities allow in granting the culture greater normative force as a "serious conversation partner."[32] With Bloesch, Grenz references "Scripture as the primary source for theology," but points to a "trialogue" consisting of "the biblical message, the theological heritage and the contemporary culture."[33] Bloesch acknowledges the theoretic relevance of culture to which theology must respond. However, in practice, he does not develop a substantive cultural apologetic in a manner that would satisfy Grenz.

Erickson offers tempered, but pointed, commentary from a more traditional evangelical position. In light of Bloesch's dialectical and paradoxical biblical theology, Erickson would like him to better clarify something of "the exact nature of the connection between personal truth" revealed by the Holy Spirit "and the propositions of Scripture and theology."[34] Specifically, given his critique of the rationalistic assumptions of traditional evangelicalism, Erickson wants Bloesch to identify the philosophical presuppositions that grounds his theology of Holy Spirit by giving more explicit consideration to the underlying existentialism upon which it is based.

Erickson also wants Bloesch to provide an apologetic rational to complement his claim that the revelation of Christ "is essentially self-certifying."[35] If Bloesch is to present the claims of the gospel within highly secular cultural contexts that can be heard, he will need to better address the questions raised by those who challenge the fundamental precepts of the biblical revelation and provide more of an intellectual defense. Os Guiness's

---

32. Grenz, "Fideistic Revelationism," 57.

33. Ibid., 60. Grenz points to "a host of traces of divine grace present in the midst of human brokenness." It is for this reason that he is "willing to speak of culture as a source for theology (to the horror of some evangelicals), albeit not in the sense of being the normative standard determining the nature of the gospel message itself but as a conversation partner that as theologians we must take seriously in our constructive articulations of the 'faith once delivered.'" Ibid., 57.

34. Erickson, "Donald Bloesch's Doctrine of Scripture," 95.

35. Ibid., 96.

Dust of Death could serve as one such example of making the case for the radical particularity of Christianity "in a society characterized by empirical religious pluralism."[36] Erickson also wonders about the extent to which the evangelical and Barthian elements of Bloesch's theology "can be held together in a stable combination."[37] This is a concern of Bloesch himself, who nonetheless defines his theological vision from a different set of epistemological assumptions than Erickson's.[38] In Bloesch's words:

> Against the rationalists who reduce faith to intellectual assent to verbal truth and the experimentalists and spiritualists who appeal to private illuminations over the written Word of God, I affirm the paradoxical unity of Word and Spirit so that the reception of the Word is both a rational apprehension and a redeeming experience. I have considerable difficulty with the view, so appealing to those of a rationalist bent, that the Bible is impregnated with universal, unchanging truths that are waiting to be discovered or reformulated. Instead, I hold that the Bible is filled with the Spirit of God, who brings new light to bear in ancient wisdom—light that leads us not only to renewed understanding but also to obedience.[39]

Like Grenz and Erickson, Olson also provides an assessment of Bloesch's mediating project and the invariable tensions within it, noting that Bloesch

> wishes to be and is *progressive* compared to fundamentalists and neo-fundamentalists who cherish and defend a particular, narrow view of tradition that is more indebted to Scottish common sense realism and Princeton theology than it is to the genuine Reformation and revivalist heritage of evangelicalism; yet he is *conservative* compared to evangelicalism's postconservative

---

36. Ibid.
37. Ibid., 97.
38. Bloesch, "Donald Bloesch Responds," 191. "Erickson questions whether I have offered adequate grounds for adopting a particular religious perspective. This may show a trace of rationalism in Erickson, for it seems he is asking for rational and experiential corroborations of the claims of faith. If faith rests on rational corroboration, then reason, not faith, becomes the ground of religious certainty. Yet I wish to affirm the rationality of faith, and this means that faithful reasoning has a role in elucidating the claims of faith. I have real reservations about justifying the claims of faith in the light of extrabiblical rational criteria." Olson also notes that "Bloesch criticizes even sophisticated evangelical biblicalism for overemphasizing the propositional facticity of the Bible to the point that revelation is reduced to conceptuality or logic." Olson, "Locating Donald G. Bloesch," 29.
39. Bloesch, *Holy Scripture*, 20.

revisionist party that calls for genuine dialogue with moderates among the mainstream of liberal Protestant thought.[40]

Bloesch critiques what Olson refers to as a conservative tendency in his (Bloesch's) theology through what Bloesch understands as the full catholic tradition of Christian orthodoxy, mediated through a perspective grounded in the vision of the Protestant Reformers. Bloesch does seek to confront the operative assumptions of contemporary thought and culture, in their various secular and theological guises, with the unvarnished gospel truth, but rejects its association with neo-fundamentalism. At the same time, he is more reluctant to engage in the same level of open-ended dialogue with the culture than are Olson, Grenz, Dorrien, and Pinnock. In principle, Bloesch embraces a methodology of critical dialogue, yet he has not developed a substantive culturally focused apologetics. Rather, his objective remains highly focused on the desire to persuade others to accept the indubitable truth of the gospel illuminated by the Spirit. He does so by drawing on whatever sources are available that help him increase his understanding of the infinite dimensions "of an enlivening and liberating" rather than "enervating"[41] Christian orthodox revelation. His more pressing aim is to expound upon its significance to a potentially receptive readership for the purpose of expanding the ecumenical evangelical community.

Bloesch acknowledges that the Christian revelation is variously expressed in diverse cultural and historical settings—a realization that gives force to his dynamic theology of Word and Spirit. At the same time, he stresses the universality of the message in which "Jesus Christ is the same yesterday and today and forever" (Heb 13:8), however much that revelatory truth needs to be explicated in any given historical context. In the process, he places historicism within a relativistic viewpoint under the sovereignty of God in which Scripture serves as the prism to evaluate and ultimately judge the culture. Bloesch acknowledges the inescapability of historical influence with which he is willing to grapple, though not to the degree that would satisfy Dorrien, Olson, or Grenz. His primary emphasis remains a biblical universalism expressed, however paradoxically, within and through the dynamics of historical and cultural change.

---

40. Olson, "Locating Donald G. Bloesch," 30–31.
41. Bloesch, *Theology of Word and Spirit*, 23.

THE PARADOXICAL MYSTERY OF GOD IN CHRIST: A THEOLOGY OF WORD AND SPIRIT

The centerpiece of Bloesch's theology of Scripture is the fullness of God in Christ revealed by the Holy Spirit as "communicated to us through" the biblical text. Bloesch describes the relationship between Scripture and Spirit as dynamically transactional in which the Spirit is "the ultimate author of the Bible."[42] What is written is the revealed will of God, strictly speaking, in *potential form*, regardless of whether perceived as such by specific individuals in any given reading. This potential only becomes actualized when it "derives its efficacy from the Spirit." "It is not the Bible, as such, but the divine revelation that confronts us in the Bible that is the basis and source of spiritual authority,"[43] as it breaks forth in the world in any given context. As Bloesch explains, the Spirit "was the ultimate author of the Bible and is the ongoing interpreter of the biblical message to the church in every age."[44]

Notwithstanding other statements where Bloesch draws tighter connections to the Bible as a source of revelation itself, Colyer views Bloesch's theology of Word and Spirit as "uncomfortably close to occasionalism."[45] Since he does acknowledge an "ontic difference between the Bible and other books,"[46] Colyer encourages Bloesch to more precisely clarify the relationship between the Bible and the Spirit. According to Bloesch, "the biblical writers and their writing participated in the event of revelation," even as "revelation is not to be equated with the objective verbal representation of this reception." In his interpretation, the Bible is binding as witness, which also "mediates revelation, since the Spirit acts through the persons and words that he inspires."[47] Colyer wants Bloesch to draw out more precisely the relationship "between the sign"—the written biblical text—"and the thing"—the revelation of God. Because Colyer believes Bloesch is "reluctant to say that" the revelation of God "resides exclusively in the Spirit speaking,"[48] he wants Bloesch to elaborate upon the conjunction of Word and Spirit, particularly to explain how the relationship between the two is mediated.[49]

42. Bloesch, *Theology of Word and Spirit*, 13.
43. Ibid., 2.
44. Ibid., 13–14.
45. Colyer, *Theology of Word and Spirit*, 7.
46. Ibid.
47. Bloesch, *Holy Scripture*, 56.
48. Colyer, *Theology of Word and Spirit*, 7.
49. Colyer states that "Bloesch needs to clarify the nature of the reverberation or participation between the sign and the thing if he is reluctant to say that it resides

For Bloesch, "the Spirit is not inherent in . . . creaturely structures—Bible, church, sacrament—but enters them from above again and again."[50] Strictly speaking, this does sound like occasionalism, which Bloesch is at pains to deny in his effort "to affirm God as logos as well as spirit."[51] Bloesch also argues that the Bible is not only the *vehicle* through which the transmission of the Spirit of God in Christ is mediated. It is the language itself that, through the intercession of the Holy Spirit, God has chosen, century after century to communicate to fallible human beings who, on faith have dared to commit their lives to Christ. The gift of revelation that the Spirit opens up through the Bible is intricately enmeshed in the flow of human historicity, in which God speaks through appropriate illumination. According to Bloesch, the scriptural model teaches a "derivative infallibility." That is:

> The Bible does not have infallibility within itself, but through the power of the Spirit it carries the infallibility of the very truth of God. We may also speak of the Bible as having a functional infallibility in its role as the supreme rule of faith, conduct and worship. At the same time, it would not infallibly convey the truth of faith unless it had an infallible basis and goal. The Bible bears the stamp of infallibility through its unique inspiration and transmits infallible truth through the ongoing illumination of the Holy Spirit to people of faith.[52]

Drawing on Barth, Bloesch points to the "objective-subjective"[53] dimension of revelation, both inscribed in the Bible and in the heart and minds of past believers and the recorded testimonies they left. His focus is the dynamic presence of God when and as revelation occurs, including the role of the Bible in mediating that presence. Bloesch contends that

> the Bible and other signs of grace mediate God's Word through the action of the Spirit, but they do not contain divine grace and truth. The Bible is not itself a mirror or echo of the living Word of God, but the Bible penetrated by the Spirit becomes a conduit of salvific meaning.[54]

---

exclusively in the Spirit speaking and therefore affirms an ontic difference between the Bible and other books." Ibid., 15.

50. Bloesch, *Response to Elmer Colyer*, 1.
51. Ibid., 2.
52. Bloesch, *Holy Scripture*, 43.
53. Bloesch, *Theology of Word and Spirit*, 15.
54. Bloesch, "Response to Elmer Colyer," 1.

The perception of such an "actualist" tendency in Bloesch concerns many in conservative evangelical circles where more emphasis is placed on the Bible *as such* as the inscripturated source of revelation conveyed directly from the mind of God.

On the one hand, certain evangelicals, schooled in various rationalist hermeneutics, are troubled by the Barthian emphasis on dialectical theology in twentieth-century biblical studies and Bloesch's embrace of it. On the other hand, advocates of a more "open theology" chide Bloech for not going far enough in allowing greater say to the Spirit in discerning the shedding of new light from the Word in any given particular context. Bloesch identifies strengths and limitations in both traditional and postconservative evangelical perspectives in his quest for an inclusive Protestant theology that holds the potential to speak to the most basic exigencies of each. Whether there is sufficient potency in his paradoxical theology of Word and Spirit to resolve these conflicts in order to achieve the level of Protestant comprehensiveness he seeks is another matter. His quest for its attainment drives his embrace of Scripture—that is fundamentally sacramental in nature—as well as his entire theology.

THE BIBLE AND MYTH

One can further probe the tensions Bloesch attempts to resolve between theological liberalism, neo-orthodoxy, and traditional evangelicalism through an analysis of his chapter in *Holy Scripture: Revelation, Inspiration, and Interpretation* titled "The Bible and Myth."[55] Bloesch notes at the opening of chapter 8 that "the presence of myth and legend has been a continuing source of embarrassment to conservatives and a pretext to liberals for dismissing large parts of the Bible as anachronistic."[56] He reproves conservatives for clinging to literalism in adherence to biblical statements related to untenable historical and scientific claims. He also critiques liberals because they relegate large portions of the Bible as myth, thereby dismissing as a historical residue the claims of an ancient worldview based on a different set of epistemologies than those that give shape to historical consciousness in the contemporary era. According to liberal hermeneutics, the Bible requires considerable de-mythologizing in order to re-mythologize in a manner that can link the underlying meaning of the text to the cultural and intellectual exigencies of contemporary life in an era dominated by secular paradigms. This includes a discrediting of theism within certain streams of liberal the-

---

55. Bloesch, *Holy Scripture*, 255–77.
56. Ibid., 255.

ology and that of marginalizing core ontological claims about the nature and character of the transcendence and immanence of the triune God of classical Christian faith.

Bloesch draws heavily from Barth's concept of saga in establishing a mediating perspective between biblical literalism and the de-mythologizing project of the Bultmannian school of exegesis.[57] Extending his critique of Bultmann made in chapter 7, Bloesch focuses, in chapter 8 of *Holy Scripture*, on the need to posit an intelligent counterproposal to what he takes as the historical reductionism of theological liberalism. In the process, he builds on his underlying thesis that the Word of God is revealed paradoxically in the very human words that comprise the biblical text, while acknowledging their canonical validity as the unique place where God in Christ, in conjunction with the Holy Spirit, condescends to reveal himself to finite human flesh.

Bloesch references Barth's concept of saga "as the wondrous events in Scripture that, though inaccessible to historical investigation, are related to real history."[58] In contrast to certain streams of traditional evangelical exegesis, Bloesch maintains that there are no straight correlations between the events portrayed in the Bible and empirical history. He carefully points out that key events such as the incarnation, atonement, and resurrection need to be accepted as historically true even as they are not capable of proof by historical methods and sources of evidence. The core doctrines of the Christian faith represent "the reality that binds together all the other realities mirrored and recorded in Scripture."[59] They transcend history even while being immersed within it.

Drawing on an array of biblical scholarship, Bloesch identifies sagas as "events [that] do not rise out of history, but concern divine intervention in history." "They are superhistorical not historical." That is, "a saga has a historical setting but a theological focus" in which the latter possesses interpretive privileges over the former without denying the contextual importance of the former.[60] Bloesch echoes Gerhard von Rad's definition that a biblical saga "comprises the sum total of the historical living recollections of peoples." It is "history of a people" defined by themselves; "the form in which people thinks of its own history."[61] A prime example is the Pentateuch, which, while grounded within historical events—including the theo-

---

57. Ibid.
58. Ibid., 256.
59. Ibid., 269.
60. Ibid., 256.
61. Ibid., 257.

logical literature of ancient Israel—makes superhistorical claims through a realistic-like historical genre of God calling his people to live in special covenant relationship with him.

Even a biblical narrative can be described parabolically—for example, the exodus story as a primary source of memory and revitalization that reverberates throughout the Old and New Testament in the imagery of God's people in perpetual search of the holy land and the restoration of the full covenant relationship with a holy God. In turn, the new covenant, as depicted in Jeremiah 31:31–34, becomes reinterpreted in the New Testament in Jesus as the greater Moses leading a redeemed people (Jews and Gentiles) to the promised land of right relationship with God through the sacrificial blood of the lamb that takes away the sins of the world.

In short, Bloesch adheres to a view that can be described as "biblical realism" with serious theological intent.[62] Viewed in this way, the mystery of the eternal God is embedded within the lived experience of human historicity, specifically, in the Old Testament narrative of the people of Israel and ultimately in the singular particularity of the Christ event as interpreted by the early church through its canonical literature. While noting that the full breadth and depth of God's reality extends beyond what is recorded in the Bible or could be conceivably disclosed within the finite vehicle of human history, Bloesch defends this central claim against certain strands of theological liberalism. His use of the literary term "saga" also pits him against certain aspects of rationally grounded evangelical literalism, particularly his notion of historically depicted events perceived parabolically.

Bloesch prefers the term mythopoeic to characterize the more figurative portions of the Bible rather than what Bultmann refers to as myth or what certain strands of evangelical scholarship might depict as history, for example, the first eleven chapters of Genesis. On Bloesch's reading, "myth exists in the Bible. . .[but only] in a qualified sense."[63] Drawing on the biblical scholarship of Catholic theologian Avery Dulles, Bloesch argues that the various pagan myths that the biblical writers drew upon were "progressively purified, broken and sublimated" as they were integrated into the biblical plot line and in the process fundamentally transformed.[64] Thus, as Bloesch notes, the first chapter of Genesis places the creation story within time in which there was a beginning,—"a real creation ex nihilo"—that "history is

---

62. Ibid., 265.

63. Ibid., 259.

64. Ibid., 260. Bloesch references, Dulles, "Symbol, Myth, and the Biblical Revelation," 39–68.

powerless to record or certify."[65] While this God is very much invested in the salvation of the world, he is not of it. He is over and above it as transcendent other in contrast to certain eco-theologies in the contemporary period that describes the earth as the body of God.[66]

Through such a distinction Bloesch observes that the mythopoeic world of the ancient near east became de-sacralized in the Old Testament. Specifically, its many gods were deconstructed by the monotheistic God "I Am Who I Am," "the Lord, the God of your fathers—the God of Abraham, the God of Isaac, and the God of Jacob" (Exod 3:14, 15) who delivered Israel from the bondage of Egypt and set it on pilgrimage to the holy land. In calling upon this God alone, Israel repudiated idolatry "in the form of anything in heaven above" such as the stars, the sun, or the moon, "or on the earth beneath, or that is in the waters below" (Exod 20:4). In short, whatever mythopoeic elements the Old Testament writers may have drawn upon to construct their narrative, they fundamentally transformed those sources to fit into the very different cosmology of the biblical text.

Bloesch encourages evangelicals to "avoid hard and fast positions regarding every event or recorded miracle in the Bible." He nonetheless stands firm with them on the historical validity of "events that are integral to the message of faith." Even here, however, there is no obligation "to accept everything recorded as being exactly the way it is described, even in the stories about Jesus," including, one presumes, the literal historicity of the resurrection narratives as described in variously different ways in the four gospels. What Bloesch argues for is "the historical reliability of their [the biblical writers'] witness without being bound to modes of expression or understandings of life and the cosmos that belong to another age."[67] In this, Bloesch exhibits a subtle dialectic between rigor and fluidity governed by the overarching fideism of his paradoxical Word and Spirit theology. Bloesch anchors this view in the firm commitment that the Spirit cannot

65. Ibid., 267.

66. Ibid., 259–63. Bloesch notes that "the imagistic language of Scripture generally has a solid anchor in real happenings, but these events are inaccessible to historical investigation or confirmation." In commenting on the resurrection of Christ, Bloesch maintains that the witness of the New Testament does not make the event "even a historical probability. It proves only that a series of extraordinary occurrences moved a great many persons to assert that it really happened. From the perspective of natural reason the resurrection of Christ is a historical impossibility, but faith grasps what reason cannot comprehend." Ibid., 267. For Bloesch, this does not mean that Christ did not rise from the dead, but that such an event, which took place in history, also transcended it, in which, to use the Pauline phrase, mortality was swallowed up in immortality (1 Cor 15:53 KJV).

67. Ibid., 269.

contradict the core biblical meaning, even as there is new light to be shed in novel historical and existential situations. As he explains:

> Only faith can lay hold of the spiritual reality to which the text or sign points, and faith itself is a gift of God. Faith does not deny critical reasoning but turns reasoning around so that it is made to serve the search for deeper and fuller understanding of the mystery of God's self-revelation in Christ, including his atoning death on the cross and his glorious resurrection from the grave.[68]

This faith, a product of grace itself, is not given in any doctrinal creed or biblical text. It is only revealed again and again in ever fresh breakthroughs of the Holy Spirit in which all human resources, including the Bible, core dogmatic formulations, and the historical church are profoundly ministerial. God reveals himself in history, in and through the biblical text, the historical church, and in the minds and hearts of believers through the interiority of their consciousness and in their communal gatherings wherever two or more are gathered. Yet the full mystery of God remains transcendent to all human experience in which no human effort or even act of God can change. This is because God remains infinite in his plenitude and partially hidden, even in his revelation as a suffering servant hung on a cross. Thus, the Bible, written in a particular historical context by human beings inspired by the Holy Spirit, is a God-given gift to other human beings, who through faith are able to obtain glimpses of his holy majesty. As Bloesch concludes:

> The Bible is essentially neither history nor myth but a historical witness to the dramatic intersection between time and eternity in Jesus Christ, often depicted in mythopoeic language. It is *Geschichte*—focusing on the divine intrusion into historical events—rather than *Historie*—a recording of events as they appear to an objective observer. It is saga—an imaginative poetic narration that takes into account the interaction between God and humanity. It is the perception of what transpires on the plane of history through the eyes of faith.[69]

As various commentators reflecting divergent theological perspectives have observed, there is room to critique Bloesch's mediating vision, which by definition, can only be an aspiration toward evangelical comprehensiveness. His biblical hermeneutics provides an indeterminate and alluringly imaginative potential that requires additional exploration. Morrison, and,

68. Ibid., 270.
69. Ibid., 274.

with a less blunt edge, Erickson and Colyer raise important questions on the ways in which Bloesch has left unresolved critical relationships between the Bible and the Holy Spirit. From an opposite direction, Dorrien—and with more nuance, Grenz, and Pinnock—questions Bloesch on what they perceive as the rigidity of his theological orthodoxy in the face of new light in which a more open theology more fully attuned to the dynamics of the Holy Spirit might evoke.[70] The various critics of Bloesch's biblical interpretation from the theological right and left raise many provocative issues. The more pressing matter is whether the tensions in his biblical hermeneutics are an essential by-product of the mediating theological project Bloesch proposes. I envision Bloesch's theology of Word and Spirit as an unrealized trajectory toward a theological unity, which—in its aspiring telos—is greater than the sum of its parts. I briefly address prospects of moving toward and potential roadblocks impeding Bloesch's comprehensive Christian orthodox vision in the concluding section of this chapter.

BLOESCH'S THEOLOGY OF GOD

Bloesch draws more directly on the Bible as the inscribed Word of God in what he views as his most important book in the Christian Foundation series, *God the Almighty*, than in *Holy Scripture*. In the latter text, his dominant interpretation is God speaking *through* the Bible via the inspiration of the Holy Spirit. As with *Holy Scripture*, Bloesch maintains a dialectical tension in *God the Almighty*. In the latter text, the dynamic impetus depends less on the tension between Word and Spirit than toward a vision whereby God maintains his omnipotence and transcendence, on the one hand, and his vulnerability and participation in human affairs, on the other. More by usage than by direct theological statement, the biblical text comes across in *God the Almighty* as the most enduring and reliable source that describes and mediates Bloesch's dynamic portrayal of God.[71]

Against certain tendencies that he attributes to classical theism, Bloesch posits a view of "God [who] is free to act in history and does not

---

70. For Pinnock, see "Holy Spirit in the Theology of Donald G. Bloesch," 119–35.

71. Bloesch states that the Scripture "contains an objective meaning that the inquirer must bow before and accept by virtue of the Bible's past inspiration by the Spirit and its present illumination in which the Spirit confirms and clarifies what he already affirmed and revealed through the mouth of human authors." *God the Almighty*, 76. The emphasis on the illumination of the Holy Spirit in revealing the objective meaning of the text parallels his biblical hermeneutics in *Holy Scripture*. In *God the Almighty*, Bloesch punctuates his discussion of the character and attributes of God by Scripture, which he draws upon in a largely illustrative manner.

simply tower above history." He defends the Christian understanding of divine transcendence by depicting God's involvement in history as "an act of freedom, not as a quality of his being." As creator, "he remains with the world in its struggle for fulfillment and happiness."[72] The notion of God's vigorous reach into human affairs resonates profoundly with the immanent impetus in theological liberalism. Yet, Bloesch argues that this engagement occurs on God's terms, not that of the world's, as one might find in certain strands of liberationist and process theology. With classical theology, "God is other," yet by his own choice he does not remain distant. Rejecting descriptions such as "'Absolutely Other' (as in mysticism and existentialism)" and God as "'Creative Force' (as in process thought and New Age religion)," Bloesch calls for a profoundly biblical naming of God "as the majestic Lord and loving Savior."[73] Bloesch aims to flesh out the attributes and character of this God in *God the Almighty: Power, Wisdom, Holiness, and Love*.

As part of his dialectic interpretation, Bloesch points to "the mainly figurative language of the biblical narrative" and "the conceptual language of philosophy" as key sources that provide access to God's revelation to humankind. Bloesch does not fully develop this latter emphasis. He identifies philosophy as a potential resource in knowing or describing God, but rejects any correlative approach—such as existentialism or process metaphysics—as the primary pathway through which God communicates to human beings.[74] In a representative statement, Bloesch notes that "theology is free to use philosophical terms to elucidate biblical meanings, but it must not become bound to this terminology."[75] That is because, for Bloesch, there is no other language to draw upon than the Bible itself as the ultimate reference point to establish theological norms that can only be illuminated by the Holy Spirit. As he states, "The God of theology remains hidden and inscrutable until he makes himself known."[76] Philosophical reflection and related "concepts and images are necessary and useful" to the extent that they point "beyond themselves" to the revelation of God who "is both hidden and revealed in Jesus Christ."[77] Bloesch otherwise holds that that the viability of philosophy remains questionable if it serves in any way to displace or marginalize the unfathomable depth and range of biblical revelation.

72. Bloesch, *God the Almighty*, 24.
73. Ibid., 24, 25.
74. Ibid., 31.
75. Ibid., 32.
76. Ibid., 32.
77. Ibid., 34.

In conjunction with a broad range of neo-orthodox and liberal theology, Bloesch acknowledges the importance and inevitability of symbolic and analogical reflection in coming to a partial knowledge of that to whom Isaiah refers to as the Holy One. However it is processed, his ultimate grounding point remains the indisputable reality of God's revelation in and through Scripture, whose fullness remains inscrutable to human consciousness, even through the efficacy of the Holy Spirit. Bloesch contends that what is given through Scripture, almost two thousand years of church tradition, and wherever two or three are gathered in Christ's name, "is adequate for our salvation and vocation as his ambassadors and heralds"[78] within the ministry of our everyday lives. The manna comes when given, but cannot be clung to or stored up lest the vehicle of transmission (the sign) be turned into a source of creation worshipping idolatry. The focus, in radical faith, needs to remain solely on the quest for the indwelling power and love of the Holy God whose revelation breaks through where it will within the crucible of living reality.

In stressing the need for radical fidelity to the broad essentials of evangelical faith grounded in the tradition of the Protestant Reformers, Bloesch critiques what he perceives as the rationalistic excesses of twentieth-century fundamentalism. In his theology of Word and Spirit he envisions nothing less than that of bringing to bear a broadly inclusive Christian orthodox perspective both to mainline and evangelical practice and theological construction. Taking his stance within evangelicalism, he wants to revitalize mainline denominations through a solid embrace of biblical principles in a manner that can be appreciably acknowledged, if not fully accepted in the contemporary secular era. Against Tillich, Bloesch does not seek a dynamically interactive pathway between faith and culture in which each is taken equally on its own terms and brought into dialectical engagement. Instead, he posits an infinite-like gap between human perception and divine revelation that can be bridged, but only in part, through the risk of faith and the indwelling power of the grace of God revealed in Christ. With Barth and Reinhold Niebuhr, Bloesch puts forward a dogmatically grounded dialectical theology that—based on his evangelical faith stance as premise—seeks to establish a comprehensive interpretation of God that draws on resources from a wide range of theological perspectives.

Bloesch carries out these themes on the nature of God in a way that Torrance refers to as "a very powerful and welcome contribution to contemporary theology."[79] He notes that one of Bloesch's primary contributions to

---

78. Ibid., 36.
79. Torrance, "Bloesch's Doctrine of God," 147.

evangelical theology is the clarity of his biblically grounded concept of God as profoundly transcendent and uniquely revealed in Jesus Christ. Rejecting the "immanentalism associated with existential and process theology," Bloesch seeks "to recover a robust supernaturalism that avoids the overt dependence on Hellenistic philosophy as well as a naïve biblicalism that reduces God to 'the Man Upstairs.'"[80]

A thorough analysis of the entirety of *God the Almighty* would require more space than possible to cover here. The topics alone of his chapters are significant: "The Self-Revealing God" (chapter 2), "Transcendence and Immanence" (chapter 3), "Power and Wisdom" (chapter 5) and "Holiness and Love" (chapter 6). As one example of his mediating theology of God, Bloesch maintains that

> the mystery of God's self-manifestation in Jesus Christ is neither absurd nor opaque. Rather it is translucent to reality, since we see partly, but not exhaustively. God's disclosure of his grace and mercy is intelligible but not finally comprehensible.[81]

Whether serious evangelical theologians, such as Carl Henry, Millard Erickson, or J. I. Packer, would deny that this is so is not so certain; clearly, Packer does not. As illustrated by this passage, Bloesch seeks to maintain a dynamic tension that preserves what he views as essential and truly catholic in the orthodox position while repudiating anything approaching a metaphorical interpretation of the biblical God that obscures the core claims of Scripture. In rejecting notions of God as utterly opaque as well as bordering on full transparency, Bloesch wishes to maintain the traditional understanding of God as mysteriously transcendent, and therefore radically other, as well as communicable, at least in part, to finite human beings.

In accordance with a broad stream of orthodox theology, Bloesch sustains his mediating argument by noting that "God controls all events." However, at least partially in line with process theology, "he is not the exclusive actor in all events," even as he remains sovereign in the most fundamental sense. Moreover, while there is evil in the world of which God is not the author, "His hand is in all events—always working to bring good out of evil"—sometimes in cooperation with human beings; at other times despite their intended thoughts and actions.[82] According to Bloesch's substantially Barthian perspective,

---

80. Bloesch, *God the Almighty*, 84.
81. Ibid., 62.
82. Ibid., 115.

human freedom and divine providence are by no means mutually exclusive. Our freedom comes from God, and is realized as God works with us and in us. God's sovereignty liberates the human creature for responsible obedience. The paradox is that the more the human will submits to God the more free it becomes. Human freedom is upheld and fulfilled by divine providence, not annulled.[83]

Bloesch places God's love in creative tension to his holiness. He maintains that God expresses love, as his most fundamental attribute, in "his outgoing, tenderhearted embrace of the sinner." Bloesch describes holiness as God's "majestic purity that cannot tolerate moral evil." It is both the means through which God seeks to reconcile the world and an essential attribute without which—as radical "separateness from all that is unclean and profane"—God would not be God.[84] As Bloesch more fully elaborates the apparent paradox in the dynamic relationship between these two attributes:

> God's love and holiness constitute the inner nature of the living God. These two perfections coalesce in such a way that we may speak of the holy love of God (as did Forsyth) and of his merciful holiness. In the depths of God's love is revealed the beauty of his holiness. In the glory of his holiness is revealed the breadth of his love. The apex of God's holiness is the holiness of his love. The apex of God's love is the beauty of his holiness. God's love transcends his holiness even while it infuses and upholds it. His holiness is adorned and crowned by the magnitude of his love.[85]

In linking God's holiness to his "anger and jealousy" when his people do not walk in his way, Bloesch rejects any notion that these are merely "figurative expressions reflecting the projection of human feelings upon God"—an anthropomorphic residue of an earlier era. Rather, Bloesch insists, God's wrath is an indispensable function of his holiness, a "necessary reaction . . . against sin,"[86] which nonetheless "is qualitatively different from human anger." Bloesch contends "that God's wrath is a real, objective power." It is "the necessary reaction of God's holiness against sin." However, "it is not"—given its functional purpose in restoring the creation to its God intended purpose—"identical with his true nature, which is revealed"

---

83. Ibid., 116. Packer also maintains that God's power rightly appropriated is humankind's source of liberation of the profoundest sort even as the pathway to it is by way of the cross. See *Truth and Power*, 11–55.

84. Bloesch, *God the Almighty*, 140.

85. Ibid., 141.

86. Ibid.

most fully in the incarnation of Jesus Christ.[87] Viewed in this light, Bloesch characterizes wrath as "the highest strained energy of the holy will of God,"[88] a righteous outpouring against intransigent sin which flows forth at the time and circumstance of God's own choosing.

Perceived in this way, the attribute of wrath is "provisional whereas his love is enduring" even unto hell. This supposition leads to the consequent "need to envision hell as a creation of God's love as well as of his justice." More fundamentally, it is "incumbent . . . to see the grace of God reaching into hell" (which arguably, is nothing other than the cross itself in its stark nakedness) "as well as reigning in heaven." God is Lord of heaven and hell, "for otherwise we are forced to posit a co-eternal evil that would take away from the glory and beatitude of heaven" and the absolute sovereignty of his divine will.[89] It is this tension between God's holiness and love where Bloesch seeks to dialectically work through the complex terrain between various liberal and conservative theologies on the goodness and severity of God. It is here that Bloesch most fully seeks to navigate the sense of the paradox and mystery of the biblical revelation of God within the context of our human fallibility and sin. The grappling with this issue, in turn, leads logically to a more than partial, albeit far from complete, resolution in chapter 7 of *God the Almighty*, "The Mystery of the Trinity."

THE MYSTERY OF THE TRINITY

Bloesch describes the Trinity as "the apex and goal of [Christian] theology," a doctrine that is "drawn out" and inferred "from the total biblical and apostolic witness concerning God."[90] The ontological basis for the Trinity is the claim that "God interacts with himself before he acts on the world."[91] Intra-triune communication, then, is the basis of God's interaction with the world. As Bloesch explains, "there are distinctions within God himself and these distinctions constitute a fellowship of subjectivities that in their perfect unity mirror one divine intellect and one divine will."[92] "God does not simply act in a threefold way" as Father, Son, and Holy Spirit. Rather, at the very essence of his being, he exists within himself in a tripersonal

---

87. Ibid., 142.
88. Ibid., 143.
89. Ibid.
90. Ibid., 166, 166–67.
91. Ibid., 37.
92. Ibid., 185.

relationship."[93] This intrapersonal characterization is what is technically referred to as the immanent or ontological Trinity. It is distinct from the economic Trinity which has a functional purpose in bringing the entire created order into right relationship of its God intended purpose (Rom 8:19–23). The immanent and the economic Trinity work together in which the latter "follows . . . and is not to be equated with" the former.[94] Stated otherwise, "Because God . . . interacts dynamically within himself . . . *this is why* he can also go out of himself and interact dynamically with his human subjects."[95]

Bloesch maintains that the Trinity is altogether congruent with biblical exegesis if not—unlike Torrance's claim—exhaustively included within it.[96] Bloesch bases the substance of his exposition, not only on New Testament "allusions to three modes of God's being and activity," but also on "certain underlying motifs that run through the apostolic testimony." Of foremost importance is "the preexisting Word, the core claim that the Word [or Son of] of God existed before the Incarnation in unity with the Father."[97]

Bloesch identifies several references to the plurality of God's being and activity in various passages throughout the Old Testament, which "attests that the God of revelation was conceived from the very beginning as a composite rather than a solitary unity."[98] Christianity extended the depiction of God as both majestically holy and transcendent of all human control while simultaneously immersed in the work of healing the inherent flaws within the human condition and searing fissures within the created order. It was not that the biblical God *had* to do this to fulfill some aspect of his own being. Rather, compassion and the desire to communicate are inherent attributes of his character that existed before the foundation of the world. After creating "man in our own image, in our likeness" (Gen 1:26), God desired fellowship not only with humankind at its best. In the most poignant yearning, God embraced humankind at its worst while always insisting upon repentance in the call to fidelity to his holy law. This twin reality is reflected in Psalm 119, one of the Old Testament's most comprehensive statements of the character and essence God's holy law.

For Christians, radical faithfulness to, and fulfillment of the law, is established by faith in Jesus Christ, who "is the propitiation for our sins" (1 John 2:2 KJV). The agency and work of the Holy Spirit, which "came to

---

93. Ibid., 184.
94. Bloesch, *God the Almighty*, 185.
95. Bloesch, *Jesus Christ*, 141.
96. Bloesch, "Donald Bloesch Responds," 98–199.
97. Bloesch, *God the Almighty*, 170.
98. Ibid., 168.

be seen as the power of God . . . in action," especially in the Gospel of John and the Acts of the Apostles, closes the circuit of a solid biblical basis for the ultimate development of a formally articulated Trinitarian doctrine.[99] This theological work was an incarnational effort in its own right of the early church that emerged amidst the need to expound upon and defend the truth claims of its faith in the first several centuries of its history. The primary doctrines that came to fruition in the Council of Nicea (325 CE) and the Chalcedonian Creed (451 CE) on the incarnation and Trinity have remained an indispensable center of settled orthodox Christian dogma for nearly seventeen hundred years even as "new light" has emerged over the centuries by necessity and grace.[100]

Bloesch maintains that it is best to describe the Trinity, "as an outcome of the church's reflection of faith than as ground or basis of faith." That is because the Trinity, as an "object of faith," affirmed in revelatory mystery is "a later development." It is not in itself a "part of the original testimony of faith."[101] Bloesch identifies the incarnation rather than the Trinity as the foundational source of the Christian faith—the "saving mystery of salvation."[102]

In his effort to gain maximum clarity within the midst of the paradox of revelation, Bloesch draws a distinction between "the reality of the Trinity"—in pointing to the distinctive, but unifying modes of God's identity—"and the conceptualization of this reality,"[103] which can only be conveyed in symbolic and analogical imagery. He sees the formal articulation of the Trinity as an essential interpolation of the first order based on the original apostolic and broader biblical witness. As he states:

> The doctrine of the Trinity is both an analytic development of the central facts of divine revelation (as Barth maintained) and a synthetic construction drawn from the church's reflection upon this revelation. We do not project upon God the human experience of personal relationships, but we find in God the perfection of personal interaction as this is mirrored in the self-revelation of the Father in the Son and through the power of the Spirit.[104]

---

99. Ibid.

100. For an extensive discussion of the historical developments that led to the early church's embrace of the doctrines of the Trinity and incarnation, see Pelikan, *Emergence of the Catholic Tradition*, 172–277.

101. Bloesch., "Donald Bloesch Responds," 199.

102. Ibid., 198. Apparently, the quote is an uncited reference to Torrance's *Doctrine of Grace in the Apostolic Fathers*.

103. Bloesch, "Donald Bloesch Responds," 199.

104. Bloesch, *God the Almighty*, 167.

A systematic theology is based on a hermeneutical reflection on the Bible in light of particular issues or challenges that arise in a given historical setting. While the context needs to be taken into account, at stake in any period or culture is the viability of the kerygma in light of competing constructions of reality. Bloesch notes that the "dogma of the Trinity emerged in the church only through a constant struggle with heresy." In the first few centuries of its history several heterodox movements "infiltrated the bastions of the church."[105] The challenge these posed to an emergent orthodoxy required a more articulated response than early church theologians had previously provided on the relationship between the divinity and humanity of Christ and on the ways in which the Father, Son, and Spirit interacted within the Godhead.

One such challenge was the widespread influence of Gnosticism—"a syncretic movement" that identified evil with the material world and the need for the spiritually faithful to "rise into the purely spiritual realm." On the Gnostic account, the spiritual journey consists of the search for and ultimate "ability to discover this divine element"[106] within the interiority of the released soul. The Christian influenced Gnostic identified the "true self" with Christ, "the revealer of the unknown, high and all perfect God."[107]

Bloesch references Arianism as another major heresy that confronted the early church. On the Arian account, Christ was deemed divine, but not one with God; rather, the Son was an intermediate being between God and the world"—a "demigod." The Arian account denied the eternal nature of the Son as explicated in the prologue of the Gospel of John. Bloesch notes that in the Arian vision the Logos was perceived as "preexistent but not eternal."[108] The influential Gnostic and Arian heresies shared a sub-biblical perspective that required the early church to formalize its understanding of the relationship between Christ and God. Both envisioned the Son as divine in some way, but denied the eternal significance of the deity of Christ as well as the descent of God in bodily flesh, whether in the life and earthly ministry of Jesus or in the post-resurrection revelation.

Bloesch discusses an additional set of heresies that placed the superiority of God over and above the Son and the Spirit, particularly the Sabellian heresy in its emphasis on God as "a single person." While the Sabellians

105. Ibid., 171.

106. Ibid., 172. See 172–76 for Bloesch's broader discussion of the various "syncretistic movements" facing the Christian community in its first several centuries. The problems posed by these and related challenges to an emerging orthodox vision led to the crystallization of the Trinity beginning at the Council of Nicea in 325.

107. Ibid., 173.

108. Ibid., 171.

understood God as taking "different forms," the primary emphasis remained on his singularity. In this depiction, the "divinity of Christ was merged into the essence of the Father," including the incarnation interpreted simply "as a mode of existence or manifestation of the Father." This included acceptance of a "a threefoldness in God in relation to the world" as "three successive phases of his being, but a rejection of any understanding of God that could be construed in an intra-triune manner.[109] These and related theological conflicts over the nature of Christ and the relationship between the Father, Son, and Spirit engaged church fathers in the search for a coherent orthodoxy within the very heart and soul of the early church.[110]

In direct response to these various challenges, the doctrine of the Trinity posits Christ as existing "of one substance with the Father . . . not only a mediator between God and humanity but God himself in human flesh."[111] Bloesch interprets this teaching as each person of the Trinity having its own existential function in the economic Trinity, while, in essence, the three persons are of equal importance in the fullness of God's being in the imminent Trinity. Consequently, "it is more theologically felicitous to affirm a relationship of dependence between the three persons in their mode of operation than to speak of subordination in any ontological sense."[112]

Bloesch's analysis of the constructed nature of Trinitarian dogmatics reflects tight parsing since the New Testament itself contains "a fundamental Trinitarian awareness, expressed in many triadic formulas."[113] He lays out a variety of passages in the gospels and letters that references Father, Son, and Spirit, in which "each is presented as equal to the others."[114] Bloesch also notes that "the equality of the three subjectivities that compose the Godhead is only implied," even as such equality of persons "was fully in accord with the intention of the Bible."[115] Moreover, while there is "no ontological superiority of the father in the immanent Trinity," Bloesch points to "an

---

109. Ibid., 172.

110. See Pelikan, *Emergence of the Catholic Tradition*, 172–277, 332–57, for an extended discussion of these various heresies and the various ways the early church worked through them in the doctrines of the incarnation and the Trinity.

111. Ibid., 171.

112. Ibid., 174–75.

113. Scheffczyk, "God: The Divine," 564; cited in Bloesch, *God the Almighty*, 168.

114. Bloesch, *God the Almighty*, 168–69.

115. Ibid., 169. Bloesch "agree[s] with Barth that there is no clear statement of equality in the New Testament. In his [Barth's] view the church in positing the equality of the three persons went beyond the Bible, but it was in full accord with the Bible." Ibid.

order of succession" in "the economic Trinity" in which the Son proceeds from the Father.[116]

This theologically constructed distinction between the immanent and economic Trinity provides a way of explaining passages in the gospel where the Son, while remaining God, is subordinate to the Father. Bloesch refers to "an order of procession within the Trinity itself" in which the relationship between the three persons is one of equality and "interdependence." He places Christ's "voluntary subordination" in the economic Trinity in which God in Christ, as suffering servant, becomes the means of reconciling the world.[117] In a more direct manner than Bloesch sees it, Torrance views the Trinity as "fully implicit throughout the New Testament in God's historical manifestation in Jesus Christ as Father, Son and Holy Spirit"—and therefore, at the very beginning of the formation of the early church in the first century.[118] Bloesch takes what Torrance refers to as a more "synthetic" approach to the Trinity that guided the church "through continuous reflection on its faith that lasted several centuries." He hesitates, therefore, to associate the formal doctrine of the Trinity that crystalized in the fourth and fifth centuries "with the self-revelation of God as triune."[119]

Nevertheless, Bloesch is in primary agreement with Torrance in viewing the essential unity of Father, Son, and Holy Spirit as implicit within the biblical testimony itself. As Bloesch further argues, the three persons of the Trinity "are symbols" that point "to ontological realities" on the "objective" nature of God, even as any human understanding of God's infinite plenitude can only remain shrouded in mystery that is only partially revealed through grace by faith.[120] It is the struggle of faith to work with the signposts that are available—particularly Scripture, early doctrinal formulation, theological reflections through historically informed ecclesial traditions, and the body of Christ in its local and global expressions—to gain glimpses of that to which the signs point. Whatever differences separate Bloesch and Torrance on the origins of the Trinity, both theologians are in close accord on that to which it points: the incarnation and the intra-triune nature and character at the very essence of God's being.[121] To minimize the Trinity, therefore, is to

---

116. Bloesch, "Donald Bloesch Responds," 199.

117. Bloesch, *God the Almighty*, 189.

118. Torrance, "Bloesch's Doctrine of God," 144.

119. For Torrance's reference, see ibid. Bloesch's quotes are from "Donald Bloesch Responds," 198.

120. Bloesch, *God the Almighty*, 185.

121. As Bloesh states, "The fullness of [God's] being is in the Trinity itself, and each member of the Trinity is to be found in the perichoresis, the mutual indwelling of the members of the Trinity." Ibid., 188.

dismiss the basic claims of the entire tradition of orthodox Christianity in its classical Protestant, Catholic, and Eastern Orthodox expressions and to place the Christ story within another metannarative—whether within the pantheon of the ancient Greco-Roman cosmology or within the relativistic and pluralistic worldview of the contemporary era.[122]

For these reasons, Bloesch maintains that without a solid doctrine of the Trinity anchored in the more foundational theology of the incarnation, any evangelical project of revitalizing a biblio-centered Christology can only falter on the shoals of prevailing modernistic anthropological assumptions such as have influenced contemporary liberal Christian perspectives.[123] In short, without the Trinity and the incarnation as grounding points, the Christian understanding of God as fully transcendent, while totally immersed within the fragmentations, fissures, and aspirations of humanity and the entire created order through a partially realized and anticipatory eschatology, has little chance of radical acceptance within setting of contemporary mainline Protestantism.

Trinitarian challenges to prevailing mainline theological constructions are several, including the very notion of Christ as God in human flesh (hence, the incarnation). To hold to this kerygmatic claim in any profound sense is to accept nothing other in our day, as well as in days of old, than the radical particularity of the scandal and folly of the cross (1 Cor 1:18–25) in its full New Testament significance. While Trinitarian theology requires perpetual explication in changing historical and cultural settings, any diminishing of the significance of the Trinity and corresponding claims about the nature of God, Christ, and the Holy Spirit can only lead to the diminution of core claims of orthodox Christianity.[124]

The Trinity, in its organic relationship to the incarnation is, as in ages past, an indispensable dogmatic truth claim of the most fundamental sort. Dislodging either of these central doctrines of the Christian faith involves great loss, with little or no obvious gain for the strengthening of a scripturally grounded theology of God. As Bloesch well knows, mainline Protestant theologians would need to work through many of its core assumptions before such a robust Trinitarian prospect, as he presents it, becomes a vital

---

122. See ibid., 205–60, for Bloesch's discussion of ancient and modern challenges to the orthodox interpretation of the Christian faith within respective religious and secular cultures, which includes various Christian efforts of theological adaptation.

123. See Ogden, *Doing Theology*, and Spong, *New Christianity for a New World*, as representative examples of some substantial note. See also Bloesch, *God the Almighty*, 178, for his assessment of Tillich's understanding of the Trinity.

124. See Bloesch, *God the Almighty*, 177–84, for his assessment on contemporary Trinitarian perspectives.

source of revitalization within its religious culture. He does not hold out much prospect for such a movement within the contemporary liberal Protestant sector, even as he longs very much for it.[125]

CONCLUDING REMARKS

One takes costly theological positions on faith without full assurance of conclusive evidentiary support (Heb 11:1). Thus it is with Bloesch in his commitment to a catholic evangelical orthodoxy rooted in the theology of the Reformers through which he seeks to mediate the profound tensions that mark twentieth-century Protestant theology between what H. R. Niebuhr typologically refers to as *Christ and Culture*.[126] Bloesch calls Christians "not to flee from the world but to bring the world into subjugation to the advancing kingdom of God." He argues that this mission occurs both within and beyond history.[127] With Reinhold Niebuhr, Bloesch views social meliorism as a proximate good, a task to which Christians must be engaged, while keeping their most focused attention on both heralding and advancing the realm of God whenever and wherever opportunity arises.[128]

---

125. Bloesch is appreciative of Jürgen Moltmann's contribution to Trinitarian theology in the latter's highly influential *Trinity and the Kingdom*. Nevertheless, Bloesch remains concerned that Moltmann's social Trinitarian emphasis is so extensive that it "breaks with . . . monotheism altogether, since his God is not one being but three movements or processes that converge and complement one another." *God the Almighty*, 181. As Bloesch elsewhere notes, "Moltmann endeavors to move beyond a Trinitarian monotheism to a tritheistic panentheism." *Theology of Word and Spirit*, 251. These statements do less than full justice to the breadth and depth of Moltmann's theological project. Still, Bloesch has a point in highlighting the imminent emphasis in Moltmann's theology at the expense of a robust transcendent vision. Moltmann is also susceptible to criticism for his all-encompassing focus on God's suffering love, with the result of marginalizing the attribute of holiness and God's wrath in the light of enduring sin. Bloesch, *God the Almighty*, 97. Despite his reservations, Bloesch remains grateful for Moltmann's significant contribution to contemporary theology in the areas of Trinitarian theology, eschatology, social justice, and ecology. In bringing these themes into a wide-ranging theological framework, Moltmann has established important theological bridges between various Reformed, Lutheran, evangelical, liberal, and Eastern Orthodox perspectives. For a similar interpretation of the strengths and limitations of Moltmann's Trinitarian theology, see Grenz and Olson, *20th Century Theology*, 172–86.

126. As part of my discussion on the enduring significance of the neo-orthodox influence I comment on *Christ and Culture* in chapter 7, along with Niebuhr's equally influential *Radical Monotheism in Western Culture*.

127. Bloesch, *Last Things*, 110.

128. Ibid., 112. On Niebuhr's social ethics, see *Interpretation of Christian Ethics*, esp. 62–83, and Lovin, *Reinhold Niebuhr and Christian Realism*, 72–118. I also focus on Reinhold Niebuhr in chapter 6.

Bloesch does not dismiss the questions posed by the culture. He seeks to contextualize them in light of the core values and beliefs of orthodox Christianity, as he depicts them, in his "centrist evangelical" vision.[129] He is skeptical of liberal theological approaches to culture, which he views as possessing an inordinate influence on mainline Protestantism. For Bloesch, this theological dead end needs to be substantially deconstructed for any contemporary Protestant revival to flourish beyond avowedly evangelical congregations and movements. His call for a broad-based orthodoxy across denominational lines cannot remain past oriented. It requires reformulation in changing historical and cultural contexts without any diminution of its apostolic core in the faith once for all delivered to the saints. Bloesch differs from Tillich and Dorrien, both of whose dialectical theologies are based on a more correlative relationship between culture and faith.

As depicted throughout this chapter, Bloesch may be viewed as a dialectical theologian within the context of an unequivocal orthodox baseline. He refuses to compromise on his most fundamental dogmatic precepts by ceding too much to prevailing cultural predispositions in giving the social context more legitimacy than warranted, even on Reinhold Niebuhr's terms, as a proximate reality. Bloesch views as problematic the very concession to take cultural stances on their own terms among liberally oriented mainline theologians. However much the integration between Christ and culture may have seemed credible among progressive theologians of the early twentieth century when Protestantism functioned as a vital force in US culture, this plausibility has become utterly eroded in the postmodern, post-industrial, post-Christendom, and increasingly global religious milieu of the current period. Bloesch's emphasis on paradox, dialectics, and mystery needs to be grasped as part of his vision to fashion a comprehensive orthodoxy through a synthesis of selective strands of mostly Calvinist theology, evangelical pietism, and neo-orthodoxy, and in his desire to establish an apologetic counterpoint to theological liberalism.

By staying firmly focused on the core essentials of the tradition of the Protestant Reformers—as articulated in his *Essentials of Evangelical Theology* and more comprehensively in his seven-volume *Christian Foundation* series—Bloesch offers a flourishing panoramic of the breadth and depth of the orthodox worldview. Both works are infused with solid biblical explication, profoundly ruminating theological discourse, subtle probing into the nature and character of God, and a passionate call for a faithful renewal of the church in the contemporary period.

---

129. Bloesch, *Jesus Christ*, 11.

Accepting Bloesch's orthodox premises greatly facilitates entry into his theological vision. Those who do seek, or are driven to this pathway, will be richly rewarded with an understanding that is thoroughly grounded in the fundamentals of the faith and theologically attuned to the main currents of confessing Christ movements within the mainline Protestant denominations and centrist evangelical perspectives. They will also have a framework to provide reasonably effective responses to the challenges posed to serious evangelical discourse by Protestant liberalism that will need to be further worked out beyond where Bloesch goes in substantially addressing such liberalism on its own terms. I will attempt such an effort in chapter 5 through the "evangelical ecumenical" vision of Bloesch's esteemed colleague, Gabriel Fackre and in chapter 6 in my discussion of the postliberal Old Testament scholar, Walter Brueggemann.

For those adhering to a postliberal perspective, there is also a great deal to ponder in Bloesch's work, even though such advocates will be less persuaded by what they take as his excessively dogmatic leaning orthodoxy. For someone like Dorrien, who rejects Bloesch's orthodox vision primarily through rhetorical dismissal, this would require placing Bloesch among the evangelicals he views as on the cutting edge of remaking evangelical theology at the dawn of the twenty-first century.[130] Such a sensibility to the rich nuances of Bloesch's theological vision is more fully evident in Elmer Colyer's collection *Evangelical Theology in Transition: Theologians in Dialogue with Donald Bloesch*. What remains an open question is the extent to which those within the Protestant mainline who seek a substantive encounter with the Great Tradition will view Bloesch as a serious conversation partner.

---

130. Dorrien, *Remaking of Evangelical Theology*, 189–209. Dorrien distinguishes Bloesch's modernist sensibilities from the postmodern perspectives of those postconservative evangelicals exhibiting an "open theology." Dorrien points to an important difference. As he notes, in his emphasis on paradox, dialectics, mystery, and the central role of the Holy Spirit as the interpreter of Scripture, Bloesch has traveled a good distance from more traditional evangelicals like Henry, Erickson, Packer, and Donald Carson, who put more stress on the inerrancy of Scripture, in which the Bible in itself, is the inscripturated Word of God. Dorrien also notes that, despite his critique of "paleoorthodoxy," Bloesch belongs "to a group of 'Great Tradition' evangelicals who are clearly more interested in pursuing dialogue with conservative Catholic and Orthodox theologians than with progressive evangelicals." Ibid., 193. There is much here in what Dorrien contends. However, his caricature of Bloesch, as exhibiting a form of evangelical theology and piety "that lives decidedly in the house of authority" (ibid.), is a reductionist depiction that does not adequately account for the significance of Bloesch's contribution in expanding critical thought within the broader Protestant community he seeks to address. In fairness, Dorrien provides a balanced summary of Bloesch's role in contemporary evangelical culture, even though his critical assessment of it is shaped by his obvious affinity for the open theology of the postconservative evangelicals. Ibid., 189–93.

Throughout this chapter, I have sought to make the case that his "ecumenical evangelical" vision—particularly, his theology of Scripture, God, and the Trinity—could play an important role in coordination with other key perspectives in mediating the interface between evangelical, postliberal, and neo-orthodox theology.[131] Gaining greater credence within the UCC denomination and in seminaries like Yale, Union, and Andover Newton (that have a strong UCC influence) for Bloesch's work would play a significant role in establishing such credibility. This aspiration is eminently plausible, however difficult may be its actual attainment. Much hangs in the balance.

---

131. In his desire to reclaim "the dynamic center of biblical and apostolic faith," Bloesch seeks to "appeal to two groups: those coming out of fundamentalism in search of a biblical alternative to liberalism, and those who have become disillusioned with liberalism and sense the need to recover the transcendent truth of the gospel kept alive in church tradition by the Spirit of the living God." Bloesch, *Jesus Christ*, 11, 12. Thanks to Fackre, in particular, Bloesch's theology is well-received in the UCC based Confessing Christ network. It is another matter whether his work will gain sufficient visibility for critical assessment within the broader UCC culture and throughout Protestant mainline denominations and theological centers.

5

Restoring the Center
Gabriel Fackre's Evangelical Ecumenism

The basic interpretive principle of scriptural authority is Jesus Christ, the "lens" through which we read the text. What is biblically authoritative is, as Luther put it long ago, what "urges Christ."[1]

While Scripture is the sole teaching authority, contra the functional occupancy of this role by the then [Catholic] church's magisterium, this point of decision does not preclude a process for discerning the Bible's meaning that includes the community of faith and its wisdom. Nor does it exclude from the process any means to be found in a fallen but still graced creation that can also aid in the discernment and clarification of Scripture's intent. . .[These are, however,] *ministerial* to the understanding of a Scripture that remains always *magisterial*.[2]

Dogmatics is a science . . . No act of man can claim to be more than an attempt, not even science. By describing it as an attempt, we are simply stating its nature as preliminary and limited. Whenever science is taken in practice completely seriously, we are under no illusion that anything man can ever do can ever be an undertaking of supreme wisdom and final art, that there exists

---

1. Fackre, *Christian Story*, 2:39.
2. Ibid., 94.

an absolute science, one that as it were has fallen from Heaven. Even Christian dogmatics is an attempt—an attempt to understand and expound, an attempt to see, to hear and to state definite facts, to present them in the form of a doctrine.[3]

FACKRE AND BLOESCH BRIEFLY COMPARED

In progressing toward a centrist Protestant vision, there is no finer voice than that of Gabriel Fackre to move us forward in our exploration of the theology of Scripture and God in contemporary US Protestantism. Like Bloesch, Fackre is committed to a mediating theology that holds in radical tension a wide stream of highly conflicting perspectives. While exhibiting much appreciation for the work of Bloesch—whom he refers to as an "ecumenical evangelical"—Fackre characterizes himself as an "evangelical ecumenical."[4] The differences are subtle in that Bloesch and Fackre have more in common than what separates them. Henry's astute observation warrants much consideration that "it is debatable whether Fackre is best characterized as an evangelical theologian with ecumenical sympathies, or an ecumenical theologian with deepening evangelical commitments."[5]

One finds a subtle difference in Bloesch's emphasis on a sacramental reading of Scripture where God has the power to speak in and through each individual passage without necessarily making an expository linkage to the arc of the biblical trajectory, as depicted in Fackre's narrative theology. Considering that both theologians accept what each identifies as important, the distinction, while slight, does point toward Bloesch's evangelical orientation and to Fackre's appreciation of postliberal and narrative theology within the more fundamental context of their broad convergence. Bloesch and Fackre also differ in the latter's greater willingness to incorporate themes within theological liberalism in his comprehensive Christian centrist vision.

This feature is particularly evident in Fackre's greater appreciation of the "hermeneutics of suspicion" on any alleged "innocence" of biblical texts as well as the centrality of culture in the liberal claim that traditional orthodoxy too easily dispenses with matters of dominance and oppression. As Fackre states in a passage that echoes a similar refrain to that of Walter Brueggemann:

---

3. Barth, *Dogmatics in Outline*, 9.
4. Fackre, "Jesus Christ in Bloesch's Theology," 98.
5. Henry, "Evangelical-Ecumenical Dialogue," 39.

The hermeneutics of suspicion that looks for the power agendas of texts and their interpreters, regularly cloaked in piety, is also consonant with the Christian doctrine of the fall, which sees the will-to-power in all human ventures, and is particularly sensitive to the self-righteousness that smokescreens its self-interest. How these insights are used as instruments in the hermeneutical venture, rather than full-scale ideologies that take charge of it, is the challenge we...[need] to address.[6]

In liberationist and feminist readings, this impetus leads to a critique of legitimizing discourses that require considerable deconstruction of many of the basic premises of traditional biblical perspectives before any theological reconstruction can take place.[7] As orthodox theologians exhibiting broad ecumenical sensibility, both Fackre and Bloesch reject interpretations of the biblical canon that remain fixated in this deconstructed mode. They differ in that Bloesch is "more pessimistic than Fackre concerning the possibility of evangelical renewal in"[8] both the UCC and the broader Protestant mainline in a way that holds the potential of incorporating liberationist and feminist theologies within a comprehensive ecumenist oriented orthodoxy.

Where Bloesch remains skeptical, Fackre lays greater stress on balancing fidelity to the fundamentals of the faith with openness to new light. It is this dialectic that Fackre envisions in his narrative theology that could create space for the type of mainline renewal of its own heritage in the tradition of the Protestant Reformers. Given his firm commitment to the magisterial authority of the Bible that he holds in common with all evangelicals, along with a deep affinity to the theological legacy of the Reformation—that he shares with *some* evangelicals such as Bloesch and Packer—Fackre defines

> an evangelical *ecumenical*...[as] one who joins... commitments [to the Bible and justification by faith] to a classical trinitarian faith, as transmitted in creedal, liturgical, and sacramental traditions, and who vigorously participates in an ecumenical movement that both seeks ecclesial unity and is deeply immersed in today's struggles for justice, peace, and the integrity of creation.[9]

As an essential component of his strong catholic commitment to ecumenism, Fackre adheres to a rigorous dialectic between the biblical Grand Narrative and the breaking in of new light that may be evoked through

---

6. Fackre, *Christian Story*, 2:214.
7. Ibid., 102–24.
8. Bloesch, "Donald Bloesch Responds," 192.
9. Fackre, *Ecumenical Faith in Evangelical Perspective*, ix.

changing historical exigencies.[10] This includes keeping the many points of tension within contemporary theology in dynamic balance, within an overarching fidelity to the biblical magisterium through the prism of Christ revealed as the incarnation of God in flesh reconciling the world (2 Cor 5:19).

FACKRE'S THEOLOGY IN BRIEF

In his probing commitment to theological comprehensiveness, dialogue, and ecumenism, Fackre has written a nuanced theological systematics that will require considerable unpacking in order to address sufficiently. I will take on that task in the subsequent sections of this chapter. This introductory preview provides a broad sketch based on the introduction of the first volume of Fackre's *Christian Story*.[11]

Fackre grounds his theology in what he refers to as the arc of the storyline from creation to consummation. He views the narrative mode as a "metaphor 'translation' . . .used for the systematics of communicating Christian faith" in the contemporary era.[12] Playing off the "translation" metaphor, he characterizes his narrative hermeneutics as providing a "dynamic equivalence" for explicating the traditions of the Christian faith in light of the diversity of challenges confronting the contemporary body of Christ.[13]

He provides three reasons for the narrative focus. At the most foundational level, he views the Bible as a "Storybook" in which its basic plot line unfolds as "chapters in the biography of God."[14] Second, as a contemporary theologian, Fackre draws on the recent work in narrative theology in giving structure to his own systematics. He references the importance of "imagination," "story," "metaphor," and "visual symbol" as better ways to depict something of the ineffability of God's revelation, which can be grasped only through analogical reasoning and language. As an ecumenical bridge builder, he argues that "discursive exposition" needs to stand "alongside" the more imaginative modes of expression in addressing the intrinsic truth of the biblical revelation.[15] As a final reason, he points to the need for a

---

10. I discuss this in the section of this chapter titled "External Hermeneutics." As an example, one might consider the impact of the Holocaust on supersessionist readings of certain New Testament texts (e.g., 2 Cor 3:7–18).

11. Fackre, *Christian Story*, 1:1–45.

12. Ibid., 9.

13. Ibid., 10.

14. Ibid., 1, 15 for "Storybook" reference.

15. Ibid., 28. See 27–32 for Fackre's fuller discussion of narrative theology and its significance in his own work.

theological systematics that is faithful to the biblical storyline and congruent within the contemporary theological context. For Fackre, this requires factoring in critical biblical scholarship, the more constructive insights of feminist and liberationist theology, and the impact of a postmodern consumer culture on the collective conscious of the modern Christian. Given the importance he attributes to analogical thinking, Fackre reasons that narrative hermeneutics represents a more persuasive way of "relat[ing] the ancient formulas to our contemporary context"[16] than what can be gained by rigorous systematics or rational apologetics.

Fackre acknowledges that his storied account is "from one angle of vision, not from a God's-eye point of view."[17] He accepts the inevitable contextualization that shapes his vision. In depicting the narrative mode as a metaphor, Fackre distinguishes between types of translation, which include the literal and what he refers to as the "paraphrastic" (paraphrasing) approaches, both of which he rejects. In positing "dynamic equivalence," the "translation" "follow[s] the original context line by line," yet is not rigorously "tied to the exact repetition of the original words." Rather, such translations can be changed in a manner "that reflect[s] original intent, attempting thereby to be 'dynamic'" with need for only "modest alternatives" in language and original meaning.[18]

In articulating his theological rationale, Fackre is not only interested in "get[ting] the *story* out," but "get[ting] the story *straight*."[19] On his interpretation, getting the story straight necessitates identifying the Bible as the *source* of revelation and therefore foundational in terms of authority. He points to the church and the broader theological and ecclesial two thousand-year tradition as primary *resource*, and a fundamental mode of illumination. Finally, and third in terms of priority, he points to human experience and culture as the *setting* in which the faith is situated in any given time and place through which new light on God's word can break forth as a result of new contextual contingencies.[20] The underlying standard to which all of these modes of revelation open up is "Jesus Christ, before which all our efforts to tell the Story are judged."[21]

Fackre presents the storyline of the biblical trajectory through various "chapters" that allow him to play out the fullness of his theological vision.

16. Ibid., 11.
17. Ibid., 4.
18. Ibid., 10.
19. Ibid., 2.
20. Ibid., 24.
21. Ibid., 14.

Each of these chapters, from creation to consummation, maintains their own revelatory integrity while their meaning becomes enriched, and ultimately, clarified only as the story progresses, ultimately beyond human history in the coming of the eschaton.[22] In a series of pictorial vignettes Fackre depicts this vision through the following creative imagery:

> God brings the world into being, the stretching of one hand toward the other as captured in Michelangelo's painting of God's reach toward Adam, *creation*. The response of the world is the rejection of the divine initiative, the *fall*. The recall of God, the new reach of the Creator toward creation, takes place in the *covenant with Israel*. The depth of human alienation requires a correspondingly deep plunge into a resisting world, issuing in the suffering Love at the center of human history, *Jesus Christ*. The new age to the end is the time of the *Church, salvation* and *consummation* when that drama through which we now are living proceeds toward the intended unity of God and the world.[23]

Fackre describes this storyline in various simple and highly subtle ways in rigorous dialogue and in generous encounter with the broad range of mostly twentieth-century Protestant theological perspectives. He intricately weaves narrative and formal systematics in the construction and explication of a vision that is ecumenically broad and evangelically faithful, while acknowledging that, in seeing in a mirror dimly, his reach invariably extends beyond its grasp.

SCRIPTURE AS SOURCE OF THE REVELATION OF GOD

Fackre bases his claim on "the authority of the Bible . . . in its testimony to the decisive events in the faith narrative" of the Old and New Testament as mediated through the unique occurrence of Christ revealed as the incarnation of the living God.[24] One cannot sharply distinguish the sources of authority in the Bible from those of revelation upon which faith claims are based in the various means of grace empowered through the efficacy of the Holy Spirit.[25] Nevertheless, for purposes of theological clarity, Fackre does

---

22. Ibid., 37–42. Fackre provides an extensive synopsis of the chapters through much of the rest of the first volume of *Christian Story*.

23. Ibid., 5–7.

24. Ibid., 15. See *Christian Story*, 2:14–15. On Jesus Christ as the "central truth claim" of the Christian faith, see ibid., 14. For an expanded discussion on the central role of Christ to which the Bible is the primary source, see ibid., 1:99–151.

25. Fackre, *Christian Story*, 2:49–59.

so, as reflected, respectively, in volume 2 of *The Christian Story*, subtitled *Authority: Scripture in the Church for the World*, and the next volume, titled *The Doctrine of Revelation: A Narrative Interpretation*.[26]

Given the massive evidence of critical biblical scholarship to the contrary, Fackre maintains that it is no longer credible to base the authority of New Testament Scripture on direct apostolic authorship. However, he does maintain that the twenty-seven books that comprise its canon are based on the "reliable transmission of original apostolic testimony," confirmed by the Holy Spirit, the ultimate source of illumination. As he states, "the layers of subsequent tradition" that have shaped the final editing process of its various books "have not obscured the proclamation of salvation," and for this reason, "its apostolic authority . . . remains."[27] Such apostolic authenticity includes the authority of Paul, called by Christ as the "apostle to the Gentiles" who represents the most authentic singular voice of the entire New Testament because of the scope and dating of his letters as well as the central role he plays in the Acts of the Apostles.[28]

As Fackre expresses it, the Bible as source is the *what*. The question that he grapples with throughout the second volume of *The Christian Story* is the *how*. His explanation is ultimately clear, even as it is more allusive than straightforward, as one finds, for example, in Packer.[29] The *how* includes not "mistaking the setting," that is the culture, or for that matter the resource—the church's two thousand–year tradition in its varied manifestations and expressions—"for the *source* and *substance*" of the revelation of God, as embodied first and foremost in the Bible. In theologies that mix these up therein "is the problem."[30]

---

26. Fackre notes that while working on the third volume of the *Christian Story* series the editors of the *Edinburgh Studies in Constructive Theology* asked him to contribute a book to that series. The result was a refashioning of the materials he prepared for the initial project in meeting the editorial needs of the series. See Fackre, *Doctrine of Revelation*, ix. Fackre never formally completed a third volume. Yet, he refers to *Doctrine of Revelation* as vol. 3 of part of a five-part series subtitled *A Pastoral Systematics*. Fackre completed his *Christian Story* series when he published vol. 5 in 2007 on the church.

27. Fackre, *Christian Story*, 1:16.

28. Schnelle identifies 1 Thess, Gal, 1 & 2 Cor, Rom, Phil, and Phlm as the authentic extant writings of Paul. He views Col, Eph, 1 & 2 Tim, and Titus, which are sometimes attributed to Paul, as "deutero-Pauline" texts, and adds Acts to the list of New Testament texts as central to the church's understanding of its meaning and mission in the second half of the first century. Schnelle, *Apostle Paul*, 44.

29. This does not mean that the Packer's exposition is not sophisticated and compelling in its own right, but that his prose does not contain the allusive and metaphorical resonances that one finds in Fackre writing style. One might argue that Fackre's image eliciting prose is, itself an expression of his theological commitments.

30. Fackre, *Christian Story*, 2:17.

Fackre subtly draws out something of the intricate relationship of these three dimensions of faith in a manner that seeks to give each of these "macro-options" their respective due. He does so even while acknowledging the ultimate limitations of these "ideal types" in "the exactitude suggested" but not realized "by their [functional] distinctions."³¹ There is, at a certain level, not all that difference between what Fackre and Packer propose in terms of the delineations of the hierarchy between the Bible, church tradition, and personal experience and the historical context, through which faith is expressed in given place and time. However, Fackre offers a more sophisticated presentation of the *context* underlying contemporary Protestant discourse, along with a willingness to incorporate significant aspects of neo-orthodox and liberal perspectives into his theological model. He also draws on progressive political and social thought within his comprehensive biblical social ethic. He does so in a manner that remains both evangelically attuned and unequivocally ecumenical in spirit.

The *how* also pertains to the interpretation of the Bible that includes a long exposition on various schools of inerrancy and biblical infallibility.³² Fackre shares an affinity with evangelical hermeneutics in highlighting the importance of a common sense, plain meaning reading of the Bible. With Packer, Fackre accepts the principle of *analogy of scripture* where texts that are more opaque are interpreted through passages which are clearer and more central to the overall direction of Scripture and authorial intent. Fackre and Packer are at one in maintaining that "Scripture is its own best interpreter" in the clarification of meaning of any passage.³³ On this and related aspects of biblical interpretations, Fackre shares much in common with his primary evangelical interlocutors, Carl Henry and Bloesch, even as he diverges in substantial ways, especially with the former.³⁴ What he shares in particular with these two is a firm belief that "the Bible has an overall coherence and directionality that constitutes the horizon against which the reader views the biblical drama and declarations."³⁵

This core evangelical principle of the ultimate authority of the Bible interpreted through the incarnational prism of Christ revealed is a durable axiom in Fackre's theology. Based on this foundation, Fackre discusses, in the second volume of *The Christian Story*, what he refers to as a combinationist

---

31. Ibid., 60.

32. Fackre, *Ecumenical Faith in Evangelical Perspective*, 7–19.

33. Fackre, *Ecumenical Faith in Evangelical Perspective*, 52.

34. Fackre compares and contrasts his views of Henry's biblical interpretation in ibid., 171–97, and *Doctrine of Revelation*, 153–78. I review Fackre's assessment of Henry in the second half of this chapter.

35. Fackre, *Ecumenical Faith in Evangelical Perspective*, 52.

and contextual hermeneutic. He provides a conceptual overview of his interpretive framework in his second chapter, "The Context of Authority," which he elaborates upon in his third chapter, "The Text of Authority" and his fourth chapter, "The Context of Authority."

His second chapter also includes a tight twenty page exposition on feminist theology.[36] He is quick to point out that in his analysis of feminist theology he is providing a case study example of his hermeneutical methodology, which he carries out through a discussion of a broad range of contexts in the course of his book. In the process, Fackre gives expansive scope to the breaking forth of new light in a manner in which the context opens up fresh insight into Scripture. In the case at hand, he does so, particularly in referencing the important role that women played in the ministry of Jesus and the early church that had become largely repressed through centuries of ecclesial and theological patriarchal domination. In the presentation of his expansive theology of Scripture, Fackre carefully assesses what can and must be drawn upon from the insights of feminist theology in support of the type of inter-subjective ecumenical reading of Scripture for which he advocates. He also points out what he believes needs to be attenuated and even outright rejected in feminist theology if the integrity of orthodox Christianity conceived in both its ecumenical and evangelical prisms is to be upheld.

Stated in the briefest of terms, while remaining faithful to the broad scope of orthodoxy as depicted in his ecumenical and narrative vision, Fackre places feminist theologians in the role of "critic-in-residence" in expanding the horizon of Christian theological witness. He notes that this is difficult space to maintain both for critic and the church.[37] It is nonetheless crucial in order for the church's ministries of remembrance and vitality to work synergistically in a manner that empowers the body of Christ in its central work of fulfilling the Great Commission (Matt 28:19–20).[38]

Whether the center holds between the midpoint and the periphery by incorporating the insights of the pioneer feminist theologians that Fackre

---

36. Fackre, *Christian Story*, 2:102–24.

37. Ibid., 120–24. The question for Fackre is whether feminist theology, particularly in its pioneering formulations as discussed in chapter 2 of my book, can be incorporated within the wider ecumenical Christian body that he envisions. While he is critical of the whole-scale rejection of fundamental themes in traditional biblical and systematic theology, as evident in certain streams of feminist theology, he also believes that the church loses a great deal if "it does not make a place for women-church and its witness" in the important "role of critic-in-residence." Ibid., 121.

38. The critic-in-residence function extends well beyond Fackre's discussion of feminist theology, which is precisely his point in highlighting it as an example of the ways in which the historical contexts can shed new light on God's word in bringing out aspects of the faith not previously identified or emphasized.

highlights is another matter. This is a concern of major proportions. Both Fackre and I are vitally concerned with the extent to which a confessing Christ movement can provide that underlying cohesion through a dynamic Christian orthodoxy within mainline Protestant denominations to bring its evangelical, Reformed, and progressive wings within a single tent as envisioned in 1 Corinthians 12. This issue will be examined briefly at the end of this chapter and more extensively in chapter 8 of this book.

INTERNAL HERMENEUTICS

Chapter 3 of the *Christian Story*, volume 2, titled "The Text of Authority," highlighted in this section, focuses on internal hermeneutics through what Fackre identifies as the common, critical, and canonical sense of Scripture. Chapter 4, on external hermeneutics—which is discussed in the following section—centers on the various social, cultural, intellectual, and religious contexts that give shape to biblical interpretation and authority largely in the second half of the twentieth-century Western world. In these two chapters, Fackre presents his fourfold hermeneutics through the ways in which the Bible, the church, and the culture interact in any legitimizing hermeneutics. In chapter 3, Fackre addresses the issue of *how* the Bible is authoritative as well as the *what*, in terms of its meaning. Without ignoring the salience of these questions, chapter 4 focuses more on the *why*, or the significance of the text as defined by interpreters of the faith in relation to the prevailing questions and issues of the day.

Common Sense

Fackre identifies three historical sources in describing the role of common sense in biblical interpretation: the Scottish Enlightenment, the Protestant Reformation, and the socio-cultural context of the late twentieth-century Western world. The term stems from the "common sense realism" that emerged in the philosophical reflections of Thomas Reid and other eighteenth-century Scottish philosophers, in the quest to base "reasoning upon self-evident first principles,"[39] sifted through empirical observation of the natural world. Reid's philosophical analysis represented a direct response to the epistemological skepticism of eighteenth-century philosopher David Hume on whether knowledge is accessible through direct intuition and sense perception. Throughout the late eighteenth and much of the

---

39. McConnell, "Old Princeton Apologetics," 651.

nineteenth century, the "rational intuitionism" of Common Sense Scottish Realism gave structure both to the "self-evident truths" of early American republicanism and to a very broad range of Protestant theology.[40] As Fackre observes, through a "chaste induction" this philosophical strand provided a framework for assuming "that sincere minds furnished with similar inductive capacities will come to the same conclusion"[41] in assessing any issue or consideration.

The influence of the school of Common Sense Realism included the philosophical precepts both of the mid-nineteenth-century liberal New Haven Theology of the Congregationalist minister Nathaniel Taylor and the Calvinist Princetonian Theology of perspective of Charles Hodge. More broadly stated, the school of Scottish Common Sense Realism provided an overarching philosophical framework in self-evident reasoning, objectivity, and scientific analysis underlying a wide spectrum of secular and religious thought in the mid-nineteenth-century American thought and culture. It was only in the late nineteenth and early twentieth centuries that this philosophy took on a more rigid hue in the linkage of biblical claims to precise propositional statements and the doctrine of inerrancy that gave fundamentalism its peculiar flavor.[42]

Fackre acknowledges a plain sense meaning of the many didactic and promissory statements embodied throughout the Bible. As he states, "The image of God in us is not so delimited by historical finitude or damaged by sin that a common grace cannot facilitate common understandings" of the Bible.[43] Moreover, the "common sense of Scripture" is a gift of God "discernible through the eyes of committed persons in the people of God"[44] regardless of formal training in biblical and theological studies. He notes that the plain meaning of Scripture "is accessible to ordinary people through the methods of communication common to their everyday life." He speaks of

---

40. Turner, *Without God, Without Creed*, 62.

41. Fackre, *Christian Story*, 2:161.

42. McConnel, "Old Princeton Apologetics," 647–72. As McConnel notes, "Common Sense Realism is much more readily apparent in the theology of antebellum Unitarianism and the New Haven Theology, and especially in the anthropology of Charles Finney at Oberlin . . . The acceptance, in some sense, of Scottish Common Realism by the Old Princetonians would have been in general agreement with the America culture of the day." Ibid., 650. Fackre references the impact of common sense realism on the Princetonian theologians, "Charles Alexander Hodge and Benjamin Warfield, who believed that one could construct a 'science of theology' from a rigorous induction of Scripture, just as the natural sciences gathered and tested their facts." *Christian Story*, 2:161.

43. Fackre, *Christian Story*, 2:163.

44. Ibid., 167.

"rudimentary rules of communication through texts and across personal and social boundaries" that provide a way for individuals to read given biblical passages with a common enough understanding of its meaning to engage in fruitful biblical interpretation and application. He also argues that a "doctrine of general revelation undergirds this" plain reading of the text.[45]

Fackre presents a common or plain sense reading of Scripture as an antidote against radical historicism that renders any universal or "transcultural aspect of biblical truth"[46] academically illegitimate. He notes the inevitable impact of historical influences on any and all readings of Scripture. He seeks to account for them through his tripartite analysis of Bible, church, and contextual setting cross-referenced to the fourfold interpretation under discussion here: common sense, critical sense, canonical sense, and contextual sense. In doing so, he remains critical of historical absolutism—a powerful tendency within contemporary scholarship, which has had a great deal influence, particularly on German academic biblical studies. Fackre argues, that if taken to its logical conclusions, "a consistent radical perspectivalism ends in the narcissism and individualism so rife in modern society."[47] Instead, he posits an ecumenical commitment to inter-subjective communication on the assumption that "there is some common ground sharable in space and over time"[48] that at least partially counteracts the more radical tendencies of historicism. On this assumption, he shares strong similarities with philosopher Jürgen Habermas that

> engaged interpreters relinquish the superiority that observers have by virtue of their privileged position in that they themselves are drawn, at least potentially, into negotiations about the meaning and validity of utterances. By taking part in communicative action, they accept in principle the same status as those whose utterances they are trying to understand. . .[in which] interpreters give themselves over to a process of reciprocal critique. Within a process of reaching understanding, actual or

---

45. Ibid., 166. As Fackre further maintains: "No elite group takes the text out of the hands of the faithful. The Bible is the 'church's book' in this wide-ranging sense, belonging to the *laos*, the whole people of God." Ibid., 165.

46. Ibid. As Fackre states: "The view set forth here . . . respects the historical consciousness of modernity that necessitates the historical study of texts and requires self-critical understanding of the receptor's appropriation process. But it also seeks to honor the transcultural concerns of traditional hermeneutics. The latter comes to the fore in the recognition of a common sense in a biblical text, a sense common to both the creator and the receiver and, as such, available to the ordinary people of God in any and every time and place." Ibid.

47. Ibid., 163.

48. Ibid.

potential, it is impossible to decide a priori who is to learn from whom.[49]

Like Habermas in the realm of philosophy, Fackre—in his radical commitment to communicative action—could best be depicted in a late modernist mode in much of his *philosophical* style even as his *theological* premises are radically opposed to the operative assumptions of the Enlightenment project, which Habermas seeks to fulfill. With Habermas as well, Fackre's commitment to inter-subjective communication is not free flowing, but based on a set of substantive values, which for the philosopher is democracy through the aegis of rigorous and broadly inclusive public discourse. For Fackre, such discourse is empowered by ecumenical communication across the body of Christ in which the varieties of denominational and theological perspectives enrich and correct each other in a continuous process of "mutual affirmation and admonition."[50]

Fackre views the common sense reading of Scripture, as he presents it, as insufficient without broader frames of reference that the other "senses" bring to an informed reading of the biblical text. In this respect, "advocates of the common sense of Scripture," therefore, "must have enough common sense to recognize the limits of common sense" and consider insights from various critical, canonical and contextual readings of the text.[51]

Critical Sense

Fackre briefly discusses "lower" biblical criticism, as reflected in conservative evangelical study, which he links with "word studies, knowledge of the customs and history of scriptural locale, and the accuracy of textual transmission and translation."[52] Such aids as *Strong's Exhaustive Concordance of the Bible* are staple features of the types of critical tools drawn upon in conservative biblical exegesis. He intends this introduction as a brief counterpoint to his main focus on the "higher" criticism of critical biblical scholarship as reflected in modern historical and literary scholarship grounded in the "antitheological bias(es)" of the secularized modern university.[53]

The contrast is well taken to a point, although his description bypasses a much richer evangelical biblical and theological scholarship, as reflected

---

49. Habermas, *Moral Consciousness and Communicative Action*, 26.
50. Fackre, *Restoring the Center*, 123.
51. Fackre, *Christian Story*, 2:167.
52. Ibid., 170.
53. Ibid., 171.

at such seminaries as Gordon-Cornwall, Fuller, Trinity Evangelical, Dallas, and Bethel. Scholars at these seminaries also examine such issues as hermeneutics, exegesis, epistemology, and apologetics. They also address the historical accuracy of the biblical text and the influence of culture on the contemporary Christian believer and church. Fackre's appreciation of conservative and moderate evangelical biblical interpretation and theology is clearly evident in his many assessments of its strengths and limitations, always in conjunction with the broader purpose of "restoring the center."[54] Nonetheless, in the second volume of the *Christian Story*, Fackre—while at Andover-Newton in the 1980s—placed most of his focused attention in critical engagement with liberal theology.

Fackre refers to the scholarship that undergirds theological liberalism as "historical-literary criticism." He notes that the emphasis of such work is to disclose "the world underneath the text." He locates the impetus for such scholarship as having its origins in the Enlightenment with its "associated stress . . . upon 'reason'" in sharp juxtaposition to "dogma" in directing biblical studies toward "the quest for natural explanations of the text."[55] Whether the focus is on the literary composition of the Bible or the rich array of social, theological, and political forces that gave rise to the text, scholarship based on the "historical-literary" perspective interprets the Bible as it would any other ancient text. This scholarly tradition presupposes a naturalistic epistemology based on the "principle of analogy," which posits that explanations are acceptable only if they "conform to our contemporary experience." Disallowed is any notion of "divine agency in the description of events" that cannot pass the threshold of a tight "causal nexus" based on verifiable empirical evidence grounded in naturalistic presuppositions.[56]

Fackre maintains that such scholarship could be incorporated into a critically attuned theological vision to the extent that it becomes "freed from ideological accompaniments," by a naturalistic epistemology, which itself needs to be evaluated from a critical perspective. Such a critical turn

---

54. Fackre notes that "the Modern Theology course" at the evangelical seminary he studies "gives first hand encounter with major exponents of alternative views, an exposure to the 'other' that has no counterpart in mainline seminaries—for all the rhetoric of inclusivity." "Seminary Cultures—Evangelical and Mainline," 166. He is also hopeful that, despite a stereotypical contrastive polarity that has some basis in fact, there are also moves toward a "center-left" theology at some mainline seminaries and a similar "center-right shift" at some evangelical seminaries. Ibid., 168. See also his review of Wells's *No Place of Grace*, which Fackre titles, "An Alter Call for Evangelicals," 112–19.

55. Fackre, *Christian Story*, 2:172.

56. Ibid.

"means a refusal to abandon reference to God's action in, with, and under the phenomena discerned by critical instruments."[57]

Fackre allowance for the possibility of "divine agency"[58] is of a programmatic rather than a substantive nature. His real focal point is not so much secular intellectuals, but liberal theologians highly influenced by secular intellectual discourse. Of course, any postulates derived need to be grounded in the coherency of logical analysis based on substantive sources of evidence if theology is to come into the realm of serious academic discourse in the modern university. Without this unlikely prospect, the position to which he adheres can only be severely constrained. H. R. Niebuhr (1960) argued similarly three decades prior to Fackre that "theology "takes its place . . . alongside other inquiries," neither as irrelevant nor as queen of the intellectual universe, "never separated from" such inquiries, "never dependent upon them, never isolating itself with them from the totality of the common life which is the universe."[59]

It is from such a reference point freed from artificial academic constraint that both Fackre and the historian, George Marsden—along with Niebuhr—argue that the Christian scholar can engage the modern secular intellectual on both its and the academy's own terms.[60] Assuming God's agency as an active power within history, the theologically attuned scholar will be in a position to perceive aspects of reality that may not be evident to her secular counterpart which on faith, the Holy Spirit opens up to the trained and discerning eye.[61] Fackre argues, as related to this point, that a "critical scholarship . . . relatively free of ideology . . . is an expression of trust in reason as the way to reality," but does not exercise hegemony over it.[62] Based on such a premise in which theology is viewed as a legitimate field of studies, a subfield of Christian studies could, in principle, be viewed just as legitimate as did feminist, African American, or urban studies in the gaining of intellectual legitimacy for their respective fields in the 1970s and 1980s.

Perceived in this way, all disciplines and sub-disciplines need to be evaluated from their own respective merits rather than—as it is with current university-based study of religion—a reductive subset of culture—a

57. Ibid., for initial quote; 172–73 for second quote.
58. Ibid., 172.
59. H. R. Niebuhr, "Theology in the University," 99.
60. Marsden, *Soul of the American University*; H. R. Niebuhr, "Theology in the University," 93–99.
61. Fackre, *Christian Story*, 2:172–73.
62. Ibid., 173.

naturalistic bias, in which the biblically depicted God is ruled out by virtual fiat as a possible causative factor in his own right. Such efforts would require much academic translatability to carry weight in the discourse community of the contemporary university. Given the radical nature of such theological premises required to evoke what I refer to as the "God hypothesis," the quest for legitimacy would likely demand a good deal of academic canon reconstruction from which could emerge new knowledge and a fresher vision of the contemporary university as a vital learning community. The viability of the "divine agency"[63] as a causative factor in contemporary academic scholarship does not appear a likely prospect. The substantive reach of such Christian scholarship extends beyond Fackre's immediate purposes in volume 2 of *The Christian Story*, even as he suggests that such a task could be taken on by the contemporary seminary. Whether at the university or seminary, its plausibility (if only as a serious utopian proposal) is of no minor importance to his centrist objectives of bringing liberal theologians into its orbit, even in the critic-in-residence role.[64]

Canonical Sense

The "capstone" of Fackre's internal hermeneutics is the canonical sense in which the meaning of individual biblical texts can only be properly discerned within the trajectory of the entire scope of the biblical revelation.[65] In the process, he merges narrative theology with a complex systematics that is at least as conceptual as it is a storied approach to biblical interpretation. Fackre rejects any notion that the "full" truth can be grasped through any quest for biblical comprehensiveness. At the same time, he argues that a canonical approach to Scripture represents a "fuller"[66] manifestation than that accessible through a more fragmented hermeneutics that one finds, for example, in the postmodern narrative theology of Walter Brueggemann. Fackre appreciates the importance of such imaginative readings of Scripture provided by Brueggemann and others. Nonetheless, he is concerned about placing so much emphasis on the significance of *reception* for various communities of readers that it blunts any durable *meaning* of the text, as interpreted within the canonical integration of the Grand Narrative. For Fackre, what is ultimately at stake in such postmodern readings is the very notion

63. Ibid., 171, 172.
64. Ibid., 176.
65. Ibid., See 177 for "capstone" reference.
66. Ibid.

of truth in the core Christian claim of Christ revealed as the incarnation of the living God.

Fackre identifies the gospel at the substantive core of the canonical perspective. His use of this term extends beyond the four books commonly denoted by the collective term "gospels," or even in the entirety of the New Testament. The gospel, as Fackre defines it, is nothing less than "the Good News of God"[67] as manifested throughout the Old and New Testaments. In this expanded meaning (from creation to consummation), the gospel extends beyond the scriptural text into the historical church communities through the ages and into the broader world, wherever God in Christ indwells. Fackre notes that the breadth of this application reflects a shift from "the source to the resource level of authority" in Christian theological and ecclesial tradition as well as to that of the historical setting of any given era. The latter two areas attain validity to the extent that they shed new light on the "canonical intention" of God's revealed Word.[68]

Notwithstanding this expanded gospel definition, Fackre focuses first and foremost on the disclosive word of Scripture in which any biblical text is most authentic to its authorial intention "when it articulates the gospel of Jesus Christ."[69] Viewed in light of 2 Timothy 3:16, "All Scripture [which] is God breathed" is most completely "useful" to the extent that it is revelatory of Jesus Christ. This, Fackre claims, is no reductionism of the Grand Narrative, which includes the entire scope of the biblical story in "dialectical relation to a familiar delimitation of it to Christ's redemptive work."[70]

Fackre acknowledges that there is no direct relationship between narrative theology and a canonical sense of Scripture, but only a mediating one based on the theologian's imaginative construction in light of the resources of the church and the setting of the contemporary cultural context. He argues that "*narrative* is a legitimate translation of *gospel* to the extent that it clarifies for us the biblical intention of the term and/or enriches our understanding of it."[71]

His specific claim is that "the use of the narrative metaphor in twentieth-century theology" takes better "account of the revelatory dynamisms within Scripture" than other theologies.[72] He compares his own account with those exhibiting "antisystematic and contradiscursive tendencies" within certain

67. Ibid., 179.
68. Ibid., 182.
69. Ibid.
70. Ibid., 180.
71. Ibid., 184.
72. Ibid., 184, 186.

schools of narrative theology and to the "progressive revelation in orthodox appropriations"[73] that could be applied to supersessionist interpretations of the New Testament indicative of certain evangelical biblical theologies. Both approaches are limited to the extent that they do not account for a more "complex relationship between the past, present, and future, including the active influence of the past on the future"[74] as Fackre posits in his narrative systematics, including the ongoing impact of Israel's story.

Fackre acknowledges the gap between his theological reach and his grasp in his narrative construction. Yet, he maintains that an ecumenically searching narrative theology accompanied by a rigorous systematics provides a highly effective way of presenting the gospel in its canonical comprehensiveness in the contemporary era. "As such it functions as the 'perspective' in hermeneutics and systematics, seeking to be both faithful to Scripture and fruitful in interpreting the faith to the contemporary world in its own drama of suffering and hope."[75] Fackre holds his ground despite the tendency toward over-complexity characteristic of much of the second volume of *The Christian Story* that his mediating approach seems to require in the quest to properly account for all of the dynamics and divergent movements he seeks to include in his comprehensive canonical vision.

EXTERNAL HERMENEUTICS

Internal hermeneutics pertains to the *meaning* of the biblical text within its various common, critical, and canonical senses, as described above. As Fackre discusses in chapter 4, "The Context of Authority," external hermeneutics refers to the *significance* of the text within the frame of a given contextual setting. This is an exceedingly complex matter in that contextualization and recontextualization are embedded in the canon itself. A prime example is the New Testament interpretation of Jesus Christ as Isaiah's Suffering Servant in fulfillment of the new covenant revelation as envisioned by the prophet Jeremiah. Such recontextualization is also evident in each of the testaments separately as both the Jewish people and the early Christian church encountered dynamic historical change which required re-appropriation of their faith traditions in the given contingencies

---

73. Ibid., 186.

74. Ibid.

75. Ibid., 185. As he also states: "The various forms of narrative theology all teach that through this medium they engage ultimate reality at a profounder level than do discursive modes of communication." Ibid. Whether that is so is another matter in which Packer might take issue.

of new circumstances. Old Testament examples include the impact of the Babylonian captivity in the fifth century BCE and the reinterpretation of the Mosaic exodus in the ingathering of all people into the promised land of God's holiness (Isa 55:3–5). In the various editorial constructions of the New Testament canon, one can point to the influence of the destruction of the Jewish temple by Rome in 70 CE, the delay of the Parousia, the mission to the Gentiles, and the incorporation of Greek philosophical categories into certain New Testament books.

The impact of historical contingency also influenced the formation of doctrine in the early church. As noted in the previous chapter on Bloesch, theological conflicts over the relationship between the divinity and humanity of Christ and the relationship of the Father, the Son, and the Spirit stimulated "a doctrinal debate more vigorous than any the church had ever experienced." The "reformulation of . . . dogma"[76] that ensued established the creed of the Trinity, which has become settled doctrine throughout orthodox Christianity.

Such contextualization can lead to an expansion of what the orthodox faith tradition is able to bring into its orbit since the infusion of new historical contingency has the capacity to open up Scripture in new ways. The danger is that of cultural cooptation in the ever present apprehension that the quest for contemporary significance can override the canonical meaning of the text. Fackre insists the risk must be taken, and not only for the sake of relevance. The more compelling reality is that the contextual influence is inescapable. That is so, he argues, because all interpretations are partial and invariably influenced by the cultural matrix.[77] This is the case even among theologies that claim a Bible only allegiance through a "plain meaning" hermeneutics. Fackre contends that such "Bible only" interpretations have a propensity to disregard the overarching meaning of the biblical canon.[78] Such flat-line readings foster textual interpretations that do not adequately reflect the breadth and depth of the human conditions that new

---

76. Pelikan, *Emergence of the Catholic Tradition*, 172.

77. Fackre notes: "Historical awareness is an outworking of the assumption of human finitude, a premise integral to the Christian doctrine of creation. We are all creatures rooted in biological and cultural soil, living now in time and not in eternity. As such our thought is perspectively shaped, and always short of the realm of Light in even the most inclusive formulations." As he further states, the issue revolves around whether insights gleaned from a given context can be "used as instruments of the hermeneutical venture, rather than as full scale ideologies" that override the authority of the canonical text. *Christian Story*, 2:214.

78. Writing in the mid-1980s, Fackre references a "neofundamantalist" misreading "of Scripture" in which its religious culture became linked to "the political agenda of the New Right." Ibid.

ideas or movements within history can open up about both the meaning and significance of the Bible.

Fackre argues that it is better to attempt to identify the context that gives shape to biblical interpretation and to struggle in the search for faithful recontextualization than to deny a process that is already at work.[79] In his characterization, biblical "textualization as the intended meaning . . . in every context is the teacher and critic of contextualization." Nevertheless, the canonical text is also "a student learning from" the context, albeit within its parameters as the illuminated setting of revelation.[80] In such readings, new light breaks forth from God's Word through dynamic encounter with the culture. When this becomes efficacious the result is that the new historical context illuminates aspects within Scripture not formerly attended or given as much attention as previously warranted. Whether or not actualized, the potential for such reinterpretation of Scripture remains plausible and sometimes essential for the survival and vitality of a vigorous Christian orthodoxy.[81] The challenge from an orthodox perspective is that of remaining faithful to the Great Tradition while speaking authentically to the exigencies of a given era.

To summarize, one of Fackre's key insights is that the context in any given era illuminates certain facets about scriptural or theological interpretation that would not have emerged without the provocation unleashed by conditions specific to that historical time. This is the case in the fundamental

---

79. See ibid., 243–551, for a discussion of Fackre's "Models of Contextualization" on the interpretive relationship between the Bible and the culture. He organizes his model from the most conservative to the most liberal application. Fackre refers to these interpretive moves respectively as: "translation," "transition," "traduction," "transformation," and "trajection." While he favors the latter model, in typical fashion, Fackre draws something of value from each in illustrating the depth of his external hermeneutics. The following statement sums up a good deal of Fackre's core meaning in the realm of external hermeneutics: "Trajecton is the development of the inner meaning of the text: drawing out the text's implications, educing its intended meaning. This intentionality refers . . . not to the human author but to the purpose of God in the scriptural words. This developing insight into the divine Author is its *sensus plenior*. The fuller sense of the meaning is in continuity with the original trajectory. As such it is a development along this line, coherent with it and extending into a new setting." Ibid., 250. Such interpretive scope allows for new light, even as the issues raised—abortion, the role of the government in fostering social justice, modes of biblical interpretation, same sex marriage, the role of revelation in non-Christian religions, to name a few that are currently central—are anything but easily settled in determining authentic contextual frames of reference for legitimate biblical justification.

80. Ibid., 217.

81. H. R. Niebuhr's *Christ and Culture* provides a broad overview of various ways in which the Christian faith tradition and Western culture have intersected throughout the history of the church.

matter of Christology where only certain issues come to the fore in any given time and cultural setting. While, in principle, the entire scope of the New Testament depiction of Christ is available, only certain emphases attain particular saliency in a given context. For example, in the early theological conflicts that led to the doctrines of the Trinity and incarnation, advocates placed less emphasis on the earthly ministry of Jesus, particularly on his healing and teaching as depicted in the synoptic gospels, than on the incarnational theology reflected in the Johannine tradition.

Fackre draws on the *munus triplex* of prophet, priest, and king to illustrate both the person and work of Christ.[82] He interlays this imagery with the theological functions of thinking, doing, and feeling, any dimension of which may attain significance in a given historical setting. Within this imaginative interplay, Fackre locates the range of the "contextual problematic(s)" that the person and work of Christ addresses in the overcoming of the enduring problems of "sin, suffering, error, [and] death" in every age.[83]

In the early church, the thinking function featured prominently in the effort to interpret Judeo-Christian beliefs through the prism of Greek philosophical thought. The problem the early church faced was that of conceptual error in the construction of the person of Christ that gained substantial resolution in the doctrines of the Trinity and the incarnation. During the Reformation, the doctrine of justification by faith became the conceptual response to the centrality and inescapability of sin, with Christ interpreted through the sacrificial vision of his own priestly person. The Reformation emphasis on the thinking function in developing new theological constructions was balanced by other elements, especially feeling, through an ever present pietism that provided the Reformation with much of its spiritual power. This was the case especially with Luther, but also with Calvin, and as Packer has amply demonstrated, with the English Puritans.[84]

In illustrating the significance of external hermeneutics, Fackre highlights the centrality of suffering as a dominant theme of twentieth-century theology. This focus provides a wide angle vision on an array of theological reflections on the powerful impact of the Second World War on both Jewish and Christian imagination. The range includes Barth's rejection of any voice but Christ's in response to the Nazi onslaught against Christianity and every other form of decency. Barth's Barmen Declaration may have been viewed as heroic in the midst of the most intense suffering and evil the modern

---

82. Fackre, *Christian Story*, 1:134.
83. Fackre, *Christian Story*, 2:231.
84. For Packer, see *Quest for Godliness*.

world has ever known.⁸⁵ Nevertheless, an important stream of Jewish and post-war Christian theologies painfully veered toward a more critical assessment of traditional theistic notions of an all knowing, all powerful God in light of the unimaginable suffering in the concentration camps and ghettos of Eastern Europe.⁸⁶ Bonhoeffer's highly theistic interpretation of secularization was also born out of a profound theology of suffering in the need to confront Nazi power from the grounding point of faith to the point of martyrdom in the surrendering of his personal future to the all-embracing vision of Christ as crucified and resurrected Lord. Reinhold Niebuhr's key texts, written between the 1930s to the early 1950s, issued a similar refrain on the ever presence of evil within the ambiguities of human history in ineradicable tension to the unconditional love of Christ as a regulative ideal beyond history that subtly acts as a solvent within the fabric of human time.

Moltmann's *Crucified God* had a direct lineage to these various theologies emerging from the Second World War in refashioning faith along the motif of suffering, with reverberations in the death of God theology of the 1960s and the liberationist themes emerging out of Latin American theology in the later decades of the twentieth century. All of these threads emphasize the strong accent of suffering in the midst of the profound evils and injustices of various twentieth-century political and social realities. Such experiences extend from that of war, to political oppression, to sexism, to profound existential angst, and to the pervasive reality of poverty. Such problems are exacerbated by the increasing gap between the haves and have nots throughout the world amidst a persisting conflict between the classes that knows no end.

Another refrain emerged in the post-war period from Moltmann: a counter theology of hope within history, which Fackre links with the "humanization accents of the sixties" grounded in the revealed promises of the reign of God rather than in purely secularization energies.⁸⁷ Vatican II, the civil rights vision of Martin Luther King Jr.—in its rich blending of demo-

---

85. The Barmen Declaration, written in 1933 in response to the failure of the German Protestant churches to oppose efforts to justify Nazi ideology through the angle of natural theology. See Barth, "Barmen Declaration," 148–51. The key statement that became the signature for Barth's theology of the Word is the following: "Jesus Christ, as he is attested for us in Holy Scripture, is the one Word of God which we have to hear and which we have to trust and obey in life and in death." This statement stood as a bulwark against "the false doctrine" that attempted to associate the Christian church with "the 'blood and soil' philosophy of Nazism." Ibid.; Fackre, *Christian Story*, 2:22n31.

86. Fackre, *Christian Story*, 2:233.

87. In delving into the themes that Fackre discusses in chapter 4, suffering and hope need to be interpreted as part of a broadly unified post-war theological tradition in which hope represents the other side of despair. See Fackre, *Christian Story*, 2:233–40.

cratic idealism with the biblical concept of social justice—and Pannenberg's future oriented theology were examples of this more optimistic resonance of a more transformative vision of culture than the dialectical and crisis theologies of or influenced by neo-orthodoxy.

Fackre draws out the experience of suffering and the counter-response of hope as among the great themes of twentieth-century theology in order to illustrate the ways in which the contextual setting influences given interpretations of Scripture. The result is that theologians draw out certain themes often at the expense of others. Such selective emphasis is less an inherent weakness than an inevitable reality of an incarnational faith mediated to and through the living context of human history by the awesome Lord God seeking to communicate to our often non-listening ears. The influence is potentially text enriching in drawing out crucial themes that are latent in Scripture or even overtly present, but which have either lain dormant or have hardly come to the fore. A prime example is the importance of social justice against the onslaught of oppression, the key leitmotif of the theology of liberation of the post-1960 era and a central theme, particularly in Old Testament theology.[88]

Fackre notes that an overplaying of the theme of social justice holds the potential of marginalizing other important biblical themes in the realm of the personal on the perennial issues of sin, death, and alienation. Viewed in the light of canonical comprehensiveness, he argues that the influence of the context in shaping certain readings of the biblical text are counterbalanced by the text's own claims as the ultimately privileged basis for evaluating any given context. In Fackre's terms, in its role as *source*, the biblical text has interpretive priority over the context, which he identifies as the *setting* in his hierarchy of values on the means of revelation. For Fackre context has a ministerial relationship to Scripture and church tradition.

Fackre is well aware of the difficulties in concretely working through the relationship between the biblical text and the context in any particular situation. Quests for certainty can only remain elusive. He deals with the problem methodologically through his theological model. His emphasis on narrative theology provides a resource into the Scripture in showing how the different biblical storylines illustrate the ways in which God interacts with his world. This narrative interaction is multiform: before the creation of humankind, before the creation of the Bible, within the biblical plot line itself, and out into the broader world in the creation of the church and the historical space God opened up between the first and final coming of Christ.

---

88. See Brueggemann, *Social Reading of the Old Testament*, for a particularly strong statement on the significance of social justice in the ancient Israel religious tradition.

Each "chapter" in the Bible discloses different dimensions of the ways in which God and his world interact, the details of which will be discussed throughout the remaining sections of this chapter.

Fackre also draws on the narrative metaphor to highlight the "doing," "thinking, and feeling" aspects of human existence.[89] These human attributes became the basis for the playing out of particular ways of relating the biblical text to the context as we have seen. As Fackre explains, the human "narrative is the *perspective* that takes shape within the worldly context in which we interpret the text." The result is that the "way we state the problem, as well as the [particular] problem itself has repercussions in the kind of perspective developed." Even so, whatever "metaphors and motifs are chosen and *how* they are used must always be under the scrutiny of the Christian tradition that employs them."[90]

Stated otherwise, the Bible as *source* and church tradition as *resource* have ultimate interpretive privileges over the *setting* of the context, however complexly the interaction of these three factors may be in any given historical environment or personal circumstance. The discernment process is an ongoing effort of "working out...[our] faith in fear and trembling" with the hope and expectation that "it is God who works in...[us] to will and to act according to his good pleasure" (Phil 2:12–13). Fackre maintains that the Christian faith is mediated most comprehensively through the ecumenical body of Christ through a constructive dialectic of mutual affirmation and loving admonition. The fuller meaning and significance of the church's catholic fullness unfolds as it careens through time, drawing on resources from its past, present, future embodiments. Whether his focus is internal or external hermeneutics, Fackre is working out his faith between "the already" of what has transpired and "not yet" of what is to be.

THE ORIENTING FRAMEWORK OF FACKRE'S NARRATIVE THEOLOGY OF REVELATION

Ontology precedes epistemology in that reality in all of its infinite vastness is unsearchable. The problem is the impossibility of moving outside the realm of human experience, however imaginative the effort. At the level of human knowledge, there is no escape from the hermeneutical circle of radical historicism, including the awareness that the absolutism of any such

---

89. Fackre, *Christian Story*, 2:240. See ibid., 137–56, for an extensive discussion of the thinking, doing, and feeling dimensions of faith.

90. Ibid., 241.

claim is an article of faith that transcends the human capacity to prove or even to understand.

Viewed from this vantage point, "god," like the scientific method, is a construct of the human imagination in which no theological argument or source of accessible evidence can prove to the discerning critical eye. Any "beyond" this where "the wind blows wherever it pleases" (John 3:8) can only be an imaginative one. It is an un-provable axiom that the referent is a source that transcends the human mind and has given shape to it rather than the reverse. From both anthropological and theological perspectives, the religious impulse emerges in the human experience of profound need and infinite searching. It is a quality of reality that, at its most sublime, can be defined by what one influential student of spirituality refers to as "numinous." By this Otto means the awesome mystery that transcends human rationality that nonetheless, speaks profoundly to and through the human condition.[91]

The indwelling presence of the Holy is not only a subjective phenomenon, but an ontological reality that in terms of words may be referred to as the presence of God. The revealing indwelling that one has encountered—at least from the perspectives of the Abrahamic faiths—is not some aspect of a higher self or social consciousness. On the claim of faith, it is something of the ineffable presence of what the biblical tradition refers to as the living God, the Holy One of Israel, to whom Ezekiel refers to as the Sovereign Lord. While the mystery between flawed human finitude and the awesome holy God can never be transcended, increase in understanding is possible through the prism of faith. As Fackre notes, church doctrine, illuminated by the Holy Spirit, represents an effort to shed light on important aspects of the character and will of God. Yet, as Fackre also maintains, however anchored such doctrine may be in human logic, evidence, and firm biblical claims, the ultimate mystery to which they point can only remain profoundly elusive, however much they speak to the internalized experience of those who make or embrace them.

For Fackre, ontology resides within the mystery of the triune God in the "*immanent* Trinity." The imminent or ontological Trinity is the very "'being' of God." On the axiom of faith, the Father, the Son, and the Spirit, as "co-equality of Persons," commune with each other in the very process of maintaining their underlying oneness as God.[92] No human analogue is parallel to the "coinherence" of the three Persons of the triune God. No "human experience of total reciprocity can be found in which one 'inexists' another

---

91. Otto, *Idea of the Holy*.
92. Fackre, *Doctrine of Revelation*, 26, 27.

with each maintaining its identity and integrity."[93] Yet, it is this Trinity that is the foundational presupposition of the Christian faith, inferred in Scripture through the inspirational Word of God and proclaimed by the early church community through the illumination of the Holy Spirit.

Fackre distinguishes the imminent from the "*economic* Trinity," which is related to the "'doing' of God" in his revelation to humankind through the exigencies of lived history.[94] The economic Trinity is revealed first and foremost in the particular ways in which the Father, Son, and Spirit interact in the gospels, the New Testament as a whole and, in a more oblique manner, throughout the Old Testament, as interpreted through the prism of the New. With the Bible as the primary *source* of revelation, the economic Trinity continues to do its work within the body of Christ and within the broader world in every age. That work is nothing other than the reconciliation of the world. In the final analysis, "God will be all in all" (1 Cor 15:28 KJV), yet even in the space between the times of Christ's first and final coming, the faith community receives the first fruits of God's revealing love through the power of the Holy Spirit. The Trinitarian prologue, in its imminent and economic forms, is the axiomatic grounding point of Fackre's narrative theology, which is the basis of his model of revelation.

In contrast to anthropomorphic reductionism, as posited by radical historicism, the Trinitarian presupposition is a profound theological claim that is accepted on faith as transcendent truth upon which all else is grounded. However problematic the claim may seem from an anthropological basis, without such a presupposition, a thoroughly grounded Christian theology could not follow. With the eradication of any mention of God as an underlying reality, theology as the study of its supreme subject becomes disallowed by the intellectual conventions of contemporary academic discourse. The God hypothesis demands such an ontological claim as its primary operational assumption. It is the reality of this triune God that Fackre draws on—as prologue—to construct the various biblical storylines of his narrative theology. The particular "chapters" are designed to illustrate the different "phases of revelation"[95] through which God in Christ reconciles the world to himself. Fackre sets forth the substance of this story in *The Doctrine of Revelation*.

To recap, Fackre provides a variety of reasons in support of his theological focus. For one, he contends that the narrative metaphor more authentically reflects the flesh and blood exigencies of the twentieth-century

---

93. Ibid., 28.
94. Ibid., 26.
95. Ibid., 18.

history than a great deal of formal academic theology that Fackre has grappled with through the course of his career. For another, he finds that storied theology provides a way of imaginatively "find[ing] coherence in apparent incoherences" inherent in any formal theological system.[96] This includes Barth's system, which has had such a formative influence on Fackre's own theological construction. He also argues that narrative theology represents a formidable school of contemporary thought in its own right. For that reason alone it is of value to incorporate into a formal systematics.

Fackre finds all of these reasons compelling, "but not decisively so." The critical linchpin for him is that "the shape of faith itself" is substantially grounded in thick narrative description, as reflected throughout Scripture. The narrative mode is reinforced not only through the many specific biblical stories, but through the trajectory of the text, "the overarching story," a phrase he borrows from George Lindbeck.[97] As Fackre further explains, the biblical narrative, "while imaginatively portrayed . . . is no fictive account." Rather, it is the power of the gospel itself, a "story traced by canonical hand" through the inspiration of the triune God. The story is narrated in chapter units through "meaningful sequence[s]. . .[and] unrepeatable occasions with a cumulative significance internal" to the thematics of its overarching narrative framework.[98] In taking this approach, as a systematic theologian, Fackre never neglects the importance of formal doctrine. In his model, the narrative mode does not override rigorous theology, but provides a frame to better understand and interpret it. To specify, Fackre visualizes the narrative genre as a metaphor through which "the standard *loci* of systematic theology, may be understood as 'chapters' in the biblical and ecclesial macro-narrative: creation, fall, covenant, Jesus Christ, church, salvation, consummation, with the triune God as prologue and epilogue."[99]

Fackre organizes these "chapters" into distinctive "phases." *Preservation*, which subsumes the creation, fall, and the Noachic Covenant, "refers to revelation vis-à-vis universal experience." *Action*, by which he includes the covenant with Israel and the disclosure of Jesus Christ as the incarnation of God in human flesh, "refers to revelation in [the] definitive historical deeds of God." By *Inspiration* Fackre refers "to privileged accounts and interpretations of the Deeds of God in Scripture." By *illumination* Fackre points to subsequent acts of disclosure through ecclesial traditions and theological reflection. Fackre further organizes these constructs into a

---

96. Ibid., 2.
97. Ibid., 3.
98. Ibid.
99. Ibid.

tripartite typology. Hence, "General Revelation" includes all of the chapters highlighted above under *preservation*. "Special Revelation" parallels what Fackre places in the *action* phase along with the *inspiration* of Scripture. "Revelation as Reception" includes what Fackre refers to as Ecclesial Illumination, Personal Illumination, and Eschatological Illumination.[100]

In a final move, Fackre links each of the major phases of his biblical storyline to among four of the most exemplary theologians of the twentieth century. Specifically, he draws on the theology of culture of Paul Tillich to amplify the role of preservation and God's common grace. He looks to the dialectic theology of Karl Barth to detail the mighty acts of God in the election of Israel and the incarnation of Jesus Christ as prophet, priest, and king. Fackre calls upon evangelical theologian Carl Henry to explore the central theme scriptural inspiration. He engages Catholic theologian Karl Rahner to discuss the critical "chapter" of the role of the church.

These four, in particular, embody contrasting points of reference in twentieth-century Western theology. Tillich and Barth represent sharply conflicting perspectives on whether God alone through his Son is the primary source of revelation or whether a correlative role for culture is required, without which claims of revelation can only be viewed as vacuous. Similarly, Henry and Rahner represent sharply contrasting perspectives on whether Scripture or the church has primary interpretive authority in determining matters of ultimate theological significance. In Fackre's mapping, these four "interlocutors" epitomize pivotal nodal points of twentieth-century theology.[101] Fackre establishes the range and depth of his own evangelical ecumenical theology through his probing dialogue with each of the four in mutual affirmation and discerning admonition.

GENERAL REVELATION: PRESERVATION

As part of the process of reconciling the world to himself, God has put a seal of divine preservation into the natural operation of the created universe. Even if they do not recognize it, human beings made in the likeness of God's image have "a derivative freedom for partnership,"[102] with the responsibility to exercise this gift under the auspices of God's broad direction rather than to usurp it for some vaunted personal gain or vainglory. This underlying propensity for partnership with God "derives from the harmonies of the

---

100. Ibid., 18. For an overview of Fackre's organizational constructs and their subdivisions, see also his contents page.

101. Ibid., 9–11.

102. Ibid., 39.

divine "*perichoresis*" through which humankind's "partnership [with] God is stamped on all creation."[103]

Humankind's most authentic vocation of right relationship with God is found only in such a "*co*-humanity that mirrors the divine coinherence" of the immanent Trinity. The one man and one woman partnership, as reflected in the Adam and Eve story, is paradigmatic—a knowing together as in the divine partnership, which for humankind can be known only "under the conditions of finitude."[104] It was the failure to accept the exigencies of natural creaturely existence which led to the Adamic fall from right relationship with God. The original sin was not in the desire to possess knowledge, even as there was "a divine commandment *not* to know" anything like the full disclosure of God's will either for humankind or the created order other than "to work . . . and take care of" the Garden (Gen 2:15). The more fundamental problem was the desire to know *as* God. In effect, the temptation was to become like God instead of remaining in one's called vocation as made in the image of God—and finite in every way.

Regarding the Genesis account as saga rather than history, as Fackre does, still requires "correspond[ence] to *some* temporal state before the human race's first act of idolatry." Thus, on Fackre's reconstruction, there is within the human experience "an ability to know the truth, corresponding to a pre-fall 'innocence' as the capacity to do the truth."[105] Without this equivalence there can be no spiritual baseline through which to judge humankind's fallen condition from the perspective of right relationship with a holy and loving God through unbroken covenantal partnership. In this section, Fackre draws upon the Noachic Covenant to flesh out the biblical theme of general preservation of the created order and humankind, which he explores with the assistance of the first volume of Paul Tillich's *Systematic Theology*.[106]

---

103. Ibid., 38. The technical Greek term *perichoresis* refers to the triune relationship of the Trinity. For additional information, see *Theopedia*, s.v. "perichoresis," http://www.theopedia.com/Perichoresis.

104. Fackre, *Doctrine of Revelation*, 39.

105. Ibid., 41. The entire passage is as follows: "In revelatory terms at the very least there is a *posse cognoscere*, an ability to know the truth, corresponding to a pre-fall 'innocence as the capacity to do the truth. That there is such a possibility before the fall is the premise of classical Christian teaching. But what its nature is is not required of that teaching and is not integral to a theological-cum critical exegesis of the Genesis tale." Ibid.

106. Ibid., 61–102. In this section, I focus on those aspects of Tillich's thoughts that highlight the theme of preservation as Fackre defines it. In chapter 7, I include a more extended discussion of Tillich's theology, particularly in relationship to Barth's.

The covenant with Noah is that of the rainbow sign that God "will never again curse the ground for man's sake [even though]. . .the imagination of his [i.e., the human] heart is evil from childhood." Nor will God "again . . . curse the ground because of man" (Gen 8:21). Fackre refers to this as "the promise of *preservation*." This sustaining work is supported by "a common grace that both enables and enlightens"[107] human society and culture regardless as to specific religious orientation of given communities of people. The common grace upholds the world based on its God-given natural resources, including all of the arts and sciences common to human civilization. In this common grace, the Noachic covenant plays an enduring role and will continue to do so until the eschaton is realized. It is because the original covenant with Adam is broken that God needs to establish other means to sustain the world, despite a now inherently contrarian human nature in the "the elementary laws of life."[108] Such preservation is precisely what is introduced in the covenant of common grace.

Enter Paul Tillich, the premier twentieth-century theologian of culture. Like Barth, Tillich was a dialectical theologian in situating faith in the dynamic nexus between Christ and culture. However, as Barth gravitated toward the dogmatic pole while retaining a rigorous dialectic with culture, the opposite can be fairly stated about Tillich. The prioritizing pole of culture provided the matrix for the emergence of his core concept, "ultimate concern," which Fackre summarizes as "'the courage to be' in the face of non-being."[109] This was a central doctrine of existential philosophy through which Tillich sought to correlate the Christian faith to the then modern mid-twentieth-century setting of post–World War II US and European theology.

Notwithstanding the importance Tillich placed on the "medium" of experience, the centrality of the revelation of Jesus Christ as God's word for humankind was never compromised. Fackre notes that for Tillich "the integrity of the Christian message must be protected and accountability to the christological norm maintained."[110] In Tillich's words, "man's religious experience could become an independent source of systematic theology only if man were united with the source of all religious experience," which emphatically is not the case given humanity's anxious fallen state. From the premises of this reality, "insight into the human situation destroys every theology which makes experience an independent source instead of a

---

107. Ibid., 63.
108. Ibid., 64.
109. Ibid., 70.
110. Ibid.

dependent medium of systematic theology,"¹¹¹ as reflected in the dynamic presence of a yet exceedingly veiled God of the Old and New Testament. While Tillich gave culture a type of prioritization and his Christology gravitated more toward Bultmann than Barth, he did not turn culture into an absolute, however much his practice may have veered in that direction.

Fackre draws valuable resources from Tillich in his emphasis on existential experience and culture to illustrate the importance of the doctrine of preservation in the contemporary setting. With the possible exception of Reinhold Niebuhr, no other contemporary theologian has explored the border between theology and culture to the level of depth of Tillich. As Fackre notes, Tillich's theology may well be skewed toward the pole of culture. At the same time, Fackre is cognizant of the value that Tillich's rich contextualization provides in linking the source of revelation, Scripture, to the setting. Without the focused attention that Tillich gives to the horizontal dimensions of life, a powerful apologetic resource would be sorely lacking in contemporary Christian theology.

The extent to which Tillich's correlation theology of culture can be incorporated into a comprehensive orthodox perspective, as Fackre envisions it, is another matter. In Tillich, "the presence of human experience in its rich and varied sense enters so decisively into the hermeneutical conversation that the integrity of the centre, source and resource of authority is called into question."¹¹² Fackre is critical of Tillich not for what he affirms—a dynamic theology of culture—but in what Tillich denies—namely, "the event of the Word incarnate and the biblical testimony to it. . .[as] authoritative disclosure points in their own right."¹¹³ Clearly, Tillich's theology provided him with a framework to explore the dynamics of culture to the depths he believed necessary in giving it its due. For Tillich, no antiquated dogmatics—however vitally it may have spoken to another era—could function as an effective substitute. "Put in terms of the narrative of revelation," Fackre's concern is that in Tillich, "the chapters on Christ, Scripture, the Church, and its tradition are read in the light of the covenant of Noah, rather than the other way around."¹¹⁴ A major plank in Fackre's evangelical ecumenical vision is reversing this while maintaining a rich cultural theology. It is because of Tillich's extensive work in the theology of culture that Fackre draws on him in *The Doctrine of Revelation*. As Fackre highlights Tillich's contribution for the purposes of his own theological construction:

111. Tillich, *Systematic Theology*, 1:46.
112. Fackre, *Doctrine of Revelation*, 91.
113. Ibid., 84.
114. Ibid., 91.

Narratively framed, Paul Tillich's doctrine of revelation...[is] a study in the covenant with Noah. Tillich's philosophical analysis and cultural commentary presuppose a common grace that legitimizes such inquiry and invites theological attention to both the questions posed by a given era and universal human sensibilities. The Word that enlightens everyone by the power of the Spirit sufficient for the Story of alienation and reconciliation to go forwards is the giver of that grace.[115]

That grace is the common grace of preservation, an essential part of the biblical narrative. Such grace allows broad scope for a theology of the whole people of God within their various callings and locations through what is commonly referred to as the secular sphere. However perpetually present as an underlying thread of God's grace, it is only one phase in the storyline that when given more emphasis than its due becomes a form of culture idolization. There are other story chapters to be told, such as God's active presence in the history of the Jewish people and the ultimate and irrevocable revelation of Christ as the incarnation of the living God, the inspiration of Scripture as the primary source of revelation, and the secondary witness of the church and corresponding theological and ecclesial traditions that spawned from it, including the final dawning of the eschaton.

SPECIAL REVELATION: DIVINE ACTION THROUGH GOD'S REVELATION IN HISTORY

As Barth claims, "no attempt is made in the Bible to define God." What exists is the ever present voice of God speaking, as well as depictions of his actions, mighty and small, as detailed with concrete specificity in both the Old and New Testaments. Because there is so little effort in Scripture to define the nature of God—particularly in abstract categories—"the Bible is not a philosophy book." In its narration of the "deeds and the history of this God in the highest," the Bible is more of "a history book." It is through his recounted deeds as well as God's specific teachings, as embodied in the Bible, that "God becomes knowable to us."[116]

As it was with Barth, so it is for Fackre; narrative faithfulness is a goal that is not always achieved. This is because of the need of both of these theologians to explore the complex interaction of the biblical plot line through rigorous theological reflection while working through the complicated issues of historical contextualization. The problem is embedded in the very

---

115. Ibid., 97.
116. Barth, *Dogmatics in Outline*, 38.

nature of the faith. As Fackre states, "revelation in its fullest sense," as sight, "is reserved for Last Things."[117] In this, he accepts the view of Thiemann and Pannenberg, in which faith "makes no claim to *knowing*," at least in the secular scientific sense.[118] Faith presupposes nothing less than some leap—as grounded in biblical revelation and supported by accompanying devotional practice—in which the complete revelation of God can come to fruition only "beyond history" in the fullness of the eschaton. Stated in Fackre's imagistic language:

> Opened by the power of the Holy Spirit all along the revelatory pilgrimage—from the common grace of preservation to the particular grace of Israel's election and the Word's Incarnation and the appropriating grace of inspiration and illumination—the eye of faith is given the Light it needs to make its way to the final moment of truth.[119]

For both Fackre and Barth, the need that drives the effort *toward* narrative clarity supports the depth of the theological construct that emerges. That is, both Fackre and Barth draw upon formal theology to bring greater coherence to a revelatory narrative that cannot be fully grasped from a human perspective, even as in faith, sufficient light is given to move forward in the journey from Egypt to the promised land. Faith is grounded in the illumination of the Holy Spirit that contains its own epistemological persuasiveness. As human knowledge grapples with the reality that ultimately transcends it, we are called to go forth to seek that for which we are searching, in fear and trembling as well as in hope: that God is leading the way. In its suppleness, precision, and metaphorical complexity, language is the preeminent tool that Fackre and Barth draw upon in explaining a narrative reality that transcends discourse while simultaneously depending upon it for the construction of their respective theologies.

I give light treatment to Fackre's discussion of the critical storyline of God's revelation within Israel, in order keep the focus on the central "chapter" of Christ, with a special spotlight on Barth, who is Fackre's second interlocutor in *The Doctrine of Revelation*. Fackre interprets "'God's history with Israel'. . .essential to the Great Narrative because it is the entry point into a fallen world of both deliverance and disclosure."[120] In Paul's words, to the Israelites "is the adoption as sons;. . .the divine glory, the covenants,

---

117. Fackre, *Doctrine of Revelation*, 219. See 213–24 for Fackre's final chapter on the eschaton.

118. Ibid., 218.

119. Ibid., 223.

120. Ibid., 106.

the receiving of the law, the temple worship and the promises...[and] the patriarchs...from [whom]...is traced the human ancestry of Christ" (Rom 9:4–5). In contemporary terms, "the bonding with Israel is the expression among us of who God is and what God does, pointing back to the primal Life Together that God is, and forwards to the reconciliation to be realized."[121]

The Israelite storyline occupies an indispensable "chapter" that gives the biblical plot its definitional shape and texture. This storyline continues to play itself out metaphorically in any unrealized eschatology that looks anticipatorily to a future more through the guise of faith than of sight. From this perspective, the construct of the First and Second Coming of Christ can be viewed as a profound Judeo-Christian midrash that symbolizes this tension of anticipatory hope and longing—that however much the reality may appear otherwise—God's justice will ultimately rule. As Fackre puts it, "The Covenant with Israel is 'forever' (Ps 111:19). But it is also a stage on the way" toward the fuller and definitive revelation in Jesus Christ.[122]

Fackre's challenge in presenting the pivotal "chapter" on Christ is that of sifting through vast and potentially conflicting theological perspectives toward a mediating view that is broadly coherent with the dominant threads of the historical tradition of the Protestant Reformers. As an example, he refers to "the thirty-nine plus theories of the atonement," which he distills into four broad categories to drive home his broader point that an evangelical-sensitive ecumenical vision of Protestant Christianity encompasses them all within a comprehensively integrative Christology.[123] For support, he turns to Barth whose broad-based Christian catholicity represents "the most searching twentieth-century restatement of the three-fold office"[124] of Christ as prophet, priest, and king upon which Fackre's grounds his ecumenical vision.

Fackre points to the dynamic tension in Barth's theology between "objective and subjective revelation," which Hunsinger describes as the motifs of objectivism and actualism.[125] These opposing tendencies cohere with other critical components of Barth's integrated framework to comprise what Hunsinger views as a very comprehensive theology.[126] Objectivism is

121. Ibid.
122. Ibid., 116.
123. Ibid., 120.
124. Ibid., 122.
125. For an overview of Barth's six motifs of actualism, particularism, objectivism, personalism, realism, and rationalism, see Hunsinger, *How to Read Karl Barth*, 27–64.
126. Hunsiner notes that, "like Mozart, Barth preferred to work with sharply contrasting themes resolved into higher unities and marked by regular recapitulations. Themes or fragments of themes, once dominant, are constantly carried forward into

indispensable to Barth's project of placing the "strange new world within the Bible" front and center of theological reflection as a counterpoise to the dominant trends of nineteenth- and twentieth-century liberal theology. Barth's emphasis on objectivism is a response to Schleiermacher and those influenced by him in elevating human consciousness as the pivotal axis of Christian interpretative focus.[127] As expressed by Barth:

> When we Christians speak of "God," we may and must be clear that this word signifies *a priori* the fundamentally Other, the fundamental deliverance from that whole world of man's seeking, conjecturing, illusion, imagining and speculating. It is not that on the long road of human seeking and longing for the divine a definite stopping-place has in the end been reached in the form of the Christian Confession. The God of the Christian confession is, in distinction from all gods, not a found or invented God or one at last and at the end discovered by man. He is not a fulfillment, perhaps the last, supreme and best fulfillment, of what man was in the course of seeking and finding. But we Christians speak of Him who completely takes the place of everything that elsewhere is usually called "God," and therefore suppresses and excludes it all, and claims to be alone the truth. Where that is not realized, it is still not realized what is involved when the Christian Church confesses, "I believe in God."[128]

In "man's meeting with the Reality which he has never of himself sought out," there is a knowing among professing Christians, which can

---

new settings where other themes take the ascendency. Materials are constantly being combined, broken up, recombined, and otherwise brought into contapuntal relationship. Part of what Barth seems to share with Mozart, in other words, is a certain taste for thematic interplay, a taste which includes the custom of complex recapitulation, modification, and allusion." Ibid., 28. Fackre is not so persuaded that Barth has successfully resolved the tension between actualist and objective tendencies in his theological vision. See *Doctrine of Revelation*, 137–42.

127. As Hunger explains, "Barth was convinced that the knowledge of God as confessed by faith is objective in the sense that its basis lies not in human subjectivity but in God ... In light of modern liberal theology (as associated with Schleiermacher), he had to show why what faith says about God cannot be collapsed, as Feuerbach had powerfully argued, into nothing but statements about human nature. He had to show why such anthropological reduction was not warranted by the church's internal knowledge of God." *How to Read Karl Barth*, 35. As Fackre explains: "The triune God *hears* as well as utters the divine Speech, establishing it as a Word, freeing it from all dependency on us to validate it as such. The 'objectivity' of the Word made flesh in Jesus Christ, therefore, constitutes the primal meaning of the prophetic office of Christ." *Doctrine of Revelation*, 124.

128. Barth, *Dogmatics in Outline*, 36.

only be profoundly partial and fragmentary. Nonetheless, Barth contends that "there is no other way in which we can speak of" God "in the sense that the Christian Confession is and exists in a completely different way from that which is elsewhere called divine."[129] Without that reality which underlies Christian revelation—and transcends human experience—there is nothing that can be described as truth, but only experience. Without the reality of the transcendent God, who is equally majestic and lowly, nothing can challenge the gods of this age. Thus, without this Divine counterpoise—in which "Jesus Christ, *attested by Holy Scripture* is the one Word of God whom we have to hear"[130]—it is only false gods—whatever their specific manifestations—that can be perceived as the utterly real. Simply put, our God is a jealous God who will brook no rivals.

Within the context of the objective motif, Fackre points out that Barth "does not want revelation"—the self-revelation of the triune God—"to be confused with anything else," including "our reception of it even with the enlightening work of the Holy Spirit that enables us to hear the Word."[131] For Barth and Fackre such attention to objectivism is a primary focal point. Both theologians are simultaneously on the same accord that there is no faith without reception. They each incorporate actualist and objectivist motifs in their theology.[132] Thus, in his *Church Dogmatics*, volume 4, Barth includes a section on the call to discipleship in which the theme "follow me"[133] requires a profound receptivity to the prompting of the still, small voice of the Holy Spirit. Nonetheless, it is the truth claim of God's reality, "whether or

---

129. Ibid.

130. Fackre, *Doctrine of Revelation*, 196. Fackre's reference is "The Barmen Declaration" with its Christocentric emphasis that is so crucial to Barth's theology. See Green, *Karl Barth*, 148–51, for a reprint of "The Barmen Declaration." See *Doctrine of Revelation*, 134, for Fackre's statement on Barth's "christocentricity."

131. Fackre, *Doctrine of Revelation*, 124.

132. Hunsinger, *How to Read Karl Barth*. By actualism Barth means the indwelling of God in the immediacy of the revelatory moment. In the actualist motif, as Hunsinger explains: "Our relationship to God is . . . an event. It is not possessed once and for all, but continually established anew by the ongoing activity of grace. Paradoxically, however, although befalling us from the outside and exceeding our creaturely capacities, the event of grace is thus not the negation, but the condition for the possibility, of human spontaneity and fulfillment. God's sovereignty in our lives is enacted as God establishes with us a history of love and freedom." Ibid., 31. Though he does not use the same terms, Fackre also incorporates objective and actualist themes in his narrative theology. He does so through a model of prioritization in which the triune God is at the center point as divine "self-disclosure" in Jesus Christ. *Doctrine of Revelation*, 15. Scripture follows as the primary source of inspiration, followed, in turn, by the illumination is given to the church through the Holy Spirit. Ibid., 18–19.

133. Barth, *Call to Discipleship*, 1.

not there is a human receiver attuned by the Holy Spirit to its vibrations,"[134] that provides the basis for the possibility of practical obedience.

Obedience to the call in whatever context it is issued is the *epistemological* basis upon which any meaningful response to the *ontology* of the triune God must be grounded. That is, assuming one does hear the voice of God in response to the divine indwelling—what Barth refers to as the objective reality of God injected into the fabric of the human condition— as reflected most fully in the incarnation of Christ. Thus, "the call of Jesus makes history when it is heard and taken seriously." Moreover, "it is by this that we may know whether it is heard and taken seriously; whether or not it is heard and taken seriously as a call to self-denial,"[135] including an embrace of courage in the face of danger, ridicule, or ostracism whenever such a stance is warranted. For without some such response, Barth maintains that there can be no serious and sustained challenge to the idols of our time that otherwise reign by the force of their own penultimate and highly persuasive power. In short, one of the key factors of Barth's compelling theology is the dynamic interface *between* the objectivist and actualist motifs, which—in combination with the other facets of his theology—make his work so architecturally elegant and such a fundamental counterpoise to the immanent thrust of so many dominant theological threads of the last two centuries.[136]

There is much in this that Fackre accepts, particularly Barth's linkage of revelation "to the Word that God spoke to us in the historical event of Jesus Christ."[137] Nevertheless, Fackre issues an admonition that in emphasizing both "the *divine sovereignty*" of God and "*the internal testimony of the Holy Spirit*" to the extent that he does, Barth may "exclude other critical accents."[138] This concern includes Fackre's critique of Barth's overreliance on the discontinuities between divine revelation and human experience. The result is that Barth minimizes important continuities between the claims of faith and the reliability of Scripture, church tradition, and the world in the respective mediating roles they play within the plot line of God's journey with nature and the human race from creation to consummation.

Specifically, in his central focus on the sovereignty of God, Fackre points to a de-emphasis in Barth of the Noachic chapter, declaring "the constancies of an epistemic grace" in divine acts of preservation " that must not

---

134. Fackre, *Doctrine of Revelation*, 124.
135. Barth, *Call to Discipleship*, 34.
136. Hunsinger, *How to Read Karl Barth*, 27–64.
137. Fackre, *Doctrine of Revelation*, 147.
138. Ibid., 137.

be censored."[139] Also, in his over-dependence on the internal testimony of the Holy Spirit in the actualist moment of revelation, Fackre is troubled by Barth's dismissal of the enduring inspiration of Scripture and the illuminative influence on "the ecclesial form"[140] of the historic church as graces that the faith community can rely on because they are bestowed by God.

In Fackre's terms, there are other chapters in God's storyline that contribute in their respective ways to the fulfillment of the Grand Narrative that undergirds God's central revelation in Christ's incarnation. Whether addressing God's sovereignty or the indwelling presence of the Holy Spirit, Fackre argues that Barth overstresses the discontinuities between divine revelation and human experience. As a counterpoise, Fackre wants us to be cognizant of the dialectical tension of both the disjunctures and the continuities between the sovereignty of God and the various sources of grace that mediate the gap without collapsing the difference.

Fackre raises important matters. Yet, it is one that assumes that in the economy of God the ecumenical quest has a uniquely privileged place in Christian theology and ecclesial practice. In some cases the opposite may be so; namely, that God's revelation is flashed into the human experience at least as much by sharp theological conflict as by the quest for rich catholic concord. The dialectic nature of Barth's theology and the entire neo-orthodox movement in challenging liberalism and opening up a new impetus based on the tradition of the Protestant Reformers that, in principle, can be squared with twentieth-century critical biblical and theological scholarship is widely acknowledged as one such phenomenon.[141] Given also Barth's critical impact in bringing the Bible back to serious consideration on its own hermeneutical terms beyond the boundaries of various evangelical and traditional Reformed centers, it is difficult to downplay the pivotal contribution that he has made to twentieth-century European and American theology. Fackre acknowledges all of these critical influences.

My point is that such influence cannot always be squared with the type of ecumenical centrist vision that drives Fackre's theological search.

139. Ibid., 144.

140. Ibid., 136. Fackre further comments on Barth's interpretation of the revelatory role of the Bible: "While necessary to protect Scripture from bibliolatry, the accent on divine sovereignty-cum-internal-testimony is not sufficient warrant for the authority of Scripture. Standing alone, it precludes the promise of a trustworthy epistemic presence 'in,' 'with and under' the Word written." Ibid., 40–141. The role of biblical inspiration in Fackre's theology will be explored in the next section on his third interlocutor Carl Henry.

141. Dorrien examines Barth and the neo-orthodox movement in light of the broader nineteenth- and twentieth-century critical theological scholarship in *The Word as True Myth*, and *The Barthian Revolt in Modern Theology*.

Sometimes major contributions are made among those who step outside a given consensus and by doing so open up new theological light. It would be difficult to deny that this was not so with Barth, as Fackre readily notes. In fact, one might surmise that the very power of Barth's theological vision was embodied in the sharp antinomies that characterized his vision even in his search to transcend them, so eloquently depicted in Hunsinger's *How to Read Karl Barth*. That the effort remained elusive speaks to the ongoing search, which, by the very nature of what it is can only remain a longing. That longing for a reach that perpetually exceeds its grasp is also the case with Fackre's own theological project, in which the search for the center is the taproot that unleashes his own passion and creativity.

SCRIPTURAL INSPIRATION: BETWEEN DIVINE ACTION AND CHURCH ILLUMINATION

Fackre associates scriptural *inspiration* with God's divine action in the "prophetic' testimony" of Israel and the "'apostolic' witness" to Jesus Christ, as reflected throughout the entire New Testament. He refers to the spiritual *illumination* of the church catholic as a result of the "enlightening work of the Holy Spirit" that was and continues to be active through the course of human history in "the post-apostolic community."[142] In Fackre's idiom, Scripture is magisterial, to which the ecclesial practices and theological reflections of the ecumenical church through the ages are ministerial. In Fackre's highly cogent theoretical parsing, the distinctive "phases" of "inspiration" and "illumination" may be more difficult to disentangle in practice than may be initially evident in his typological view of revelation.[143] For his scriptural interlocutor, Fackre draws on the rich resources of evangelical theologian, Carl Henry.[144] He does so not only because of the importance of the "Scripture chapter" in the trajectory of the Grand Narrative and Henry's biblical acuity. In drawing on Henry, Fackre also seeks on "to end an academic hauter that regularly excludes the evangelical from the wider table of theological conversation."[145] Linking Henry with Tillich, Barth, and Rahner is very much part of Fackre's commitment to evangelical ecumenism, in

---

142. Fackre, *Doctrine of Revelation*, 153.

143. Ibid., 17–19.

144. For this section, Fackre draws on the fourth volume of Henry's magisterial six-volume *God, Revelation, and Authority* series. Volume 4 is subtitled, *God Who Speaks and Shows*.

145. Fackre, *Doctrine of Revelation*, 154.

which God is best revealed through critical, but loving "mutual affirmation and admonition" of all major expressions of the Christian faith.[146]

Fackre notes that Henry embraces a moderate form of inerrancy based on a view of flawless original scriptural "autographs" that have, to date, been lost to history. For Henry, then, "textual criticism. . ."becomes a tool for seeking approximations of the inspired writings."[147] The process is facilitated through the agency of the Holy Spirit, which "watches over the transmission process to assure the 'infallibility' of Scripture, that is, its total reliability in matters of faith and morals."[148] Fackre elsewhere draws out this moderate view which he refers to as *trajectory inerrancy*:

> Moderate inerrantists do not engage in extensive [textual] harmonization. Acknowledging the human side of the text allows for oriental hyperbole and inexactitude in numbering and in the specifics of ancient chronicles. An epistemic Providence does watch over transmission but secures the center, not the circumference of Scripture. Acceptable Greek and Hebrew texts are infallible—trustworthy in doctrine and morals and in general not error-prone. Yet mistakes appear in marginal matters of science and history. The quest for autographical purity becomes very important, hence the emphasis on textual criticism. Confidence in the inerrancy of autographs, but the freedom from tight divine control after the launch from the inspired autographs, prompts the label, "trajectory."[149]

Historians such as Marsden maintain that inerrancy is a formal doctrine of late nineteenth- and early twentieth-century vintage drawn upon by fundamentalists and doctrinally conservative Reformed theologians as a means of preserving the viability of Scripture against the onslaught of post-Darwinian modernity and theological liberalism.[150] Viewed from this perspective, the doctrine exhibits a pragmatic overtone in the challenge of maintaining a central theological focus on the Bible as the fundamental source of Christian truth, without which—proponents argue—only a hopeless subjectivity would prevail. In this respect, inerrancy became a means of preserving the doctrine of theism as well as any sharply defined belief in Christ as the incarnation of the living God. While noting Henry's view on

---

146. Fackre and Root, *Affirmations and Admonitions*, 1–43.

147. Ibid., 157.

148. Ibid., 157–58.

149. Fackre, *Ecumenical Faith in Evangelical Perspective*, 9–10.

150. Marsden, *Fundamentalism and American Culture*, 55–62, 107–8; Marsden, *Understanding Fundamentalism and Evangelicalism*, 36–40.

inerrancy, Fackre draws out what he believes to be the more important influence of Henry's theology of Scripture; the centrality of biblical inspiration as the primary source of revelation.[151]

Henry means something very specific by the "revelatory underpinnings" of inspiration, namely that the writing of Scripture itself was inspired by the Holy Spirit.[152] Although the text was written through the hands of fallible writers, Henry's emphasis on the ideal standard (the autographs) represents a purified inerrant ideal, even as the original texts are currently lost to the historical record. The more important point to which Fackre is in agreement with Henry was the infusion of

> a supernatural influence upon divinely chosen prophets and apostles whereby the Spirit of God assures the truth and trustworthiness of their oral and written proclamation. Historic evangelical Christianity considers the Bible the essential textbook because, in view of this quality, it inscripurates divinely revealed truth in verbal form.[153]

Henry's emphasis on the propositional nature of biblical truth stems both from his doctrine of inerrancy as God's own "epistemic Word" and the central role he gives to reason. Marsden links the impetus of reason to the "Baconian Ideal" and the enduring influence of "Common Sense" Scottish Philosophy on certain sectors of the evangelical mind of which Henry is a major representative.[154] A key concern of Henry's is the need for a clear response to very broad streams of twentieth-century theology based upon the presupposition that "Scripture functions only expressively and evocatively, making no cognitive truth claims, withholding assertions about reality that have abiding truth."[155] This is also a major concern of Fackre, who, in drawing on Henry for this part of an ongoing storyline, does not equivocate on the matter of biblical truth claims.

Even though Henry does not ascribe to the precepts of narrative theology, Fackre welcomes Henry's acceptance of the importance of the entire

---

151. As Fackre summarizes Henry's view on this point: "Allusion to . . . inerrancy . . . will be made here, but the focus will be on its revelatory underpinnings in the Spirit's work of prophetic and apostolic disclosure through the words of the original biblical documents. Or, in terms that Henry employs to sharpen the distinction between his view and that of Karl Barth, the Bible is God's own 'epistemic Word.'" *Doctrine of Revelation*, 155.

152. Ibid.

153. Henry *God, Revelation, and Authority*, 4:129. Cited in Fackre, *Doctrine of Revelation*, 155.

154. Marsden, *Fundamentalism and American Culture*, 55–62, 111–12, 214–15.

155. Fackre, *Doctrine of Revelation*, 159.

arc of the Grand Narrative for any comprehensive understanding of biblical truth. While challenging Henry on the doctrines of inerrancy and propositionalism, for which he is better known, Fackre echoes Henry's appreciation "of a wider and longer view of the Holy Spirit's revelatory activity" within Scripture, in which "the elements of larger narrative of revelation are discernible."[156] With Fackre, Henry accepts the importance of the trajectory of the biblical arc from creation to consummation. Both agree that "only in the *eschaton* will the fullness of God's revelatory glory shine forth."[157]

In his allusive style, Fackre probes further into both the doctrinal and revelatory aspects of Henry's theology. He does so through an exploration of the role of language in contemporary biblical and cultural studies in which concentration on "the 'verbal' is commanding new attention."[158] Fackre draws on work in "metaphor study and cultural anthropology," which, while not incorporated into a "new theological magisterium," represents a stream of contemporary scholarship based on "figural language" that has the capacity "to shed light on the Scripture's own self-testimony." Through various "master images" the Bible draws on "figural language" in describing God, Christ, or the work of the Holy Spirit. "In each case, some aspect of human experience is taken up and transfigured by its biblical usage."[159] Thus, "the role and meaning of image, symbol, analogy, metaphor, simile, and story in both Scripture and Christian theology," as well as in broader cultural studies, play a major expository role in contemporary biblical interpretation.[160] Fackre's incorporation of a broad range of religious and secular cultural studies roams far and wide of the main thrust of Henry's intent. Nonetheless, his deep-rooted ecumenical instincts propel him to establish a connection.

Fackre's main contention at this point—one shared by Henry—is that "words do count."[161] Along with Henry, Fackre argues that "a fully-orbed faith includes 'knowledge of the mind.'" Critical to this is "the validity of reference—states of affairs, historical or transcendent" in any biblical "recovery of the power on metaphor and story."[162] In short, any emphasis on the Grand Narrative of the biblical revelation must have truth claims as its

---

156. Ibid., 160. On the centrality of propositionalism in Henry's biblical theology, see Dulles, *Models of Revelation*, 46–52.

157. Fackre, *Doctrine of Revelation*, 161.

158. Ibid., 164.

159. Ibid. Fackre references Farrer, *Glass of Vision*, 42–44, for the types of "master images" that he cites.

160. Ibid., 165.

161. Ibid., 164.

162. Ibid., 167.

primary referent and not merely story as such, standing in as a *metaphor* for truth. In getting at the "cognitive truth-claims"[163] of Scripture, Fackre makes the key argument, in accordance with Henry, that the "truth of the symbol" is ultimately more important than the any referenced "symbolic truth."[164] However much "expressed in imagery and the language of story," what is ultimately fundamental about the biblical narrative is its truth claims "about reality," in short, Scripture's core "propositions."[165] Notwithstanding this basic agreement with Henry's insistence on truth, Fackre maintains that the biblical revelation comes primarily through "the symbolic form of image and story." Because of the range of the literary genres of the biblical text and the multiplicity of potential interpretations, the truths that are conveyed in and through Scripture "are better described as 'affirmations' than by the more exacting term 'proposition.'"[166]

Henry appreciates "Fackre's desire to maintain continuity with the biblical heritage." However, he worries that the narrative approach "leaves [too] open the function of a transcendent revelation," which may also "leave indeterminate the perspectival nature of the story" in a manner that could cloud its unequivocal truth claim. Henry also wonders whether Fackre's narrative approach "preserve[s] the propositional nature of the story" and, therefore, provides a sufficiently clear basis upon which "the normative role of the scriptural account" can be made.[167] Fackre's counterthrust is the claim that ambiguity and paradox are part of the storyline and inherently embedded in the basic biblical tension between the "already" and the "not yet." In response to this tension, the narrative mode includes reference to analogical as well as univocal language, the former, in which, in Fackre's view, Henry downplays. Fackre places his ultimate hermeneutical commitment on the trajectory of the storyline, including the future-oriented eschaton as the final source of revelation rather than the emphasis Henry consigns to the original autographs.[168]

---

163. Ibid.

164. Urban, *Language and Reality*, 443; cited in Fackre, *Doctrine of Revelation*, 167.

165. Ibid., 168.

166. Ibid.

167. Henry, "Evangelical-Ecumenical Dialogue," 41.

168. Fackre acknowledges that Henry incorporates eschatology into his interpretation of Scripture. At the same time, he critiques Henry's "failure to honor the distinction between the ultimate and penultimate. The problem is that Henry's "inordinate claims for the univocal nature of biblical assertions" results in his understanding of such propositions as 'sentences' protected from error by the Holy Spirit." Fackre's concern is that this stance "affiliates the human words themselves with the clarity of Light reserved alone for the End." *Doctrine of Revelation*, 170.

Given also the enduring influence of sin, Fackre argues that the level of certainty upon which Henry seeks to ground his understanding of revelation is based on a faulty polarity between the "saved" and "sinners." According to Fackre, this polarity conforms neither to the reality of human experience nor to the fullness of the biblical revelation in its documentation of the persistence of evil, failure, and the ineradicable nature of sin even amidst the saints. Moreover, in Henry's evangelical emphasis on the individual, he does not provide sufficient attention to the church as *resource* and culture as *setting* for the type of fully developed catholic comprehensiveness Fackre views as vital to any revitalization of an evangelically faithful ecumenical Protestant religious culture. With these critical "admonitions" identified, Fackre views Henry as a vital "ecumenical conversation" partner due to the crucial emphasis he places on scriptural inspiration. The role of biblical inspiration is a central "phase of the revelation narrative"[169] that Fackre depicts in his narrative theology. It is one that he finds largely missing in mainline-based ecumenical seeking perspectives.[170]

ECCLESIAL ILLUMINATION: CHURCH AS RESOURCE

The trajectory of the Grand Narrative continues to move within history as depicted in *The Acts of the Apostles*, which provides a descriptive account of the formation of the early church. In its portrayal of the eschatological end of human history, the finality of the story is dramatically brought home in *The Revelation of Jesus Christ*. Thus arises "a new heaven and new earth" (Rev 21:1) of the New Jerusalem in which "the Lord God Almighty and the lamb [of God] are its temple" (Rev 21:22). The original Edenic vision is restored to its pristine purity, as both sin and death are conquered for the redeemed. However literally or figuratively either of these New Testament books is interpreted, the significant point for our discussion is the theological import of God's continued revelation in history and his ultimate control

---

169. Ibid., 175.

170. Fackre's summative statement on Henry provides a succinct overview of what he is getting at in the scriptural "chapter" of his storyline: "The evangelical voice, often muted or missing in the ecumenical conversation, makes its most important contribution in this phase of the revelation narrative. Carl Henry's detailed defense of the inspiration of Scripture is such a word to be reckoned with. Ecumenical and academic theology that excludes the evangelical presence in the conversation impoverishes itself. Yet, inspiration, while part of the revelation story, is neither the whole nor the heart of it, and must find its derivative place under the Word enfleshed and its relative place before the Word eschatological. Thus the need for mutual affirmation and admonition from ecumenical conversation partners." Ibid.

of, and care for, the created order. Throughout the various "illuminations" in the last three chapters of *The Doctrine of Revelation*, Fackre evokes the dialectical tension between the already attained revelation of the first coming of the ascended Christ and the not yet anticipatory climax of human history, as symbolized in the second coming. Fackre imaginatively engages this tension from the living perspective of the present, with particular concentration on the role of the church.

For the "chapter" of the Christian Story on the role of the church, Fackre draws on the Catholic theologian Karl Rahner. Fackre's key argument here is that the church ecumenical is the primary location where "new light and truth *from God's holy Word*"[171] breaks forth, yet with no expansion upon the original revelation of Christ as the definitive "image of the invisible God, the firstborn over all creation" (Col 1:15). While his treatment of the role of the church is brief in *The Doctrine of Revelation*, Fackre devotes volume 5 of *The Christian Story*, *The Church: Signs of the Spirit and Signs of the Times*, to this crucial topic. As our focus here is on the *trajectory* of the Grand Narrative, the detailed presentation provided in volume 5 is not included in the current discussion.

Given Rahner's grounding in philosophy—especially the existentialist philosophy of being of Martin Heidegger—Fackre could have drawn on Rahner's vast corpus in support of his focus on general revelation, as detailed in his discussion of Tillich.[172] The key point for Rahner's existentialism is his linkage of the phenomenology of being to that of Catholic theology through which the authentic fulfillment of the human project comes to complete fruition in the incarnation of Christ.[173] Based on this anthropological impetus—which in its emphasis on indwelling grace is also transcendent—the most deeply rooted questions grounding individual identity find their ultimate resolution in the divine presence of God incarnated into such experience. The phenomenology of being as described by Rahner—when it is graced by the transcendence of God's being—is a "supernatural existential" occurrence.[174] Rahner contends that "nature should remain nature for the

---

171. Ibid., 181.

172. Ibid., 185; Heidegger, *Being and Time*.

173. Fackre, *Doctrine of Revelation*, 188–93.

174. Kelly, *Karl Rahner*, 114. See ibid., 43–44, for Kelly's formal discussion of Rahner's "supernatural existential" theology. As Kelly explains, the "primal transcendental relationship with God—which is so immanent to the process of becoming more human and, therefore, more open to the attractive lure of truth and goodness—emanates from a gratuitous gift of God." The result is that "while remaining wholly other, God's presence in grace becomes intertwined with the entire process of the creative transformation of the self." Ibid., 43. While his Reformed accents on sin, grace, and modified biblical inerrancy are clearly different than Rahner's, Packer shares a strong similarity with Rahner

sake of grace and yet always . . . grasped by Christians as an intrinsic element in the single object willed by God when God willed human beings as [he did] God's beloved in God's son,"[175] to mirror the incarnational presence of God.

Referencing the Second Vatican Council of the early 1960s, Fackre draws out the importance of the incarnation of Christ as "the decisive event of disclosure in the history of God." This is synonymous with his own position on the absolute centerpiece of the Christian revelation.[176] The centrality of Scripture was also highlighted at the Second Vatican Council to which the Church held itself ultimately accountable. However, Fackre notes that "the task of providing an authentic interpretation of God's Word in Scripture or Tradition has been entrusted only to the Church's living magisterium, whose authority is wielded in the name of Jesus Christ."[177] Fackre acknowledges that in the post-Vatican II setting, even "the interpretive authority" of the Church magisterium "is always accountable to 'God's Word,' never the source of a new revelation." Yet, as observed by Fackre, this claim is somewhat belied by the persistence of "the clear statement of the accountability of biblical interpretation to [the] magisterial authority" of the Church, which "tells another story."[178]

Fackre highlights Rahner's concept of "categorical revelation" in grounding the church's interpretive magisterium to the often-cited "disputed Petrine passage":[179]

> And I tell you that you are Peter, and on this rock I will build my church, and the gates of Hades will not overcome it. (Matt 16:18–19)

---

in equating true human freedom with radical obedience God. Packer, *Truth and Power*, 11–55. As Packer succinctly states, "God's law corresponds to created human nature, so that in fulfilling his requirements we fulfill ourselves. The gospel of Christ answers to actual human need, as glove fits hand, so that all our responses to God work for our good, and no touch of authoritarianism enters into his exercise of authority over us." Ibid., 15. In Rahner's terms, as capsulated by Kelly, "'obediential potency' for fulfillment in being is transformed through the advent of God's unending presence. In such a way, a person's concrete existence or the 'existential' becomes ordered to God and touched irrevocably by God." Kelly, *Karl Rahner*, 44.

175. Kelly, *Karl Rahner*, 117.

176. Fackre, *Doctrine of Revelation*, 186.

177. *Dogmatic Constitution on Divine Revelation*, 66. Cited in Fackre, *Doctrine of Revelation*, 188.

178. Fackre, *Doctrine of Revelation*, 188.

179. Ibid., 184, 190.

According to Fackre, what Rahner means by "categorical" is this "definitive disclosure" in "Jesus Christ" as "the culmination of all that has come before, either in particular or universal revelation history, and unsurpassable by all that comes after."[180] In Rahner's words, this revelation has its grounding point "in an irreversible direction toward a highest and comprehensive self-interpretation of humankind"[181] as definitively embodied in the incarnation of Christ. It indwells within the fabric of lived human experience through the illumination of the Holy Spirit in a manner that can be at least partially grasped, while always requiring an existential wager of faith.

What distinguishes Rahner from Tillich is that the revelatory vehicle of "New Being" (Tillich) "comes through the church."[182] As Fackre more fully explains it, "Rahner finds support for the magisterial doctrine of the church on the basis of the 'social nature' of human beings—the self as a 'being of interpersonal communication.'"[183] While accepting this; as the Reformed theologian that he is, Fackre argues for the magisterial role of the Bible and the ministerial role of the church. Nonetheless, in his ecumenical quest for a richly centrist perspective, Fackre draws on Rahner in fleshing out the significance of the church in his interpretation of the Christian story. Fackre seeks to give the church its due, which he maintains is oftentimes blurred by "the ahistorical and individualistic temptations of the Protestant tradition."[184]

The church is an important chapter, in which "Christ is epistemically present," however, "not unbrokenly so."[185] Fackre takes a cautiously critical stance that, notwithstanding the assured presence of Christ in his body, the church remains persistently fallible in its dispensational temporality residence between the First and Second Coming. Such fallibility allows Christ "to be free to speak *to* the church and even *against* the church rather than speaking only as the church" without substantial critical remainder.[186]

In this respect, "the church is not the '*one* word,' but is other than and, thus, always accountable to that Word" in which a sharp line needs to be made "between the Word incarnate and the words ecclesial."[187] As Fackre

---

180. Ibid., 188–89.

181. Kelly, *Karl Rahner*, 131.

182. Fackre, *Doctrine of Revelation*, 190.

183. Ibid. As Rahner expresses it, "The church is the historical and social presence of God's self communication to the world in Christ." Kelly, *Karl Rahner*, 258.

184. Fackre, *Doctrine of Revelation*, 193.

185. Ibid., 195.

186. Ibid., 196.

187. Ibid.

draws out the hierarchy of authority in his theology, the grounding point is the incarnation of Christ as revealed through the *inspiration* of Scripture and *illuminated* to the church through the Holy Spirit. As he sees it, the two are inseparable, yet, "narratively conceived, the chapter on Christ is distinguishable from" and prior to "the chapter on the church."[188] Fackre contends that Catholicism overreaches the importance of the church. At the same time, the Catholic tradition bears witness to the gift of Christ indwelling in the body, which offers an important corrective to an over-reliance in Protestantism on Scripture and the focal point on individual consciousness.

Throughout his ecumenical vision, Fackre highlights "the importance of the mutual corrigibilities and complementaries"[189] of divergent theological perspectives in search of a vital center. This dynamic is embodied in the very selection the four formative figures that Fackre draws on as critical twentieth-century conversation partners to punctuate the four "phases" of revelation which characterizes his narrative theology: preservation, action, inspiration, illumination.[190] In following Fackre's revelatory trajectory through the medium of his four conversation partners, I end my discussion of *The Doctrine of Revelation* with the chapter on the church. Fackre completes the illumination phase of his doctrine of revelation with two additional chapters: one on salvation ("Personal Illumination") and the other on the consummation of the Christian revelation in the final coming of Christ ("Eschatological Illumination").[191]

CONCLUDING REMARKS

At the core of Fackre's theology are some very basic tenets: the centerpiece of God's revelation to humankind in the incarnation of Christ, the inspiration of Scripture as primary witness to and source of revelation, and the illumination of God's presence throughout the course of the Grand Narrative

---

188. Ibid., 197.

189. Ibid., 200.

190. Ibid., 18. As it is with his model of revelation, his selection of critical interlocutors is influenced by typological motivations. It is not that the four theologians literally provide a tight causal fit with the key "phases" of his narrative theology—his discussion is marked as much by allusive digression as by direct application. In his theological "translation," Tillich, Henry, Barth, and Rahner symbolize the polarities of twentieth century theology along the axis of which Fackre seeks to synthesize into his ecumenical vision. The four phases of revelation and the four theologians alike contribute to Fackre's project of establishing a "dynamic equivalence" of God's revelation through the typology of narrative theology.

191. Ibid., 202–24; see also Fackre's contents page.

from creation to consummation. Crucial to Fackre's project are the foundational priorities that enable him to ground his narrative theology within the hierarchies laid out in his model. This structure provides him the latitude to consider the truth claims of a very divergent theological landscape. He is well aware that his typology is fallible. He offers his evangelical ecumenical vision as an ideal construct open to the whole people of God.

One can question the viability of the tightly woven interlocking framework of Fackre's narrative theology. Notwithstanding its dialectical probing, the breaking in of God's voice in the stream of human history may be—to draw on a term of Walter Brueggemann's—considerably more "angular" than the mediating comprehensiveness of Fackre's proposal. Granting this, one would do well to consider the trajectory of the Grand Narrative that Fackre depicts as a metaphor for the revelation of God within the affairs of the world, from creation to consummation, in the mediation of the already and the not yet. My broader point is the potential Fackre's probing opens up in establishing a centrist vision by incorporating sharply divergent perspectives within the framework of the finely tuned intricacies of his narrative theology. The question at hand is the extent to which the restoration of the center can prevail in the realm of mainline Protestantism and in the mediating evangelicalism of Packer and Bloesch with any degree of reasonable plausibility.

The question pivots around two fundamental concerns. The first is the extent in contemporary theological discourse to which Christ can be interpreted as the incarnation of the living God. The second is the extent to which Scripture, in coordination with the Holy Spirit, can hold as the primary source and witness of revelation. Both of these are problematic claims within the camp of contemporary mainline Protestantism as exhibited in its more liberal accents. Notwithstanding how intricately integrative his evangelical ecumenism seeks to be, the viability of Fackre's narrative theology pivots on these two foundational points.

Fackre goes a long way in shaping a timely theological construct that is as exceedingly dialectical as it is mediating and ecumenical. Given the attractiveness of a neo-Barthian vision in significant quarters of mainline Protestantism—particularly in the various denominational movements similar to Confessing Christ of which Fackre is a major pioneer—this effort holds intriguing promise. Drawing deeply from Reinhold Niebuhr as well as Bonhoeffer, Fackre's consensus-driven theological model provides some indication as to what *could* be construed as theologically feasible in the contexts where he seeks influence: first, the United Church of Christ and secondarily within the various Reformed-based denominations in which much of his theology is rooted. With an ecumenical probing that extends to Lutheranism, and to some degree, to the Episcopal and Roman Catholic Churches, Fackre has extended his vision widely in search of a vital center.[192] Whether the center holds is a matter of profound significance that extends to the very heart and soul of what he has envisioned through means that he readily acknowledges moves well beyond his own substantial capacity to fully fathom.

In viewing some of the tensions in Fackre's construction, the relationship he sets out between Scripture as source, church tradition as resource, and culture as setting merits additional consideration. Fackre notes that the relationships among these factors are considerably more fluid than his theological model allows. Nonetheless, he feels required to set up this tripartite model of revelation in order to stabilize a perspective that give pride of place to the sources and resources of faith *over* the setting of culture. There is in his theology a dialectical receptivity to the nuanced working of God within history, which, in God's radical otherness, may or may not follow the path lines broadly conceived by Fackre's typology.

As a Christian, Fackre is well aware of the breaking in of the vitality of God's presence wherever the Spirit dwells in the very midst of our feeble designs. On this realization, Fackre makes a strong distinction between the homiletic dynamic of the preaching moment and the much longer thread of theological construction. Nonetheless, he premises his interpretation on strong dogmatic assumptions that veer toward a certain stabilization over dynamism, however much he keeps space open for the latter, as long as it flows, at least broadly, from the theological edifice that he has constructed.

Such stabilization is not inherently problematic since without some such orienting framework it would be difficult to proceed with theological construction at all. Moreover, there is much value in Fackre's theological configurations, given the need to make coherent sense of a transcendent reality that perpetually defies our capacity to exhaustively grasp. Still, there are fissures in his thought which a more postmodern reading such as Brueggemann's would emphasize.

I raise this postmodern critique in the very process of considering the many values of Fackre's work in light of contemporary challenges facing mainline Protestantism in establishing potential dialogue with practitioners of evangelical theology. Of particular concern is the absence of theological rigor, especially in Fackre's own denomination, the United Church of Christ. The result is a pervasive lack of clarity toward a cognitively penetrating understanding of the very meaning of Christian identity, including a reasonably exacting perception of critical points of contention within the

---

192. Fackre and Root, *Affirmations and Admonitions*.

household of faith amongst clergy and laity alike. If the matter of Christian identity were more critically attended to—particularly in light of the many challenges of the contemporary setting—this could lead, in principle, to greater clarity, if not to the catholic concord sought by Fackre. Regardless of whether any such identity construction could emerge from a broad-based foundational acceptance of Scripture as the primary source of revelation, it is one of the central pivotal points upon which any viable restoration of the center depends.

There are at least three issues upon which this may turn. The first is the acceptance by the Protestant mainline of their increasing social and cultural marginality and the capacity to engage in creative theological construction in this changed milieu.[193] The second is the extent to which the Protestant mainline can engage in searing and sustained critique of the fundamental presuppositions of secular culture from a sharply defined and publicly articulated biblical and theological perspective. This would include drawing from the culture whatever may be needed to enrich its own resources in a growing critical and ever deeper canonical understanding and defense of its own core message. A closely related third is the capacity to accept the Bible as the primary text of faith in a manner that can incorporate critical scholarship. This would include scope for a hermeneutics of suspicion, while reading the text first and foremost as God's primary source of communication to the body of Christ.

Any wholesale restoration of the center is an exceedingly unlikely prospect in the foreseeable future. For Fackre, such a vision serves as a regulative ideal with very serious intent. More feasible is the prospect that centrist voices in the UCC and other mainline denominations can be substantially strengthened. This is plausible, even as the prospect of persisting tensions within the denomination and the broader Protestant mainline on the relationship of the Bible to that of contemporary culture may well endure for a long time without significant resolution.

Fackre has contributed much toward the buttressing of a vital centrist perspective within the UCC. This is evident not only in his formal theological project—*The Christian Story* series—but also in his founding work with the Confessing Christ network and the annual Craigville Colloquies.[194] These conferences have been held since 1984 on a wide variety of themes through the perspective of an evangelically grounded ecumenical vision.

---

193. This topic is addressed in some depth in Hall, *Confessing the Faith.*

194. For a list of topics, see "Twenty Seven Years of Craigville Theological Colloquies" (http://craigvillecolloquy.com/_Archive/General/historytitles.html). The Craigville Colloquy website, esp. the Archive/History link, provides additional background (http://craigvillecolloquy.com/wordpress/?page_id=60).

Through his cumulative work, Fackre has engaged in a great deal of creative grappling with the various issues that divide the household of Christian faith in the contemporary era. Both the strengths and limitations of Fackre's rigorous theological constructions have grown out of his quest for a comprehensive evangelical ecumenical vision to consolidate a dynamic Protestant center. In his dual role of theologian and churchman, Fackre has sought to bring the riches of his insights to a broader lay adult public.

6

Reading Walter Brueggemann through a Fluidly Canonical Lens

Texts That Linger in a Fragile World

Scripture . . . is the chief authority for moderates and it's the chief authority for me as long as one can qualify that to say that it is the chief authority when imaginatively construed in a certain interpretive trajectory.[1]

I believe that the "canonizing process" was a vigorous one, but not as singular as Childs thinks and in the end not as reductionist toward "church truth" as Childs insists . . . Thus in my judgment Sanders is correct in speaking of a "canonizing tendency," but a tendency that did not run roughshod over ancient textual claims and one that did not completely impose itself upon the ongoing textual tradition. The matter of completeness and comprehensiveness of the canonizing process is one that will remain contested and under adjudication. I suspect that for all parties to that contestation, the conclusions we draw reflect more the perspective of the interpreter than they reflect upon the text itself. My own inclination is to think that the Old Testament is "canonical" in its rich variegation and that the polyvalence of the text itself is an important part of the canonical claim. It matters, of course, if one believes that such variegated textual realities threaten "the core of the truth" or if they in an important way

1. Brueggemann, "Gospel vs. Scripture?"

understood something of the truth, that is a refusal to excessive closure that characteristically runs the risk of settled idolatry.[2]

In principle, the hearer of this text who listens for its theological cadences refuses to go behind these witnesses. This means that theological interpretation does not go behind the witness with questions of history, wondering "what happened." What happened, so our "verdict" is, is what these witnesses said happened. In complementary fashion, this means that theological interpretation does not go behind the witnesses with questions of ontology wondering "what is real." Nothing more historical or available is available. But this mode of "knowing" finds such a claim to be adequate.[3]

BRUEGGEMANN AND FACKRE COMPARED: NARRATIVE THEOLOGIANS IN DIVERGENT VEINS

Walter Brueggemann shares significant points of convergence with Gabriel Fackre in his embrace of narrative theology and in his substantial grappling with critical biblical scholarship. With Fackre, Brueggemann has been highly influential within the United Church of Christ and speaks to "moderate" groups among varying Protestant mainline (though less so among those reflecting evangelical) perspectives. Also, like Fackre, Brueggemann adheres to an evangelical identity, in his case, in the importance he ascribes to "imaginative construal,"[4] with a sharp focus on the relationship between particular biblical texts and the social context of ancient Israel and the contemporary era. Similarly, he, like Fackre, is highly suspicious of the claims of theological liberalism, while gravitating more so than Fackre toward the postliberal/liberationist edge of an ecumenical evangelical identity.

The differences are equally notable. While Brueggemann is more canonically grounded than some of his critics assume, a good deal of the critical commentary about his work is based on some of his own polemical claims.[5] The primary critique is his postmodern contention that the biblical

2. Brueggemann, *Introduction to the Old Testament*, 394.
3. Brueggemann, *Theology of the Old Testament*, 206.
4. Brueggemann, *Introduction to the Old Testament*, 8.
5. The following reflects Brueggemann's essential faithfulness to the tradition of the Protestant Reformers: "Praise is the duty and delight, the ultimate vocation of the human community; indeed, all of creation. Yes, all of life is aimed toward God and

text funds postmodern imagination, only "one text at a time."[6] On his highly "angular" (a favored term of Brueggemann's) reading, there is no prospect on the near-term horizon for any wholesale canonical reinterpretation of the Bible within the contemporary household of Christian identity that one finds in different ways in Barth, Packer, Bloesch, and Fackre.

With Fackre, Brueggemann views his interpretation of Scripture as compatible with canonical fidelity. However, given the inscrutable freedom of the text to speak with fresh insight in new situations, Brueggemann assumes a dialectical approach in his grappling with the significance of particular biblical texts that do not allow for any singular interpretation. For Brueggemann, the Old Testament needs to be read with pluralistic, dialectical and bipolar lenses.[7] This is in contrast to Fackre, who relies on ultimate textual harmonization through the entire storyline of Scripture.

Also, in contrast to Fackre—who views the ecclesial and theological repository of a two thousand-year tradition as a major resource of revelation—Brueggemann—while acknowledging its indispensability—does so with a great deal of unease. In contrast, he puts more emphasis on the hermeneutical significance of the cultural context. Fackre places the interpretive importance of the contextual setting third in the hierarchy of values, preceded by ecclesial and theological tradition as a primary *resource* and Scripture as the primary *source* of revelation. Both theologians are in full agreement that if cultural analysis is not handled well—however differently they interpret the challenge—the result can only lead to inadequate interpretation, with consequences told and untold, in the pulpits and the pews as well as in seminary halls.

For Brueggemann, each biblical passage is more susceptible to the hermeneutics of suspicion than typically ascribed by orthodox biblical

---

finally exists for the sake of God. Praise articulates and embodies our capacity to yield, submit, and abandon ourselves in trust and gratitude to the One whose we are. Praise is not only a human requirement and a human need, it is also human delight. We have a resilient hunger to move beyond self, to return our energy and worth to the One from whom it has been granted. In our return to that One, we find our deepest joy. That is what it means to 'glorify God and enjoy him forever.'" *Israel's Praise*, 1.

6. Brueggemann, *Texts under Negotiation*, 25. I explore Brueggemann's postmodern argument, primarily through an evaluation of this book, in the next section.

7. See Brueggemann, "Biblical Theology Appropriately Postmodern," 131–40, for a basic overview. Brueggemann correlates his dialectical Old Testament theology to the fissures within contemporary postmodern construction of societal, personal, and cultural experience. He is "endlessly dialectical" in pitting the "plurivocal" nature of the biblical text in critical tension with the ultimate goal of canonical harmonization that one finds in Fackre and Childs as well as with Packer and Bloesch. Ibid., 137, 138. I explore the various polar tensions that mark Brueggemann's biblical theology throughout much of this chapter.

theology. Each passage is also potentially evocative of revelatory power and has the capacity to break into human experience as it will in whatever form and manifestation it may take.[8] The power of such indwelling is inscrutable when torch lit by the imagination which blows where it will, which no orthodoxy, however dogmatically sound, could ever contain. As Brueggemann puts it, "a theological statement is not concerned with the process and character of the text, but with the process and character of God met in the text."[9]

Both Childs and Fackre—who ascribe to the progressive view of biblical revelation through the arc of the entire scriptural storyline—reject any notion of easy scriptural harmonization. They are on the same plane with Brueggemann in their adherence to the enduring election of God's covenant with Israel in light of the revelation of Christ. The difference is that Childs and Fackre seek an ultimate coherence in Scripture in the triune revelation of Jesus Christ, even as they acknowledge that the fullness of God's revelation in Jesus Christ extends beyond history to the eschaton. Brueggemann rests uneasily with Childs's "programmatic" canonical approach. Instead, he places more attentiveness on the inescapability of the interpretive process that particular readers bring to the Bible. He gives priority to the polyphony of voices and emphases that comprise individual scriptural texts, which defy easy harmonization. I believe Brueggemann misreads Childs as being "flatly cognitive, as though the Bible were simply a set of ideas."[10]

Brueggemann is not without hope that, over time, the many individual "pieces" of the biblical text he analyzes can become "stitched together into a sensible collage."[11] This will require a great deal of subtle re-assemblage as readers confront the biblical text in response to new circumstances and locations. These new readings—which can only be "*contextual, local, and pluralistic*"[12]—will lead at most toward greater coherences while avoiding the temptation of flat line dogmatics that absolutize the text. The challenge, in the postmodern era, is "to provide the pieces, materials, and resources out of which a new world can be imagined" that can no longer rely on "a grand theme or a coherent system."[13] Brueggemann maintains that whether

---

8. The substance of this claim will be laid out throughout this chapter.

9. Brueggemann, "Shape for Old Testament Theology I," 4.

10. Brueggemann, "Against the Stream," 169. In various texts Brueggemann also includes more subtle commentary on Childs where he acknowledges his significance to the study of canonical scholarship, though he does remain critical in characterizing his work as "massively reductionist." Brueggemann, *Theology of the Old Testament*, 92.

11. Brueggemann, *Texts under Negotiation*, 25.

12. Ibid., 9.

13. Ibid., 20. Brueggemann also notes that "we voice a claim that rings true in our

Reading Walter Brueggemann through a Fluidly Canonical Lens 171

in theology, personal or cultural identity, or intellectual coherence, any semblance of a stable world order is no longer plausible.

Neither Facke nor Childs deny the continuing challenge of humankind's capacity to grapple with the inscrutable mystery of divine revelation in diverse and often contentious settings. Nevertheless, these latter two emphasize the overarching unity of Scripture within and beyond our knowing, as embodied in the trajectory of the entire biblical arc and the Christian theological tradition. For Brueggemann, the intrinsic destabilization within the biblical text has particular poignancy in the contemporary setting in which so many of the dogmatic assumptions of traditional Protestant theology have been profoundly deconstructed, including any vestige of a coherent Christian identity.[14]

BRUEGGEMANN'S APOLOGETICS

As with Fackre, so with Brueggemann, the intersection of Scripture and the contextual setting are crucially important. While Fackre's main purpose is to infuse a greater ecumenical sensibility within mainline Protestant theology and ecclesial practice, Brueggemann focuses on addressing the needs and sensibilities of those within the mainline pews who have become disaffected with religious orthodoxy. It is principally to this group that he writes: those whose main theater of everyday consciousness is shaped as much, if not more so, by the precepts of the contemporary secular culture than the "faith which was once for all delivered to the saints" (Jude 3 KJV). As a postliberal narrative biblical theologian, Brueggemann is unequivocally committed to the revelatory power of scriptural text—and for that matter, the ontological reality of God as revealed in the Bible. Nonetheless, Brueggemann argues that biblical texts are not static statements of veritable truth. They require critical and dialectical exposition in relation to the range of prevailing cultural, religious, and socio-political narratives that possess their own imposing power to shape various taken for granted constructions of reality. This is the case, he insists, in assessing the context of the original meaning of a given set of biblical passages as well as their application in the contemporary context.

The first chapter of *Texts under Negotiation: The Bible and Postmodern Imagination* contains one of Brueggemann's clearest apologetic postmodern

---

context, that applies authoritatively to our lived life. But it is a claim that is made in a pluralism where it has no formal privilege." Ibid., 9.

14. For Brueggemann's most extensive statement on contemporary biblical scholarship, see *Theology of the Old Testament*, 61–114.

statements. The question underlying this book is the discernment of the times—the *kairos*—the manner in this case in which God indwells in the contemporary United States, largely middle class setting. Brueggemann's key argument stems from a "wholly new interpretive situation," namely, the post-Christendom, pluralistic value system in which mainline Protestantism has been profoundly dethroned from any mid-twentieth-century vestige of normative cultural influence. Brueggemann notes that "this new pluralistic, postmodern situation is perceived by many as a threat to 'mainline' churches."[15] Regardless of whether that is the case, Brueggemann argues that the deconstruction of its cultural status represents the prevailing condition through which Christianity in the United States—if it is to speak with persuasiveness at all in this era—must find its voice.

Brueggemann is cautiously optimistic, despite the dangers of co-optation, that Christianity can find its voice afresh in the midst of profound historical change. To do so will require new adaptations as the impact of locale and circumstance invariably intrude on the construction of Christian identity in this current era. He argues that this is so because it is God himself who acts, stimulating hope within history. Thus, in what otherwise could be viewed as the direst of circumstances, such as the exilic period in ancient Israel, the Major Prophets reconfigured the Mosaic tradition in a manner that accounted for the great loss in identity and land, as reported in Israel's ancient narrated history.[16] The result was a profound theological embrace of pain, in which Mosaic triumphalism—in its foundational grounding in God's deliverance from Egypt—became reconfigured to fit Israel's exigent realities after the Babylonian onslaught. Within the contemporary cultural setting, Brueggemann sees "a positive opportunity to which church interpreters of the Bible may attend with considerable eagerness"[17] to their own profound loss of socio-cultural influence. This opening for new voice of an old familiar message gives shape to the apologetic impulse that grounds much of Brueggemann's work. Reflecting on the current climate, Brueggemann argues "that we are in a quite new interpretative situation that

---

15. Brueggemann, *Texts under Negotiation*, viii.

16. Brueggemann, *Hope within History* and *Hopeful Imagination*. This latter book brought home to me the daring nature of the proclamations of the Major Prophets in light of the profound loss Israel experienced in the Babylonian captivity. At issue was the potential loss of Israel's identity, were it not for the nervy counter-speech by Isaiah, Jeremiah, and Ezekiel in juxtaposition to very powerful constructions of reality to the contrary. Such an insight had never crossed my mind until I read Brueggemann's small and highly accessible book on these three pivotal prophets.

17. Brueggemann, *Texts under Negotiation*, vii.

constitutes something of an emergency."[18] The urgent present crisis is the profound destabilization of loss of power at the dethronement of American Christendom that provided mainline Protestantism with much of its texture through the early and middle decades of the twentieth century.[19]

Brueggemann notes that the question of whether we have entered a truly postmodern era or are experiencing "a move inside modernity," is moot in the sense that the changes accompanying the contemporary crisis situation are enduring and irrevocable. He highlights "the end of Enlightenment modes of certitude and certain patterns of political domination" as embedded within prevailing Western modes of hegemonic practice.[20] It is not so much that this world vision has totally collapsed in that it is "a world that is still with us"—although I think more so than he is willing to acknowledge. In his view, the world that everywhere is "very much in retreat, if not defeat" provides the grounding point for the sense of urgency, crisis, and radically new interpretive situation that Brueggemann analogizes to Israel's exilic crisis.[21] For the contemporary period, he seeks to bring to bear the crisis in objectivity, universality, and theological absolutism that—he argues with some exaggeration—a substantial tradition of Protestant orthodoxy has relied upon from the Reformation to the early twentieth century.

"In that world"—basically the Cartesian world writ large—as paradigmatically "practiced with shameless confidence, there is no need for insecurity, self-doubt or embarrassment."[22] In the world of modernity, great scientific, philosophical, political, and theological systems of thought and practice provided substantial contours in the shaping of reality within the United States and Western Europe at the end of the nineteenth and into the early twentieth centuries. With the scientific, intellectual, cultural, and political impact of Darwinism, Einstein's transformative breakthroughs in physics, the social, political and cultural upheaval of World War I, fascism, the Great Depression, de-colonization, identity politics, the rise of critical biblical scholarship, and the emergence of liberation theology, the modernist world construction—never as certain or objective as Bruegge-

---

18. Ibid., 1.

19. Brueggemann maintains "that the loss of the authority of the dynasty and temple in Jerusalem is analogous to the loss of certainty, dominance, and legitimacy on our own time." Regardless of whether this analogy fully holds, there is much merit in Brueggemann's observation that "in both cases the relinquishment is heavy and costly." *Hope within History*, 6. I explore the Protestant mainline loss of status and its potential theological significance in chapter 8.

20. Brueggemann, *Texts under Negotiation*, 2.

21. Ibid., 4.

22. Ibid., 5.

mann depicts it—began to deconstruct. Voices previously not heard found articulation—women, African Americans, various patriots of de-colonization, and others without power in the First World of modernity.

Brueggemann's contention that all positions are contextual, "including those that claim to be objective and noncontextual," is well noted.[23] There is no escape from the hermeneutical circle of historicism this side of the eschaton, an event upon which we place our hope from the temporal ground upon which we stand. It is not the ineradicable reality of history and the inherent limitations in our capacity to perceive with which I am concerned. It is the apprehension that the all-engulfing embrace of radical historicism serves as a naturalistic absolute in which the biblical notion of God the almighty becomes interpreted as a relativistic precept of the human imagination.

Given the intrinsic human propensity toward making absolute claims—which includes the anti-foundational assumption that underlies postmodernism—I am countering with the dogmatic profession that the ultimate truth in relation to the human condition lies in the full embrace of Christ as the incarnation of God in human flesh. It is this claim that the epistle writer James tells us to embrace without disbelieving as a praxeological ideal with real intent (Jas 1:5–8). This core faith stance provides an evangelical bedrock—one about which Brueggemann is highly suspicious—as counterpoise against the many secularizing forces of the contemporary period. No doubt, a cautionary note is needed—we see in a mirror dimly. Still, I make the evangelical claim that without this core foundation, radical historicism can only prevail as a naturalistic absolute to which the Christian faith itself can only become subordinate.[24]

Brueggemann does not argue for an "end to objectivity," or a rejection of the ontology of God; matters, which, in my estimation, he too quickly brackets in order to focus on describing "how it is with us." His key argument is that, given our current pluralistic setting, "we are in a situation in which all rival claims are present to us at the same time, without any transcendent arbiter."[25] Notwithstanding the enduring reality of the unfathomable ever present Lord our God, the "macho God at the edge of modernity" of a too present orthodoxy can no longer suffice in the current setting in

---

23. Ibid., 9.

24. In this evangelical assertion, I stand on Paul's bedrock claim that "there is but one God, the Father, from whom all things came and for whom we live; and there is but one Lord, Jesus Christ, through whom all things came and through whom we live" (1 Cor 8:6).

25. Brueggemann, *Texts under Negotiation*, 10.

which any faithful "articulation of God will need to begin again in local, contextual ways."[26]

Comprehensive theologies presented by Bloesch, Fackre, and Childs will have to be set aside. Nonetheless, the search for greater coherencies may emerge from the margins of power where, in Brueggemann's view, God acts most dynamically, especially at the interface between pain embraced and the delight of praise uttered. The following provides an apt summation of Brueggemann's project up to this point in our discussion:

> The new mode of theology now permitted and required reflects an acknowledgement that all claims of reality, including those by theologians, are fully under negotiation. Theological discourse is prepared to and capable of participation in these negotiations, no longer pretending to be a privileged insider, no longer willing to be a trivialized outsider. Reality, so far as our social conversation is concerned, is no longer a forced arrangement inhospitable to theological categories, but is an ongoing, creative constitutive task in which imagination of a quite specific kind has a crucial role to play. The core of our new awareness is that the world we have taken for granted in economics, politics, and everywhere else is an imaginative construal.[27]

In giving culture its due, Brueggemann assumes the only viable option in the current setting is for the biblical text to "work its way in the presence of other, rival, and competing acts of imagination, none of which can claim any formal advantage or privilege."[28] In his interpretation, our Sunday gatherings are not "a place to come to affirm the great absolutes" of the faith of our fathers, which Brueggemann views as too "allied with a modernist hegemony."[29] The primary value of doctrinal and ethical probing is less an effort to grapple with the eternal truth of God's Word revealed than a means of providing an entry point into the nervy counter-world of evangelical imagination. "What is yearned for among us is not new doctrine or new morality, but new world, new self, new future."

"This new world is not given whole," but only in the moment of its pure unveiling, "one text at a time, one miracle at a time, one poem, one healing, one pronouncement, one promise, one commandment," one revelation at a time. "A sensible collage" may emerge if we are so fortunate.

---

26. Ibid., 11.
27. Ibid., 17–18.
28. Ibid.
29. Ibid., 20.

Any such work is, at best, "idiosyncratically, stitched together"[30] in which the quest for greater coherence is a nostalgic yearning which lacks viability in the *kairotic* moment that characterizes our times. To put this in biblical terms, our moment is a wilderness/exilic one in which the daily manna of the Holy Spirit is bestowed in the immediacy of our need and in which to seek more is idolatry itself in the lack of willingness to depend on the generosity of God's grace—given in God's time and way.

BRUEGGEMANN'S BIPOLAR THEOLOGY OF SCRIPTURE IN AND BEYOND THE FRAY

The pivot points of Brueggemann's dialectical theology of Scripture are—in his terminology—idolatry and ideology, structure legitimation and embrace of pain, and royal theology and shattered transcendence in the midst of exile. Brueggemann calls for an embrace of risky faith in mediating the tension between bedrock certainty—whether of the theological left or the right—and excruciating doubt veering toward disbelief in the ambiguous midst of human history. He claims that such risk-laden tension is not only an apt characterization of the contemporary *kairos* in the postmodern era. It is also rooted in the depth and mystery of the revealing yet inscrutably hidden God—especially the character of Yahweh of the Old Testament. This is the nub of Brueggemann's entire theology: that his expositions are firmly rooted in the dangerous texts of persevering, though revisable scriptural interpretation points to the distinctive character of Israel's God. This is a God who sometimes changes his mind in grappling with ambiguous human actors in the midst of shifting historical exigency. Brueggemann depicts this God as simultaneously in the midst of and beyond human history—a tension that cannot be resolved—in which the character of God itself is unsettled. This dialectical tension within God is normative for the faithful community. Acceptance of only one side of the dialectic results either in deadened orthodoxy or despair. In either case, a sense of hopelessness prevails in the underlying suspicion that nothing of significance will emerge.

To describe Brueggemann's dialectical theology in strictly bipolar terms assumes an equality of value that he rejects. Rather, Brueggemann views God as siding most unequivocally with the embrace of pain and the "shattered transcendence" that rose up in the midst of Israel's most abject defeat in the time of exile.[31] To put this in Christian terms, Brueggemann

---

30. Ibid., 25.

31. Brueggemann addresses this issue in "Shattered Transcendence?," 183–203. I take up this essay in the last subsection of this section.

contends that the God of the Bible is more authentically found in the theology of the cross than in any triumphal theology of glory. Brueggemann identifies the processing of loss, weakness, and pain as the grounding point of Israel's most authentic worship. It is the basis, in turn, for the scriptural emphasis on justice over power, mercy over justice, and hope in the midst of despair, as variously reflected in the exodus, the exile, and the cross. Brueggemann contends that worship of Yahweh brings "hope in history, hope through history, and hope beyond history," but never "hope from history"[32] in some transcendence reality beyond hope and despair.

Between Idolatry and Ideology

Brueggemann defines ideology as any world constructed "social system . . . that cannot change or be criticized." His primary reference points are Egypt, Assyria, and Babylon, as well as Israel in the ancient world and the United States and the West in the contemporary period. By idolatry, he means anything less than that of worshipping Yahweh as the true king of Israel, whether in or outside of Israel. The counterworld of Israel's theological imagination rejects both of these forces of oppression. Brueggemann cedes a legitimate religious role to the Davidic throne within the broader context of Israel's Grand Narrative. Nonetheless, he is acutely troubled by the dangerous exaggeration of monarchial authority in muting the transformative power of the exodus story as a source of continuous enactment in Israel's life. This is the case, whether the monarchial referent is Egypt's Pharaoh, Israel's king, or the Babylonian emperor.

Brueggemann holds that the Psalms—at least without the most discerning imaginative exposition—reflect a "distorted view of the power of God." To be more precise, at least certain Psalms have all too readily been distorted, "to symbolize a god (idol) who cannot act, and a social system (ideology) that cannot be changed or criticized."[33] In pressing his point on the "constitutive"[34] nature of social and theological reality, Brueggemann argues that "we are here at the difficult point between ontology which wants to say what always is, and a dramatic claim which wants to assert just what is happening in this moment."[35] He maintains that the ontology of the given—

---

32. Brueggemann, *Hope within History*, 5.

33. Brueggemann, *Israel's Praise*, xi.

34. Ibid., 6, 22. The first chapter of *Israel's Praise* is titled "Praise as a Constitutive Act." Ibid., 1–28.

35. Ibid., 34. Brueggemann does not "suggest that such speech-construction finally shapes the ontology of God, but it does decisively shape the life-world in which we

never as all-encompassing as claimed by its "world-building" proponents—needs to be bracketed, even if in principle, it "need not be denied."[36]

It is precisely at this postmodern moment in the life of the church and in formal biblical and theological studies that a "shift" has taken place "from the valuing of *facticity* [ontology] to the celebration of *imagination*."[37] In both the Old Testament narrative and the contemporary era, the shift from facticity to critical imagination opens up fresh space for alternative constructions of reality. In Brueggemann's view, fresh encounters of God's gracious power break forth in the dramatic moment of unsettled and contentious history where all that seems in order is not so decidedly so.

According to Brueggemann, the new world of God's holy power breaks forth not as a form of "remembering, but [as] an enactment" through the constructive power of authentic doxology. The liturgical imagination unleashes "a fresh drama in this [that is, any] moment"[38] in the dialectical encounter between idolatry and ideology. The Psalms most fully become the vehicle for religious renewal when they appropriate the exodus narrative as a primary text in opening space for new life in God in the midst of the most abject loss. For Brueggemann, such loss is symbolized by the exile in ancient Israel and the Holocaust in the contemporary era.

Brueggemann acknowledges that "'world-making' is done by God. This is foundational to Israel's faith. But it is done through human activity which God has authorized and in which God is known to be present." It is in unfettered praise to God—in spite of other constructions of reality that appear more powerful—through which transformative "world-making is indeed effected." Brueggemann identifies the breaking in of the grace and power of God within the midst of old worlds lost as a "dramatic" one of imaginative reconstruction. He does not deny the reality of the dominant powers and principalities (Eph 6:12) to exercise their force within the world. Yet, these worlds are constructed realities, however much the world-making that has gone into their creation is masked in their persuasive claims of representing the world as it is. In delegitimizing their totalistic claims, Brueggemann seeks to open space for the power of God to act within the

---

encounter God." Ibid., 25. The extent to which Brueggemann successfully processes the tension between ontology and rhetoric is a theme I take up throughout this chapter.

36. "The process of 'world-building' requires that society assert its world as authoritative, accepted as a given without a doubt or reservation, and without any entertainment of a plausible alternative. Ibid., 14. See ibid., 34, for the second quote.

37. Ibid., 12. See also Perdue, *Collapse of History*, for the various ways in which contemporary Old Testament studies have moved beyond historical description and analysis.

38. Ibid., 34.

liturgical moment of utter praise. As Brueggemann contends, "Praise is not a response to a world already fixed and settled, but is a responsive and obedient participant in a world yet to be decreed and in the process of being decreed through this liturgical act."[39]

In his later work, Brueggemann gives greater attention to the many narrative threads that give shape to Old Testament theology, including "The Loss and Recovery of Creation in Old Testament Theology,"[40] in which no singular scheme will do. By contrast, much of his earlier writing is characterized by sharp polarities in which the core texts of "Israel's primary memory"[41]—the exodus narrative and its prophetic re-appropriation in the exilic period—stand as a radical counterpoint to royal theology and the power of the conquering state. When Yahweh is enthroned as Israel's king in the existential moment of unfettered praise, fresh interpretation breaks forth in the crucible of conflict between Israel's slave narratives and claims of the oppressor forces within and without the Israelite state.[42]

Brueggemann acknowledges that royal theology is not "necessarily bad theology." Yet he calls for the stinging counter-narrative of Israel's most primal voice in issuing sharp rebuke to the power of the Davidic king to submit to the true king who led and continues to lead his people from tyranny to liberation in the promised land. Without this dialectic between royal power and the slave narrative, the unrestricted tendency of royal power rolls irresistibly "on its way to an absolutizing of the present order."[43] In the expression of his truest character, the God of Israel most identifies with the marginalized, the oppressed, and the enslaved than with agents of the status quo, whether Israel's king or Egypt's Pharaoh. This is the case, even though the dialectical tension between Israel's royal theology and the exodus narrative is never fully resolved.

Between Structure Legitimation and Embrace of Pain

Brueggemann further draws these themes out in the first three chapters of *Old Testament Theology: Essays on Structure, Theme, and Text*. I focus here on the first essay where he posits a bipolar tension between

---

39. Ibid., 11.

40. Brueggemann, "Loss and Recovery of Creation in Old Testament Theology," 83–96.

41. Brueggemann, *Israel's Praise*, 91.

42. Ibid., 29.

43. Ibid., 110.

"structure legitimation" and the "embrace of pain."[44] By structure legitimation, Brueggemann refers to any worldview that associates the authority of God with the legitimization of the social structure. In terms of the ancient Near East, Brueggemann links such legitimation to a "common theology" across nations and civilizations whose god (or gods) "is one who punishes those who offend him or her and rewards those who please him or her." He identifies this in contractual terms based on a "theology of strict retribution." He accepts that "this common theology is all around Israel" and appropriated in distinctively particular ways in Israel's monotheistic identity.[45] Brueggemann's contends that this legitimizing theology was embodied most fully in the Torah (i.e., the Law) and the Davidic monarchy.

Such legitimization was sometimes liberating, particularly in the early "egalitarian" period in Israel's history.[46] Nonetheless, the social and political structures legitimized by the theology of Torah and Monarchy have also resulted in the oppression by the powerful of the marginalized within Israel itself. Such domination required a "*sharp critique*"[47] of the power structure based on Israel's primal narrative of liberation from bondage, which had force as a continuous strain throughout Israel's biblical history. Brueggemann identifies a "key element in this critique" as the embrace and articulation of pain by those so disaffected, expressed most fully in the lament psalms "and in the public outcry that leads to liberation."[48] He maintains that "Israel's faith" is embodied in dynamic "interaction between the *full assertion* of common theology, which is relentlessly contractual, and the *protest against* it." The most dynamic and authentic "moments of faith are the moments of tension between the two."[49]

The dialectic remains unresolved. What is crucial is the "corrective" function of each pole, in which the tension itself "may be the central dynamic of Old Testament faith."[50] Brueggemann positions this tension both

---

44. Brueggemann refers to these terms throughout "Shape for Old Testament Theology I."

45. See ibid., 5–10, for Brueggemann's overview of the ancient near East depiction of a common theology. For quotes, see ibid., 5–6, 8.

46. Ibid., 8. Brueggemann draws heavily on Gottwald, *Tribes of Yahweh*, for his understanding of the relevance of the social structure in its synergistic role in theological formation in early Israel.

47. Brueggemann, "Shape for Old Testament Theology I," 17.

48. Ibid., 18. Brueggemann references Exod 2:23–25: "The Israelites groaned in their slavery and cried out, and their cry for help because of their slavery went up to God. God heard their groaning and he remembered his covenant with Abraham, with Isaac and with Jacob. So God looked on the Israelites and was concerned about them."

49. Brueggemann, "Shape for Old Testament Theology I," 18.

50. Ibid., 2.

within and above the fray of Israel's and human history, a tension resident in the very heart of God, as constructed in the biblical text. Holding the two together is exceedingly difficult work.[51] Yet, it is one that faithfulness to the Old Testament script demands. The dialectic, to which Brueggemann refers, is a pointer to God's ultimate overcoming of Israel's pain and loss against a great deal of power and skepticism to the contrary. The Old Testament literature speaks to such overcoming in the midst of the most profound loss within Israel's narrated history and in God's ultimate coming in the messianic period.

By juxtaposing the canonical perspective of Brevard Childs and the sociological standpoint of Norman Gottwald, Brueggemann sets up a critical *theology* that includes sociological analysis as an essential, often overlooked dimension of the biblical interpretation. In so doing, he seeks to move beyond sociological reductionism toward full theological integrity. Brueggemann shares certain affinities with Childs's quest for comprehensive biblical integrity. Nonetheless, he maintains that the canon is more fluid than Childs allows in placing the Bible "beyond critical dissection and historical development." By contrast, Brueggemann notes that Gottwald's analysis is relentlessly sociological and historically informed. What stands out for him is not only Gottwald's analysis of "societal conflict" in ancient Israel, but the notion that "the canonical literature" embodied the social ideology of the early tribes of Israel, and therefore, reflected "a certain partisan experience of reality."[52]

By incorporating neo-Marxian sociology and the cultural anthropology of Clifford Geertz on the symbolic construction of reality into his perspective,[53] Brueggemann is keenly appreciative of the positive value that a hermeneutics of suspicion opens up to an authentic Bible interpretation. He argues that such an interpretation is discernible within the pages of Scripture and in application to the current climate. In such a reading,

---

51. Brueggemann notes that the "point is not to choose one to the disregard of the other, although holding them together" in dialectical tension "is not easy." Ibid., 3.

52. Ibid. Brueggemann further notes: "With Gottwald, it is important to see that the text has reached its present form and shape by *being in the fray*. These theological claims did not come out of the sky, nor did they have any prior claim to authority; but with Childs it can be argued that the text as we have it is *above the fray*, the fray of historical interaction and historical-critical analysis. Whereas Gottwald is sociologically relentless, Childs is theologically reassuring. That tension is part of the richness of this faith claim and is also part of the problematic that we must study. We know that the Bible is fully engaged in the struggle for faithfulness, and yet at the same time we also claim that it is out of reach of that struggle. I suspect anyone who chooses either Gottwald or Childs alone too easily escapes the issues that must be faced." Ibid.

53. Geertz, *Interpretation of Cultures*.

the theological is inherently political, even as Brueggemann contends that God is both in and beyond the fray of Israel's formative history (and ours). Brueggemann identifies this bipolar struggle within God's very being as the most authentic voice of Israel's religious vision—a God that transcends history while being fully enmeshed within it.

Brueggemann identifies the structure legitimation-embrace of pain dialectic as most pitched in competing creation-royal, exodus-exilic theologies. The reality, as he notes, is more complex in that the theme of structure legitimation undergirding covenant theology is pervasive throughout the Old Testament. It permeates Leviticus, Numbers, Deuteronomy, and the later half of exodus. It is also found throughout the recounted history from Samuel to Nehemiah in the waxing and waning of royal theology.

The contractual mandate of covenant theology is pervasive in much of Job—both in Job's questioning of God in light of his understanding of his own righteousness and as depicted in the speeches of his "friends," who draw implicitly, as well as overtly, on the tight morality strictures of Proverbs. Brueggemann notes that the climactic final chapters of Job challenge this dominant discourse. These later chapters support a common view of Job as a counter-discourse that moves beyond any just reward thesis based on the call to obedience as the basis for God's enacting of the covenant. Nonetheless, the main thread of covenant theology is also operative here in the very nature of Job's questioning of God's purposes and of his own unrequited suffering in light of his own perceived morally upright life. So it is with the prophets, who point to new hope amidst the pain of Israel's tremendous loss of stature in the exile, and thereby fundamentally repositioned the very fabric of the identity of "the chosen people" beyond the land to the messianic vision of New Israel. This literature has a "solid basis in contractual theology," as well, in which, for "the prophets, the entire historical process" of Israel's story "is read through the prism of the law court metaphor."[54] Viewed in this this way, Israel, time and again, came up short of the rigorous strictures of their covenant with God, as depicted throughout the Old Testament.

Brueggemann finds "a basic commitment to *contractual theology*" throughout the Old Testament. He concludes, "If that is foundational to the Mosaic traditions, Deuteronomic theology, the prophets, and the wisdom materials, then we may say that it is the foundational construct for Israel's faith."[55] From an Old Testament perspective, obedience to the law is one's due religious obligation, the failure of which results in negative consequenc-

---

54. Brueggemann, "Shape for Old Testament Theology I," 12.

55. Ibid., 15.

es of varied and many sorts. To short change this reality—which is reflective of the theologies of both testaments (e.g., Rom 6:15–23)—for a too easy theology of grace and forgiveness is nothing less than to give short shrift to one of the dominant themes of the Bible itself.

The Old Testament does offer a counter-narrative, one that Brueggemann places as more primal in significance than the dominant one, at least in terms of God's ultimate relationship to humankind, though for Brueggemann it remains a close call.[56] From the vantage point of the exile, the agony of loss and God's longing quest for reconciliation is ultimately more significant, whether the pain is the result of self-infliction or of oppressive social structures in the domination of the weak by the strong. Brueggemann implies that this is so, even as the covenantal mandate is more textually prevailing, as paradoxical as that may seem. Such longing comes across in the prophetic yearning of Isaiah and Jeremiah for covenant renewal in the midst of the most abject loss. Through the Suffering Servant, God takes in Israel's anguish into his own self; in so doing he provides a fresh resource for hope in the midst of much compelling evidence to the contrary.[57]

Continuity and Discontinuity in an Era of Radical Historical Dislocation

Hope within history is a key signature in the hermeneutical lexicon of Brueggemann's theological vision—God and humankind grappling in the "fray" with the issues of the day where certainties are displaced by risky ventures and new breakthroughs. Brueggemann contends that that the exile—587 BCE as metaphor—had a profound impact on Israel's self-definition as a chosen people. He contends that the exile also "constituted a significant crisis in God's own life"[58] in the need to respond to Israel in light of the grief and loss the event provoked. That signature event turned Israel's world upside down. During the exile, any notion of the Holy Land, as envisioned in the Mosaic Covenant and in the royal lineage of David's legacy, teetered on the verge of annihilation. Brueggemann argues that, in the midst of the "shatter[ing] [of] the old settled categories of Israel's faith," the Major Prophets spoke their powerful voices in radical continuity *and*

---

56. "God's mind is not closed on this question, because God in Israel must decide about the practice of contractual theology and the embrace of pain that permits and requires life outside the contract." Ibid., 19.

57. Even so the dialectical tension between the law and God's gracious response to Israel's pain remains unresolved in the agonized mind and heart of God. Ibid.

58. Brueggemann, "Shattered Transcendence?," 188.

discontinuity of Israel's covenantal tradition. This led to new hope against "abandonment of faith or . . . despair"[59] when the world that was known by Israel could no longer hold. The prophets maintained a sharp-edged focus on covenantal theology. Yet they also issued a new promise of God's gracious forgiveness and maternal nurturance of forlorn Israel in the midst of her seemingly irredeemable loss.

The crisis evoked by the exile was the extent to which "the character of Yahweh continued to be the same character in, and through, and beyond the exile," or the extent to which "the character of God is decisively changed by the crisis of exile; that is, if God ceases to be in some crucial way who this God was heretofore."[60] According to Brueggemann, this remains an open issue in the prophetic texts. In either case, "the displacement and suffering of exile break something of God's own self, both permitting and requiring Yahweh to be presented in a different way."[61] Brueggemann poignantly links such redemptive suffering to the homecoming imagery of Second Isaiah.

> For a brief moment I abandoned you, but with deep compassion I will bring you back. In a surge of anger I hid my face from you for a moment, but with everlasting kindness I will have compassion on you, says the Lord your redeemer. (Isa 54:7–9)

Brueggemann contends that in this passage God actually abandoned Israel. The "abandonment by God was . . . without qualification." It was "massive, total, and decisive."[62] The break was for a moment, but in that moment God hid his face from his chosen people. The impact of such abandonment was sufficiently decisive to crush God's heart and to commit himself to his beloved "with an everlasting kindness" (Isa 54:8b). In line with his dialectical theology, Brueggemann contends that the scriptural evidence on the relationship between continuity and discontinuity is inscrutably ambiguous; it is ultimately hidden in the opaqueness of God's infinite mind.[63] Whether continuous or discontinuous with the Mosaic and Davidic legacies, what emerges in the prophetic literature is sufficiently new for a fresh imaginative encounter of the relationship between God and Israel in the hope of a

---

59. Ibid., 188, 185.

60. Ibid., 188.

61. Ibid., 188–89. Brueggemann draws on Deut 4:23–31, Isa 54:7–10, and Jer 31:35–37 to discuss the relationship of continuity and discontinuity in God's response to Israel before, during, and after the exile.

62. Ibid., 194.

63. "It is for Israel a close call; whether or not the . . . break for Yahweh determines continuity or discontinuity for Israel." Ibid., 195.

new covenant built upon a more enduring basis than the justice/retribution model of the old.

Whatever the impact of the exile on the character of the Old Testament God, Brueggemann is highly suspicious of "settled" theologies that tend to exempt divinity from the ravages of the historical process. Consequently, the character of Yahweh appeared in some profoundly new ways that "permit[ted] God to become toward Israel whom God [previously] was not."[64] Brueggemann maintains that what emerges in the prophetic literature is a radically new level in degree of God's compassion beyond the retributive boundaries of the Mosaic covenant system, though never in total repudiation of the law. He asserts that the issues surrounding the exile are as relevant to our own historical moment as to that of Ancient Israel. They are also prototypical of the New Testament interpretation of faith "recast in the form of crucifixion and resurrection."[65]

CONCLUDING REFLECTIONS ON BRUEGGEMANN'S THEOLOGY OF SCRIPTURE

Imaginative construal underlies Brueggemann's bipolar theology of Scripture. By this, he refers to the capacity to re-envision God's revelation with a zest and freshness that overcomes the many counter narratives that hold an alluring pull on the constructed thoughts that give shape to more dominant worldviews, whether in the ancient Near East or the contemporary period. His emphasis on imagination is not meant to diminish the role of the biblical text, which Brueggemann accepts as the ultimate baseline of Judaic and Christian faith. As he states in the spirit of 2 Timothy 3:16:

> The task of retexting requires the scribal preacher to be a textman or a text-woman, to engage in study, to trust the text and be led by the text, to have confidence that the text, in all its vagaries and complexities, in all its characteristic and confounding cadences merits our primal attention as a word of life. This perspective requires that we submit our modernist rationalistic assumptions to the text and, even when the text sounds in violence and all of its unbearable harshness or other objectionable

---

64. Ibid., 200. Brueggemann notes that "the tone of God's speech toward Israel is dramatically transformed through this terrible jeopardy that God shares with Israel." Ibid.

65. Ibid., 183. In *Hopeful Imagination*, Brueggemann "seeks to make a hermeneutical move to our own theological situation by drawing a 'dynamic equivalent' between Israel's exilic situation and that of the American church." *Hopeful Imagination*, ix.

cadence, still to assume that engagement with this text is a primal engagement out of which comes missional energy, imagination, and identity. To be sure, such engagement with the text does not consist in blind acceptance of the text. Such engagement evokes, as well as assent, desperation and protest. Nonetheless, such engagement makes possible a new field of freedom and courage.[66]

Brueggemann's emphasis here is on the freedom and courage to imagine with fresh power nothing less than God's counter world against the seemingly more viable world constructions of a given dominant world order. Thus, in addition to "attentiveness to the text," effective preaching also "requires attentiveness to the listening congregation in a particular way." This includes paying heed to the largely "*textless*" reality pervasive in contemporary mainline denominations, the "'expressive, experiential' perspective, which believes that one can live out of one's autonomous experience without any text."[67]

On the postmodern assumption that there is nothing beyond the text, Brueggemann refers to "the *weak, thin text* of technological, therapeutic, military consumerism that is an odd mix of moralism, market ideology, self-congratulations, and anxiety."[68] His reference here is to the "American way of life," which has a pervasive textual power on the imaginative formation of many of those who habituate the pews of mainline congregations, notwithstanding some faint or more earnest hope to hear an authentic word from the biblical text. If it is the authentic Word rather than some ersatz similitude that breaks into the settled reality of the middle class congregants, the preached text has the capacity to exert its power in perhaps the only way it can—in the immediacy of the revelatory moment in creating space for new revelation.

Given the fragmenting dislocations of our contemporary period, such breakthroughs take place at the critical edges of the dominant world constructions in a manner that will likely have effect only at the far from unimportant margins. It is an open question for Brueggemann whether a more coherent Christian worldview ultimately emerges through such constructive work. He places his more immediate focus on the power of "the third world of evangelical imagination" to create fresh space amidst the settled

---

66. Brueggemann, "Proclamatory Confrontations," 37. By "retexting," Brueggemann means reinterpreting older texts in light of the contingencies of any current context such as Esra's reading of the Torah (Neh 8:1–2) or the prophetic reading of the Deuteronomic law in light of the "shattered transcendence" of the Babylonian exile. Ibid., 36. The quoted phrase is from Brueggemann's essay, "Shattered Transcendence?"

67. Brueggemann, "Proclamatory Confrontations," 37.

68. Ibid.

realities of the dominant social order and the anxiety experienced in the mainline pews among those resigned to seek their place within it.[69]

There is an exaggerated rhetoric in the parallel that Brueggemann draws between the metaphor of 587 BCE and the shattering of the Enlightenment worldview of the liberal intellectual culture of the West. As Brueggemann notes, a great deal of the constructed force of the modern worldview collapsed as a result of the political, economic, social, intellectual, and cultural upheavals in the preceding 150 years. The theological significance of this breakdown was, perhaps, no more poignantly depicted than in the paradoxical ruminations of Reinhold Niebuhr.[70] The crisis of the post-1960s era further intensified centrifugal forces in society and culture. Still, the claim that the postmodern era represents a fundamental break with modernity ignores the enduring influence of the fundamental tenets of rationalism, technology, belief in progress, and secularism in the contemporary period. This is, so even with the end of cultural hegemony which underplays the ways in which the dominant threads of modernity became assimilated into a broad array of countercultural and postmodern perspectives. This is the case, even with the loosening of personal identity and the wider acceptance of the value of pluralism, traits commonly linked with postmodernism—tendencies that are built into the most fundamental precepts of "late modernist" epistemology.[71]

There is a certain caricature in Brueggemann's analysis. Perhaps it is an unavoidable feature of his theology, which is not to argue against the value of the many keen insights that flow from his illuminating essays. Brueggemann softens his own rhetoric in his less polemic moments. Nonetheless, his dialectical theology is characterized by "an overly simplistic polarization"[72] that masks some of the more subtle nuances missing in the analogy he draws between the ancient Israelite exile and the postmodern deconstruction of the Enlightenment worldview. His many "angular" readings of the biblical text and his countless contemporary applications are made with much rhetorical power. Even so, the dialectical polarity between structure legitimation and embrace of pain creates an exaggerated rift against the possibility of an ulti-

---

69. Brueggemann, "Third World of Evangelical Imagination," 9–27.

70. For Niebuhr's acute analysis of the relationship between early and mid-twentieth-century US and Western culture and his neo-orthodox assessment of Calvinist theology, see *Interpretation of Christian Ethics*; *Moral Man and Immoral Society*; *Beyond Tragedy*; and *Irony of American History*. In chapter 7, I subtitle the section on Niebuhr "Reinhold Niebuhr's 'Impossible Possibility.'"

71. For two influential studies on implications for the middle class self in "late modernity," see Giddens, *Modernity and Self-Identity*; Kegan, *In Over Our Heads*.

72. Sharp, "Trope of 'Exile' and the Displacement of Old Testament Theology," 161.

mate harmonization in the biblical canon, as variously advocated by Packer, Bloesh, and Fackre. The extent to which such harmonization is ultimately viable is an ongoing question in contemporary biblical hermeneutics; I do not want to close off the possibility that it may be so. I will continue to assess the strengths and limitations of Brueggemann's Old Testament hermeneutics through the remainder of this chapter.

ISRAEL'S TESTIMONY CONCERNING YAHWEH IN LIEU OF A MORE FORMAL THEOLOGY OF GOD

I have alluded to Brueggemann's theology of God in much of this discussion. A key point includes the need to bracket ontological claims in order to focus imaginatively on the God who speaks with dramatic power at the interface between Scripture and history in the immediacy of each and every moment of personal and public time. This God revealed in the midst of Israel's narrated history sides with the marginalized and oppressed, as reflected in its most representational themes in the exodus, exile, and cross. This is the case even as the revelation—inexorably mixed with much ideological self-interest—is also embedded in what Brueggemann refers to as more power-centered creation and royal theologies. Given the inescapable ambiguity of human history, the God of Israel sometimes changes his mind in response to new situations, including the insistent pleading of key individuals at selective climatic moments. In Brueggemann's view, this God characteristically reveals himself through terse dialectics, in response to the various antinomies of the human experience, where nothing is indubitably certain and all is potentially at risk.

Brueggemann accepts the radical sovereignty of God revealed in the Old Testament as his most enduring quality, in which any "finished portrayal" is impossible for a God who comes to human actors in the midst of history and takes the subject of his action with radical seriousness.[73] The ineradicable gap between the unfathomable depth and breadth of God and the unique revelation inexplicitly given to Israel remains inherently fragile, particularly in times of the most compelling stress. Re-negotiation, as a stimulant to revitalization, is required if the dynamic of faith is to remain vitally alive in response to the contingencies of the flow of historical change. In the process, matters of risky venture and theological re-definition are inescapable.

---

73. Brueggemann, *Theology of the Old Testament*, 206.

For Brueggemann, such emphasis on "*processes, procedures,* and *interactionist potential*"[74] of the relationship between Israel and Israel's God leads to the courtroom metaphor through which he constructs his opus magnum, *Theology of the Old Testament: Testimony, Dispute, Advocacy*. In this key text, testimony and countertestimony (dispute) are sharply pitted. By testimony, Brueggemann refers to the declarative statements of the sovereign power of God, as reflected in much of the Torah, which he identifies as the Old Testament's normative speech. By countertestimony, Brueggemann refers to the collective witness of Israel in the lament of exile, where Israel and Israel's God speak in a very different cadence—one that cannot be easily reconciled with God's normative speech—where Israel talks back to the God of the Torah out of the depth of her pain and loss.

In a dramatic sense, everything is put at stake in response to the contingency of historical change and the dynamics of human decision making as played out in and through the stream of time. This dialectical tension between testimony and dispute in Israel's narrated story leads to advocacy in the midst of rebirth that bursts forth in the stream of time only after the most profound loss, as reflected paradigmatically in the theology of the exile. What emerged in the prophetic vision was not a synthesis in any enduring sense, but a temporal reconstruction which allowed faith to flourish in a manner authentic to the Torah in a way that brought out new accents, such as the suffering servant (Isaiah), the new covenant (Jeremiah), and the holy city (Ezekiel). Such imagery, in all of its poignancy and pathos, gave fresh vitality to a faith that had veered perilously close to extinction—as narrated by the text—because of Israel's persistent faithlessness. Such a counterassertion took tremendous imagination—to say nothing of courage—in the persisting faithfulness of the prophets to hold up a vision of New Jerusalem against the onslaught of a persisting Babylonian reality brought about by Israel's backsliding, as the wrath of God poured into the living reality of a disobedient people.

Despair and abject surrender to the new reality may have been the more realistic response. Yet, what Brueggemann depicts is the daring prophetic countervoice, that—whatever the ontological reality of God's eternal purposes may have been—was anything but assured at the level of history and drama. As Brueggemann sees it, only by giving full weight to historical reality that the exile forced upon Israel would the ontological reality of God's enduring presence, as reflected in the prophetic voice, have penetrated the phenomenological exigencies of Israel's plight, as it found itself in an utterly new context. Stated in related terms, when the promised land of New

---

74. Ibid., xvi.

Canaan was no longer in Israel's possession, faith [re-]formation had to take place in some radically new ways.

In Brueggemann's courtroom metaphor, Israel's various "testimonies" are sharply juxtaposed, with a strong accent on contradictory evidence, as portrayed in the voice of Israel's God. The discussion is constructed along four major parts: Israel's core testimony, Israel's countertestimony, Israel's unsolicited testimony, and Israel's embodied testimony. I concentrate on the pivotal first two in my main discussion of Brueggemann's theology of God, while focusing on the latter two in a less structured manner. His opus includes a stimulating two chapter overview of critical issues in Old Testament scholarship—for the most part throughout the twentieth century—the gist of which has been embedded in my discussion up to this point. The book concludes with brief commentary on the relationship of Old Testament theology to critical issues related to historical criticism, the New Testament and church theology, the relationship to Jewish theology, and to themes of social justice.[75]

ISRAEL'S CORE TESTIMONY

At the outset, Brueggemann notes that "the primal subject of Old Testament theology is . . . God."[76] In this nonnegotiable stance, he takes a foundational position in the radical acceptance that there is ultimately no truth beyond that revealed in, and through, Scripture, however tenuous may be any human capacity to grasp such a transcendent claim. In this uncompromised grounding in Israel's core testimony, Brueggemann exhibits his purest evangelical and Reformed impulses. However, he seeks to distinguish himself from his characterization of a wide swath of traditional Protestant theology by rejecting the notion that the Old Testament provides a "coherent and comprehensive" picture of God, particularly as "classically understood as Being or Substance."[77] Informed by a searing postmodern sensibility, Brueggemann points out that "this subject matter is more difficult, complex and problematic than we might expect."[78]

---

75. See Perdue's excellent synopsis of *Theology of the Old Testament* in his review essay, "Adhering to Israel's God."

76. Brueggemann, *Theology of the Old Testament*, 117.

77. Ibid., 126.

78. Ibid., 117. In reference to the God of Israel, he states that *"the elusive, but dominating Subject of the Old Testament cannot be comprehended in any preconceived categories."* Ibid.

Brueggemann is well aware that there can be no merely textual reading based on an unadulterated authorial understanding of the text. For this reason, he acknowledges that philosophical probing into the character and definition of God is epistemologically inescapable. However elusive—and problematic—the effort may be, Brueggemann's quest to peel back extratextual layers serves as a core strategy that enables him to structure his courtroom model of dramatic narrative presentation. This includes God speaking through weighty sentences with strong verbs that attest to Yahweh's action in Israel and throughout the world and "direct objects" of the "subject" of such sentences, variously defined as Israel, the nations of the Near East, or creation itself.[79] Such mighty acts of God gain some of Brueggemann's most prescient attention.

Brueggemann's stated aversion to formal theological reflection might be seen as a rhetorical strategy against what I believe is one of his major targets—the importation of Greek philosophy into the New Testament.[80] He maintains that it is this that provides the early church with a speculative metaphysics that grounds such concepts as the incarnation and the Trinity. Whether this is actually the case, what is clear is Brueggemann's suspicion of absolute claims as indicative in a great deal of the New Testament, particularly any supersessionist interpretation of Jesus as Lord, "whereby Jewish religious claims are overridden in the triumph of Christian claims."[81] Brueggemann rejects any unequivocal embrace of a predominant New Testament claim that "Jesus is the embodiment and fulfillment of Israel's normative revelatory literature through whom all of Israel's hopes now come to bodily fruition." Rather, he takes a "more critical and distanced reflection" that "might make it possible to see that Jesus is understood as *one* fruition of the durable expectation of Israel's hope."[82]

Brueggemann is skeptical of Childs's proposal of a biblical theology based on the "Christian Bible," consisting of its two related yet far from easily reconcilable testaments. Childs posits that both testaments possess their

---

79. Ibid., 125.

80. Brueggemann maintains that "the Jewish markings of elusiveness, materiality, and concreteness that belong to the very character of Yahweh . . . are most problematic for Hellenized, Enlightenment Christianity." Ibid., 730.

81. Ibid., 729. See also Brueggemann, "Contemporary Old Testament Theology." "Insofar as Old Testament theology is Christian, it is still deeply problematic to assume uncritically that the text leads directly to or can be delivered innocently for the classic formulations of Chalcedon, that is Trinitarian and incarnational claims. It may be that these linkages can be voiced afresh, but we must recognize that such linkages are not easy or obvious, and surely must be dealt with in an awareness of their contested quality." Ibid., 120.

82. Brueggemann, *Introduction to the Old Testament*, 260, 26, italics added.

own distinctive integrity. At the same time, he maintains that the ultimate grounding of the entire biblical canon is based on the fundamental presuppositions of the Christian kerygma to which both testaments, in their distinctive ways, contribute. He also argues that biblical, historical, and systematic theology need to mutually inform each other in an ongoing process of clarification grounded in the presuppositions of faith in search of greater knowledge.[83] Rather than rejecting speculative metaphysics, Childs maintains that it is better to accept it as a resource in the ongoing quest for clarity in linking the core kerygma of Christ revealed as God incarnate within the context of any and every historical time. This includes dialectical probing of the two testaments, both in the development of their distinctive canonical trajectories and in the Christian Bible's final form, in terms of the relationship between promise and fulfillment, as exhibited in the temporality of historical experience.[84]

Despite a somewhat underdeveloped New Testament reading, in seeking to place the text center stage, Brueggemann enacts the most basic principle of the Reformed tradition—the sovereignty of God as mediated through the Bible. Nonetheless, there is no pure reading of the text in that the perpetual quest for contextualization requires grappling with the relationship between biblical, historical, and systematic theology, a critical

---

83. Childs, *Biblical Theology of the Old and New Testaments*, 55–69. See 65–67 for various references to the "Christian Bible."

84. Ibid., 77–79. Childs notes: "The two testaments have been linked as Old and New, but this designation does not mean that the integrity of each testament has been destroyed. The Old Testament bears its true witness as the Old which remains distinct from the New. It is promise not fulfillment. Yet its voice continues to sound and it has not been stilled by the fulfillment of the promise." Ibid., 77. As Childs further argues, "a major task of Biblical Theology is to reflect on the whole Christian Bible with its two very different voices, both of which the church confesses bear witness to Jesus Christ. There is no overarching hermeneutical theory by which to resolve the tension between the testimony of the Old Testament in its own right and the New Testament with its transformed Old Testament. Yet the challenge of Biblical Theology is to engage in continued activity of theological reflection which studies the canonical text in detailed exegesis, and seeks to do justice to the witness of both testaments in the light of its subject matter who is Jesus Christ." Ibid., 78–79. For Brueggemann's discussion of the relationship between the Old and New Testament see, *Old Testament Theology*, 729–33, esp. the following: "Old Testament theology . . . must prepare the material and fully respect the interpretive connections made in the New Testament and the subsequent church; but not make those connections, precisely because the connections are not to be found in the testimony of ancient Israel, but in the subsequent work of imaginative construal that lies behind the text of the Old Testament." For that reason, "the task of Old Testament theology, as a Christian enterprise, is to articulate, explicate, mobilize, and make available the testimony of the Old Testament in all its polyphonic, elusive, imaginative power and offer it to the church for its continuing work of construal toward Jesus." Ibid., 732.

directional focus that grounds Childs's work as well as Brueggemann's when taking into account the latter's various exegeses, expositions, and apologetic probing.[85]

Through his critical scholarship Brueggemann acknowledges this tension, even as his underlying purpose remains fresh interpretation of the primary narrative in a manner that does justice to the various contexts in which it is situated and appropriated. In this, he is first and foremost a narrative Old Testament scholar seeking to explicate Israel's God in the midst of the wide range of contexts, ancient and modern, which influence the shaping, direction, and significance of the text. There is much in this to which Childs agrees. The key difference is that Brueggemann is more of a dialectical Old Testament scholar who focuses on the disjunctions and points of seemingly irreconcilable tension not only manifest in the biblical text, but in the very character of God, as portrayed.

The "Character" that both Israel and we have come to know is the God who speaks in Scripture through the various witnesses that give testimony to his presence within the contestable stream of human history.[86] Brueggemann claims that for "Old Testament faith, *"utterance is everything."*[87] This is not mere speech, but the very presence of God breaking forth in the midst of human experience in the varied ways that he does, whether through praise, devotion, processed pain, or intense study. The presence of God's holy utterance makes it possible for Israel to grasp something of the ontological reality that underlies his elusive presence. Brueggemann accepts the sovereign reality of the God revealed in Israel's text that is both transcendently majestic and intimately invested in the fate of the human story. He does so, even as these mutual tendencies of God's core characteristics are not easily reconcilable. In terms of epistemology, Brueggemann maintains that human understanding cannot go beyond testimony and witness in the acceptance, on faith, of God's ontological reality, which works through and transcends human perception. Brueggemann accepts this latter claim as ultimately foundational for faith, even if, *for us,* "speech is the reality to be

---

85. According to Childs, "What is now required is fruitful cooperation, not only between these two fields [systematic and biblical theology], but among a whole variety of other disciplines which impinge on the study of the Bible, such as philosophical, literary, and historical scholarship." *Biblical Theology of the Old and New Testaments*, 89. Notwithstanding Brueggemann's rhetorical strategy to let the Old Testament narrative speak on its on its own terms, he is in accord with Childs on the synergistic relationship between a broad array of critical academic disciplines and biblical theology. See *Theology Old the Old Testament*, 61–114.

86. Brueggemann refers to the God of Israel as the "central Character" of the Old Testament. *Theology of the Old Testament*, 87 and elsewhere.

87. Brueggemann, *Theology of the Old Testament*, 122.

studied," the most viable pathway into God's elusive presence whose back, at most, we may be given an occasional glimpse.[88]

What comes across here is the depth and range of Brueggemann's probing of the nexus between God's incomparable sovereignty and his persisting fidelity to Israel. At its core is the centrality of covenantal relationship in the joining of Israel's exodus narrative and the creational theme of God's primary ordering of the world. This is brought out most extensively in Brueggemann's discussion of "the God who creates."[89] Israel's core testimony is also exhibited by "the God who makes promises,"[90] "the God who delivers,"[91] "the God who commands,"[92] and "the God who leads."[93] To provide some sense of the ways that Brueggemann understands the power of Israel's testimony through God's "verbal sentences," I focus on his discussion of the God who commands, which he identifies as "the foremost mode by which Yahweh communicates to Israel."[94]

In its most elemental expression, God's authority is "understood" in terms of "an utterance of a lordly sovereign who has a legitimate right to command, who expects rightly to be obeyed, and who has the power to match legitimacy in order to force the commands." Brueggemann does not equivocate on this core testimony. His view here resonates with the most fundamental heart pulse of traditional evangelical and Reformed theology. Only a God of such awesome power and majesty is worth obeying. Not to do so is to cut oneself off from the most viable source of life accessible to humankind in the known universe. Whatever common theology may have been pervasive in the ancient world, it was Israel to whom this God was revealed, which "is the community that understands itself as bound in this relationship of obedience," whether "in glad compliance," or in active "resistance and recalcitrance to Yahweh's command."[95] As depicted throughout the Old Testament, the dialectical relationship between obedience and rebellion defines Israel relationship to her God.

The Decalogue (Exod 20:1–17) grounds the core of God's commands both to the entire human race and to his royal people, those called out of slavery—whether of their own internal chains or of Pharaoh's oppressive

---

88. Ibid., 118.
89. Ibid., 145–64.
90. Ibid., 164–73.
91. Ibid., 173–81.
92. Ibid., 181–201.
93. Ibid., 201–5.
94. Ibid., 145, 181.
95. Ibid., 182.

rule—to enter the promised land of full restoration under the pathways of God's life affirming sovereignty. Such unequivocal fidelity is required *just because* this God "*deabsolutizes every other claimant to ultimate power*"[96] to which anything less than full commitment of heart, mind, strength, and soul is idolatry of the first order, with consequences to bear onto the third and fourth generations. At the center of such faithfulness is the command to holiness in reverence to God's sovereignty and to the formation of a civic polity within Israel that promotes justice among the poor and oppressed, those still coming out of bondage requiring new exodus in the unique contexts of their own historical settings. Stated epigraphically, the call to the obedient life is "to act justly and to love mercy and to walk humbly with your God" (Mic 6:8).

Brueggemann draws on the Sabbath to demonstrate the correlation of the two primary commands. Thus, in Exodus 20:10, "*we find at the core of creation the invitation to rest*." The foundation of holiness is reflected in the absolute reverence of God in the First Commandment's unequivocal call to loyalty to the one true God and in the Fourth Commandment mandate of solemn Sabbath rest. In its Deuteronomic version, the Sabbath is a perpetual reminder and memorial of being brought out of slavery by "a mighty hand and an outstretched arm" (Deut 5:15b).[97] This example interweaves the calling of Israel to an orderly life within the inexhaustible nature of God's life-affirming covenantal boundaries of holiness and justice; the God who gives life-breathing shape to the elemental chaos of the created order.

In this respect, creation motifs are an expansive metaphor for Israel's called destination to re-establish the world to its pristine harmonization and beauty. The God of Israel seeks this both for the created order and for a redeemed humanity under the aegis of a new covenant restoration where "all will know me, from the least . . . to the greatest" in a new world order where "I will forgive their wickedness, and will remember their sin no more" (Jer 31:34b–c). Thus, Sabbath rest—which needs to be understood in its various Old and New Testament motifs—underscores the foundational commandment of absolute fidelity to God almighty in the rejection of "other gods" which creeps into Israel's experience as they do our own.

As the leitmotif of all of Israel's core testimony "the commands, rightly understood, are not restraints as much as they are empowerments," allowing Israel "to participate in the ongoing revolution of turning the world to its true shape as God's creation." The commandments, as well as all of Israel's core testimony, can be only understood from the vantage point of the

96. Ibid., 184.
97. Ibid., 185.

covenantal bond between God and Israel. It is this intrinsic desire for right relationship to the Holy One, as articulated most fully, perhaps, in Psalm 119, which militates against any "caricature of command as legalism,"[98] given a God who feels the full depth of human experience in the midst of Israel's narrated story in both triumph and exile.

ISRAEL'S COUNTERTESTIMONY

Brueggemann argues that the Old Testament's core testimony of the mighty acts and commands of God could no longer gain traction as convincing discourse as Israel went through various disjunctions before, during, and after the Babylonian exile. A different linguistic construction between the boldness of the normative claims of the Torah and the reality of the Israel's lived experience was needed, if the very notion of God as depicted in the Pentateuch was going to find resonance in the prophetic era. Brueggemann argues that after Marx, Freud, the deconstructive discourse of French philosopher Jacques Derrida, and most poignantly, the Holocaust, a similar reconstructive language is required to give force to any viable theistic vision of the God of the Old and New Testament in our contemporary context.

As a first level countertestimony discourse, Brueggemann draws extensively on the wisdom literature, particularly Psalms and Proverbs, to reference the hiddenness of God. Throughout his discussion, he maintains that the Old Testament's emphasis on God's hiddenness is "an alternative mode of theological speech." Such hiddenness adds depth and range to the more primary discourse, which, when taken together, reflects a more complete range of speech in the articulation of God's presence in the midst of Israel's narrated history. As he notes, any reasonably informed student of the Bible would be hard pressed not to "recognize that the Old Testament articulates more than one way of doing theology."[99] This is an important acknowledgment. If that were the whole of it, Brueggemann's contention of placing God's hiddenness within the category of *countertestimony* in support of his bipolar thesis would be less than fully warranted by the evidence.

In his discussion on this topic, Brueggemann lays out a wide range of scriptural examples that illustrate a more subtle textual representation than the active verbal sentences characteristic of God's mighty acts in history. The language is more plaintive, subtle, and elusive, as depicted in Proverbs 16:1–2:

---

98. Ibid., 200.
99. Ibid., 335.

> The plans of the mind belong to mortals, but the answer of the tongue is from the Lord. All one's way may be pure in one's own eyes, but the Lord weighs the spirit (Prov 16:1–2, WB's translation).

> The human mind may devise many plans, but it is the purpose of the Lord that will be established (Prov 19:21, WB's translation).[100]

As Brueggemann explains this apparently enigmatic discourse:

> An authoritative human act or decision is set alongside and contradicted by a counter-act or decision on the part of Yahweh. The effect of the contrast is to assert that human acts, even "deeds" that produce "consequences," are penultimate. What is ultimate and decisive are the predisposition and inclination of Yahweh, who may override human intentionality and therefore deny a deed its anticipated consequence—that is, break the moral certainty given by the "deeds-consequences" construct.[101]

"Yahweh's hiddenness is commonly understood as an affirmation of Yahweh's providence." Yet, Brueggemann places it in the broad category of countertestimony in positing that the more "direct and visible ways of Yahweh's working were not adequate and credible for much of Israel's life."[102] As he elsewhere notes:

> I have no particular disagreement with the notion of wisdom as [simply] an alternative model of theological speech. But I am here seeking to understand the Old Testament in terms of testimony [i.e., dialectics], so I advance the notion of wisdom as an alternative in order to suggest that wisdom is not simply an unrelated, second effort, but is an attempt to speak of Yahweh in all those contexts of Israel's lived experience wherein the main claims of the core testimony are not persuasive.[103]

As Brueggemann further argues, the sharp juxtaposition between core and counter-discourse, as experienced in and through the stream of the Old Testament's narrated history, breathed authenticity into Israel's God talk. The hiddenness of God as articulated, for example, in Deuteronomy 29:29, is refashioned through a more elusive, yet more believable rhetoric that

---

100. Ibid., 349.
101. Ibid.
102. Ibid., 352.
103. Ibid., 335.

takes into account the dislocating experience of the exile. In Brueggemann's own poetic diction:

> *Where now is your God?* Here and everywhere, but in ways that one cannot administer.
>
> *How long?* Until I am ready.
>
> *Why have you forsaken?* My reasons are my own and will not be given you.
>
> *Is Yahweh among us?* Yes, in decisive ways, but not in ways that will suit you.[104]

As Brueggemann notes, these are haunting questions, although one may argue that such elusiveness is built into the very fabric of the Torah in the very travails of the wilderness toward the Holy Land. As posited by Grudem, an evangelical theologian, all "the words of the Bible are God's words" in which the various discourses need to be posed and juxtaposed in light of what they shed in relation to changing contexts wherein "*God responds differently to different situations.*"[105] Brueggemann does not disagree, even as his hermeneutics do not require an ultimate textual harmonization, as posited by traditional evangelical theology, and allows for a greater diversity of discourse, including scope for greater discordance within the speech and very mind of God.

Brueggemann raises the stakes in highlighting the ambiguity and negativity of God's articulated voice, in which core testimony and countertestimony are more sharply contrasted. In this increasingly problematic shift in the character and language of God, "Yahweh emerges not only as hidden . . . but also on occasion as devious, ambiguous, irascible, and unstable." Thus, under the category of ambiguity, Brueggemann identifies the attributes of God's "abusiveness, contradictory conduct, and unreliability."[106]

As a case in point, Brueggemann draws on Jeremiah 20:7 as his core text: "O Lord, You have deceived me, and I was deceived; you have overpowered me, and prevailed." He notes that the original Hebrew (*pth*) meaning "deceived," also holds a second meaning linked to "illicit religious affection," which is treated in the Old Testament as "a sexual metaphor of promiscuity that violates one's proper loyalty."[107] In the Jeremiah text, Brueggemann argues that the key passage (as well as a good deal of the entire chapter) is

---

104. Ibid., 357.
105. Grudem, *Bible Doctrine*, 40, 74.
106. Brueggemann, *Theology of the Old Testament*, 359.
107. Ibid., 360.

"uttered by a voice that reflects profound disturbance." There is much within the text that bears this out, where the writer is "assult[ed] and reproache[d] all day long," confronted as he was with much "whispering" and "terror on every side." Like Job in his severest moments of affliction, Jeremiah cursed the day in which he was born. He was consumed for his faithfulness to God with an overwhelming burden of "trouble and sorrow" (vv. 8c, 10, 14, 18). Brueggemann notes that the same Hebraic word is used in Hosea 2, where the pivotal passage in v. 14 can be linked to metaphors of nurturing, homecoming, and unconditional love, notwithstanding the abject repudiation of the scorned lover Yahweh, as found in the first half of the chapter.[108]

Brueggemann ups the ante by drawing out "feminist hermeneutical considerations" to critically examine authorial motivations in using the same term (*pth*) in Jeremiah 20:7 and Hosea 2:14 for the NRSV translated "enticed" and "allure," respectively, in which "love-making implied here [Hosea] includes deceptions of exaggeration and overstatement." Based on this reading, "Yahweh is at least available for the types of deception characteristic of passionate love."[109] Pushing further, Brueggemann wonders whether the language, reflecting the strong possibility of God's deceptiveness with those he allegedly loves best (the prophet and fallen Israel), "also speaks something forcible, coercive, or violent about Yahweh." Noting the likely exaggeration of the feminist analysis in the spousal imagery critique in Hosea, Brueggemann nonetheless "wonder[s] what the poet intends us to imagine happens in the hidden places where the relationship is restored. Is wife-Israel willing? Or did she have no alternative" but to go back to an abusive relationship because of empty promises and nowhere else to go? Brueggemann suggests that throughout the twentieth chapter in Jeremiah, there is a strong lingering likelihood of being "forcibly, deceptively, abusively pressed into a relationship for loyalty toward Yahweh" in which Jeremiah's compliance reflects masochistic tendencies. As Brueggemann presses the argument, Jeremiah had little choice but to respond to a rather dubious "relationship for loyalty in which Yahweh has not been fair, supportive, or constructive."[110]

This is tough rhetoric. Any literal reading of what Brueggemann is suggesting at this point is subject to searing criticism from various evangelical, Reformed, conservative Catholic, and Eastern Orthodox perspectives on the principle argument that Brueggemann treats these texts in a profoundly reductionist manner. That would be the case, particularly if Brueggemann

---

108. Ibid., 361.
109. Ibid.
110. Ibid., 362.

meant for such an interpretation to stand alone as an ultimate statement. This is not his intent when taking the wider thematic project in *Theology of the Old Testament* into account. His broader aim is to lay out something of the problematic nature of—in the case of Jeremiah—the severity of the struggle through which the prophet issued his polemics. This, in turn, points to the perilous nature of so doing in the light of very convincing claims to the contrary in a milieu where God's mighty acts of intervention had zero sum credibility in the exilic era. The post-exilic prophets still grappled with the core claims of Torah faith, yet they required another hermeneutic, born out of anguish, oppression, and the severest of self-doubts. Such attributes were not missing altogether from Moses, but the prevailing sense of triumphal overcoming is almost completely foreign in Jeremiah's rhetoric.

Rather, the very undergirding of the Torah faith in the promised land was torn asunder. The radically changed context required a new covenant where remnant faith would emerge through penultimate fidelity to Babylon in the God ordained work of building up the captor's city (Jer 29:5–7). Jeremiah's covenantal reconstruction reconstituted the very viability of the continuation of the Mosaic tradition, however much in a new covenant key. Brueggemann's broader intent is to demonstrate that this was a far from foregone conclusion. The profound grappling of the nexus between faith and culture in the cataclysmic events surrounding 587 BCE required a tremendous act of faithful imagination in which Jeremiah, in much angst and tribulation, bore witness, more than often despite himself.[111]

I cannot follow Brueggemann's discussion of "Yahweh and Negativity" in depth. I simply note that this is the sharpest dialectical counterpoint to the powerful affirmations of what he describes as Yahweh's core testimony. His reference points are key passages in the complaint laments, such as Psalms 35, 39, 60, and 88, "Yahweh's capacity for violence"[112] as interspersed throughout the Torah, the prophetic emphasis on God's abandonment of Israel, Job on the issue of theodicy, and Ecclesiastics, which he refers to as "the far edge of negativity."[113] What is depicted in such texts is the seemingly "drastic rejection of Israel by Yahweh," what Brueggemann refers to as "a decisive and irreversible reality in Israel's self-discernment." In short, "what Israel has been given by Yahweh"—promised land and a favored

---

111. Brueggemann, *Hopeful Imagination*, 10–47.

112. Brueggemann, *Theology of the Old Testament*, 381, bold print and caps removed.

113. Ibid., 393.

relationship—"is now matched by what Israel has suffered at the hands of Yahweh."[114]

According to Brueggemann, God's apparent rejection of Yahweh's own claims in the core testimony were likely the result of some combination of Israel's violation of the covenant with "the inordinate fury of Yahweh . . . incommensurate" with the depth and range of Israel's disobedience (e.g., Deut 28). To these imponderables, Brueggemann adds the inescapable reality of "the hubristic self-assertion of Babylon"[115] that set its own state authority as an idolatrous absolute in sharp juxtaposition to the power of Yahweh's supremely royal throne. Whatever the causes—including Israel's own culpability—the writers of these counter-scripts held God to the fire through their own risky speech, even to the point of *"accusing Yahweh of not having honored the covenant"*[116] in allowing Israel's unrelenting and seemingly unending pain to go unhealed. In the most radical about face from the basic premises of the core testimony, it is God and not Israel who is on the precipice of violating the covenant.

Brueggemann notes that such disjunction—abandonment in its most graphic depiction—represents a critical moment in time, wherein homecoming is ultimately revisited: the result of the very working through the abyss of the profundity of loss so tightly linked to promised land and Israel's temple splendor. Notwithstanding this ultimate return, the impact of loss was of sufficient intensity to become an essential part of the reality that characterized Israel's post-exilic experience. Brueggemann rightly characterizes this loss as a profound historical reality. Without undergoing something of the actual angst that was experienced in the midst of the breach, its precariousness cannot be skimmed over in any notion that characterizes the events of the exile and the restoration promises in terms of eschatological inevitability. Such hope—veering toward what Brueggemann would depict as dogmatic certitude—may have been present based on the high point of Israel's core testimony in the unequivocal sovereignty and majesty of God. Yet, from the perspective of the historical process itself—including the impact of history on God—such a result was not so evidently obvious in the post-exilic period. Brueggemann argues that to make such a claim is to place too much on certainty at the expense of much else, including that

---

114. Ibid., 440.

115. Ibid.

116. Ibid., 375. The entire passage reads: *"Whereas the prophets hold to the sanctions and consequent indictments in asserting that Israel has betrayed the covenant, the complaining palms hold to the sanctions accusing Yahweh of not having honored the covenant."*

of a dynamic faith in the midst of complex and often dangerous historical change.

Brueggemann concludes his discussion on negativity with special treatment of Psalm 88. In this text, he notes that there is not even a hint of hopeful resolution in the unrequited pain articulated by the author, who remains utterly faithful in the very act of calling out to God in the acutest midst of the harsh reality that characterizes his experience. In speaking from the place in which he lives, the author rejects any pious similitude of "God talk," as depicted, for example, in Psalm 138, 148, and 150, which could be read as a dogmatic embrace of God's core testimony, yet which would have been an utter denial of the existential reality encountered in the lived experience of the writer of Psalm 88. As Brueggemann summarizes it:

> Israel has no answer against this reality of its experience. It does not seek to justify. It does not acquit Yahweh or indict itself. Israel is left with its psalm always to be uttered one more time, always more shrilly, uttered as an act of profound need, of intense indignation, and of relentless, insistent hope. But Israel will in any case refuse silence. And so the psalm stands as testimony to Yahweh . . . and against Yahweh.[117]

The countertestimony, even in the sharpest negative portrayal, opened up fresh theological space in the midst of the most abject pain and exile of Israel's experience. This led to a novel form of doxological praise uttered most poignantly in Second Isaiah in the ever revealing heart and mind of God, where loss articulated found new resonance in the pain that was borne by the Suffering Servant. For it was this elusive character who "was numbered with the transgressors" and bore the sins of many" (Isa 53:12b), even those who despised and rejected him. Whether read with a Christian exegesis in mind or in Israel's tongue, the Suffering Servant points to God's pathos, at its starkest, in his willingness to suffer, at least in a vicarious sense, for his people's sake, even when the most ardent sacrifice of his Servant is rejected and viewed as utterly of no account. This radical embrace of such sacrificial love may be interpreted as the counterpoint of God's abandonment of Israel as suggested by Brueggemann, a breech—however brief—that was endured for sufficient length and depth of poignancy to have really mattered in the life of Israel (Isa 54:7–8).

To push the point, to the extent that God was intimately linked to Isaiah's Suffering Servant, whether through Jewish or Christian exegesis, God's "repentance" of his abandonment was that of absorbing and, to some extent, vicariously displacing the abandonment onto his own self through

---

117. Ibid., 381.

the unjust suffering of his innocent Servant. On Brueggemann's most passionate reading, it was only through such a tense yet ultimately faithful dialectical engagement between core testimony and countertestimony that the richness and depth of Israel's narrative experience came to fruition in the crucible of encounter between faith and history. Both Israel and God were subtly changed as a result of the exile even as both remained clearly identifiable from the disclosures that emerged in the earliest of testimonies. Brueggemann's interpretation of God's and Israel's faithfulness in the light of the perplexity of the most abject loss is one of his boldest and most prescient claims.

CONCLUDING REFLECTIONS ON BRUEGGEMANN'S THEOLOGY OF GOD

At the heart pulse of Brueggemann's dialectical hermeneutics is the need to keep as sharply poised as possible to the tonality of God's utterances, particularly in the places of the most radical marginality and abandonment, where any vestige of worldly wisdom is fundamentally turned on its head. For it is here, as nowhere else, that the still, small presence of the softer and more subtle manifestations of God's presence may become available, where anything less than the authentic indwelling of God (in whatever ways that may be perceived) will not do. As it is with these most extreme moments, so it is the case for all human experience in the search for the indwelling of God, wherever and however such presence becomes discernable. This is Brueggemann's broader frame of reference, even as he finds particular poignancy at the interface between the majesty and sovereignty of God and the fulfilling presence of divine healing in the midst of the acutest loss.

An analysis of Brueggemann's bipolar leanings could be indefinitely extended. Perhaps enough has been presented here to provide a sufficient overview of its influence on his theology of Scripture and theology of God. This section concludes with a few illustrations on the ways in which he modulates the dialectical tension in his depiction of God, as embodied in the Torah, the prophets, wisdom literature, and temple worship, all of which provides some degree of stability in Israel's normative religious practice.

Mediation (*embodied testimony*) is indirect evidence and part of the broader testimony through which Brueggemann constructs his courtroom analogy. Mediation presupposes theophany—God's direct presence in key decisive moments. For the Old Testament, the events surrounding Sinai are definitional, for which Brueggemann cites Exodus 19:9–25 and 25:4:9–18. The Decalogue (Exod 20:1–17) is also represented in the Old Testament as a direct revelation in which "the fundamental Torah requirements are lodged in Israel's originary experience."[118]

Based on the core claims of Brueggemann's narrative theology, we have only the text in its final canonical form with which to work. What is given in the mighty acts and proclamations of God is "beyond explanation, criticism, or management." These acts and utterances lay out the foundational assumptions upon which the legitimacy of Old Testament faith rests. It is this very ontology of God's dynamic Presence which "evokes great fear in Israel, fear that requires a mediator," that is, a series of mediators as "Israel moves promptly from immediacy to mediation," as depicted in the great bulk of its narrated history.[119] The mediation gives shape to the forms which the testimony takes that provides Israel with its enduring sense of identity between times of absolute certainty and most urgent crisis.

The Old Testament text, in its entirety as well as in its component parts, is a prime mediator, particularly in its "stylized final form" substantially "removed from the concrete practice of the ancient community."[120] Stated in other terms, the "stylized" text of the final editorialized formation mediates the gap between the lived experience of Israel's actual history and the core claims of Israel's narrated canon. It is the many traces embodied in this testimony and the analogues drawn from them between ancient and modern times that require the hermeneutics of vigorous imagination.

The mediation of the text is twofold. The first is its rhetorical power in pointing to a "reality" in the constructed given in which "everything is possible, everything is imaginable, and everything is utterable" as expounded in the text.[121] The second consideration Brueggemann brings to our attention is the enormous elusiveness of God that "the speech of the Bible conceals . . . even while it discloses" (e.g., Deut 29:29). On this, Brueggemann is concerned about certain orthodox "self-deceptions," particularly "bibliolatry" which are in "serious disregard of the text in its daring specificity,"[122] where, in his account, revelation takes place one single moment at a time within the maelstrom of historical change. Broader textual coherencies might emerge to give greater body to counterworld kingdom claims. They are attained, to the extent that they are realized, often at only the greatest of cost in a manner that requires risky ventures, in which outcomes are far from evident. The canonical integrity of the text—which Brueggemann accepts with much

---

118. Ibid., 569.
119. Ibid.
120. Ibid., 573.
121. Ibid., 573–74.
122. Ibid., 574.

reservation as to what this implies—provides one more enduring source of stabilization, although wrought within the contestability of risk-laden historical encounter.

To the extent that Brueggemann accents bipolarity, prophetic and monarchial influences are sharply distinguished. Drawing in the sociological critique of Gottwald,[123] Brueggemann's great concern is that monarchy-based theology becomes too easily conflated with the ideology of royal power in the secular sense. In the later parts of *Theology of the Old Testament*, he articulates a more modulated presentation of royal theology. Without diminishing ideological critique, in these sections, he points to royal power as "a genuine *novum* in Israel's faith," an exemplar of God's fragile, but righteous justice in which Israel's monarchial authority depended very much on the unswerving Torah obedience of the king.[124]

Notwithstanding Brueggemann's concern for the enduring specter of false consciousness, the monarchy was subject to a higher power, as was Israel itself. The kings—including Saul, David, and Solomon—who, in varying ways came up short, were held to account to the rigorous standard of Torah righteousness. Even for them, disobedience resulted in dire consequences on a personal level, for the monarchy, and for the state of ancient Israel in marring the quality of its own inner life and in its standing in the international arena. However problematic monarchial authority was, the "novum" of David's truth reverberated throughout the later sections of the Old Testament and into the New Testament.[125] The image of the just king pointed toward God's reign over Israel, and by extension, the world, one mediating presence among others in service to the overarching vision of the Abrahamic promise of world restoration.

As Brueggemann points out, the gap between the promise and the reality flowed into post-exilic apocalyptic longing for a redeemed kingdom where lion and lamb shall lie down together in harmonic acceptance of radical world restoration. In the new world order of Zion's restored city, Assyria and Egypt will be bonded with Israel in an Edenic-like return to original purity through the righteous reign of David's redeemed progeny (Isa 19:23–25). This was a vision that inspired Israel's imagination in the midst of the acutest pain and loss. Despite the reluctance upon which God bestowed the gift, "kingship is authorized by Yahweh. . .[as] the human,

---

123. Gottwald, *Tribes of Yahweh*.
124. Brueggemann, *Theology of the Old Testament*, 605.
125. Brueggemann, *David's Truth in Israel's Imagination and Memory*.

anointed agent to do Yahweh's will in the earth,"[126] a vision that extended to the exile and beyond and substantially transmuted in the process.

Brueggemann also draws out the mediational role of the prophet, the cult, and the sage, which, together with the Torah and the king, provided Israel with the daily sustenance to maintain the enduring faith in a single religious monotheistic tradition with its rich diversity of strands. He contends that these mediations were the principle means which God used in keeping the covenant intact throughout the varied circumstances of ancient Israel's living history. None of these roles stood alone, and each, when overemphasized, possessed their own temptations to idolatry. Both the king and the prophets were called to live out of and articulate the primary mandates of the Law. Under certain limited conditions they worked together in support of a common tradition. However, the very need for the great prophetic tradition that arose in the eighth and seventh centuries emerged from the failure of the monarch to live out its calling, which placed in jeopardy the viability of Israel's radical faith in Yahweh.

Such was also the case for the priestly role of the cult in providing a "regularized, stylized practice of symbolization . . . indispensable for the sustenance of intentional ethical practice" over time.[127] The great care that the priestly tradition took in laying out the intricate details of tabernacle and temple construction often gets short shrift in various Christian supersessionist readings, based on the "better covenant" vision of the Epistle to the Hebrews. Without minimizing the centrality of the new covenant, Brueggemann's support of the Jewish integrity of the Old Testament for the shaping of both Jewish and Christian theology is duly noted. In its place and in its given contexts within ancient Jewish practice, the priestly emphasis in Exodus and Leviticus had an important and enduring mediating function in worship and maintenance in the preservation of Israel's "peculiar [religious] identity" over time and substantially changing historical situations.[128]

Brueggemann's theology of God is deeply influenced by his bipolar reading of God's presence and absence. His scriptural perspective reflects the twin influences of the biblical theology movement of the mid-twentieth

---

126. Brueggemann, *Theology of the Old Testament*, 695.

127. Ibid., 678, italics removed.

128. Ibid., 653, italics removed. Brueggemann notes that "Israel understood, as the Western disestablished church is only now having to learn again, that *there must be important and intentional lines of defense and maintenance if a peculiar identity is to endure*, and worship is the most likely place in which such an identity is to be guarded and maintained. Without such intentional worship, a community of an odd identity will first be co-opted and domesticated, and then it will evaporate. I understand the worship materials of the Old Testament to be precisely practices, proposals, and acts of imagination whereby Israel sought to maintain its oddity as the people of Yahweh." Ibid.

century—especially through the mediation of his textual mentor, Gerhard Von Rad—and his profound engagement with postmodern theology and culture. Faith can only be grasped within the lived context of on the ground experience which cannot *but* substantially shape the most elemental understanding of one's religious identity and the corresponding cultural matrix of our, or any, time. In the most fundamental sense, the dynamic between faith and culture plays out in any and in every context. Operative assumptions are often pushed to their most logical extreme in periods of the acutest crisis—thus, Brueggemann's twin emphasis on the exilic period in Israel and the postmodern Christian disestablishment era of our contemporary setting as particularly defining moments.

While bipolarity is a central thread in Brueggemann's theology, he accepts the importance of qualifying mediations, without which any enduring sense of religious identity would be virtually impossible to maintain over any durable length of time. His finely tuned dialectical sensibility militates against what he views as exorbitant claims of religious certainty. He qualifies this critique by the recognition that claims cannot *but* be made that require proclamation. The profession of faith at some axiomatic level of dogmatic verity needs to prove its mettle time and again in the midst of any and every historical reality.

CONCLUDING REMARKS

Throughout this chapter, I have sought to probe into the dynamic strains between dogmatics and dialectics in Brueggemann's theology. He is relentlessly dialectical in the very engagement of the relationship between dogmatics and dialectics, which, by the logic of his hermeneutics, does not and cannot, come to settled resolution. This is so even with his acceptance that "after our imaginative interpretations are made with vigor in disputes with others in the church . . . we must regularly, gracefully, and with modesty fall back on our best extrapolations to the sure apostolic claims that lie behind our extremities of imagination, liberal or conservative."[129] For Brueggemann, even these anchoring points are only critical moments of revelatory time, incredibly fleeting in the nexus where faith must live in the crucible of human historicity.

As Brueggemann depicts the tension in specific Christian terms—our place is a perpetual Saturday dwelling, "the longest of days" lodged between the excruciating pain of Good Friday and the inexpressible joy of Easter.[130] It

---

129. Brueggemann, "Biblical Authority," 30.

130. Steiner, *Real Presences*, 5; cited in Brueggemann, *Theology of the Old Testament*, 402.

is this day that is ever before us as promise. It is reality as hoped for and not lived except within the immediacy of the revelatory moment. Within the midst of this terse dialectic that he refers to here as Saturday, Brueggemann is always grappling with the perpetual search for the actual indwelling of God in each and every moment. This is so, whether focusing on exegesis or exposition, or more typically, a subtle interfacing at any particular point. Through his effort at faithful construal, Brueggemann seeks to bring to his readers something of awesome poignancy and problematic nature of that to which the quest alludes within the context of any given historical experience. This is his objective, whether his immediate reference point is to times of old or the current era.

Brueggemann's work offers a great deal to his primary audience—particularly those in the mainline denominations seeking to maintain a connection to the Christian faith, but who are disaffected with traditional orthodoxy. I will illustrate this by blending my personal experience based on an initial encounter with his work in the mid-1990s with the theological issues evoked by his work. As stated in chapter 1, my own religious grounding point stemmed from a "born-again" conversation to Christianity in 1972. I maintained a reasonably stable evangelical identity throughout the 1970s, which became de-stabilized throughout much of the 1980s and early 1990s.[131] During these latter decades I was influenced by various strands of death of God and process theologies, less as modes of formal theological positions and more in terms of personal religious reconstruction at the level of felt experience. The upshot is that by the 1980s I could no longer resonate with what is sometimes pejoratively referred to as "God talk." I was no longer able or desired to embrace the evangelical religious subculture that consumed much of my energy in the 1970s. I did not reject Christianity in the 1980s, but could no longer function within overtly religious frames of reference without coming to terms with the primary issues that pulled me away from many of its prevailing assumptions.

I attended UCC and American Baptist congregations regularly during the 1980s and 1990s. While seeking engagement with God through the worship service, I typically experienced milder to stronger forms of disengagement from many of the hymns, liturgies, and sermons that I encountered as the sum and substance of mainline Protestant practice. Even when I did experience resonance, to some greater or lesser degree, little of that had much of an apparent effect on my Monday to Saturday reality, as my identity was firmly anchored in the presuppositions of a more secular perspective.

---

131. See my online essays "Born Again" and "Seeker's Journey" for a personal overview of my religious journey from the early 1970s to the mid-1990s.

I experienced more of a connection through participation in church-based adult education classes and small group discussions, even as my broader sense of self-perception continued to be more influenced by various precepts of the secular culture than by any intentional Christian identity. Still, I continued to probe for some new potentialities that could lead to a revitalized born-again faith in a manner that I could embrace in some authentic and sustained manner. However much I sought to move "beyond" the born-again identity of an evangelically grounded faith, its core precepts remained foundational to my personal understanding of Christianity. I drew on the characterization of a polarized consciousness during this period to describe the pull of tensions that tugged at my identity.

I viewed myself as open to the promptings of the Holy Spirit as I understood it. However, I was not particularly seeking spiritual illumination in a consciously religious way. My pursuit of careerism, secular intellectuality and more broadly based secular identity, particularly through the prism of John Dewey's naturalistic philosophy, seemed more pressing to the fundamental concerns of my life.[132] I sought neither to repress the religious impulse nor to embrace a sharply defined Christian identity unless called back into it through what I could perceive as the authentic voice of God, however mediated by the peculiarities of my own self-construction. I persistently accepted as implicitly true the fundamentals of the orthodox Christian worldview, even in the midst of a substantial embrace of a predominant secular identity. Given the particular reference to the potency of Dewey's naturalistic focus in the construction of my own imagination, his philosophy could act, as I intuited it, only as a blockage point to any unfettered evangelical stance as an alternative anchoring point to the secular credo.

It was not a rejection of the ultimate significance of God's existence. Rather, I was working within a theological perspective that reinforced a mode of thinking *as if* God did not exist, even while, at another level, I intuited that he did. Through this limiting framework I hoped to disallow "God talk" from "illegitimately" intruding on my encounter with the world. I held this position simultaneously with an unquenchable quest, however sublimated, for a full-fledged re-encounter of a Christian orthodox worldview processed through my born-again sensibility. It was in the midst of this search that Brueggemann's postmodern credo of one text—one revelation at a time—spoke very much to my reality in a more compelling manner than what reams of dogma, pages of Scripture, or pietistic claims were, at that point, likely to bring about. Stated otherwise, encountering Brueggemann's imaginative probing stimulated my own reading of Scripture. This

---

132. Dewey, *Experience and Nature*, Demetrion, "Re-Inventing the Self."

re-ignited a searching pursuit for meaning within the context of a more intentional self-articulated Christian identity.

Given the power of the many competing metanarrative construals both within contemporary Christian theology and in the broader secular arena, vigorous imagination is the critical pathway Brueggemann relies on for opening up some facet of God's reality among those who otherwise would dismiss doctrinal claims as a form of religious obscurantism. For Brueggemann, what is most deeply sought and most significantly needed are actual *encounters* with God's living presence in each and every moment. However fleeting, such theophanous moments are the baseline experiences for whatever fragile religious coherencies may emerge. Brueggemann argues that our times require a grappling with perceptions of loss and abandonment, from the ashes out of which new birth can burst forth. Such energy has the power to give shape to the formation of new religious communities or the revitalization of existing ones. In my case, the encounter with Brueggemann opened up "a third world of evangelical imagination"[133] that turned a deconstruction of an initial born again evangelical identity into a new frame of reference congruent with orthodox Christianity in a manner that enabled me both to embrace and partially transcend the secular. Clearly, any such new construction remains a work in progress.

Brueggemann's many expositions have the capacity to speak with a great deal of verve to those who need to encounter the text in a manner that first and foremost excites the imagination *before* attaining any fuller encounter with a more centralized Christian identity. For those on the boundary of coherent Christian identity formation, the avenue opened up by Brueggemann's emphasis on the imagination may be the only conceivable way that faith claims can pass muster in the crucible of engagement with contemporary culture. This is particularly the case where other narratives speak with compelling and seemingly more pressing power than the claims of dogmatic assertions that seem to miss the mark among those operating from the boundary line of faith and doubt in the existential moment of engagement. For those able to embrace a more centered Christian identity, there is also much in Brueggemann that is of value, including that of an imaginative engagement with the text in which no *merely* doctrinal reading of Scripture can ever convey. Even if one disagrees with some of Brueggemann's postmodern sensibilities, his bipolar courtroom biblical hermeneutics is so rich and wide ranging, that there is a great deal within his insights for those more evangelically inclined to critically appropriate.

---

133. Brueggemann, "Third World of Evangelical Imagination," 9–27.

The tension that Brueggemann fleshes out in the dialectic he posits between the "timeless document" of the Bible and interpretations that are "always timeful"[134] also offers much gist for critical reflection among Protestant mainline and evangelical readers. In this, he calls for a perpetual grounding in the biblical literature over and against any other normative standard, while rejecting what he views as false closure that he associates with certain inerrant and infallible interpretations of the text.[135] In the process, Brueggemann wants discerning readers not "only" to attend to "the normative [biblical] credo, crucial as that normative credo is." He also brings out the importance of "the dangerous stories at the edge which protests the center"[136] of dominant orthodox biblical interpretation. In this dialectic between the biblical text as given and interpretations that keep the horizon open to new insights both from the center and margins, there is sufficient depth and nuance in Brueggemann's biblical theology to stimulate critical engagement from evangelical and Protestant mainline perspectives alike.[137]

Also of vital importance for evangelical revitalization and critical dialogue with the Protestant mainline is the extensive work Brueggemann has undertaken in identifying justice and equity toward the poor and marginalized as a major biblical theme. This is not typically denied by serious readers of the Bible across the theological spectrum. However, its emphasis is often downplayed. Brueggemann's contribution lies in the range of coverage and depth of analysis that he brings to the topic. This includes that of embracing holiness and justice, which are inextricably conjoined, along with his extensive analogizing of Old Testament texts to the contemporary period. Whatever the degree in which the themes of equity and justice get played out in terms of any proposed Christian interpretation of political culture, they cannot simply be viewed as secondary. The critical linkage between justice and holiness as a core *biblical* theme within both mainline Protestant and evangelical theology needs to be viewed as a major focal point of biblical

---

134. Brueggemann, "Canonization and Contextualization," 121.

135. Brueggemann, "Biblical Authority in the Postcritical Period," 4.

136. Brueggemann, "Canonization and Contextualization," 128.

137. The following is an apt summary of Brueggemann's hermeneutical theory: "The canon . . . is not a settled truth. It is an ongoing conversation in which the ongoingness is an epistemological decision about the character of truth. The hope is to keep the conversation going without excluding any voice or giving any voice a veto. The conversation must be attentive to the role, function, gift, power, and claim of different voices." Ibid., 132. I argue that in his acknowledgement of the ultimate normative value of the Bible, which holds a finality of loyalty "as no other" (ibid., 122) literature, Brueggemann's dialectical hermeneutics opens up a source of critical engagement for which critical evangelical readers would have much to gain, even in their rejection of significant aspects of his argument.

ethics *and* theology. Brueggemann offers much insight on the centrality of justice throughout the Old Testament that can inform Protestant thought and practice across a wide theological landscape.[138]

As one who has shifted back toward a more centrist evangelical theological perspective, I continue to find a great deal to draw upon in Brueggemann's extensive project, even while holding some critical concerns. This includes his valuable commentary on the social and cultural disestablishment of contemporary Protestantism—along with his emphasis on postmodernism as the decisive moment through which faith needs to speak if it is to be heard with authenticity in the contemporary era. The critical factor underlying disestablishment is the fundamental shift of mainline Protestantism from its central location in US society and culture in the mid-twentieth century to its marginalized socio-cultural status in the current setting—a trend of decline evident throughout the past half century.[139] The shift is noteworthy for a variety of compelling reasons. For Brueggemann, its key significance is the increasing improbability that it highlights for prospects of cultural transformation through theological alliance with the prevailing cultural and intellectual centers of Western modernity.

It may have been of strategic value for early and mid-twentieth-century mainline denominations to have constructed their theologies through the prisms of modern secular intellectual life and culture. Given the persisting mainline declension of the past fifty years, continuing energies spent in such a direction are a reflection of a culture lag that has lost its purchase in the current era. In short, cultural marginality may open up certain theological possibilities that were not so evident when mainline Protestantism was more closely aligned with the broader notion of civil religion characteristic of a great deal of the religious and civic culture of post–World War II America. This is a topic I further discuss in chapter 8. For the purposes of the present chapter, Brueggemann's analysis of the current marginality of Protestant religious culture could serve as a potent resource in stimulating an evangelical countercultural claim, in concert with critical Protestant mainline perspectives.

Brueggemann makes an important contribution in presenting postmodern culture as a powerfully shaping metanarrative construal. Evangelical literature occasionally caricatures this view. In doing so it fails to come to grips with one of the most powerful source of cultural energy at the center

---

138. For one of Brueggemann's most extensive statement on the relationship between theology and social justice, see his collection of essays, *Social Reading of the Old Testament*.

139. Hall, *Confessing the Faith*, 201–64; Robinson, *Transforming Congregational Culture*.

of middle class popular and contemporary intellectual life. Brueggemann's counterproposal of "funding" postmodernity one text at a time is a novel insight that has found its primary audience in that sector of the Protestant mainstream that would like to embrace the Bible with radical seriousness in a manner that proponents could come to characterize as authentic. As stated, it has also had significant purchase on my own imagination which I internalized in some ways different than from what Brueggemann may have intended.

Brueggemann's indicates that greater coherences may emerge through a stitching together of individual fragments that break forth in the radical particularity of any given time and place.[140] Such a quest tapped into my own imagination. However, something more also was at work that stimulated a type of paradigm switch that pushed me to the boundaries of a threshold. Specifically, the released energy opened up by Brueggemann's insights moved me toward a creative *re*-construal that had the potential of enabling me to imaginatively move beyond the hermeneutical circle of his postmodern logic in which I had been tightly locked well for over a decade. The release prompted by my internalization of his hermeneutics of imagination stimulated the rhythmic heart pulses of my own evangelical consciousness. This, in turn, opened up the vital prospect that I could re-encounter a deepened evangelical sensibility processed through the original motif of the conversion experience that initially drew me to Christianity within the context of my more recent life setting.[141]

The shift in the direction to Barth's "strange new world" may be an exceedingly difficult one to make for those on the boundary of faith and culture without some similar perceptual impetus gravitating toward Christian orthodoxy in the full Trinitarian and incarnational sense. This may not be a feasible prospect for mainline Protestantism as a whole. Energies within its prevailing religious culture may be blowing in some other directions. Nevertheless, its own theological heritage, rooted in the tradition of the Protestant Reformers, provides the baseline for a viable rebirth of a fully developed Christian orthodoxy. Such a focus could be incorporated within a context that gives full justice to contemporary scholarship—both secular

---

140. Brueggemann, *Texts under Negotiation*, 25.

141. This paragraph reflects my current thoughts on an experience that took place over a decade ago. What I refer to as a paradigm shift back to an intentional evangelical consciousness was a gradual process of which I was only partially conscious, particularly at a high level of cognitive or formal theological precision. My *TheoTalk* essay "Small Still Prompting of the Shadow Voice of Secular Modernity," written in 2004, was my first formal statement of a distinctively formed evangelical identity during the period under discussion.

and theological—as suggested in the postliberal theology and in certain strains within evangelical thought. Brueggemann's biblical theology may open some doors to such a vision, which, I argue, will require an intentional shift toward a more centrist orthodox theology than he proposes. For this, Fackre's probing theology serves as an important complement for the type of project I propose.[142]

In addition to Brueggemann's appeal to certain tendencies in Protestant mainline theology, evangelicals can benefit from his analysis of postmodern culture. This requires a sophisticated understanding of contemporary culture that someone like Brueggemann can open up while simultaneously questioning what may be his too easy acceptance of the prevailing premises of postmodernism as the basis of shaping scriptural interpretation. To put this in the typological terms that H. R. Niebuhr identifies in his classic text, *Christ and Culture*, the breaking in of the *kairos* at this time and place in history may well call for a substantial re-direction from a *Christ of, above*, or a *transformer* of culture that characterized the mainline Protestant response through the middle decades of the twentieth century. The shift needed at this time, as part of the process of Protestant disestablishment, may be toward a *Christ and culture in paradox*, and even the possibility of a *Christ against culture* paradigm.[143] Any such paradigm shift of the relationship between Christ and culture from an embrace of the prevailing mid-twentieth-century intellectual and cultural assumptions, as embodied in Cox's iconic *Secular City*, toward one of increasing distance would require profound restructuring for mainline and evangelical identity and religious practice alike. There is scope within mainline Protestant and evangelical theology for doing so.[144]

Coming to terms with such a shift would require much courage and imaginative insight, necessitating a fundamental alteration in the prevailing religious culture. Such a transition would include that of recasting the evangelical community as the primary dialogue partner of the mainline Protestant denominations. For the evangelical community, a more critical embrace of tragedy and irony in interpreting American history—along with a more skeptical stance against the siren call of American exceptionalism—may be needed to ground an orthodox centrist perspective in a broader ecumenical concord with postliberal leaning sectors of the Protestant

---

142. If such a shift is not made within the mainline Protestant denominations, then I am left to wonder of what a Christianity otherwise defined might actually consist in the concrete terms of its theological grounding.

143. *Christ and Culture*. See chapter 7 for a discussion of the various typologies Niebuhr identifies in *Christ and Culture*.

144. Hall, *Confessing the Faith*, 201–64; Wells, *No Place for Truth*, 57–92

Reading Walter Brueggemann through a Fluidly Canonical Lens 215

mainline denominations. As discussed earlier, for these profound shifts, Brueggemann's cultural analysis of the nation's post-Christendom's status offers much keen insight, notwithstanding certain evangelical reservations about his postmodern reading of the biblical text.

What also merits examination is Brueggemann's critique of any supersessionist interpretation that the New Testament represents the better covenant "whereby Jewish religious claims are overridden in the triumph of Christian claims."[145] Brueggemann finds reasons for such a view in the need for certainty among dogmatic theologians and certain evangelical biblical scholars. He associates supersessionist theology with "the classic modes of Hellenistic thought" that influenced early Christian theology. Such influences have made "it nearly impossible for Christians to attend to the riches of Judaism"[146] in coming to terms with a text "that remains as elusive as its Subject and that relentlessly resists closure."[147] The concern is not his critique of a simplistic supersessionist Christian interpretation of the Old Testament that he sometimes caricaturizes, but his ideologically rooted anti-supersessionism that claims too much. This is particularly disconcerting to find in a biblical scholar who seeks to disclose something of the inimitable revelation the Bible opens up, given the predominant theme of the New Testament that, in Christ, the New Covenant fulfillment has reached its apotheosis, even as a first eschaton revelation (e.g., 2 Cor 3:7–11).[148]

In fairness to Brueggemann, he is an Old Testament theologian who draws essentially on the New Testament in a supplemental manner. Nonetheless, critical issues remain. First, in his definition, and that of Childs, Old Testament theology is a *Christian* discipline. That stands whether or not all Old Testament scholars are Christians. As discussed by Childs, interpreting both testaments through the prism of Christ's revelation does not preclude

---

145. Brueggemann, *Theology of the Old Testament*, 729.

146. Ibid., 735. The following is one of Brueggemann's more discerning statements: "We have yet to decide how christological exclusiveness is to be articulated so that it is not an ideological ground for the dismissal of a co-community of interpretation. Thus our most passionate affirmation of Jesus as the 'clue' to all of reality must allow for other 'clues' found herein by other serious communities of interpretation. And of course this applies to none other so directly as it does to Judaism." Ibid.

147. Ibid.

148. The term supersessionism carries an excessively pejorative connotation. Any supersessionist notion that the orthodox Christian view "has permanently replaced Israel in God's plan" with Jesus Christ is overstated when one takes into account Romans 9–11 or Hebrews 11. See Vlach's *Theological Studies* blog entry, "Defining Supersessionism." Nonetheless, Brueggemann cannot rely on anti-supersessionist polemics. He still needs to more directly address the core New Testament claim that in Christ the better covenant has been fulfilled.

taking the Old Testament on its own terms." This acknowledgement can be drawn upon in support Brueggemann's position that fulfillment in Christ was only one future option and not something that could be discerned through the Old Testament, itself.

However, in Child's canonical interpretation, the interpretive center of biblical theology as a subset of *Christian theology*, can be nothing other than Christ revealed as the fulfillment of the New Covenant, however fluid may be definitions of what this means.[149] Brueggemann is obviously reluctant to go in this direction because of what he takes as a profound reductionism of the Old Testament and the proclivity such a move has toward transmuting the biblical text into a dogmatic certitude that extends beyond the claims of Scripture itself. A major problem as well is an implicit anti-semitism that simply cannot stand in light of the horrific events of the twentieth century.

These concerns have much merit. Brueggemann has done great service in fleshing out a multi-dimensional reading of the Old Testament and linking its core claims to the critical issues of the day.[150] Still, his interpretation of the New Testament can veer toward one dimensionality with a tendency toward simplification and occasionally caricature. There is also an occasional tendency to conflate the New Testament's core claim (1 Cor 8:6) with the "tyranny of the church" linked to "the ideological claims of the religious community."[151] Notwithstanding these concerns, in his Old Testament ponderings Brueggemann provides many powerful insights that could be appropriated in a dialectical reading of the New Testament. Such an approach would need to come to terms with core Christian Trinitarian and incarnational claims without equivocation (Jas 1:6), while taking into account the existential power of God Holy Spirit's innermost dynamic (Heb 4:12).

Critical issues of ontology and formal theological argumentation also need to be discerned in any evangelical effort to critically appropriate certain themes and emphases from Brueggemann's project. In his search for an almost pristine narrative theology, there is an evasive tendency in his bracketing of ontological claims and interpreting the epistemological ones, accurately, as a second order interpretation. On the ontology of God,

---

149. Childs, *Biblical Theology of the Old and New Testaments*, 73–79.

150. Such a reading is especially evident in Brueggemann's highly discerning collection of essays *The Book That Breathes New Life* when contrasted to his earlier essay collections with their sharp emphasis on the theme of bipolarity. Brueggemann continues to press the theme of bipolarity in *The Book That Breathes New Life*, though he shapes his discussion within a wider theological framework that allows scope for more voices in the center in this later work.

151. Brueggemann, "Biblical Authority in the Postcritical Period," 11.

Brueggemann stresses the importance of the revelatory moment. This is a critical emphasis in an era dominated, as he portrays it, by claims of dogmatic certitude on the one hand, and radical doubt and cynicism, on the other. Without something of the substance of an actual encounter with God as a phenomenological reality that penetrates to the heart and soul of the human experience, the very claim of faith is in grave danger of losing whatever fragile credulity it may possess. This is a point well taken.

At the same time, an evangelical theologian will want to push Brueggemann further than he goes in identifying the source of truth itself in God, whose existence as ultimate reality extends to the foundational claim of his sovereignty, as attested to in Scripture. However much the gap remains in human experience, in faith, God's sovereignty is utterly reliable beyond any conceivable human perception. This is an ontological, not a phenomenological claim. A felt sense of God's presence is still essential. Without this, such faith would seem vacuous, a danger for which there is an ample biblical warrant. Nonetheless, we have the enduring testimony as an even surer foundation of faith beyond the lived encounter of the revelatory moment (Heb 6:16–20). As Brueggemann argues, both epistemology and ontology are important. However, greater stress on ontology is needed to more thoroughly ground evangelical theology in articulated truth claims. Such a stance in faith is required without any semblance of a dogmatic certitude that fails to respect the dynamic elusiveness implicit within and throughout the biblical text. What comes to mind is something along the lines of working out our salvation in fear and trembling as God is working in us both to will and to do for his good pleasure (Phil 2:12–13).

There is much to draw on from Brueggemann's narrative perspective to inform and challenge an evangelical theology. I believe he is on solid ground in arguing against any dogmatic claims of inerrancy because there is nothing intrinsic in the Bible that assumes or requires a literal or even a radically reliable account that equates biblical claims with precisely what happened within history. While revelation takes place within history, and a great deal of the text comes across as a realistic-like narrative—as Brueggemann argues for the Old Testament—its revelatory power comes from a source other than from what can be discerned from empirical historical sources. He contends for this case while insisting that the power of God cannot be interpreted by human actors beyond history. I contend that it is not the Jesus of history that fulfills the claims of John 1:14. Rather, it is the power of God in Christ reconciling the world (2 Cor 5:19), as reverberated throughout the entire New Testament canon. Issues like the historical accuracy of the New Testament and related claims of biblical inerrancy remain important points of contention, but they are secondary to the more fundamental proclamations of faith. Of foremost importance is the centrality of the Bible as the primary source of Christian revelation.

Finally, I would like to see Brueggemann grapple more directly with the central claims of orthodox Christianity as expressed throughout the ages. On this, I am pushing for a more subtle reading of Childs's canonical interpretation grounded in the normative claim of Christ revealed as the underlying incarnational presupposition of what Childs refers to as the Christian Bible. In my view, that is essential work of a Christian theologian, even one whose primary medium is Old Testament theology. This is a call for a profession of faith, without equivocation that "there is one God and one mediator between God and men, the man Christ Jesus, who gave himself as a ransom for all men" (1 Tim 2:5–6). At this point, how such an intentionally emphatic Christian reading would impact on Brueggemann's Old Testament theology remains largely in the realm of an intriguing counterfactual hypothesis.

7

Re-Envisioning the Neo-Orthodox Legacy

Theologians are historically conditioned persons whose attempt to comprehend the eternal are relative.[1]

Barth maintained throughout *Church Dogmatics* that theology is a work of Christian proclamation. It does not defend the reasonableness of Christianity to outsiders, nor does it look for a common ground on which the superiority of Christianity over other perspectives might be defended. Theology cannot move to neutral apologetic ground without forsaking its basis in the circle of Word-inspired faith. Neither can it prove the truth of God's Word "either directly or indirectly," Barth argued. "It can only trust in the Word's demonstration of itself."[2]

The Christian message is, let me repeat, not one truth among others; it is *the* truth.[3]

The whole man stands before the whole earthly and eternal reality, the reality which God has prepared for him in Jesus Christ. Man can live up to this reality

---

1. Hall, *Remembered Voices*, 100.
2. Dorrien, *Word as True Myth*, 96.
3. Barth, *Dogmatics in Outline*, 70.

only if he responds fully to the totality of the offer and the claim.⁴

In Christian theology at its best, the revelation of Christ, the God-man, is a revelation of the paradoxical relation of the eternal to history, which is the genius of mythical-prophetic religion to emphasize. Christ is thus the revelation of the very impossible possibility which the Sermon on the Mount elaborates in ethical terms . . . In genuine prophetic Christianity the moral qualities of the Christ are not only our hope, but our despair. Out of that despair arises a new hope centered in the revelation of God in Christ. In such faith Christ and the Cross reveal not only the possibilities but the limits of human finitude in order that a more ultimate hope may arise from the concrete recognition of those limits.⁵

It is not essentially the problem of Christianity and civilization; for Christianity, whether defined as church, creed, ethics, or movement of thought, itself moves between the poles of Christ and culture. The relation of these two authorities constitutes its problem.⁶

OVERVIEW

The discernment of the *kairos*—Christ's indwelling in the contemporary setting—is as important as it is problematic in any Christian effort to find voice in the complex context of the contemporary era. Such discernment in relation to the current US setting requires much grappling in the effort to work through the issues that underlie the many tensions in contemporary Protestantism in its relationship to culture. I have sought to address the Christ/culture issue through a critical encounter with key Protestant theologians and biblical scholars whose cumulative work spans a wide spectrum across the twentieth-century US theological divide. Each of the four protagonists I have written about has taken a broad mediational perspective in bringing together disparate positions within the framework of various schools of Protestant thought.

---

4. Bonhoeffer, *Ethics*, 208.
5. R. Niebuhr, *Interpretation of Christian Ethics*, 73–74.
6. H. R. Niebuhr, *Christ and Culture*, 11.

Re-Envisioning the Neo-Orthodox Legacy

There is an inescapable historical dimension to this book situated as it is within a particular cultural location and time, to say nothing of the autobiographical signature that underlies every page. My theological focal point—implicit throughout this text—is set within the context of the prevailing intellectual and cultural currents of a largely suburban religious and secular culture that seeks critical points of connection with the urban sector from the vantage point of the Bible interpreting the world.

In addition to these broader cultural and religious trends, the autobiographical note looms large of one "born-again" through a sharply delineated conversion experience processed through a historical faith journey of over forty years. This passage has been across the Protestant landscape, extending at the outer polarities from intense Pentecostal pietism to the "death of God" rejection of any semblance of "God talk." The key autobiographical shift that has provided the focus of this book is that of moving from a distinctively born-again evangelical cast of mind to a more secular sensibility, and then to an embrace of a more centrist Christian identity through a protracted hermeneutical retrieval of the core orthodox proclamation.

Context remains essential. Yet, unless it is placed in service of the universality of the kerygma, however much contextually *conditioned*, historicist insights within the contemporary culture attain an absolutist warrant they do not merit. To put it another way, axioms beyond empirical verifiability need to be postulated as the basis for any fruitful investigation—whether in science or religion. Without an ontological vision that can make faith claims beyond *epistemological* warrant, the radical particularity of the core contention of the gospel—that "God so loved the world that he gave his one and only Son that whoever believes in him shall not perish but have eternal life" (John 3:16)—becomes relativized as an artifact of ancient religious thought.

I acknowledge that my sense of the *kairos* is invariably colored by my own perceptual encounter with the Christian faith. This admission is not synonymous with turning the contingency of historical experience into an absolute. I argue, rather, that the space opened to me through faith in the New Testament claim of Christ as "the radiance of God's glory and the exact representation of his being" (Heb 1:3) provides a taproot into the core proclamation of the Christian kerygma. To stipulate, that to which I refer to in faith as "God our Father and the Lord Jesus Christ" (Phil 1:2), transcends the vagaries of the particularities of historical relativism, even as its revelation invariably takes place through the stream of a selective set of human events.

It is with these caveats noted that I propose an embrace of the Barthian dictum of re-encountering "the strange new world within the Bible" as a core objective in contemporary US theology and religious culture.

As argued throughout this book, it is this shift that represents a critical turning that mainline Protestantism needs to address if there is going to be any sustained hermeneutical retrieval of a theological vision based on the fundamental precepts of the faith rooted in the historical tradition of the Protestant Reformers. I maintain that without this turn, contemporary mainline Protestantism will only be further eroded as a distinctively defined Christian faith. Given the various "battles for the Bible" and the great divide between fundamentalism and modernity that has attained iconographic significance in contemporary Protestant thought and culture, the proposed shift in focus in adhering to a comprehensive biblical faith as the prism to engage the culture is no simple matter.

On what absorbs what, Miroslav Volf raises a valid point that the relationship between faith and culture is more complex and perpetually interpenetrating than what may be suggested by any such polarity. There is more than a grain of merit in his argument that "the religion with which we interpret a given culture is itself always an interpreted religion."[7] This is inescapable. My central argument is based on a historical assessment that a turn to a centrist biblical perspective is needed at this time for any revitalization of US Protestant thought and culture on its own grounding values. Complexity notwithstanding, on the assumption that truth claims are foundational to the human experience, ontological claims are, by definition, inescapable, however implicitly or explicitly made. There needs to be a grounding point somewhere on the faith/culture axis. There is no free standing space outside of interpreted experience. Barth's claim—as well as that of evangelical theology—is that the content of a *particular* text (the Bible) points to a reality that is inherently transcendent, one that demands our most radical commitment in order to realize something of its fuller revelatory potential. This claim, made within the limits of finite and historically conditioned understanding, points beyond itself to the ontology of God as revealed in the Old and New Testaments. Viewed from this perspective, the Christian faith "is about recognizing the truth of Jesus Christ as Savior and Lord. It is about the perception of the truth of the gospel, and thereby the perception of the need for Christian theology to give as reliable an account as possible of its identity and significance."[8]

The position taken here—as embodied in the great stream of evangelical and Reformed theology—is the core faith assumption that God has spoken and continues to speak in and through the Bible and inspired human witnesses. I have duly noted that there is an inescapable historical

---

7. Volf, "Theology, Meaning, and Power," 46.
8. McGrath, "Evangelical Evaluation of Postliberalism," 38.

dimension to this claim. Yet, the more important point is that the revelation, which—by the grace of God can be accessed afresh as a living word through the Holy Spirit—has the potential of speaking with an utterly convincing ring of inner authority. This Word can be publicly shared, and thereby its understanding refined, through dialogue with others via what the New Testament refers to as the body of Christ. This includes communion with the Christian community throughout the ages via the written word and ecclesial practice. I acknowledge that the claims of revelation and the possibility of deception are not easily discerned; at best, we attain proximate understanding. Yet, there is the ineffable prompting of that still, small voice. It speaks where it will in its own distinctive cadence however variously revealed both among the living and the dead in the contemporary era, throughout the ages, and into the future until the holy city becomes embodied on earth on God's promised fulfillment (Rev 21:10).

The key point of contention is whether it is *this* New Testament metanarrative or some other story that shall attain an ultimate claim of truth. Either claim can be made only beyond any ultimately verifiable proof, which is not to negate the importance "of evidence of things not seen" (Heb 11:1 KJV). The question posited to the contemporary church can be nothing other than that posed to Peter by Jesus—namely, "Who do you say that I am?" (Matt 16:15). What is at stake in the radical nature of this pointed question is nothing short of whether Paul's assertion holds as an ultimate faith stance beyond which there cannot be any claim to Christian faith within the ecumenical orthodox tradition: "For us there is but one God, the Father, from whom all things came and for whom we live; and there is but one Lord Jesus Christ, through whom all things came and through whom we live" (1 Cor 8:6). Barth sought to discover this faith claim anew for the early and mid-twentieth century. Upon this faith claim he constructed a magisterial dogmatics that laid the foundation for the neo-orthodox movement in Europe and the United States. Hall seeks to draw upon this legacy in the current era.[9] I do also.

RECLAIMING THE NEO-ORTHODOX LEGACY

Hall contends that the breadth and depth of the neo-orthodox vision is sorely needed as a critical resource in empowering a revitalization movement within contemporary mainline Protestant theology. In his embrace of Bultmann and Tillich, Hall builds broadly within the orbit of the neo-orthodox movement that, in addition to Barth, includes the Niebuhr brothers,

9. Hall, *Remembered Voices*.

Bonhoeffer, Emil Brunner and the lesser known Suzanne de Dietrich. Despite their differences, all of these theologians held to a common outlook over the key themes of

> the revelatory, Christological basis of the gospel; the indispensability of the study of scriptures; keen and informed historical consciousness; an internalized and nuanced appropriation of the Reformed traditions in particular; and the attempt to address the whole church in the contexts of its real world.[10]

Taking the tack of both Hall and the historian Gary Dorrien of reclaiming the legacy of neo-orthodoxy, broadly conceived, I shall explore something of its promise as a revitalization dynamic for both mainline and evangelical Protestantism.[11] I do so through a selective reflection on the theology of Barth, Bonhoeffer, Reinhold Niebuhr, and H. R. Niebuhr. There is much in both Hall and Dorrien's dialectical sensibilities that I seek to draw into my own reflections, even as I challenge some of their key assumptions from a more doctrinal-centered, evangelical set of presuppositions. For example, I take a stronger stance than they on the proclamation in faith of revealed *truth* amidst inescapable epistemological uncertainty.[12]

---

10. Ibid., 144–45.

11. For Dorrien, see *Word as True Myth*, 73–127, and *Barthian Revolt in Modern Theology*, 81–196.

12. See McGrath, "Evangelical Evaluation of Postliberalism," 35–39. McGrath acknowledges that the Christian epistemological reach exceeds its ontological grasp. Nonetheless, he assumes the ontological claim of God's revelation as a foundational source of faith. In his words: "While acknowledging postliberalism's hesitations over potentially naïve approaches to the issue of truth, evangelicalism nevertheless insists that theology must be concerned with the question of telling the truth about God. That truth may take the form of a narrative . . . or a doctrinal framework . . . or a simple affirmation of the truthfulness or trustworthiness of God. However the concept of truth may be stated, it is firmly understood to be located *outside* the language of Christianity, as well as within it. Christianity aims to provide a systematic, regulated and coherent account of who God is and what God is like—that is to say, that there is an extra-systemic referent which functions as both the foundation and criterion of the Christian language game. Or to put it another way, evangelicalism is insistent that Christian 'truth' must designate both a reality outside the language game and the adequacy of that language game to represent it. In other words, Christian theology must accurately and consistently render the truth of the identity and purposes of God." Ibid., 39. In its emphasis on truth, such ontological claims extend beyond the dialectical sensibilities of Hall and Dorrien in their desire to reinvigorate a neo-orthodox theology rooted in the tradition of the Protestant Reformers. McGrath's claims raise an important difference between most evangelical and postliberal perspectives; one that will require considerable mediation in the ongoing effort to stimulate constructive dialogue between these two schools of thought.

Substantial differences remain between dialectical postliberal Protestant scholars like Hall, Dorrien, and Brueggemann and critically attuned evangelical theologians like Richard Lints, David Wells, Mark Noll, George Marsden, and John Stott. The point here is that one can find important threads of common agreement between postliberal (even in its dialectical variants) and evangelical thought in the basics of the tradition of the Protestant Reformers, as reflected in the quotation above from Hall. I do not deny the persistence of significant differences on such critical issues as the role of history in determining the validity of core biblical claims, the radical particularity of the Christian profession, and the viability of making foundational truth claims within the realm of faith. Nonetheless, in building critically on the insights of Hall and Dorrien, I seek to offer some mediating perspectives that can provide a level of biblical depth and theological acuity sometimes missing in mainline and evangelical circles. Any rigorous encounter between faith and culture from the grounding point of a biblically based revelation requires such depth. For that, the neo-orthodox legacy has much to offer.[13]

With Bloesch, Fackre, and Bernard Ramm,[14] I draw on the neo-orthodox legacy to foster an open-ended dialogue between Protestant mainline and evangelical theology. I do so by focusing on Barth's illuminated word-based theology, Bonhoeffer's "worldly Christianity," and Reinhold Niebuhr's paradoxical theology grounded in the dynamic tension between the penultimate reality of history and the ultimate truth of God's revelation that extends "beyond history." I conclude my discussion of the neo-orthodox theologians by drawing on the relevance of H. R. Niebuhr's *Radical Monotheism in Western Culture* and *Christ and Culture* for the current period.

I have expressed my reservations on the extent to which a revitalization of a centrist theological project is plausible in our given historical context. I perceive the diaspora to which Hall refers in *Confessing the Faith* as not only reflective of the social and cultural marginality of mainline Protestantism within the US culture. More fundamentally, and in a more problematic sense, there is only a marginal appreciation, at best, of the rich theological vision that Hall envisions pervasive within the identity of many mainline churches, denominations, clergy, and congregational members. Notwithstanding this problem, a variety of confessing Christ movements, attuned to the historical Protestant tradition rooted in the Reformation, have emerged within the mainline denominations in recent decades. What seems plausible at this time is the growth of such revitalization movements

13. Hall, *Remembered Voices*; Dorrien, *Barthian Revolt in Modern Theology*.
14. Ramm, *After Fundamentalism*.

within the Protestant mainline denominations, with the potential of becoming an enduring presence within them. Such growth could lead to a greater legitimacy for an ecumenical orthodoxy, based on the centrality of the Bible as a primary source of revelation; a stance that contradicts many of the core assumptions of both the modernist and postmodernist presuppositions that underlie contemporary Protestant mainline theology and religious culture.

The extent to which such confessing Christ movements become mediating rather than polarizing will depend on the degree to which evangelical and postliberal theologians and church practitioners find sufficient common theological ground within the heritage of the Reformation to build a broad based religious culture. I am not sure the extent to which such convergence is plausible given the need for a shift to biblical and theological dogmatics over apologetics (culture) as an ultimate grounding point of faith.

I do not deny, as Fackre illuminates in particular (as also evident in Dorrien's, historical probes), that the issues raised from various theological quarters require close attention. I have sought to address some of these through the various chapters of this book. Yet, unless such a perspective on the centrality of Scripture as the basis for engaging the culture is embraced, I do not see how the persisting declension in mainline Protestantism can be reversed. Diaspora within the culture offers its own set of challenges in grappling with the significance of the church's residency in its post-Constantinian reality where culture lags persist, pointing to an earlier era construction of broad social influence. An acceptance within the mainline denominations of a powerfully grounded Word-based faith is another matter altogether. A revitalization of the neo-orthodox legacy has something to offer in pointing to the centrality of the Bible for mainline Protestants and in providing hermeneutical resources that evangelicals can appropriate in extending the meaning of, and discerningly moving beyond, the doctrine of biblical inerrancy. In this book we have seen this convergent potentiality in Bloesch's and Fackre's theology. I envisage such refocusing as a live option, even as the great divide between fundamentalism and modernism is likely to persist as an enduringly iconographic presence within the household of American Protestantism for some time to come.

BARTH AND BULTMANN: A CRITICAL ENCOUNTER

From the vast collection of Barth's many texts, I focus on his singular theme of the illuminated word as the basis for interpreting the sum total of human and creational reality.[15] My motivation here is less historical than exemplary

15. Barth, *Dogmatics in Outline*, 9–14; *God Here and Now*, 13–33. "God's word does

in positing Barth's radical baseline as a critical theological challenge in the current setting. My core argument is that Barth's central call to turn the culture/Scripture relationship of contemporary mainline Protestantism on its head through the illuminated Word can play a significant role in mediating the fundamentalist/modern divide in the contemporary era.

As indicated in previous chapters, the Barthian vision is an underlying thread in the theology of Bloesch, Fackre, and Brueggemann. Even Packer admires Barth's substantive commitment to the Bible, which he maintained through the course of his *Church Dogmatics*. It was this enduring fidelity to the Word-inspired text that both sustained his earlier, more dialectical theology and distinguished him from all of the other leading theologians of the neo-orthodox movement. As one might discern from the following passage, it is the persistence in Barth of a Word-based theology that makes his relationship with Bultmann of continuing relevance, given the latter's influence throughout twentieth-century liberal and existential theology. As Barth put it:

> I have found myself in an intensive, although for the most part quiet, debate with Rudolf Bultmann. His name is not mentioned often. But his subject is always present, even in those places where with his methods and results before me I have consciously ignored him. I respect the man, his mind and aim and achievements, and the zeal of his following. I only wish I could do him greater justice. But If I have to choose between, on the one hand, accepting the rule which he has proclaimed and thus not being able to say certain things which I believe ought to be said, or having to say them very differently from

---

not harmonize with other words, for there exists no second and third, but only one Word of God. Thus it cannot be heard with other words, nor can it be heard inclusively. It can be heard only exclusively, or else not at all. Other words can only be its echo or a response to it, giving a contradictory or acknowledging answer. As God is unique so is his Word . . . Put the one Word side by side with others and it becomes already powerless, comfortless, and without creative might. But it would not be the Word of God we are hearing at all if it were put side by side with others. The sovereignty of the Word of God is distinguished by the fact that it has no competitors." *God Here and Now*, 22. Barth never budged from this position even in his later theology in keeping a sharp edge focus on God as wholly other. According to Metzger, Barth ultimately established a theology of constructive engagement with culture through his Christology. This enabled Barth "to truly speak of God's transcendence in such a way that it would not threaten the doctrine of the divine immanence." Only by giving "proper attention . . . to God's humanity" through his Christology "could Barth offer the assurance that humanity and human culture would be preserved and not annihilated, before God in his Word." *Word of Christ and the World of Culture*, 41. That assurance was not so clear in his earlier dialectical period, as reflected in Barth's groundbreaking text *Epistle to the Romans*.

how I perceive them, and on the other hand saying them quite freely, but making myself guilty of using what he regards as an "obscure conceptuality," then I have no option but to choose the second. His hermeneutical suggestions can become binding on me only when I am convinced that by following them I would say the same thing better and more freely. For the time being I am not so convinced.[16]

Dorrien provides illuminating insights on how each of these profoundly formative theologians processed the relationship between historical research and the nature of Christian belief.[17] The common link was their shared embrace of "dialectical theology" in the 1920s that included rejection of theological liberalism, on the one hand, and a more traditional orthodoxy, on the other. Both theologians accepted the validity of the search for the historical Jesus as a legitimate scholarly pursuit while they rejected its relevance for direct theological application. Despite this commonality, the significance they each drew from this rich German scholarship on historical research pushed the trajectory of their theological development in fundamentally different directions. What is pertinent here is the continuing importance of these differences on how the relationship between faith and culture is processed in our current setting.

In the broadest of terms, Bultmann critiqued the "outdated ontology"[18] of traditional Reformation theology that needed to be demythologized in order to preserve the core kerygma of Christian salvation in a manner that addressed the existential issues of the human condition of early twentieth-century Europe. He argued that the apocalyptical message of the historical Jesus was no longer credible as part of a contemporary Christian worldview. In rejecting a pre-scientific depictions of a "three-story structure"[19] of the New Testament world, Bultmann sought to probe into the "deeper meaning" of the kerygma "which is concealed under the cover of mythology."[20] Stated otherwise, his purposes were overwhelmingly epistemological rather than ontological in nature. "Deny[ing] that the message of Scripture and of the Church is bound to an ancient world view which is obsolete,"[21] what was

---

16. Barth, *Doctrine of Reconciliation*, ix.
17. See Dorrien, *Word as True Myth*, 76–86, 99, and *Barthian Revolt*, 104–6.
18. Dorrien, *Word as True Myth*, 100.
19. Ibid., 102; cited from Bultmann, "New Testament and Mythology," 1.
20. Bultmann, "Jesus Christ and Mythology," 293.
21. Ibid., 300.

critical for Bultmann was one's "personal response to the Word" of God.[22] At the core of what Bultmann sought to preserve was an

> open[ness] to God's future which is really imminent for every one of us; to be prepared for this future which can come as a thief in the night when we do not expect it; to be prepared, because this future will be a judgment on all men who have bound themselves to this world and are not free, not open to God's future.[23]

Anything that occluded this ineffable presence in the very midst of human temporality needed to be excised. This included rejection of outmoded word pictures of earlier world constructions that Bultmann contended had given shape to a great deal of historical orthodox theology, as well of Barth's, especially in *Church Dogmatics*. This impetus gave force to his theological project grounded in the presuppositions of Heideggarian existentialism.[24]

Bultmann pressed hard for Barth to articulate the interpretive presuppositions underlying his theology.[25] Barth understood that the epistemological issue was unavoidable, but refused to move outside of the hermeneutical circle of faith in order to respond. That would have required him to engage in what he interpreted as a form of anthropological absolutism (the bane of theological liberalism) since it was God the almighty where Barth stood his ground rather than history as the ultimate arbiter of truth and therefore of reality. Barth took what he viewed as the more radical tack in constructing his edifice on the ontological scaffolding of the kerygma as an underlying *truth* claim, in search of epistemological explanation. Whether Kant, Plato, Hegel, Kierkegaard, Dostoevsky, or a slew of liberal or more orthodox theologians, Barth drew on whatever set of philosophical and theological resources could shed needed clarity on "the self-authentic sufficiency of God's word."[26] He sought, on this core turn, to ground twentieth-century Protestant theology within the historic Reformation heritage and to undo the historicist paths of liberalism grounded in Schleiermacher's vision, from which Barth's illuminated-Word theology would never entirely escape.

The project that Barth embraced required the more pressing task of turning on its head the historicist presuppositions of theological liberalism and biblical critical scholarship. This goal entailed interpreting dogmatics as

22. Dorrien, *Word as True Myth*, 107.
23. Bultmann, Jesus Christ and Mythology," 298.
24. Dorrien, *Word as True Myth*, 99–101.
25. Ibid.
26. Dorrien, *Barthian Revolt in Modern Theology*, 76. See ibid., 47–80 for an in-depth discussion of dialectical theology in Barth's thought.

"*the science in which the Church . . . takes account of the content of its proclamation critically, that is by the standard of the Holy Scripture and under the guidance of its Confessions.*"[27] For Barth, this was the starting point to which scholarship and theology had to respond.

The trajectory of a great deal of contemporary theological scholarship has traveled broadly along the pathway laid out by Bultmann.[28] More so than Barth perhaps acknowledged, the emphasis on apologetics remains a critically important biblically mandated project (1 Pet 3:15), upon which Moltmann has done so much to bring to focus in the contemporary period.[29] Yet, historicism as an absolutizing tendency remains a central point of focus in a great deal of liberal theology and critical biblical scholarship, where one may read of Roland Barthes, but not of Karl Barth.[30] Historical and cultural determinism may also be an underlying unconscious presupposition within the pews of the mainline churches, giving force to its pervasive biblical illiteracy, thereby ceding the Bible as the inspired Word of God to the fundamentalists and conservative evangelicals without much critical or imaginative rejoinder of reclamation.[31]

As long as historicism adheres as an ultimate value within contemporary liberal biblical and theological scholarship, this trend can only continue, largely unabated. The only substantial antidote is to relativize historical and cultural determinism itself through some substantial re-encounter of the dogmatics of faith in which *its* object becomes the focal point of theological concentration. Apologetics should be conjoined in a more substantial way than Barth was able to focus on. Yet, it needs to become embodied in the service of Christian orthodox biblical interpretation and theology through a faithful ecumenical lens, where in principle, all that is proclaimed in 2 Timothy 3:16 can be richly embraced, ultimately without equivocation. This is a call for a discerning irenic lens within a broad-based orthodox tradition as the very foundation of faith itself (John 3:3–21). Viewed from these perspectives, Barth's project continues to offer much to draw on for contemporary theological renewal.

---

27. Barth, *Dogmatics in Outline*, 9.

28. For a contemporary example, see Ogden, *Doing Theology Today*, esp. 210–44.

29. Moltmann, *Experiences in Theology*.

30. Aichele et al., *Postmodern Bible*, 384. There are over twenty references to Barthes listed in the index, but not one mention of Barth.

31. See Lawson, *Cracking the Book*, for an exemplary overview of the Bible designed to appeal to interested members of mainline Protestant denominations.

BARTH'S DOCTRINE OF THE ILLUMINATED WORD OF GOD

What then of Barth's project? As a "critical science," dogmatics starts from the evidence of faith—the same basis upon which the "apostles and prophets" grounded their core revelatory claims; the reality of "God's self-evidence" perceived through the direct illumination of the Holy Spirit and the testimony (past and present) of a mighty cloud of witnesses (Heb 12:1). For Barth, such a revelatory grounding point serves as a core datum inherent within the very Word of God revealed to humankind. It was *this* illumination that underlined the focus of his dogmatic work in the biblically revealed God in Christ.[32]

It was this vision that stimulated Barth's unrelenting existential commitment to church-based dogmatics. Such faith could only be experienced through the persuasive power of the still, small voice resident sometimes even in the most abject hopelessness (1 John 3:20). In this, Barth acknowledged the inescapability of felt perception within the dogmatic frame of his theology of the illuminated Word. For without this inward capacity at some substantially convincing level, bestowed by grace, it would be impossible to believe in any meaningful sense. Yet, for Barth, the focal point was the content of faith—the sovereignty of God and the divine imminence of Jesus Christ—rather than the nature or credibility of belief in itself.[33] This shift to ontology was needed in order to move beyond the invariable reductionism in the concentration on perception, as reflected in a century's worth of liberal theological probing.

Barth found his theological voice through an "obscure conceptuality"[34] that had underlain the tremendous force of his theological project. This enabled him to change the subject of the prevailing discourse of early modern liberalism and existentialism, both of which were grounded in the experience of faith. The sum result was magnificent, even with the invariable limitations and rejoinders that a critical examination of his work brings out. In his largely appreciative stance, Hunsinger is far from unaware of these latter concerns. This irenic position enables him to focus on the substance of Barth's theological project in fleshing out something of the depth and

---

32. Barth, *Dogmatics in Outline*, 12, 13.

33. As Barth states, "We cannot pursue dogmatics without this standard being kept in sight. We must always be putting the question, 'What is the evidence?' Not the evidence of my thoughts or my heart, but the evidence of the apostles and prophets, as the evidence of God's self-evidence. Should a dogmatics lose sight of this standard, it would be an irrelevant dogmatics." Ibid., 13.

34. Barth, *Doctrine of Reconciliation*, ix.

range of Barth's emphasis on God as Wholly Other.[35] In Barth's terms, it is this very God, as revealed in and through the Bible, who chose to enter into human story, who—by the very depth of his transcendence—brought salvation to humankind that could not be accomplished by any merely immanent influence within history or nature.

In Barth's postulation, God is the unquestionable presupposition of faith. This God—rooted in history, the Bible, and most concretely in Jesus Christ—is the antithesis of anything that could pass as a human projection. According to Barth, there is a radical distinction between the Christian revelation and all other depictions of explicit or implicit divinity, whether formally religious or as manifested in natural philosophy, such as the philosopher Dewey's poignant existential study, *Experience and Nature*. It is this key text in its ardent probing of the range and limits of transcendence within human experience, along with Heidegger's *Being and Time*, that, within the intellectual history of the early twentieth-century West, stand in sharp antithesis to Barth's *Epistle to the Romans* and *Church Dogmatics*. Such "active longing" for human fulfillment as the stimulant and "object of man's homesickness"[36] that one finds in both Dewey and Heidegger is a false basis for hope from the Christian perspective. Barth did not question the longing; rather, he rejected its identification with some Absolute, including the view that the divine is synonymous with any Tillichian notion of the ground of our being.

In positing God as radical other, Barth sought to eradicate the subtle pantheistic elements that had underlain liberal theology for the preceding century, a trend that would remain pervasive throughout the twentieth century, despite the very substantial—but ultimately limited—neo-orthodox interlude. In contrast to all of humanity's projections and idealizations, this God, revealed through a particular Scripture, "is the One who stands *above* us." This God is "also above our highest and deepest feelings, [and] strivings, intuitions," beyond the most subliminal impulse "of the human spirit."[37] It is this most transcendent God who has "condescended to us" to be one of us without sacrificing an iota of his divinity. It is this God who is spoken of "in the book of the Old and New Testaments"—and from no other independent source beyond that proclaimed in Scripture—as God almighty in the

---

35. Hunsinger includes a lengthy epilogue on Barth's acknowledgment of "secular parables." *How to Read Karl Barth*, 234–80. These "parables" as signs contain truth that can and should be incorporated into the fuller truth of the revelation of God in the incarnation of Jesus Christ. Ibid., 260.

36. Barth, *Dogmatics in Outline*, 35.

37. Ibid., 37.

highest, creator and Father of our Lord Jesus Christ.[38] As Barth posits, "once a man has understood 'God in the highest' it becomes impossible for him to want any imagery in thought, or any other kind of imagery"[39] that would detract from the majestic depth and utter poignancy of this God; the one most fully revealed in the incarnation of Jesus Christ.

A TILLICHIAN CRITIQUE

Along with Bultmann, Tillich stands in the most symbolic contrast to Barth within the neo-orthodox tradition. This is a significance that does not only reside in the realm of the historical, but also in contemporary theology, given that Bultmann and Tillich remain high status iconic figures. That Tillich did not fully appreciate the dialectical power in Barth's work even after his dogmatic turn is an important matter in its own right.[40] The more pressing issue that Tillich raised was (and for our purposes, is) the very viability of Barth's biblical dogmatic turn. I cannot provide here an extended review of Tillich's critique and the feasibility of his "theonomous" project. However, a few compelling issues can be probed through a consideration of Tillich's 1936 critique of Barth's "'dialectical' theology."[41]

Tillich raised the key point that, in its most radical turn, dialectical theology positions God's sovereignty not only against the world, but also against the bourgeoisified church of nineteenth- and early twentieth-century German society. In a refrain that remained a core assumption of Tillich's throughout his career, God has the capacity "to make more of his will known through a contemporary secular movement . . . than through ecclesiastic activities and the churchly forms of piety."[42] With Barth, Tillich was highly critical of any non-dialectical liberalism. On this concern, he echoed a refrain pervasive throughout neo-orthodox theology against liberalism's substitution of sin embedded within human experience for that of "the self-developing personality"[43] and any conflation of the kingdom

38. Ibid.
39. Ibid., 41.
40. Hunsinger notes that "dialectic and analogy are merely two sides of the same coin—where you have one you have the other—and Barth had both from the early period onward. After 1931 dialectic was thoroughly subjected on principle to analogy (though not expunged. . .), because Barth found a way he had not seen before to conceive of theological language as the vehicle of positive analogical reference to God." *How to Read Karl Barth*, 17. See also Dorrien, *Barthian Revolt in Modern Theology*, 196.
41. Tillich, "What Is Wrong with the 'Dialectical' Theology?," 104.
42. Ibid., 105.
43. Ibid., 106.

of God with social reform. As reflected in his collections of sermons (such as *The Shaking of the Foundations* and the *Eternal Now*), as a "boundary" theologian, Tillich—at least in theory—affirmed the church in its calling as the body of Christ. He also adhered to the theology of the Bible as the inspired word of God. His sermon in the latter collection on the seventh chapter of Paul's Epistle to the Romans ("The Good That I Will, I Do Not"[44]) echoed refrains laid out by Barth in his commentary to *The Epistle to the Romans*—the formative text that ushered in the neo-orthodox movement.

Tillich's primary critique of Barth was his shift from a dialectical to a "supernatural" theology after *The Epistle to the Romans*. According to Tillich, this latter move cut Barth off from a critical facet of the dynamic power of God, who, through the *kairos* of the Holy Spirit, infuses the human spirit in its existentialist, social, and cultural modes. In the process, Barth settled for an orthodox stance that Tillich contended impaired the vitality "the theonomous," the "prophetic word," where "the contradiction between autonomy and heteronomy is overcome."[45] Tillich argued that Barth's supernaturalist turn skated perilously close to a heteronomy that he defined as uncritical and undialectical "submission to divine or secular authorities."[46] Further, Tillich accused Barth of constructing a Christ "above history" who is not directly engaged with "the development of human history and human spiritual life." This Barthian Christ is only "insert[ed] into history" from above and discerned only through the mystical power of the Holy Spirit.[47]

Tillich also viewed Barth's evasion of the critical biblical scholarship of the early twentieth century an escape mechanism. This provided Barth's orthodoxy with a certain protective sealing, but at the expense of distancing the Christ of the New Testament from the concrete Jesus who lived and died at a certain time and place. Other than for historical purposes, neither was Tillich fundamentally interested in this concrete figure that lived almost two thousand years ago. Rather, Tillich made the existential argument that God breaks into human reality in whatever ways he chooses, in which neither Scripture nor church tradition has any privileged status. Nonetheless, Tillich used the historical argumentation in the effort to deconstruct Barth's Word-inspired biblicalism.

According to Tillich, God's revelation may be "linked with the Bible"[48] and often is, though not necessarily so. This is an interpretation Barth would

---

44. Tillich, *Eternal Now*, 122–32.
45. Tillich, *On the Boundary*, 41.
46. Ibid., 38.
47. Tillich, "What Is Wrong with the 'Dialectical' Theology?," 107.
48. Ibid., 108. According to Tillich, the indwelling word of God "occur[s]. . .when

accept—though not Tillich's view of the Bible, given that Barth interpreted Scripture as the primary source through which God speaks to humankind. Barth identified the Bible as a privileged text, indeed.[49]

Tillich categorically rejected Barth's view of God's sovereignty as so extreme that it "is not blended with any form of human existence and action." In this, Tillich took to task "not only a criticism of Barth," but widespread traditional theological views "of the Bible, the church, and theology in general."[50] Tillich targeted theism which he referred to as "supernaturalism." To this he posited "dialectics" as the critical counterpoint through which the "impossible possibility"[51] of God's revelation breaks forth within the dynamic flow of human history. The *kairos* of God's revelation may emerge within a church context as in the Barmen Declaration of 1933, in the "worldly Christianity" of Bonhoeffer's martyrdom, or in a religiously infused socialist movement. The latter could conceivably accomplish more of ushering in God's grace within the fabric of concrete historical reality than the most exacting orthodoxy that remains so otherworldly that it leaves the fate of existing historical struggle to the forces of the non-religious and to the ever infallible mystery of God's will. In the face of the Nazi onslaught—Barmen notwithstanding—this was Tillich's most telling critique of Barth's "supernaturalist" turn.

To be sure, Tillich understood that "culture is not revelation," though it "is a human possibility" where the power of God can break through. Culture has the capacity for "divine possibility," but only if revelation is a phenomenon that can be perceived within the midst of a given cultural matrix. Tillich affirmed Barth's repudiation of "all attempts to find a point in man where he may be able to find and lay hold of God."[52] With Barth, he noted that there is no direct entrée to God's presence that is not transcendent in the most fundamental sense.

Nonetheless, Tillich insisted that the connection between our nature and God's becomes the basis for experiencing the indwelling presence of God. Without this connection between God and human experience, faith is in danger of becoming a phantom. This quest for transcendence that arises

---

the event [of revelation] happens" and nowhere else. "It is linked with the Bible, but we do not possess it when we possess the Bible." Ibid.

49. According to Barth, "The Biblical witness is the visible form of the otherwise hidden presence and Lordship of Jesus Christ." Further, "There is no other visible and, in the strict sense of the word, authoritative Word of God, no other binding form of the divine dominion, than the Holy Scriptures." *God Here and Now*, 57, 61.

50. Tillich, "What Is Wrong with the 'Dialectical' Theology?," 108.

51. Ibid.

52. Ibid., 112.

within human experience is stimulated by the various problems, aspirations, and mysteries that garner our foremost attention. The power of these forces drives us beyond ourselves to find resolutions through which the *kairos* of God's Holy Spirit may break through. Tillich maintained that this is so even when there is no correlation between the nature of our questions and God's answers. He argued that the provocations which compel us may very well be a means of knowing God in the sense that "sin could never be experienced as sin without the anthropological possibility of guilt and despair."[53] He also acknowledged that without the biblical referent it would not be possible to ground experience in anything beyond the anthropological. Tillich and Barth shared a common view on this, even as they substantially differed in their focal areas of concern. It is evident that Tillich gave greater attention to the various "hints of the Kingdom of God"[54] that break into human experience through the pathways of culture. Even so, in his later career Barth acknowledged the relative importance of "secular parables."[55]

Barth did not deny what Tillich pointed to, but did not want to lend to cultural influences greater credibility than warranted. This was the case, particularly if the cost was at the expense of diluting the ontological claims of faith that were put in peril through a century of epistemological focus on the question of human meaning. Tillich acknowledged the substantial contribution of Barth in saving "theology from forgetting the deity of God and . . . the church from lapsing into secularism and paganism."[56] It is another matter whether Barth was guilty of displacing dialecticism with supernaturalism in his foremost desire to place the focus of theological concentration on the sovereignty of God and the incarnation of Jesus Christ. Tillich's definition of supernaturalism is also questionable in that it challenges any robust sense of theism that is at the core of orthodox Christian theology. The reemergence of these issues within contemporary evangelical-mainline discourse speaks of the enduring importance of these two theological giants.

A BARTHIAN REJOINDER

According to Hall, "what distinguishes Tillich's method from the prophetic tradition" out of which Barth wrote "is a very different theory of reality," a "substantialistic" in contrast to a "relational" one at the core of the Hebraic vision. In putting its primary focus on the underlying belief in humanity's

---

53. Ibid., 113.
54. Ibid., 115.
55. Hunsinger, *How to Read Karl Barth*, 234–80.
56. Tillich, "What Is Wrong with the 'Dialectical' Theology?," 116.

created status, the prophetic view places less emphasis on the metaphysical nature of humankind. The biblical vision is based on a humanity that has "the creaturely capacity for [right] relationship" with the living God, though "not necessarily actualized."[57] Rather than being per se—which is taken as an unproblematic and relatively uninteresting biblical given—the human capacity for right and wrong thought and action in relationship to the unfathomable God, whose name is known and not known (Exod 3:14–15), is at the center of the Hebraic outlook. In the Hebraic perspective, "ontology is not about *being* as such, but *being-with*," which "presupposes the genuine prospect of *not* being with, of being-against, and being alone—in short, of discontinuity."[58]

In line with the Hebraic view, Barth embraced the full relational sense of God and humanity through the biblical imagery of God the Father. This God—both almighty and the highest, who seeks to embrace humanity with his unconditional love—is the basis of Barth's theism. It is this Father God who begot his own Son as well as his very Spirit, the Word, which was "in the beginning" (John 1:1) and manifested in the incarnation of his Son who "became flesh and made his dwelling among us" (John 1:14). The relational nature of the Hebraic *cum* Christian vision is not only a depiction of the covenant between God and a particular representative people. It is also inherent in the mutual indwelling of God within his Trinitarian existence. This relational view is at the foundation of Barth's Spirit-Word theology.

Barth acknowledged God's inscrutability beyond all human knowing. Through his incarnations in Christ and in the Holy Spirit, God becomes nothing less than "the Father for us."[59] In this capacity "he is not a lonely God," one so distant that relationship with him would be well-nigh impossible.[60] Rather than a human construct, the biblical revelation of the Fatherhood of God becomes the basis for interpreting "true and proper Fatherhood."[61] Barth subsumed dialectics within his underlying dogmatic belief in God's faithfulness to his covenantal relationship to humanity. This relationship holds, whether God is with or against us in any particular situation of obedience or disobedience. It is this understanding of theism coming through the still, small prompting of the Holy Spirit through which Barth responded to Tillich's charge of "supernaturalism." Stated in philosophical terms, Barth argued in support of a theistic ontology that privileges

---

57. Hall, *Thinking the Faith*, 359.
58. Ibid., 359–60.
59. Barth, *Dogmatics in Outline*, 43.
60. Ibid., 42.
61. Ibid., 43

the relational dynamic of a particular covenant over against any universal ontology of being.

Barth recognized that "human concepts can never be more than an indication of Him." He acknowledged that it "is inconceivable"[62] to know God in a manner that even approaches certainty. God breaks into reality when, where, and how he will as a real presence, but the human capacity to grasp and comprehend that indwelling is limited by the only means available: analogical reflection through signs and parallels which, by definition, cannot extend beyond the symbolism of language itself. God's reality (the ontological referent) exists beyond the sign; in the final analysis, the actual is not language, as depicted in postmodern philosophy. Yet it is only through language—in this case, the biblical text—through the internal witness of the Holy Spirit—that we can perceive this particular God at all. Barth did not reject such philosophical attributes (analogies) that refer to God's aseity, infinity, eternity, and omnipotence. He subsumed them within the more evocative imagery (analogical, also) of God Almighty as issued in the Apostles' Creed.[63]

It is the purity and precariousness of the felt sense of the uniqueness and holiness of God that heightened Barth's sense that human beings can only come to terms with God's revelation through imaginative appropriation of "the biblical witness." "The visible form of this otherwise hidden presence" of God "is in the "Lordship of Jesus Christ."[64] This is so whether the revelation of God in Christ is the result of direct personal experience of the power of the Holy Spirit or through the more indirect route of the mighty cloud of witnesses. Barth found practical resolution of the dialectical tension between certainty and doubt in relation to faith through prayer

---

62. Ibid., 46. As Barth further stated, "Only derivatively, only in a secondary sense can we venture to take His Word on our lips." Ibid.

63. Barth linked the concept of God's almightiness with his power, will, and purpose, as embodied in the Trinity. "He is the basic measure of everything real and everything possible." Ibid., Barth noted that statements such as these can be used in "constructing general concepts" about God. Ibid., 47. They are valid, but misleading and incomplete when relied upon as final vocabulary about God. It is biblical language that is required to get at a fuller sense of God's power which is "real power"—in fact, the only real power. It is the God as embodied in the Bible that "is superior to all other powers." It is this God who is "the Lord of Lord, the King of all kings." Ibid., It "is the power of His free love in Jesus Christ, activated and revealed in Him." Ibid., 49. It is the power of this love in apparent powerlessness that is the true power through which God expresses his almightiness. No language other than biblical language—however analogical—can (in-)adequately capture the power and character of God than that revealed in the Jewish and Christian Scripture.

64. Barth, *God Here and Now*, 57.

and surrender. Such faith can only be accessed through the appropriation of biblical language:

> There are many events, powers, forms, and truths which are important, worthwhile, and indispensable for us men, but there is only *one* Word of God, only *one* Jesus Christ, in whom the confrontation of the gracious God with sinful men took place once for all. And because not all, but only these particular men are elected, called prophetic and apostolic witnesses to Jesus Christ, there are many hidden forms but only this *one* visible form of the one Word of God. Only in this form is God's Word finally, decisively normative, binding, and authoritative. The Church of Jesus Christ acknowledges the unique Word of the unique God in this uniquely visible and uniquely normative form. In this knowledge, it sets the biblical canon.[65]

Barth also put it this way: "There is no other visible and, in the strict sense of the word, authoritative Word of God, no other binding form of the divine domination than the Holy Scriptures."[66] It is on this grounding in the Bible—not as an inerrant word, but as illuminated by the Holy Spirit—that Barth could embrace the kerygmatic witness of Scripture as a primary source of revelation. The epistemological ground remains that of self-authentication in critical dialogue with biblical testimony and the historical witness of an almost two thousand–year tradition. The ontological truth claim (to which the evidence points) is God's revelation in the midst of human experience, even in its masking within the very center of God's hiddenness. Such revealing within creation in any given context is "a particular determination" of God's triune fullness "in which the biblical witness"[67] illuminates God's actual presence to those able to receive it. Such revealing sometimes takes place even among those who may not be at least initially receptive to it.

Barth declared within this biblically based ontological grounding of truth—that is both revealing and hidden—that "God's power is different than powerlessness." Such power given in signs and wonders bestowed within and reflected through creation "is superior to other powers, and is victoriously opposed to power in itself."[68] The distinguishing characteristic is the capacity of this God, "who has not the nature of a shadow" and "is

---

65. Barth, *God Here and Now*, 60.
66. Ibid., 61.
67. Ibid., 64.
68. Barth, *Dogmatics in Outline*, 47.

opposed to every powerlessness" to be "able to do what he wills to do."[69] Such a God is not only love, but "the light [that] shines in the darkness" (John 1:5), the very logos that gives meaning to the created order. It is upon this rock that the fulfillment of the creation is proclaimed as "the theater of His glory,"[70] of which Christ incarnate is the fullest sign (Col 1:15). In his passionate desire to turn twentieth-century biblical ontology on its head, this critical aspect of Barth's theology can be summed up in the following:

> God is the content, the determination, the limit of all that is possible. And in that way He is over all that is real as the immanent God—He, the Subject, who utters this holy and good word and plies His holy and good work.[71]

It is on this framework that Barth sought to posit a compelling critique against Tillich's method of the correlation of faith and culture and of the prevailing trajectories of nineteenth- and twentieth-century Protestant theological liberalism.

From a rigorous and ecumenical Christian orthodox position one can incorporate much from Barth's core vision of turning modern secular ontology on its head through the prism of the strange new world within the Bible. The radical seriousness through which Barth embraced the biblical worldview as the only viable foundation for a modern theology serves as a potent symbol for any rigorous hermeneutical retrieval of the tradition of the Protestant Reformers in the contemporary setting.

BONHOEFFER'S "WORLDLY" CHRISTIANITY

Both Barth and Bonhoeffer laid great emphasis on the centrality of Christ as revealed in the Word. They also highlighted the importance of living out the faith in the church and the world. They both were dogmatic dialecticians seeking to make sense of the reality of God's revelation in Christ as worked out in the "crisis" theology that underlined the neo-orthodox movement, particularly in Europe from the 1920s to the 1940s. Barth's concentrated more exclusively on the centrality of dogma as revealed through the Word, while Bonhoeffer attended more to the significance of the revelation of God for right action in the midst of the contingency of living history.[72]

---

69. Ibid.
70. Ibid., 58.
71. Ibid., 49.
72. For an insightful comparison between Barth and Bonhoeffer, see Dorrien, *Barthian Revolt in Modern Theology*, 149–57.

Because of this focus, the "secular" theologians of the 1960s drew on Bonhoeffer's "religionless" Christianity to articulate what they considered a more viable vision of the Christian faith.[73] The search, in the 1960s, for a new language beyond religion, represented a *kairotic* desire for an authentic revelation among those for whom traditional pieties and orthodoxies no longer held sway. Bonhoeffer became a precursor among those theologians who rejected the traditional "three-story" theistic God that could not stand given the flourishing of critical biblical scholarship, the academic legitimacy of post–World War II liberal thought and culture, and the centrality of pluralism underlying the increasing embrace of a global worldview.[74] In a quest for a post-war vision beyond neo-orthodoxy, the "secular" Bonhoeffer (as an alter ego to that of Barth) served as an important figure in the death of God theological imagination.

Bonhoeffer pushed the boundaries of faith in his search for a "religionless" Christianity in the midst of the most searing of perplexities forced upon Germany by the Nazis.[75] This was particularly evident in light of his *Letters and Papers from Prison*. Yet it was this same Bonhoeffer who spoke of the God who resided more at the center of life than at the boundary, "not in weakness" of faith, "but in strength," the strength of authentic proclamation in the midst of life. Rather than the God "beyond . . . our cognitive facilities," Bonhoeffer emphasized the "God . . . beyond in the midst of our life."[76]

The Bonhoeffer that I draw on here is based primarily on *The Cost of Discipleship* and *Ethics*. This is both a worldly and church-focused Bonhoeffer, who searched long and hard for the indwelling of Christ in the midst of any given historical setting. *This* Bonhoeffer is not set in antithesis against the neo-orthodox Barth, but is one that shared significant affinities with him, while bringing out important themes that remained more tangential in his mentor's work. As Bonhoeffer put it in his critique of the secular/

---

73. Bonhoeffer, *Letters and Papers from Prison*, 278–82. The death of God theologians drew particularly on the following from Bonhoeffer's 1944 letter to Eberhard Bethge: "What do a church, a community, a sermon, a liturgy, a community life mean in a religionless world? How do we speak of God—without religion, i.e., without the temporally conditioned presuppositions of metaphysics, inwardness, and so on? How do we speak (or perhaps we cannot even 'speak' as we used to) in a 'secular' way about God? In what way are we 'religionless-secular' Christians, in what way are we the. . .[church], those who are called forth, not regarding ourselves from a religious point of view as specially favored but rather as belonging wholly to the world? In that case Christ is no longer an object of religion, but something quite different, really, the Lord of the world." Ibid., 280–81.

74. Grenz and Olson, *20th Century Theology*, 156–67.

75. Lawrence, *Bonhoeffer*, 104–9.

76. Bonhoeffer, *Letters and Papers from Prison*, 282.

religious polarities that provoked and stimulated Reinhold Niebuhr and Tillich:

> There are not two spheres, standing side by side, competing with each other and attacking each other's frontiers. If that were so, this frontier dispute would always be the decisive problem of history. But the whole reality of the world is already drawn into Christ and bound together in Him, and the movement of history consists solely in divergence and convergence in relation to this centre.[77]

Bonhoeffer sought to move beyond any sterile orthodoxy to the extent that doctrine impeded the free flowing power of the Holy Spirit. At the same time, he remained fully committed to the centrality of the Bible as the primary source of revelation—including the scriptural emphasis on the majesty of God in his capacity to speak within any context and idiom that he so desired. It is this more Barthian Bonhoeffer who gave shape to a worldly-sensitive Christianity as reflected in his key text—*Ethics*. This Bonhoeffer offers a great deal for the contemporary church in any hermeneutical retrieval of the ethos of the Reformation in an early twenty-first-century context.

Bonhoeffer noted that "the essence of the gospel does not lie in the solution of human problems."[78] Rather, it is in radical obedience to Christ in each and every situation. What radical commitment to faith necessitated for Bonhoeffer was nothing less than unswerving obedience to the very call of God—to surrender all for the privilege of following Christ for the entire course of one's life. Anything less is a holding back: some adherence to the idolatry of the self or culture that can only contradict the will of God in some fundamental way. Such obedience is not the Lutheran concern against works. Rather, it is the very essence of faith—costly faith in the midst of our fallen state where nothing we can do can right our relationship with the living God in which we are nonetheless called into radical obedience (Rom 3:31; 6:15–19). It is this same ethos of radical commitment to Christ, and to Christ alone, through which Bonhoeffer grounded the most elemental obligation of the church in relation to the world. For

> we know of no relation of God to the world other than through Jesus Christ. For the Church too, therefore, there is no relation to the world other than through Jesus Christ. In other words, the proper relation of the Church to the world cannot be deduced

---

77. Bonhoeffer, *Ethics*, 195.
78. Ibid., 351.

from natural law or rational law or from universal rights, but only from the gospel of Jesus Christ.[79]

The emphasis on the sovereignty of God shows the extent of Barth's influence. Bonhoeffer did not deny—as neither did Barth—that the church has a great deal to say about the broad range of human ethics since the spirit of Christ is revealed within the midst of, and through the signs of, our material existence. Bonhoeffer and Barth agreed that God can only be known analogically through the signs that his Spirit opens up to human perception. They each noted that the reality transcends the symbols which enclose the signs of God's revealing. Such signs flow forth within the context of any given time and place throughout all of the spheres of the "secular" realm in various hidden and revealing forms. The quest for the ultimate Word embedded within the penultimate experience of human history will lead to specific courses of action in given situations in accord with the prompting of the Holy Spirit. Such actions are invariably shaped by the contingencies of the historical context which, at best, results only in proximate resolution of complex human problems of both personal and collective sorts.

The dilemma over the abolition of slavery in the United States in the 1840s and 1850s among the northern clergy is a case in point. Many northern US clergy opposed the expansion of slavery and slavery itself in this time period. Most clergy also rejected abolitionism as endangering the stability of the republic, destroying any prospect of national religious unity, and potentially leading the nation into civil war. The tempered position on the slave issue taken by the northern clergy in the antebellum period spoke as much to the complexity of the issue as to any charge of moral hypocrisy. Horace Bushnell and other prominent anti-slavery leaning clergy viewed some form of gradual abolitionism through voluntary emancipation more plausible from God's eye than immediate abolitionism in the pre–Civil War era. As argued, particularly from various Calvinistic persuasions, given the historical complexity of a society and political culture rooted in sin wherein slavery had been institutionalized for almost two centuries, some form of gradualism was more akin to approximately meeting God's will than immediate abolitionism.[80]

That slavery was sin of a most egregious social and moral sort was widely accepted, at least amongst the clergy in the North by the 1850s. In this respect, a certain anti-slavery convergence was coming together over this looming issue that raised the most searing concerns in the realm of political ideology as well as a moral sensibility on the overarching need for

79. Ibid., 352.
80. Noll, *Civil War as a Theological Crisis*, 36–39.

national redemption. Nonetheless, even in the North, the ethics in how to resolve the dilemma of slavery was driven by acrimonious conflict in the two decades before the Civil War. The actual commencement of the Civil War profoundly changed the focus of the moral debate. It also unleashed a broad array of constitutional, moral, and religious dilemmas over the enduring legacy of racism that persisted for more than a century beyond the war.

To put this in Bonhoeffer's terms, God may have acted through the crisis of the Civil War. Yet, in the northern clerical mindset of the nineteenth-century evangelical imagination, the result was anything but a restoration of America as redeemer nation through the cleansing blood that was thought to have been released through the war. To put it again in Bonhoeffer's terms, whatever sense of God's ultimate will was unleashed through the Civil War became imperceptibly merged into the penultimacy of the ongoing flow of historical experience. It was here within history—in this case the century following the Civil War—that the spirit of Christ needed to be perceived and acted upon over the issue of race ever freshly anew in the midst of the most searing ambiguity and social and moral conflict. Bonhoeffer did not deny that God acts in history, sometimes in very decisive ways. The life and death issues that he faced in the 1930s and 1940s give vivid testimony to the *kairotic* energies that were operating in Europe in response to the unimaginable evil unleashed by Nazi Germany. The challenge, as Bonhoeffer posited, is the central quest to discern the will of God in every concrete situation in the midst of moral ambiguity.

Bonhoeffer's testing ground was nothing less than the most devastating war in the history of Europe in the midst of the most barbaric evil that the continent had ever experienced. In the need to surrender all for the following of God's will, as he understood it, into the very bowels of hell, if that is where it brought him, the cost for Bonhoeffer was nothing less than his life. In the process, the extremities and the centralities of his theological probing expanded in his always focused Christ the center vision as embodied within the church and within the world. What is critical for our purposes is not so much the crisis theology of the 1930s and 1940s, although that remains instructive. What is enduring is the force of Bonhoeffer's orthopraxy of pressing the Word of God to speak to the concrete historical situation in things great and small in bringing together the "secular" and the "religious" within a common interpretation.

The relevance of Bonhoeffer's "worldly" Christianity for our current setting may be further discerned by taking note of the four principle areas ("mandates") of application that he identified in *Ethics*: "labour, marriage, government, and the Church."[81] In all of these realms Bonhoeffer's underlying theological principles remain constant. Whatever courses of action or presuppositions that may emerge within the mandates, the pivotal point is that "each in its own way shall be through Christ, directed toward Christ, and in Christ."[82] Bonhoeffer rejected characterizations of the first three mandates as "secular" in contrast to the last one only as being particularly "religious."

The core concept in his vocational theology is "deputyship" which we might now refer to as stewardship.[83] Bonhoeffer emphasized the importance of social role identity as the place where theological construction takes place. He rejected claims to authentic Christian identity based on an ethos of radical individualism. Even those called to a more solitary life are so called for the purpose of servitude to Christ for the betterment of "mankind as a whole."[84] In maintaining allegiance to Christ, the deputy works against two temptations: "set[ting] up one's ego as an absolute" in establishing the pathway for one's direction, or "set[ting] up the other man as an absolute" in the simple surrender of the self to the will of the other.[85] The unity of the self within the body of Christ only comes through the deputyship of Jesus, "the incarnate Son of God." It is Christ who is "the responsible person par excellence," the image through whom the very notion of deputyship is to be formed among those who aspire to call themselves his disciples.[86]

How one applies this to the specific realms of contemporary life can only be discerned within the complexities of particular events and circumstances. Our current task is not so much that of "turn[ing] the world upside-down." It is "to do what is necessary" through the prompting of Christ's still, small voice "at the given place" and time through which the call to obedience comes. Such a mandate calls for "a due consideration of reality"[87] in the discernment of right action in which it needs to be exercised in a given situation. This applies to a decision at work on how a manager will mentor an insecure, but competent employee or on how parents of a child who has broken with them will keep open to the possibility of reconciliation even if the prospect of healing is not likely to be achieved. It also bears on the political process—not only on which candidate and which sets of issues to sup-

81. Ibid., 204.
82. Ibid.
83. Hall, *Steward*.
84. Bonhoeffer, *Ethics*, 221.
85. Ibid., 222.
86. Ibid.
87. Ibid.

port, but also in the discernment of the terms of engagement, including that of one's attitude toward one's political opponents. Similar such examples can be infinitely multiplied.

Attending to the immediacy of the situation also requires close discernment of broader cultural trends. This includes rejection of any semblance of parody that sometimes accompanies an evangelical caricature of liberal theology or secular culture. This high call also mandates rejection of any liberal caricature of fundamentalist anti-intellectualism or simplistic reductionisms of evangelical theology and religious culture. There may be grounds for such criticism across theological lines in a manner that calls for admonition as well as appropriate affirmation. In taking a cue from Bonhoeffer, such criticism should come in a somewhat reluctant vein rather than, as first impulse, seeking first the voice of God speaking through one's seemingly alter Christian identity. Such sensitivity demands close listening for the voice of God through a discerning reading of Scripture via the mediation of the Holy Spirit, including the capacity for much humility.

Whether through preaching, teaching, liturgical practice, or theological explication, the church becomes the source that gives specific articulation to God's reconciling the world through Christ. In its foremost vocation, the church is the called institution whereby God's "word is repeatedly spoken, expounded, interpreted and disseminated until the end of the world."[88] Given the importance of the lived experience of faith in the midst of its worldly setting, Bonhoeffer identified the church as playing an extremely important role. Specifically, it gives voice to the reality that shapes the identity and worldview of those called to the various vocations where God places them. The church conforms and confirms individuals to their most fundamental role as living members of the body of Christ. This mandate has much to offer in potentially bringing greater concord to the discordant sectors in contemporary US Protestantism. It also holds the prospect of lending clarity to a common Protestant identity rooted in the priesthood of the laity through a theology of vocation grounded in the original vision of the Reformation. In Bonhoeffer's Christ-centered stance, "worldly" Christianity also serves as a mediating link between the ontological radicalism of Barth's unequivocal embrace of biblical revelation and the pragmatic Christian realism of Reinhold Niebuhr.

---

88. Ibid., 288.

REINHOLD NIEBUHR'S "IMPOSSIBLE POSSIBILITY"

While counterfactual history is not usually productive, one of the largely unexplored "what ifs" of twentieth-century Protestant history is how Bonhoeffer's *Ethics* would have been appropriated within the US context of the 1930s and 1940s. Bonhoeffer had more than a passing knowledge of US religious life through his studies at Union Theological Seminary in the early 1930s under Reinhold Niebuhr as well as through brief encounters with various Black ministries in Harlem during the period of its cultural renaissance.[89] As Bonhoeffer put it, "the 'ethical' as a theme is tied to a definite time and a definite space" in which revelatory insight is given to men and women as "living and moral creature[s] in a finite and destructible world."[90] Critical discernment of this essentially Niebuhrian orientation requires nothing less than grappling with the concrete specificity of historical experience in light of the redemptive voice of God's reconciling power in Christ's unequivocal love for the world.

The extremities of the Nazi reign of terror and Bonhoeffer's determination to frontally face it deprived him of a normative middle class existence as pastor or professor of theology. Attaining such a status would have required a more extensive grappling with the seemingly more commonplace implications of the impossible possibilities embedded in his theology of vocations. In drawing out a comparison between Bonhoeffer and Niebuhr, I do not argue for precise symmetry, but for strong affinity in the mutual importance each gives to the complex relationship between the penultimate and the ultimate, particularly in their respective ethics.

Rasmussen maintains that "Bonhoeffer found Niebuhr too saturated with liberalism to be theologically compelling, just as Niebuhr found Bonhoeffer too taken with Barthianism to move from human moral experience into knowledge of God."[91] Whether that was, in fact the case, Niebuhr stressed the contingent more so than the finalities. By contrast, Bonhoeffer emphasized the sovereignty of God more than Niebuhr, even though the differences between them were more a matter of degree than absolutely irreconcilable. Despite the differences, the more compelling issue (even in their subtle variations) remains their mutual contribution to the mediation of the penultimate and ultimate in their individual work. It is from this shared sensibility that I focus on Niebuhr's ethics.

---

89. Metaxas, *Bonhoeffer*, 107–10.
90. Bonhoeffer, *Ethics*, 260.
91. Rasmussen, *Reinhold Niebuhr*, 12.

Niebuhr placed an anthropological emphasis at the core of his theology. This impetus drove what he referred to as "prophetic religion" from the sterility and obscurantism of Christian orthodoxy, on the one hand, to the naivety of Christian liberalism, on the other. That his thinking here is typological and not without caricature fits in well with a core Niebuhrian theme that the fundamental realities of prophetic revelation are embodied in truth saturated myths. Such myths carry an unavoidable element of deception without which finite human beings would lack the capacity of reaching toward the transcendent through language forms that can only be an inadequate instrument of conveying the reality of God's infinite truth and love.[92]

Notwithstanding such "deception," this theological construction gave Niebuhr a sharp intuitive grasp on a broad range of contexts and influences on the interface between politics, economics, society, culture, and religion. His keen understanding of Marxist social analysis, Freudian psychoanalysis, the pragmatism of William James, and international power politics provided him with an insightful set of tools to analyze the ways in which culture infused, and sometimes occluded, what he took to be the authentic message of prophetic religion. His theological understanding, which posited ultimate reality with God's truth as biblically discernible, gave him the capacity to reflect back on culture through a transcendent vision—however much its expression could only be depicted through cultural metaphors and influences folded back into history.[93] The dynamic of Niebuhr's theology has its grounding in

> the degree to which the transcendent truly transcends every value and achievement of history, so that no relative value of historical achievement may become the basis of moral complacency; and the degree to which the transcendent remains in organic contact with the historical, so that no degree of tension may rob the historical of its significance.[94]

Niebuhr did not shortchange the transcendent, which remained for him "above history," even as the many incarnations of God's Spirit can only take place within and through historical experience. In the process, they become merged within its flow, in which any given revelatory moment becomes immersed in "some immediate and relative value of history."[95]

92. R. Niehbuhr, *Beyond Tragedy*, 3–24.

93. For a succinct overview of Niebuhr's biography and theological influences, see Rasmussen, *Reinhold Niebuhr*, 1–41.

94. R. Niebuhr, *Interpretation of Christian Ethics*, 5.

95. Ibid., 6.

Ambiguity, paradox, and irony become invariably entwined within the transcendent. This dialectic requires perpetual discernment on the range of subtle factors impacting on any given context, resulting, at best, in proximate justice or partial fulfillment in a complex world setting.

Niebuhr accepted the message of God's redemptive love as the center point of biblical revelation which comes, as the Spirit wills, as gift into the world. He acknowledged the prospect—though not the likelihood—of embracing the Beatitudes of the Sermon on the Mount (Matt 5:3–12) on an individual basis as an ethical possibility. He rejected its attainment as an impossible ethic in any complex social context where various powers interests converge and clash.[96] Niebuhr utterly rejected its prospect as a viable basis for social policy, even in an avowedly Christian society which, despite certain conservative protestations to the contrary, did not characterize United States of America in the middle decades of the twentieth century. The persistence of social evil on a massive scale remains an enduring problem given the ultimate aspiration within Christianity of God in Christ transforming the world through the realization of a new heaven and new earth. The gap between the promise and reality requires explanation of the most discerning sort. Otherwise, the biblical vision is in danger of becoming both incredulous and incomprehensible to the audiences Niebuhr sought to address both at Union Seminary and that sector of the wider secular culture influenced more by John Dewey than the Bible.[97] This problem is compounded in that neither Jesus nor his earliest followers, as depicted in the New Testament, confronted power in any systemic way. This was so even in their willingness to stand up against the power structure and undergo suffering and persecution when failure to do so represented a direct challenge to what they proclaimed and staked their lives upon.

The primary problem that Niebuhr addressed was the relationship of power to justice which the New Testament Jesus largely averted through the prospect of apocalyptic fulfillment. It is the sublimation of power in the embrace of Christ's suffering love, which lends a great deal of persuasive rhetoric to Barth's and Bonhoeffer's defense of biblical revelation. It is this Christological standard that both theologians posited against what they took as the fundamental presuppositions of early twentieth-century-century liberal and conservative theology and culture, and politics. It was not that Barth and Bonhoeffer escaped the cultural relativism that they perceived in Niebuhr. Their theological vision, like his, was buttressed by a large dose of existentialism. Both realized with Niebuhr the impossible ideal of any

---

96. R. Niebuhr, *Moral Man and Immoral Society*, xi–xxv.
97. Rice, *Reinhold Niebuhr and John Dewey*.

human embrace of a biblically derived revelation. However, they were more troubled than Niebuhr by what they took as the rampant historicism of both liberal theology and academic biblical studies.

Against such historicism, Barth and Bonhoeffer posited the orthodox kerygma as a transcendent ideal and the basis through which to construct a viable twentieth-century-century theology, ecclesial polity, and Christian ethics. Even if this could only be an imaginative construction this side of the eschaton, their faith in biblical revelation brought them to an ontological stance beyond knowing, which on faith, points to the ultimate truth of the meaning of Christ. Niebuhr did not deny this, but his theology was considerably more apologetic in the undeviating quest to situate the Christian revelation "with the moral and social problems of our age."[98] Niebuhr interpreted what he viewed as Bath's dogmatic biblicism as undercutting the dynamic interaction of God's engagement with the uncertainties of history. Niebuhr saw this as a denial of the very meaning of an incarnational faith. That such a critique did not account for Barth's own grappling with history may have to do with some unconscious conflation by Niebuhr of Barth's project with American fundamentalism, or at the least, Princetonian orthodoxy.

However imponderable such a conjecture may be, the practical result was the impetus it gave Niebuhr to put forth a major anthropological theology of enormous significance in relation to the cultural, political, and religious life of the United States in the 1940s. This took place in an era where dialogue between faith and culture mattered, notwithstanding the secularization tendencies pervasive throughout the twentieth century. Given his work in politics and ethics, Niebuhr was an ideal candidate in the mid-twentieth century to cross cultural boundaries with the academy and the broader national culture. As summarized by Lovin, Niebuhr's project raised the following fundamental questions touched on in a more guarded fashion by Bonhoeffer and less so by Barth:

> What new claims about the human situation do we make by saying that God is present in the needs or goals that we all understand? What motives emerge that were not readily available to us? What actions are we permitted or required to take that a non-religious analysis would not also permit or require? Does belief in God make it reasonable for us to do or risk things that a reasonable person who did not believe in God would not do or risk?[99]

---

98. R. Niebuhr, *Interpretation of Christian Ethics*, 21.
99. Lovin, *Reinhold Niebuhr and Christian Realism*, 35.

Niebuhr's transcendent vision was premised on the contention that "truth about God must in the end prove consistent with every other kind of truth we can know."[100] This stance requires a confrontation with all that is contingent within human experience, including an acute awareness of the fallibility of the religious knower. In his willingness to put faith on the firing line in juxtaposition to the most treasured assumptions of contemporary society and culture, Niebuhr's faith stance was as radical as that of Barth's and Bonhoeffer's. What distinguished Niebuhr, especially from Barth, was his embrace of the most searing doubt in which "the prophet himself stands under the judgment which he preaches."[101] Because faith in God is never given to humankind in pure form, Niebuhr viewed authentic doubt, a mediating symbol of the finitude of the entire created order. Such reasoned doubt has the added benefit of puncturing false illusions that one's perceptions are synonymous with the truth itself. The church is also subject to the critical gaze of prophetic scrutiny. Its vocation of "disturb[ing] the security of sinners [is valid] only if it is not itself too secure in its belief that it has the word of God."[102]

Niebuhr held to the radical nature of faith, but only a faith that passes through to the reality of the cross. He maintained that "in its profoundest terms," authentic religion is based on "faith in the meaningfulness of existence."[103] The ultimate meaning in the universe resides in the realm beyond history. Yet, the revelation of God is given in history through various signs and myths that provide partial glimpses of God's revelation. The fundamental human vocation is to embrace in faith the radical finitude of human existence in all of its private and public manifestations and to enter into the fray of God's redeeming work of world restoration in light of the recalcitrance of human sin.

At the core of Niebuhr's theology is a radical commitment to "Christ, who expresses both the infinite possibilities of love in human life and the infinite possibilities beyond human life." The dynamic tension inherent in the "true revelation of the total situation in which human life stands" can only be in the light of "every possibility of illusion and deception."[104] It is this radical commitment to Christ that is the basis for engaging the world in all the realms of public and private life. This stance necessitates rejection of any special privilege stemming from a protective religious identity, even in the

---

100. Ibid., 240.
101. R. Niebuhr, *Beyond Tragedy*, 110.
102. Ibid.
103. Ibid., 113.
104. Ibid., 17.

very acceptance of faith as the substance of things hoped for, the evidence of things not seen (Heb 11:1). It is only on such a basis—the basis of Christ's own engagement—that one can embrace and encounter the world both on its terms and those of faith. While Christ ultimately transcends the contingency of human history, he does so only by way of the cross. Within the context of human history, the revelation of God in Christ reconciling the world (2 Cor 5:19) remains, at best, a partial gleaning.

For the purposes of this book, I am less concerned about the adequacy of Niebuhr's theology than the breadth and depth of his capacity to engage the issues he raised across the spectrum of US public life and the continuing theological relevance of such "realistic" probing. The seriousness of his inquiry and his refusal to participate in public discussion about faith without a substantive apologetics serves as a significant reminder in our current setting of the need to draw broadly on the legacy of neo-orthodoxy in any reclamation for our times. To be sure, times have changed. Any prospect Niebuhr had in substantially influencing US culture through an engaged theological reflection has become significantly diminished in what Hall refers to as the current Protestant diaspora.[105]

The critical objective at hand is not so much that of seeking to persuade large segments of the broader US public of the viability and ultimate truth of the Christian kerygma. The more important purpose in our post-Christendom era is that of developing a viable dogmatics that can be appropriated with authenticity and intelligence among those who do adhere to this faith in structuring a coherent Christian worldview. I maintain that this dogmatic turn is both a viable and essential response to the internalization of the secular culture that is pervasive in different ways among broad segments of both mainline and evangelical clergy and laity. In this vision, Barth's radical turn to God's revelation, as embodied in the Bible, provides a critical resource.

The enduring contribution of Reinhold Niebuhr is that of keeping us attuned to the illusions and deceptions that so easily creep into what we might take as our most authentic and revered sources of belief. Niebuhr maintained that the prophetic faith of the Augustinian tradition "is able to defy the chaos of any moment, [precisely] because the basis of its trust is not in any of the constructs of human genius," even the most religious ones. Neither is it with "any of the achievements of human diligence which arise periodically," including theological constructs built "to imposing heights [that]...tempt men to put their trust in their own virtues and abilities."[106]

---

105. Hall, *Confessing the Faith*, 201–64.
106. R. Niebuhr, *Beyond Tragedy*, 13.

Re-Envisioning the Neo-Orthodox Legacy 253

This piercing of our finest ideals—including those residing in the religious realm—serves as a critical remainder that even the most incisive and penetrating faith can, at best, be an approach toward the holy ever in search of its object—full acceptance of, and by God, within human experience.

In identifying more mediating space than Barth on the relationship between the secular and religious, Niebuhr's project opens important pathways to a theology of vocations in all of the critical realms of public life. Such a quest consumed some of his most passionate life ventures, particularly the realm of politics. His nuanced liberal theo-political insight on the nature of US democracy disabused any notion of national innocence or the conflation of a progressive political culture with the kingdom of God.[107] His quest for proximate justice in a sinful world included an "ironic" embrace of the imperatives of the cold war in the late 1940s and 1950s, followed by his opposition to the Vietnam War in the late 1960s. In both periods, Niebuhr sifted the complexities of power politics in light of the transcendent vision of God's love beyond history and hovering within history around the edges.[108]

Given his anthropological emphasis, Niebuhr remained wedded to liberalism through a "theological pragmatism,"[109] even in his embrace of the core kerygma through what he referred to as prophetic religion. In this quest for a relevant theology, his primary interlocutor was the renowned pragmatic philosopher John Dewey.[110] Niebuhr's most stinging criticism was to charge Dewey with naivety on the viability of education and social reform to solve complex human problems, particularly in the era of the Great Depression and World War II.[111] In our current era, Niebuhr's critical realism serves as an enduring apologetic supplement to a vibrant return to a post-critical dogmatics that underlies postliberal and a good deal of critical evangelical theology in the contemporary period.[112] Niebuhr's attunement

---

107. R. Niebuhr, *Irony of American History*.

108. For an extended discussion of the relationship between theology and politics in Niebuhr, see Lovin, *Reinhold Niebuhr and Christian Realism*, 158–90.

109. Ibid., 82–83. See also Rice, *Reinhold Niebuhr and John Dewey*, xxii–xxiii.

110. Rice, *Reinhold Niebuhr and John Dewey*.

111. Ibid., 50–66.

112. There is a direct lineage between Barth and the work of Hans Frei and George Lindbeck, the pioneers of the postliberal theology. The authors of both *Eclipse of Bible Narrative* (Frei) and *Nature of Doctrine* (Lindbeck) call for a "post-critical" return to a narrative approach to biblical theology. The postliberal theologians accept the relevance of contemporary biblical scholarship in illuminating some of the ancient and modern contexts that informs current academic study of the Bible. However, they place primary emphasis in elucidating the meaning inherent within the biblical text as a "realistic narrative" for determining what is significant about the Bible. This essentially Barthian insight has influenced a broad swath of evangelical scholars as well as those of

to the subtleties of human deception and the possibility of a more meditative theology between the natural and religious is his strongest insight. Together, with Barth's sensibility to an illuminated Word-based theology and Bonhoeffer's attention to its "worldly" implications in the dynamic interface between the culture and the beloved community, the neo-orthodox vision offers a wealth of theological insight that can be richly drawn upon in contemporary theological reflection. Much of the writing of these three has the added benefit of being accessible to the educated laity. Their cumulative work has much to offer faith-seeking mainline and evangelical congregations in the era of our current diaspora.

REPRISE: CHRIST AND CULTURE

Radical Monotheism and the Struggle over Centers of Value

In bringing the discussion of the neo-orthodox legacy to a close, I draw on two pivotal and closely related themes in H. R. Niebuhr's theology, both of which have a great deal of bearing on the mediation of the penultimate/ultimate nexus in our current theological setting. The first is the inescapable human need of making absolute commitments through what Niebuhr refers to as "centers of value"—absolutes—beyond what can be discerned from empirical evidence. The second is the interpenetration of culture in any theological or ecclesial tradition, however proximate a given faith expression purports to be in alignment with the core proclamation of the Christian faith.

For Niebuhr—"faith" which he "distinguishe[d] from religion"—is an inescapable phenomenon in mediating the unfathomable distance between human finitude and the inexorable quest for meaning beyond the merely given.[113] Based on this definition, faith is synonymous with that held, for example, in Dewey's adherence to democracy and critical inquiry, and more fundamentally to the philosophical naturalism at the center of his pragmatic theory of value.[114] God, as objective reality beyond experience may—and according to Niebuhr—*does* exist. But the human comprehension of any such actuality is only given in faith in search of greater knowledge.[115]

---

a predominantly postliberal stripe and provides one of resources that support the type of ecumenical evangelical dialogue I call for in this book.

113. H. R. Niebuhr, *Radical Monotheism and Western Culture*, 11.

114. Dewey, *Experience and Nature*.

115. Niebuhr states that "radical faith in the God who is the principle of being itself is given to men as a hope and a goal more than an achievement." *Radical Monotheism*, 63.

The crux of the matter for any serious ontological contention is twofold: the depth and range of the persuasive power that radical monotheism has on the claimant in motivating toward ultimate commitment and its capacity to incorporate lesser constructions of reality into its more comprehensive framework. The viability of a theological construction is less its formal logic than its motor force of stimulating a commitment of one's entire heart, mind, strength, and soul to its vision. Such faith is based on the twin principle of "confidence" in its validity and "fidelity" in committing one's life to the implications of its worldview.[116] Radical faith of any sort incorporates, but extends beyond the logical into a more inclusive vision of reality wherein faith transcends reason. In Niebuhr's vision of radical monotheism, trust in God as objectively present—upon whom believers place their ultimate confidence—and the ability to experience God's presence as the emotional source that stimulates loyalty and commitment—are mutually entwined. In this respect, "the subjective can no more meaningfully be abstracted from the objective than vice versa."[117]

Niebuhr linked the theological concept of radical monotheism to the "One beyond all the many."[118] It is this faith that he identified as the ultimate center of value, while acknowledging that even those most faithfully committed to radical monotheism fall short of its realization. Niebuhr maintained that that the lesser "gods of faith"—what in traditional biblical language are referred to as idols—fail to achieve that to which they are designed to realize: fulfillment of the human vocation, the quest for meaning, and ultimately, the harmonization of the universe, itself.[119] Writing in 1960, Niebuhr identified such centers of value in nationalism and other forms of "henotheism"—single sources of ultimate value. In addition to nationalism, democracy, capitalism, and communism, Niebuhr also identified civilization, nature, and humanism as the predominant henotheistic faiths of his time. Common to all of these value systems is their attempt to provide a total explanation for the human condition for which they lack the capacity to fulfill. They appear to be "movements in the direction of radical monotheism. Yet they all fall short of the radical expression; each excludes some realm of being from the sphere of value; each is claimed by a cause less inclusive than the realm of being in its wholeness."[120] Niebuhr also pointed to shifting centers of value in response to the failure of overarching world-

---

116. Ibid., 16.
117. Ibid., 12.
118. Ibid., 24.
119. Ibid., 24–37.
120. Ibid., 37.

views to provide coherent frames of meaning. Such "multiple centers of value"[121] have become more pervasive in the postmodern era—a movement that came into cultural significance sometime after Niebuhr wrote *Radical Monotheism and Western Culture.*

Niebuhr contended that "radical monotheism dethrones all absolutes short of the principle of being itself. At the same time it reverences every relative existence."[122] Specifically, it sanctifies "all [created] things" through a process of secularization by which it desacralizes the natural universe.[123] The reference to being is the critical linchpin in Niebuhr's depiction of radical monotheism, which is the fundamental scandal of particularity against the entire tradition of Western philosophy in its privileging of abstract reasoning and its corresponding belief in impersonal causation. In contrast, the principle center of value in radical monotheism carries "no hint of metaphysics" and is grounded in nothing other than "God speak[ing]"[124] from the presence and veil of his holy name (Exod 3:14). For Niebuhr, the grounding point of radical monotheism is both the unnamed "I Am" and the God revealed to Israel, "the God of Abraham, the God of Isaac, and the God of Jacob" (Exod 3:15). God as "First Person"[125] reality is counter-intuitive to the dominant direction of the Western epistemological tradition.

The biblical claim raises the specter of "anthropomorphism," a risk that needs to be taken, according to Niebuhr. Without such a First Person Being, "the cornerstone of Christian as of Jewish and all radical monotheist confidence and loyalty"[126] in the God revealed in and through the Bible, simply cannot gain traction. It is this very God that stands above all other centers of value while providing a place for them in their respective spheres—whether nationalism, a political ideology, a psychological viewpoint, or economic theory.

The challenge of radical monotheism is not only that of providing a well-argued summation of its dogmatic claims. This is difficult enough given the cogency of a host of counter-claims as embodied throughout twentieth- and twenty-first-century Western thought and culture. The more fundamental challenge is that of making this First Person God the most enduring center of value that men and women in the contemporary era can

---

121. Ibid., 28.
122. Ibid.
123. Ibid., 52.
124. Ibid., 42.
125. Ibid., 44.
126. Ibid., 45.

and do encounter.[127] Niebuhr defended the ontological reality underlying this claim and its potential cogency in evoking the level of commitment, passion, and philosophical and theological acuity needed in order to be internalized among those within the mid-twentieth-century Christian fold. That to which Niebuhr staked his theological identity is a foundational presupposition for any theological construction based on a canonically comprehensive interpretation of the Bible. Radical monotheism needs to be taken up with fresh insight as a primary grounding point of contemporary Protestant revitalization.

Christ and Culture

I close this review of Niebuhr's theology by focusing on his highly influential book, *Christ and Culture*. Niebuhr maintains that God's revelation in Christ is the ultimate value of center for Christians, however extensive the gap between the vision of what this means and any temporal realization in human history. He also argues that the Christian faith has been developed within culture and is invariably shaped by it. More radically put, the revelation that God bestows on individuals and communities of believers cannot exist outside of its cultural purview.[128] At the core of the relationship between Christ and culture is the struggle over centers of value within the Christian community on how an imperfectly realized Christian faith gets worked out within the context of a given society and culture.

No single Christian response on the relationship between Christ and culture carries absolute validity as synonymous with the will of God. Rather, there are only particular responses that have emerged in specific contexts in the quest among historical actors to seek the will of God in Christ within the immediacy of given situations. While any effort to live faithfully and fully within the framework of the Christian kerygma can only be a partial one, Christ's followers can rest "assured that he uses their various works in accomplishing his own." Niebuhr based this assumption on the belief "that Christ as living Lord is answering the question [of his will for humankind] in the totality of history in a fashion which transcends the wisdom of all his interpreters yet employs their partial insights and their necessary conflicts."[129]

---

127. Ibid., 112–13.

128. "Christ claims no man purely as a natural being, but as always one who has become human in culture; who is not only in culture, but into whom culture has penetrated." H. R. Niebuhr, *Christ and Culture*, 69.

129. H. R. Niebuhr, *Christ and Culture*, 2.

Niebuhr developed his thesis through a five-part model of Christ and culture that ranges from a sharp oppositional perspective, through various forms of cultural engagement, to an ultimate transformation of culture by the Christian worldview—Niebuhr's ideal typology.[130] He noted that the discussion of historically representative ways of being Christian within culture is endless and "warn[ed] against the danger of confusing hypothetical types with the rich variety and the colorful individuality of historical persons."[131] Nonetheless, a finite model based on "a series of typical answers"[132] provided him with a useful heuristic to probe into the ways in which Christians have mediated the relationship between radical monotheism and a range of culturally significant values that have factored into the shaping of mostly Western Christian identity.

The typologies that Niebuhr advanced are less important in themselves than what they represent in terms of working through the invariable gaps between the Christian revelation and any grasp of the full significance of what this means, as embodied in any given time and place. Carson gets at this in noting "that Niebuhr is not so much talking about the relationship between Christ and culture, as between two sources of authority as they compete within culture, namely Christ (however he is understood within various paradigms of mainstream Christendom) and every other source of authority divested of Christ."[133] What is at stake in the relationship between Christ and culture is precisely that of loyalty to what set of values garner ultimate commitment among individual and communities of Christian believers, as Niebuhr formally argued a decade later in *Radical Monotheism and Western Culture*.[134]

Given Niebuhr's underlying thesis that, at their best, Christians strive to attain an ultimate fidelity to God and Christ, there remains a divided loyalty between the authority of Christ and that of culture tugging at Christian identity—an inescapable tension this side of the eschaton. The typologies, as described in *Christ and Culture*, illustrate representative ways in which this tension has played out in the history of Christian Western civilization and continues to work itself out in the contemporary period. The relationship between Christ and culture over the issue of biblical authority is a central theme that I have pursued throughout this book. I draw on Niebuhr's

---

130. Useful summaries of Niebuhr's typology can be found in Carson, *Christ and Culture Revisited*, 9–30, and Shriver, *H. Richard Niebuhr*, 42–48.

131. H. R. Niebuhr, *Christ and Culture*, 120.

132. Ibid., 2.

133. *Christ and Culture Revisited*, 12.

134. Niebuhr, "Centers of Value," 100–113.

typological thinking here not so much because of the comprehensiveness of his categories which have undergone significant critical analysis. I do so as a resource in assessing how the Christ/culture relationship has played out on the matter of biblical authority and the orthodox theological tradition over the last century of Protestant religious culture and how that history is shaping the viability of establishing a centrist Protestant vision in this current era of Protestant cultural diaspora.

Niebuhr referred to the first type as *Christ against culture* which posits a strict opposition between the Christian worldview and the dominant norms of the host society and culture. He pointed to Tertullian and Tolstoy as historical examples of this typology. For the purposes of this book I highlight the oppositional critique of early twentieth-century fundamentalism against the prevailing mores and values of the modern secular world.[135] Niebuhr offered the following overarching value of the first typology: "The relation of the authority of Jesus Christ to the authority of culture is such that every Christian must feel himself claimed by the Lord to reject the world and its kingdoms with their pluralism and temporalism, their makeshift compromises of many interests, their hypnotic obsession by the love of life and the fear of death." Niebuhr gave credence to this perspective as an aspect of any Christian worldview, but pointed as well to "an equally necessary movement of responsible engagement in cultural tasks."[136]

Niebuhr referred to the second perspective as *the Christ of culture* motif based on an underlying accord between Christ and culture. He linked this typology to Abelard in the medieval period and to Albrecht Ritschl as representative of the nineteenth-century liberal German theological tradition.[137] An application for this study is the linkage of the social gospel to the progressive evolution of society—whether to the Progressive Era reforms in the United States of the early twentieth century or to the social and labor reform movements in England in the same time period. What Niebuhr attributed to Ritschl is relevant to the broader twentieth-century mainline Protestant theological tradition: "God and man have in common the task of realizing the kingdom: and God works within the human community

---

135. Marsden, *Understanding Fundamentalism and Evangelicalism*, 9–61. Without denying this oppositional stance, Niebuhr also associated fundamentalism with a form of "cultural Protestantism" in its uncritical appropriation of a pre-Darwinian "cosmological and biological" worldview that was no longer tenable in the light of twentieth-century academic scholarship in the fields of science, history, and literary analysis. H. R. Niebuhr, *Christ and Culture*, 102.

136. H. R. Niebuhr, *Christ and Culture*, 68.

137. Ibid., 91–101.

through Christ and through conscience, rather than on it from without."[138] The merging of the kingdom of God with cultural renewal has been a prevailing Protestant liberal theme of the past century. This has been the case, whether in the euphoric heyday of the social gospel era, the civil religion of the post–World War II period, the quest for religious and cultural renewal stemming from Harvey Cox's *Secular City* of the 1960s, or in more recent movements in the various liberationist and ecological theologies.

Niebuhr organized the five typologies into three broad categories: Christ *against*, Christ *of*, and *above* culture. He referred to the latter as "the church of the center" model. He pitted the first two constructs in sharp opposition to each other. Niebuhr identified the third as a mediating category. Within the Christ above culture centrist type, Niebuhr pointed to three distinctive positions: Christ *above*, Christ and culture in *paradox*, and Christ as the *transformer* of culture.[139]

Common to all the centrist perspectives is the emphasis on Christ as "the Son of God, the Father Almighty who created heaven and earth." Common as well is the focus on the relationship "between God and man" rather than "Christ and the world."[140] Niebuhr linked the centrist perspective with the broad themes of traditional Christian orthodox theology on the incarnation, atonement, and Trinity. The theological emphasis on God in Christ reconciling the world is central to this position, however persisting the gap remains between the reality and the sought for aspiration. Niebuhr also stressed the importance of culture as the location where the church enacts its gospel in the world. The tension between the already of a partially realized kingdom and the not yet of an anticipatory eschatology was characteristic of Niebuhr's centrist perspective in its varying forms. It is this tension between the times where the struggle for Christian identity within culture is always being played out.

In his overarching taxonomy, Niebuhr identified the third of the five types as *Christ above culture*. There is a similarity here with the second motif in the sense that Christ "is the fulfillment of cultural aspirations and the restorer of the institutions of true society." Yet, in this third motif, Christ is simultaneously "discontinuous"[141] with the dominant values and institutions of a given culture. In this synthetic vision, Christ transcends culture in the sense that God's intent can never be contained within the boundaries of a given cultural matrix. At the same time, a Christian culture, at least in

---

138. Ibid., 98.
139. Ibid., 120.
140. Ibid., 117.
141. Ibid., 42.

principle, can be so constituted that its aspirational values are aimed at the fulfillment of God's will within the contexts of its mores, institutions, and philosophical assumptions. There will always be a gap between Christ and culture, but in the ideal construct of this typology the distance between the aspiration and the attainment serves as a goad to press forward to its fuller realization.

Niebuhr identified this third motif with Clement of Alexandria. He viewed late medieval theology of Thomas as the fullest representation of the Chris above culture type. Niebuhr viewed "Thomas' synthesis . . . not only [as] an intellectual achievement but the philosophical and theological representation of a social unification of Christ and culture"[142] within a given historical context. The short-lived New England Puritan vision of Boston as "a city on a hill" was the closest approximation to the synthetic typology in American history. Both the medieval and colonial visions were limited by the press of ongoing historical change and the natural limitations of any temporal effort to incorporate the realm of God on earth. Niebuhr was attracted to the synthetic vision because the incarnational fulfillment on earth as it is in heaven is an aspirational Christian drive of major proportions that will not and should not be easily denied. Nonetheless, he stressed the importance of giving more credence to the fissures between Christ and culture than is evident in the synthetic typology.[143]

Christ and culture in paradox was Niebuhr's fourth representative model. The emphasis here is on the perpetual tension between the core values of the Christian faith and those of a dominant society and culture. There are similarities here with the Christ against culture typology in that both focus on the persistence of perpetual conflict between the two poles. The difference is that the paradoxical model acknowledges the legitimacy of both centers of value and accords due regard for "the institutions of society . . . as well as obedience to a Christ who sits in judgment on that society."[144]

Luther was Niebuhr's main representative of the paradoxical or dualist position in his absolute reliance on the grace of God, on the one hand, with his acknowledgment of the perpetual indwelling of sin, on the other. The tension is expressed culturally in Luther's radical fidelity to Christ's

---

142. Ibid., 137.

143. In the Christ above culture typology, "there is always the *more* and the *other*; there is always 'all this and heaven too'; and for the true synthesis the *more* is not an afterthought, as it so often seems to be with the cultural Christian." Ibid., 144. Yet, "the effort to bring Christ and culture, God's work and man's, the temporal and eternal, tends, perhaps inevitably, to the absolutizing of what is relative, the reduction of the infinite to a finite form, and the materialization of the dynamic." Ibid., 145.

144. Ibid., 42.

reign while seeking to enact the call within the context of sixteenth-century German society. Niebuhr represented the tension by contrasting Luther's *Treatise on Christian Liberty* to his call *Against the Marauding Hordes of Peasants*—a response to the perceived chaos unleashed by the Peasants' War.[145]

Niebuhr's broader point was that in his secular calling "as God's minister," the ruler is required to restore order, even if—by necessity—at the point of the sword.[146] Christians are called to find their true vocation—whether in commerce, law, teaching, farming, or the domestic arts—through the values and institutions that shape these callings, and learn to live with the tension between their demands and the absolute purity of God's grace. They are to absorb the paradoxes and tensions within their own Christian identity "in a single act of obedience to the one God of mercy and wrath, not as a divided soul with a double allegiance."[147] They are to live out their Christian vocation in the world, in faith, as justified sinners in the realization that in living in the world they cannot escape the consequences of their own sins and the sins of others. Still, they live in the world in the hope and expectation that in God they will attain their ultimate salvation.[148] In the twentieth century, Reinhold Niebuhr embodied the paradoxical view in a particularly compelling manner.

Niebuhr labelled the fifth type—"the *conversionist* solution"—as *Christ the transformer of culture*. Along with dualists, conversionists acknowledge the centrality of sin "as deeply rooted in the human soul, [so] that it pervades all man's work."[149] With them, they accept that "all cultural work" is infused with sin. They also contend that "culture is under God's sovereign rule." It is the prime location where "obedience to the Lord" can and needs to be worked out.[150] The conversionist's "more hopeful attitude toward culture"[151] is based on an incarnational theology emphasizing creation, including a perspective of the fall modified by the "created goodness" of humankind, and an eschatology that is more realized than anticipatory.[152] In this fifth

---

145. Ibid., 170–71.

146. Ibid., 171.

147. Ibid., 172.

148. In Niebuhr's summation: "The Christian is dealing every moment, as a citizen of the eternal kingdom and the over-arching empire of God, with the immediate transitory values of physical men, his own but above all his neighbors." Ibid., 177.

149. Ibid., 191.

150. Ibid.

151. Ibid.

152. Ibid., 191–96.

perspective, there can be "no turning of men from self and idols to God save in society,"[153] even as society is not the source of salvation.

While acknowledging a future-oriented element in the Gospel of John, Niebuhr viewed its main focus as the possibility of living in the kingdom of God in the present through the gift of the Holy Spirit. Niebuhr did not interpret the Gospel of John as a fully realized eschatology. Yet, he emphasized the "new beginning" it represents in "God's action in Jesus Christ and in sending the Spirit; not at history's end, but in each living existential moment."[154] He acknowledged that the Gospel of John does not represent a pure expression of his fifth typology. Rather, in the divisions John draws between the church and the world and between Jews and Christians, this gospel writer "combined the conversionist *motif* with the separatism of the Christ-against-culture school of thought."[155] Niebuhr found a similar tension between the conversionist and the dualist perspective in Augustine's theology.[156]

Niebuhr identified the closest approximation to the conversionist typology with the nineteenth-century socialist theology of F. D. Maurice. He did not interpret Maurice as discounting the reality of sin which, at its core, he (Maurice) identified as selfishness and self-preoccupation.[157] Rather, Maurice underlined the need to shift the focus from the concentration on sin to an exclusive focus on Christ "only and not of . . . sin."[158] He viewed the shift "from self-centeredness to Christ-centeredness" as a "universal and present divine possibility"[159] within the stream of lived time. Niebuhr interpreted Maurice's conversionist hope as a typology of religious transvaluation that would result in the radical transformation of society through the infusion of the spirit of Christ's love. This occurs "through the humiliation which comes when members of the body willingly accept the fact that they are not the head, and through the exaltation which results from the knowledge that they have been given their own particular, necessary work in service to the head of the body and to all its other members."[160] The con-

153. Ibid., 43.
154. Ibid., 201.
155. Ibid., 205.
156. Ibid., 206–18. "The eschatological hope of a new heaven and a new earth brought into being in the coming of Christ is modified [as Niebuhr interprets Augustine] by the belief that Christ cannot come to this heaven and earth but must await the death of the old and rising of a new creation." Ibid., 218.
157. Ibid., 223.
158. Ibid., 224.
159. Ibid., 225.
160. Ibid., 226.

versionist ideal envisions "every moment and period. . .[as] an eschatological present, for in every moment men are dealing with God."[161] In principle, this transformation is possible in any context. In practice, some cultural contexts are more receptive than others to the indwelling of Christ.

Christ and Culture—a classic in twentieth-century Protestant thought—has been subject to a wide and sometimes stinging assessment. The critique by John Howard Yoder has been particularly pointed in depicting Niebuhr's five typologies as so broad that they lack the differentiation required of any sophisticated sociological approach. Yoder also criticizes the notion of juxtaposing "Christ" and "culture" as ideal types when the more persisting reality is that Christian faith—including any vision of the incarnate Christ—can only be interpreted through a cultural matrix.[162]

In an important reassessment, Marsden acknowledges the legitimacy of some of the criticisms. He also notes that many of the charges would have resonated with Niebuhr's own typological thinking, which was never meant to extend beyond a representational model.[163] In addition, Marsden argues that Niebuhr never intended to portray "a culturally disembodied 'Christ' as opposed to culture."[164] Rather, his purpose was to place the challenges of theological reflection within a prevailing cultural context of a given era through which issues of faith always need to be processed.

Marsden maintains that the five types are better understood as "leading motifs" within a given historical context, in which a "dominant motif" may be widespread in a given culture and subordinate in another.[165] In addition, "something of all five of the attitudes" may be prevalent within "a particular category of cultural activities" such as politics, public culture, or education. The categories are "not mutually exclusive" since "virtually every Christian and every Christian group expresses in one way or another all five of the motifs"[166] through the course of a lifetime. Marsden's overarching point is that, with modification, Niebuhr's ideal typology provides useful modes of categorizing some of the representative ways in which Christians engage

---

161. Ibid., 229.

162. Guenther, "Enduring Problem of Christ and Culture," 6.

163. Niebuhr acknowledged that his "study could be interminably and fruitfully continued by multiplying types and subtypes, *motifs* and counter*motifs*, for the purpose of bringing conceptual patterns and historical realities into closer relations, or reducing the haze of uncertainty that surrounds every effort to analyze form in the manifold richness of historical life, of drawing sharper boundaries between the interfusing, interacting thoughts and deeds of separate men." *Christ and Culture*, 231.

164. Marsden, "Christianity and Cultures," 4.

165. Ibid., 8.

166. Ibid., 9; ibid., 8–9; ibid., 8.

the culture. These range from forms of opposition to modes of empathetic engagement, with many mediating spaces between. Marsden views the ideal types as "introductory tools" designed to probe into the relationship between Christ and culture in any given context. They have "heuristic or explanatory power."[167] If used uncritically, "they invite simplistic thought" and stereotypical categorization. Drawn upon in a discerning manner "they can be a rich resource for helping Christians think about their relationship to the world."[168]

CONCLUDING REMARKS

In Quest of a Vital Protestant Center focuses on the current challenges in US Protestantism of teasing out the relationship between the cultural matrix and the biblical text within the communities that strive to be faithful to the core kerygma of the crucified and resurrected Christ. It is here that Niebuhr's broad categories can provide a resource in working through the relationship between cultural modes of Christian expression and sources of authority in mediating the Christ/culture relationship.[169] For much of the twentieth century, the mainline Protestant denominations have veered between various Christ *of* and Christ *above* culture perspectives in the linking of the Christian faith to the more progressive elements of the American political culture. One of the major consequences of this orientation has been the muting of a robust biblically grounded worldview and embrace of a rich orthodox theology and corresponding ecclesial practice. As part of the dynamic of the modernist/fundamentalist divide, mainline Protestant religious culture has ceded much to fundamentalists and evangelicals in the critical area of biblical authority. As argued throughout this book, any revitalization of contemporary Protestant faith grounded in the tradition of the Protestant Reformers will require elevating a canonically focused biblical theology as a primary basis for shaping renewed Christian identity.

As I will argue more fully in the next chapter, this will be greatly enhanced by an intentional embrace of contemporary Protestantism's cultural marginality and a rejection of any lingering hope of merging Christianity with central themes, values, and institutions of American culture. This is a historical assessment, not a claim of timeless truth about the intrinsic relationship between Christ and culture. That is, at this time and place in history, American Protestantism has entered into a realm of unaccustomed

167. Ibid., 12; ibid., 8.
168. Ibid., 12.
169. Carson, *Christ and Culture Revisited*, 12.

cultural marginality. This can be viewed simply as a declension if the claims of faith cannot be decoupled from the progressive elements of US political culture, as reflected in much of the liberal theological tradition. The loss of cultural influence can also be interpreted as a decline from the viewpoint of certain streams of contemporary evangelical thought and culture that embrace the ideal of American exceptionalism in the acceptance of uncritical interpretations of the United States as a distinctively Christian nation. Both of these theological traditions represent forms of integration of the Christ/culture relationship in contemporary US Protestant theology and religious culture.

Marsden thinks that the current period in critical Protestant thought and culture would be well served by an embrace of a Christ and culture in paradox model—"some version of a two cities or two kingdom view." He acknowledges that "other attitudes" may be "appropriate" in certain contexts. Nonetheless, he stresses the paradoxical stance as broadly normative in relation to "Christian attitudes toward mainstream culture."[170] I concur. Such an orientation would provide mainline Protestant and evangelical theology and religious culture with creative space to work out of their respective biblical and theological frames of reference in sharp counterpoint to value systems rooted in contemporary secular culture.

For mainline Protestants, this would provide the cultural space to construct rich biblical perspectives through a range of narrative theological lenses, while critically engaging prevailing cultural modes of intellectual, artistic, social, and cultural thought and behavior on their own set of premises. For evangelicals, such cultural distance could lead to a renewed emphasis on a more purified theology rooted in the Reformation tradition without having to establish an essential religious link between the Christian faith and a justified American culture. Such theological distancing would leave considerable opportunity for mainline Protestants and evangelicals to engage the culture without compromising their own core beliefs. Chief among these are the sovereignty of God, the incarnation and atonement of Christ, the efficacy of the Holy Spirit, the Word of God revealed in and through the Bible, and the ecumenical faith community as the body of Christ within the world. Such intentional refocusing on the orthodox basics of the revealed Christian faith would leave less of a temptation of conflating core religious values with ones grounded in the secular culture, whether the progressive social ideology of liberal Protestantism or the idealized eighteenth-century political and economic ideology of the evangelical right.

---

170. Marsden, "Christianity and Cultures," 12.

Through a more paradoxical stance, the Protestant faith communities would be better positioned to assess the viability of various forms of social, political, and economic ideology on their own terms as lesser centers of value and to make their own proximate judgments accordingly. Such cultural distance would not only help create critical space for Protestant faith communities to sharpen their own respective theological visions. It would help establish openings for more creative dialogue between discerning mainline Protestant and critical evangelical voices. The hope and expectation is that many useful insights would emerge in the areas of formal theology, ecclesial and liturgical practice, personal piety, and public ethics. More hopeful still is the prospect that such engagement would strengthen the vital Protestant center.

Throughout this chapter I have sought to illustrate ways in which the neo-orthodox legacy holds the potential of contributing to this aspiration. These contributions include Barth's biblical turn, Bonhoeffer's "worldly" ethics, Reinhold Niebuhr's dialectical theology between proximate justice within history and God's ultimate sovereignty beyond history, and H. R. Niebuhr's emphasis on centers of value and their significance on the Christ/culture relationship, as variously mediated throughout Christian history. Dorrien and Hall have appropriated the neo-orthodox legacy within contemporary theology from a dialectical postliberal perspective. Bloesch and Fackre have similarly done so from centrist theological viewpoints that share an affinity with moderate evangelical perspectives. As the respective work of these four illuminate, there is much within this legacy that can stimulate fruitful dialogue across a wide span of Protestant theology. In the final chapter I incorporate such insights within my assessment of Hall's post-liberal dialectical theology and the narrative (redemptive-historical) evangelical theology of Richard Lints

8

Postliberal Dialectical and Evangelical Narrative Theology in Critical Juxtaposition

To what end are Christians asked to disentangle their movement and message from the cultures which they have been identified? What purpose is served by the deliberate disengagement of the Christian faith from the values and pursuits of the dominant culture in North America? Why would anyone feel that the message of the divine Spirit to the churches in our field of concern is to disestablish themselves, rather than waiting to be disestablished, further "sidelined"? After all, any such deliberate dissociation must prove, in practice, a painful thing. Like any divorce, Christian efforts to define the church *over against* the culture will inevitably introduce disquiet and tension into what has been, all things considered, a rather comfortable if on the whole innocuous relationship.[1]

The theologian's hope lies not in the ability to remove our cultural blinders so that we might see God but in the power of God to break through our cultural blinders and thereby enable us to see ourselves more clearly by the radiance of his glory. Strategically, this begins with conversion, but it continues most forcefully as we immerse ourselves in God's story, as we begin to think in the categories of God's revelation. The process reaches fruition when we adopt a

---

1. Hall, *Confessing the Faith*, 248.

prophetic stance within our culture. This entails understanding our culture and speaking to it in a language that is both intelligible to it and critical of it, a process that is bound to be painful, for it will inevitably remind us of our depravity.[2]

OVERVIEW

In this chapter, I focus on the cultural shift from mainline Protestant's mid-twentieth-century social location within the epicenter of US public life to its current marginality at its outposts. Hall describes the shift in status in terms of a Protestant "diaspora."[3] I also continue to draw out the challenges of postmodernity through the evangelical lens of Richard Lints.[4] The third major cultural force addressed in the conclusion of this chapter and throughout *In Search of a Vital Protestant Center* is the persistence of the modernist/fundamentalist divide in the iconography of the Protestant imagination. This split is aggravated by a widespread biblical illiteracy among the adult members of contemporary congregations, with somewhat different implications for those of mainline and evangelical sensibilities.

Any ecumenical impetus toward a hermeneutical renewal rooted in the tradition of the Protestant Reformers across the prism of the contemporary US Protestant landscape has much to overcome. Stated positively, working through the persisting tensions between mainline and evangelical thought and culture in the search for a theological center may provide a viable prospect for some healing of the breech rooted in the conflicts of early twentieth-century American Protestantism. I take this challenge on in this chapter by exploring divergences and convergences in the postliberal dialectical theology of Douglas J. Hall and the evangelical narrative theology of Richard Lints. After discussing Hall's and Lints's respective theologies, I conclude this chapter by assessing the viability of moving toward a dynamic centrist position in contemporary Protestant thought and culture.

---

2. Lints, *Fabric of Theology*, 106.
3. Hall, *Confessing the Faith*, 201–64.
4. Lints, *Fabric of Theology*, 191–256.

THE DISCERNING MAINLINE THEOLOGY OF DOUGLAS J. HALL IN THE ERA OF PROTESTANT DISESTABLISHMENT

Disestablishment—on which Hall provides much insightful commentary—is at the center of his analysis of contemporary mainline Protestant culture. Hall situates this more recent phenomenon in US religious history with the declension of the "Constantinian mode" in the trajectory of Western civilization over the past few centuries in the rise of secular modernity.[5] As part of the secularization process of the twentieth century, science, politics, art, literature, and the professionalization of academic history became detached from any overarching Christian worldview.[6] A mid-twentieth-century civil religion that sifted specific religious traditions through the filter of a common "American" identity partially held at bay the drift toward secularization. It did so at much cost to intrinsic Christian identity.

This "civil religion" had its grounding in the nation's earliest Puritan origins in a New Israel vision of "a city on a hill," which underlay the non-separating congregationalism of seventeenth-century New England religious culture.[7] The various religious awakenings in the eighteenth and nineteenth centuries transformed the Puritan vision of a holy city into an American religious identity of a nation called by God to redeem the world. Through the course of US history, a thread of American exceptionalism has persisted as a powerful strain in the nation's culture. The exceptionalist thesis has been variously linked with religion, democracy, nature, capitalism, individualism, and the good community. The exceptionalist meaning of the American experience has crossed ideological boundaries. It has galvanized the fondest hopes and deepest aspirations as well as darker illusions within the nation's history, as reflected in the nineteenth-century doctrine of conquest referred to as "Manifest Destiny."

A pervasive disillusionment swept over Europe after World War I, which reinforced the intellectual and cultural impact of the nihilistic philosophy of late nineteenth- and early twentieth-century existentialism. While influenced by currents across the Atlantic, twentieth-century US culture and religious identity were largely sheltered from such skepticism through a broad-based liberal political and religious culture through the first two decades of the new century. A sense of post-war realism entered into the political and religious culture of the nation during the two decades

---

5. Hall, *Confessing the Faith*, 210.
6. Marsden, *Soul of the American University*.
7. Miller, *New England Mind*.

following World War I. Both the neo-orthodoxy of Reinhold Niebuhr and the increasing statism of the New Deal served to shore up the most enduring fruits of liberalism on foundations more stable than the effervescent hopefulness characteristic of the Progressive Era and the advocates of the social gospel in the pre–World War I era. With the Allied victory of World War II and the emergent US consumer society, a sense of diffuse liberal optimism reemerged with a concomitant rise of a civil religion broadly associated with "the American way of life." As discussed in chapter 2, the impact of this civil religion muted the theological specificity of the neo-orthodox influence within the religious culture of the United States.

Hall posits the merging of this civic religion with the mid-century mainline Protestant culture and the continuing longing for it as a dominant echo that has persisted in the ensuing sixty years in the inexorable movement toward disestablishment. The challenge for thoughtful Christians—particularly in the declining mainline denominations—is that of reclaiming a deep theological appreciation of its core premises that are rooted in a nuanced appropriation of the Reformation tradition. Hall calls for an attendant willingness to engage in such an effort through a diaspora sensibility that can exercise the fortitude to relinquish any prospect of a recovery of the former social and cultural privileged status of mainline Protestantism. Such standing within the nation's civil religion was costly even in the 1950s in the effect of muting the primary content of faith, particularly its sharper theological contours, for the dubious benefit of social acceptability. As Hall argues, there is much to gain in terms of Christian realism and theological clarity in a mature acceptance of this unaccustomed diaspora status which, to deny, is to subscribe to a highly suspect aspiration.

An irony that holds a great deal of weight for Hall is the social displacement of the Protestant mainline by the religious right in assuming a triumphalist aspiration in the American civic polity since 1980. Hall is quick to note that, in making such an assessment, he is not aiming his critique "at individual believers, or even at churches and denominations."[8] Rather, his focus is on the larger social, cultural, political, and religious forces operating at a broader cultural level that have profoundly reshaped the landscape of American religious culture over the past thirty years. Painting this conservative revival in some very broad strokes, Hall is highly critical of its too easy embrace of the core myths of American exceptionalism. He sees this vision as buttressed by a simplistic biblicist veneer based more on "hermeneutical principles drawn from the social fabric"[9] than from any serious scriptural

8. Hall, *Confessing the Faith*, 227.
9. Ibid.

and theological analysis of the US political culture and the broader cultural matrix.

Hall's maintains that the unswerving call to justice opens space for a renewal of mainline religious culture in an unaccustomed prophetic role that can emerge in the very bearing of its social displacement. It is this prophetic call that he posits in juxtaposition to what he contends is the less than innocent political theology of the religious right. In Hall's depiction:

> The Christian Right, with its inherent religious certitude, its apparent moral rigor, and (especially!) its well-known facility for enemy imaging, is supplying what the majority culture demands in a way that the old remnants of classical Protestantism cannot (or to their credit) will not. The Christian Right sees the rebirth of Christianity in America—and through a strong America, the rebirth of Christianity in the world at large—as part of the same process. That it trivializes both American democratic ideals and Christianity belongs to its role as official cultus of an imperial people.[10]

Hall calls the mainline Protestant denominations to embrace a countercultural theology of the cross. This will not be an easy burden to bear. Nonetheless, Hall's envisions it as the *kairotic* space opened up at this time in the North American religious context. Embodying this space requires the willingness to speak out against injustice and ungodliness in all its forms from the very position of cultural marginality.[11] The Protestant mainline denominations have embraced the clarion call of justice—a clear mandate of Scripture itself. They have done so typically without a sufficient level of theological insight that, if incorporated into its vision, could bring greater clarity to a religious identity somewhat lacking in specific Christian lucidity.[12]

What is required, in part, is a clearer grounding in the legacy of the social gospel, the predominant engine of US religious reform in the early decades of the twentieth century.[13] While there is a great deal to appropriate from liberation theology, there has been too much of a romantic acceptance of some of its core tenets among certain influential leaders within

---

10. Hall, *Confessing the Faith*, 234.

11. Ibid., 211–15.

12. Hall notes that the "Protestant mainline . . . is theologically vague and forgetful" of its theological and biblical heritage rooted within the legacy of the Reformation tradition. The mainline denominations have "produced a significant minority of persons with an unusual sense of social responsibility, but it is uncertain how it did so, and why such responsibility is mandatory for Christians." Ibid., 238.

13. Ibid., 237.

the US mainline denominations. As argued by Dorrien and Hall, a nuanced dialectic between the legacy of Reinhold Niebuhr's Christian realism and the contemporary proponents of the social gospel tradition may well provide a pathway to situate some enduring theologies of justice that can speak with and to power in our current setting.[14]

Hall draws out the importance of a distinctively biblical and theological faith stance grounded in a Reformation sensibility buttressed by the neo-orthodox perspective of the twentieth century. He views this theological grounding as an inseparable part of the emphasis on justice.[15] Without such theological clarity there is the danger of sacrificing a sharply defined *religious* identity firmly grounded in the proclamation of the Christian gospel. Given the need for such a contemporary reconstruction rooted in the tradition of the Protestant Reformers, and noting the difficulties in doing so, Hall contends that "it will become necessary for the churches . . . to become knowledgeable about the Christian faith in a way that has not occurred in North America heretofore."[16] Such an embrace will require "not only a breadth but a *depth* of theological awareness, and not only a depth, but a sense of commitment, and not only commitment but a willingness to embark on critical thinking"[17] at a much more extensive magnitude than that reflected by any "Christianity of the Protestant middle classes."[18]

Hall is not overly optimistic that any such renewal is likely to gain a strong foothold given the cost required of the mainline denominations to embrace the prophetic significance of their own marginality.[19] Despite such

---

14. Dorrien, *Soul in Society*, 1–161. The relationship between social justice and the Christian realism of Reinhold Niebuhr is implicit throughout chapter 4 of *Confessing the Faith*, 201–64.

15. For a statement that defines justice as an explicit theological theme, see Hall, *Confessing the Faith*, 516–18.

16. Ibid., 247.

17. Ibid., 247–48.

18. Ibid., 248.

19. "As with every other sort of dying, people can be expected to enter into this death if they can be helped to believe that exposure to so painful an ending can become both meaningful and productive of hope. Something comparable to the intellectual-spiritual journey of the theologians themselves must be made available to those who do not have the benefits of years of professional training and full-time study. To *assume* the end of Christendom, to speak out of that assumption and to presuppose that it is both self-evident and purposeful: this is clearly not enough." Ibid., 214. According to Hall, the prophetic community must intentionally embrace its status of cultural marginality in order to clearly articulate the countercultural message of authentic Christianity in the contemporary North American setting. He views this objective as an important theological project that will require much effort if it is ever going to be embraced within the Protestant mainline denominations to any significant degree—one, despite

pessimism, his deeper tone remains that of wary hopefulness. Hall visualizes a remnant of "serious Christians"[20] who are able to articulate and live out of this dual mandate of promoting radical justice and profound theological clarity through a different idiom than the prevailing religious and secular discourses of the current milieu. As Hall sums it up:

> To walk between the dangers of absorption and ghettoiziaton is to walk a very narrow way, but it is not an impossible one. What is wanted is clear enough: a believing church with a strong sense of public responsibility. It will be a confessing church only if it continually reviews and renews its own identity with Jesus Christ through prayer, disciplined study, and nurture of its membership. And it will be a confessing church only if it continually confesses Jesus as Christ in the specific and ever-changing sphere of public life. Confession involves both inward- and outward-turning. Without the inward turning that is its spiritual-intellectual discipline the community's outwardness will lack the mark of its discipleship of the crucified one; it will be indistinguishable from other voices, and eventually incapable of grasping and articulating even for itself the "reasons for its hope." But without its outward orientation, the wisdom that it may have gleaned through its life of listening and renewal will be lost to the world for which it is intended.[21]

This is a high point in Hall's discussion. On this pivotal and meditatively balanced assessment, there is much upon which postliberal and critical evangelical Protestants can draw upon in search of a broad ecumenicity faithful to the core kerygma. This includes the importance Hall attributes to a mature Christian realism that speaks with power to both the vertical and horizontal dimensions of faith and to the emphasis he places on an intentional embrace of the cultural marginality within mainline Protestantism. Notwithstanding these strengths, I question Hall's limited critique of the evangelical Protestant tradition which he tends to paint with an overly simplistic brush. It is so sweepingly general that it leaves little account for the nuances of a broad array of serious evangelical theologians, such as John Stott, David Wells, Mark Noll, and Os Guiness, whose collective insights on both theology and biblical exegesis and exposition can rival Hall's own astute analysis.

---

the difficulties, that merits the most acute attention of the committed clergy and lay leadership.

20. Ibid., 7.
21. Ibid., 261–62.

I raise two additional points. The first is Hall's leaning toward dialectics over dogmatics in a manner similar to Brueggemann and Dorrien. This inclination is an effort to remain faithful to the most fundamental promptings of the Judeo-Christian vision in a manner that can only be grasped in and through contingent historical experience. The emphasis on dialectics reflects something of the dynamics of a living faith. At the same time it places the accent on experience over the dogmatics of faith, or—to use Hall's terminology—on apologetic over kerygmatic theology.[22] The closely related second issue is that of Hall's aversion against any substantial claims of *truth* in the awareness that any such knowing is invariably filtered through the fallibilities and deceptions of human perception.[23] Hall's apprehension is that the quest for religious certitude has been accompanied by a long history of abuse and manipulation in reinforcing a triumphal view of Christianity and American civilization. That may be so. Still, Hall has not accounted for the theological depth of serious evangelical theology that does address the issue of truth while grappling with the tension between the unfathomable gap between human finitude and the divine sovereignty of God. In earlier chapters I have sought to illuminate something of this evangelical depth in Newbigin, Packer, and Bloesch. I do so in this closing chapter through the theology of Richard Lints.

THE EVANGELICAL REDEMPTIVE-HISTORICAL VISION OF RICHARD LINTS IN CRITICAL DIALOGUE WITH POSTMODERN THEOLOGY

Richard Lints, professor of theology at Gordon-Conwell Theological Seminary, is empathetic to Hall's quest for the revitalization of Protestant theology in the contemporary period. More so than many evangelicals, he identifies critical dialogue between evangelical and postmodern theologians an important task of contemporary *evangelical* theology. To bypass this is to put at

---

22. Hall, *Thinking the Faith*, 349–67.

23. Hall is far from wholly dismissive of the importance of the search for truth as the basis of substantial theological reflection. At the least he does not want to abandon the theological significance of the search for truth for a pathway that can only lead to an emphasis on "experience" and "expedience." *Confessing the Faith*, 245. He also points to the need for "a strongly objective dimension in such theological reflection if the habit of turning theology into psychology, and hence of reverting to the criteria of 'experience' is to be avoided." Ibid., 246. Nonetheless, the dialectical emphasis on openness is pervasive in Hall, as reflected throughout *Confessing the Faith* and his companion text, *Thinking the Faith*. Dialectical theology is also at the core of his embrace of the entire neo-orthodox tradition from Barth to Tillich. See Hall, *Remembered Voices*.

risk the very prospect of being taken with seriousness by the audiences that both Lints and Hall seek to address through their divergent metanarrative construals. The positive good that Lints anticipates coming from such an encounter is that "conversation with postmodern theologians will stretch evangelicalism as it has never been stretched before" in a manner that could facilitate a moving beyond its own ghettoizing influences. He grants that "there is no guarantee that evangelicalism will not break" and be transmuted into a form of postmodern theology by giving undue predominance of some aspect of the culture, especially the specter of relativism. His hope is that "God's promise to be faithful" would result in a deepened evangelicalism through what can only be a risky journey in a radical encounter with some of the most central precepts of postmodern theology. The prospect, indeed, would likely be "discomfiting."[24] He is hopeful that, in the long run, such an effort would lead to an enriched Christian sensibility that can engage in critical dialogue with the broad trajectories of contemporary culture, while remaining faithful to the core precepts of the apostolic faith.

Lints argues that postmodern theology has taken on the "difficult task of creating *transcendent* meaning and purpose for the human community without a transcendent source."[25] In its embrace of the fundamental presuppositions of death of God theology, Mark Taylor's *Erring: A Postmodern A/Theology* is an example of theological reflection in this mode. Taylor contends that what is needed is a "theological transgression" of the most "subversive"[26] type. Such a perspective serves as a solvent in deconstructing any theology of being and concomitant centered selfhood that underlies the prevailing cultural paradigms of Western theology. Lints accepts the need to deconstruct all that occludes or limits the revelation of God's will in human history, including any false consciousness that masquerades itself in theological or biblical garb. He also insists on the centrality of the language structure and the storied trajectory of the Bible's overarching narrative as the critical grounding point for any hermeneutics of retrieval. In this, Lints emphatically rejects anti-theistic presuppositions of the death of God theology that underlies Taylor's a/theology.[27]

Lints's directive focus is toward an open-ended, ever richer dialogue between evangelicalism and certain threads within postmodern culture and theology. This is evident in his willingness, in principle, to yield up whatever is required of evangelical theology to the weaving forth of the wisdom of

---

24. Lints, *Fabric of Theology*, 256.
25. Ibid., 217.
26. Taylor, *Erring*, 10.
27. Lints, *Fabric of Theology*, 259–89.

God's revelation in creative discourse with postmodern theologians. For Lints, God remains distinctively transcendent *and* present in the very midst of profoundly entering into human history. This is so to the point of the Son of God suffering an ignominious death within history. Through this sacrifice God remains profoundly hidden even in the midst of his revelatory power and love for a fallen world (Phil 2:7–8). Lints critiques a good deal of evangelical theology as currently practiced, even as he remains firmly grounded in its core presuppositions based on the central role of the Bible as a determinative source of revelation of the first order. There is a limit, therefore, to the range of Lints's practical capacity to engage in creative dialogue with postmodern theology, though in the process he pushes a good deal on the outer edges of evangelical theology and biblical hermeneutics.

The boundary line of his theological project is based on the need to decide whether to place one's ultimate center of value on the critical precepts of radical monotheism as biblically envisioned, or first and foremost on the questions raised from "below," in privileging the sensibilities of human experience.[28] As an evangelical theologian, Lints's commitment is clearly with the former. With Hall, he accepts the dialectical dynamic of a covenantal-based faith in which revelation is grounded on both what is given (God's grace) and what is received (its reception within the fabric of human experience). However, Lints places more emphasis than Hall on the critical importance of ontology, in which faith in the God who *does* reveal himself within human history and experience has a more normative status in his theology than the realm of doubt stemming from the pain and alienation of disconfirming human experience. Lints acknowledges that doubt remains penultimately significant. It is not lightly to be treated. Both Hall and Lints emphasize theologies of the cross, however different the nuances of their particular perspectives.

Central for Lints is the importance of fleshing out what Fackre refers to as an ecumenically sensitive *evangelical* theology.[29] This includes a theology that draws richly from a broad array of academic disciplines, firmly grounded upon the fundamental "biblical categories [such] as sin, unbelief,

---

28. Lints explains the conundrum in the following manner: "Postmodern theology has to be 'from below' because the gospel is 'from below.' The postmodern will brook no compromise on this point—which is why there will always remain a theological chasm between the evangelical and postmodern theological visions. The fundamental methodological movement of the evangelical theological framework is not from the ground of human experience to the superstructure of ideology but rather from the interpretive superstructure of biblical ideology to an understanding of human experience." Ibid., 252.

29. Fackre, *Ecumenical Faith in Evangelical Perspective*.

and idolatry."[30] Hall is supportive of this emphasis. But he expresses discomfort with any such perspective if it is not rigorously processed through the acid test of a most thorough hermeneutics of suspicion. Lints assents as long as one's theological position is resolutely grounded in a deeper hermeneutics of retrieval. The critical issue is that of the starting point on whether one turns first to biblical revelation or to human experience. Both Hall and Lints exhibit a dialectical sensibility in their mutual search for a Protestant theological grounding point that provides a source of resonance *and* critical rejoinder to the prevailing discourses of the contemporary secular culture. They differ on the extent to which the Bible serves as an unequivocal starting point in mediating the relationship between faith and culture.

Lints places more significance than Hall on the entire trajectory of the biblical story as a coherent and inherently revelatory narrative. His canonical approach includes attention to the various revelatory epiphanies as embodied through the course of biblical and historical time. He argues that the Bible possesses a coherent "theological framework" that provides an organic unity to the arc of the textual narrative. It is this overarching unity, which Lints attributes to the hand of God that accounts for such development.[31]

One of Lints's key purposes is to encourage evangelical biblical scholars and expositors to come to grips with this more complex historical unfolding of the revelation of God throughout Scripture, from creation to consummation. Lints identifies God's redemption of humankind through the sacrifice and resurrection of Jesus Christ as the central biblical theme. It is the revelation of God in Christ reconciling the world (2 Cor 5:19) that drives the biblical trajectory from creation to consummation. This he posits in contrast to undue concentration on the "propositional" truth statements of individual passages or collections of passages organized to support the key themes salvation, atonement, creation, and redemption as one finds in certain evangelical textbooks.[32]

Lints identifies the importance of "epochal" events within the biblical narrative in detailing the ways in which God's redemptive power progressively emerges over time, in which each epoch, or major biblical period,

30. Lints, *Fabric of Theology*, 236.

31. Ibid., 300. See 300–303 for Lints's discussion on the relation of specific biblical "epochs" within the context of the broader biblical trajectory.

32. For examples, see Grudem, *Bible Doctrine*; Erickson, *Christian Theology*; and Bloesch, *Essentials of Evangelical Theology*. All of these texts presuppose the narrative arc of redemptive history. However, given their focus on critical topics in systematic theology, the central emphasis that Lints places on it is not always evident. In arguing for the need to restructure systematic theology in a manner more congruent with biblical theology based on a redemptive-historical narrative perspective, see Michael Williams's "Systematic Theology as a Biblical Discipline," 197–233.

contributes in its distinctive manner to the Bible's overarching narrative of redemptive history. An epochal hermeneutics requires attentiveness to narrative coherency and the theological significance of each major period—whether the Abrahamic narrative, the Mosaic period, the Davidic kingdom, the prophetic era, or the major divisions within the New Testament—the pre-resurrection life of Christ, the rise of the early church, or the eschatological fulfillment of the kingdom of God in the New Jerusalem. Each period contributes to the progressive unfolding of the Bible's underlying revelation within redemptive history.[33] With Fackre, Lints places the "modern church" in the midst of the biblical story "between the two comings of Christ, between the incarnation and the parousia."[34]

This is a common theological understanding. Its significance for Lints is that it places the attuned reader within the narrative thread of Scripture itself as a direct addressee. With Paul, the engaged reader looks forward to the ultimate fulfillment of God's reign, while looking back to the "fulfillment of the Abrahamic covenant" brought to a climax in the coming of Christ. There is no sense in Lints of disregarding the passage of almost two thousand years from the New Testament to the contemporary era. That is clear from the first six chapters of *The Fabric of Theology*. There is in Lints a profound commitment to the entirety of the Bible story interpreted from the "redemptive-historical" lens of Christ. He insists that this revelatory grid has ontological and epistemological privilege for the committed Christian over and above the contemporary influences of culture and current modes of academic biblical scholarship.[35] This stance enables Lints to argue that "with Paul, Luke, John, and Peter, we should look to the death, resurrection, and ascension of Christ for the interpretive key to the meaning of our past, present, and future." Such a perspective provides Christians with "an 'epochal reach'" in the time between the ascension and the parousia. As a people of the Book, this reach "enables. . .[Christians] to determine the way we are to think and to live even in the twentieth century and beyond."[36]

"The promise-fulfillment model" is at the center of Lints's canonical horizon. It underlies the redemptive vision of God's "divine plan of history." It is the scarlet thread that weaves together the distinctive periods and diversity of genres that comprise the biblical text as a unified document.[37] The

---

33. Lints, *Fabric of Theology*, 276–79, 300–303.

34. Ibid., 278.

35. Lints insists that in the dialogue with postmodern theology and culture, the "normative standards of the Scriptures ought to play the central role" for which "evangelicals ought not apologize." Ibid., 331.

36. Ibid., 279.

37. Ibid., 303.

canonical focus of the Bible as a unified text is based upon the progressive development within the text from one epochal period to another.

Lints points to typology as a primary mode which, through the Spirit of God, the human writers embody and convey the promise-fulfillment dynamic that underlies Scripture. He defines typology as "symbolism with a prospective reference to fulfillment in a later epoch in biblical history."[38] The "exodus event" is the "type" to which the "Babylonian captivity" is the "antitype." The original reference point maintains its intrinsic importance in biblical history. On Lints's progressive interpretation, the antitype is always more significant because its consequences are intrinsically so. Interpreted in this way, the Babylonian captivity carries more theological weight than the exodus because it factors into the ultimate release of Israel the nation's deliverance "from rebellion and sin" and not that solely of political oppression and captivity. This additional "deliverance enriched the concept of redemption and offered to Israel a greater sense of the providential activity of God."[39]

The deliverance from sin, ultimately in the atonement of Christ, goes to the core of Lints's theory of progressive typological fulfillment. It is this "fabric-like character of redemptive revelation" that Lints draws on to construct an evangelical theology. He does so by weaving together particular biblical texts and specific epochal events within a typological hermeneutics of progressive development. The result is a greater conception "of the present as existing on a continuum with the past and the future of redemptive history."[40] He connects this understanding of Scripture to specific interpretations of the biblical text and to the broader life of the contemporary Christian whose most authentic identity is grounded in the tension between "the already" of Christ's first coming and the "not yet" of Christ's ultimate coming.

LINTS AND HALL IN CRITICAL JUXTAPOSITION

The similarities are striking between Lints's biblical theology of the progressive unfolding of the biblical story and Fackre's narrative theology. A key difference is that Fackre is willing to incorporate more of the historical context into his formal theological explanation than does Lints, whose reach ultimately does not extend beyond a specifically evangelical perspective. Lints's argument is that the Bible, appropriately interpreted, has the capacity

38. Ibid., 304.
39. Ibid., 305.
40. Ibid., 309.

of "transporting the modern person back into the conceptual world of the Scriptures."[41] That may be so for evangelically minded readers who are inclined by experience and tradition to look to the Bible for foundational explanations of and resources for ongoing faith formation even in the midst of the most pressing doubt. Hall—who shares Fackre's appreciation for the role of context in shaping faith—seeks a more dynamic relationship between the Bible and culture. According to Hall:

> Humanity's ever changing conception of its world constitutes an active ingredient in the theological discipline; that the movement of interpretation, therefore, is not simply text to context but a dialectical interaction between the two, in which, being grasped by new and often unsettling factors in its sociohistorical context, the discipline community is compelled to rethink and reformulate the meaning of the story presented by its authoritative sources. In turn, the message derived through this process of interaction engages the context from the side of the text, and, in sometimes significant and sometimes inconspicuous ways, it becomes an agent in the alteration of its context.[42]

Hall accepts the "primary significance" of Scripture "because for all intents and purposes [it is] *the sole witness*"[43] to the revelation of Christ. He is critical of the prevailing liberal Protestant view of Scripture in its reductive interpretation of the Bible as "an internally inconsistent" text, one that "cannot be regarded as . . . authoritative." Hall draws a distinction between the theological liberal community that demonstrates a studious respect for the significance of the Bible and "the bourgeois ecclesiastic ethos most influenced by liberalism." It is this latter sector that "has ended by

---

41. Ibid., 316.

42. Hall, *Thinking the Faith*, 128. Hall states that "theology must be faithful to what is really present in the biblical writings, and therefore systematic theology, without being slavishly dependent upon it, must be in continuous dialogue with biblical scholarship. But theology must also be in touch with life in the here and now, and so the questions and concerns it brings to the Scriptures are not identical with those of the exegetes. What theology needs from its ongoing discourse with the biblical text is determined in large measure by its worldly context." Ibid., 263. Lints is also appreciative of the significance of the cultural context in the formation of theology. However, he views the purpose of theology as largely that of elaborating on the trajectory of the biblical story in the movement to its climatic unfolding, and applying that narrative to the human condition in the contemporary context. As he states: "The question of the relevance of the biblical text presumes that the flow of redemptive history in the biblical theological framework can appropriately give birth to a modern theological vision." *Fabric of Theology*, 315.

43. Hall, *Thinking the Faith*, 258.

apotheosizing certain sentimental 'truths' roughly gleaned from the Bible, but so thoroughly abstracted from their historical-theological context as to perform no office beyond the confirmation of the bourgeois transcendence already held by these circles."[44]

Hall is equally critical of "biblicalism," which he associates with "religious simplism." The problem Hall points to is a sense of "absolutism" in the Bible's truth that is so complete that the mainline Protestant interlocutor can only view as "impossible and fanatical." Hall notes that the linkage of an inerrant view of Scripture with the political right adds to the difficulty for those whose faith formation has been shaped in mainline denominations and seminaries. The challenge that Hall identifies is the need "to embrace a theology of biblical authority without appearing to endorse biblical literalism and much else besides."[45] In his depiction of "fundamentalism and old orthodoxy,"[46] Hall is so broad-brushed that he does not carefully account for the diverse array of contemporary evangelical theology and biblical scholarship. As stated, a more discerning analysis of evangelical scholarship could help Hall identify some resources in bridging the gap among those Christians who look first to the Bible as their primary source of identification and those who view culture as a central factor in the shaping of contemporary Christian identity.[47]

Notwithstanding Hall's lack of critical engagement with the serious evangelical sector; that which he affirms—his dialectical analysis of the role of the Bible in contemporary theological reflection—merits close analysis. For Hall, the Bible, as primary witness of the Christian faith, points to that which is most foundational—"the living God, the speaking God, the *incarnate* Word, who transcends all description and expression." This foundational focal point calls upon the faithful Christian to honor and worship God with the entirety of one's being. This, in turn, requires the need to relativize "everything [else] that claims to be absolute,"[48] including the Bible when it is so taken which, for Hall, is the primary resource, but not the primary source of revelation. Hall encourages the mature Christian to draw on the "biblical witness . . . through the divine Spirit that, by the grace of God can be evoked from it for the purpose of "illuminat[ing] the life of the disci-

---

44. Hall, *Confessing the Faith*, 298.

45. Hall, *Thinking the Faith*, 259.

46. Hall, *Confessing the Faith*, 298.

47. See Dorrien, *Remaking of Evangelical Theology*, for an in-depth analysis of twentieth-century evangelical theology from a postliberal perspective. Grenz, writing from a progressive evangelical slant in *Renewing the Center*, provides an equally substantial overview of twentieth-century evangelical theology.

48. Hall, *Thinking the Faith*, 260.

pline community in the world here and now." This is a call for the Christian community "to be faithful to what is really present in" Scripture "without being slavishly dependent"[49] on the literal words of the text. As Hall argues, this is so because the cultural context plays a major role in determining the theological issues of a given time and place, including particular biblical focal points.

Lints maintains that "the Scriptures are to be the primary interpreters of the modern era."[50] Culture is relevant for shedding light on what issues the Christian community needs to address in relation to its impact on its own membership and in apologetic response to the prevailing paradigms of a given cultural context. For Lints, culture does not carry significant theological weight in its own right in terms of determining which aspects of the Bible merit particular focus since, on his account, the world is subsumed within the canonical Bible narrative.[51] The critical difference between Lints and Hall is the place of "historicism" in their respective theologies. For Hall, the historical context is of penultimate significance as a most important source of his dialectical theology. Lints seeks to deconstruct historicism by positing the absolute truth of the biblical worldview.[52]

Lints places believers and unbelievers "on the redemptive historical index" of the Christian story. He bases this on a common humanity created in the image of God and the equally universal reality of sin that infuses the experience of believers and unbelievers alike. It is upon these assumptions that Lints identifies the biblical revelation as the foundational source for any true engagement with culture and the basis for the formation of "a modern theological vision."[53] Such a vision requires the capacity "to speak the language of the modern world," not, however, for the purpose of engaging in dialogue as an end in itself. Lints's theology is less dialectical than it is persuasive in its ultimate objective. It is aimed at "transporting the modern person back into the conceptual world of the Scriptures." For Lints, dialogue with the secular culture, however probing, is ultimately, a means to an ends.

---

49. Ibid., 263.

50. Lints, *Fabric of Theology*, 312.

51. Lints maintains that "the Bible is relevant because the present situation is but another episode in the story of the Bible—a story that has begun and climaxed and awaits consummation foretold in the Scriptures. The Scriptures offer a framework for interpreting this past, present and future, including our own past, present and future." Ibid., 314.

52. For Lints's definition of historicism, see ibid., and chapter 2n8.

53. Ibid., 315.

Its purpose is to "challenge the very assumptions that undergird cultural life today."[54]

In his focus on the relationship between faith and culture, Lints shares certain affinities with Hall, even amidst the differences that separate their respective theological visions. For example, both Lints and Hall view the contemporary church in need of much theological renewal. Hall argues that a prophetic vision can only emerge if the mainline denominations embrace their unaccustomed minority status and intentionally incorporate a theological identity rooted in the tradition of the Reformation. Lints focuses directly on the need for evangelical churches to shape their understanding of the Christian faith within a fully orbed theological perspective. The social status of the faith community is of less direct concern to him.

Lints attributes the problem of doing so to two primary sources. One is that of the "parachurch character of evangelicalism"[55] and the concomitant emphasis on the conversion experience as the central indicator of authentic faith. The result is a simplification of biblical and theological interpretation to a few key truths and a limited understanding of the broader historical Reformation tradition of which evangelicalism is a subset. Another problem is the increasing professionalization of the theological enterprise which has created a wide gap between the congregational and the seminary experience. In seeking to transcend these limitations within evangelical religious culture, Lints argues that the church needs to be the primary place where a coherent theological vision emerges and a central location where theologians practice their craft.[56] Hall is equally troubled about the low level of theological acuity and biblical literacy within the mainline Protestant denominations and the need to revitalize the churches with these concerns in mind.[57]

Lints's highlights popular culture as a primary area that merits an extended theological analysis. His focus is threefold: the influence of "distorting accretions" of culture on the "biblical faith in the believing community," a call to repudiate those aspects "of culture that are contrary to the Word of God," and the need to strengthen "and transform those aspects of culture that are consistent with God's revelation."[58] He concentrates primarily on the need to critically challenge those aspects of culture that are opposed to

---

54. Ibid., 316.

55. Ibid., 318.

56. Lints does not substantively lay out what this would look like. In this book, J. I. Packer has been the preeminent theologian in describing in detail the intricacies of a coherent evangelical vision.

57. Hall, *Thinking the Faith*, 289–99.

58. Lints, *Fabric of Theology*, 322.

the biblical worldview. In this opposition, Lints draws attention three major themes: cultural pluralism, confessional simplicity, and the cult of the self."[59] For the purposes of this discussion I focus on the first.

In his critique of cultural pluralism, Lints highlights the religious element, particularly the notion that all religions are of equal value, and the underlying value of tolerance that buttresses such an assumption. He argues that the sociological reality of pluralism should not be translated into an intrinsic "normative value." He further maintains that "most of the world's religions are monopolistic in their world views." He claims that their advocates reject any notion that discounts "truth as a relevant category of assessment."[60] He infers that evangelical Protestants should do likewise.

Hall is leery of taking an unequivocal exclusivist Christian position in opposition to other religious worldviews. This is, in part, due to the history of Christian oppression of minority groups, particularly Jews in light of Auschwitz.[61] His inclusivism is also a response to the ineradicable pluralism of North American society and the declining status of Christian social standing within it. Hall points to the need to engage the world religions on their own terms. This includes the possibility of "alter[ing] our own belief, perhaps radically" as the result of such engagement and "revisit[ing] our doctrinal heritage with genuinely critical and self-critical insight."[62] Hall's argument is more procedural than substantive at this point. Yet it underlies his broader dialectical theology that he explores with much passion and acumen throughout his *Christian Theology in a North American* series.[63]

Lints and Hall approach contemporary culture from different perspectives; ones that call for honoring the respective traditions they represent in evangelical and postliberal theology and ecclesial practice. Each opens creative space for receptive readers within the orbits in which they craft their respective theologies. They each attempt to synthesize conservative and liberal perspectives within their particular traditions and gravitate toward an ecumenical centrist position within them. Engaging their work from an irenic sensibility in a manner that does not eschew critical assessment of their respective theologies can open up fresh space for constructive dialogue across the Protestant perspective.

59. Ibid.
60. Ibid., 323.
61. Hall, *Thinking the Faith*, 210–13.
62. Ibid., 209, 210.
63. In addition to *Confessing the Faith* and *Thinking the Faith*, Hall's trilogy includes *Professing the Faith*.

A case in point is Hall's embrace of one of the most foundational assumptions of the Reformation heritage—"justification by grace through faith," which he distinguishes from the more common "formulation 'justification by faith.'" The problem with the latter construction is the emphasis it places on the power of belief and its impact on the quest for personal rectitude as a means of getting in right relationship with God. By contrast, "justification by grace through faith" depends on the unequivocal power of God to break into human experience as pure gift. It is this radical dependency that reflects the "*confessional* context" of the Protestant faith "when 'all other helpers fail and comforts flee.'"[64]

Hall is in clear accord with Packer's most Calvinistic instincts when he declares that "most people are not prepared to hear that they are justified by grace *alone* as long as they can feel they are upheld by other, worldly forms of security, including the security offered by well-regulated religion."[65] Where Hall differs is on the theological emphasis he places on the role of doubt in grappling with the gap between human experience and the sovereignty of God. Stated in other terms, Hall keeps in dialectical tension Barth's emphasis on the sovereignty of God and that which Tillich places on doubt and anxiety as essential correlates of any meaningful theology of the cross. Without necessarily accepting all that he advocates, there is much from which to draw upon in Hall's rich dialectic between faith and doubt and Christ and culture that can give embodiment to Lints's call for evangelical theology and religious culture called to "stretch as it has never been stretched before."[66]

There is also much for those like Hall to draw on through a rich engagement with the diversity of contemporary evangelical theology in the areas of biblical hermeneutics and application of biblical theology in the life of the church and the formation of personal piety. Lints's emphasis on the integrity, coherency, and truth revealed in the canonical Scripture can provide an enduring source of stability and a high degree of assurance to the vision of those like Hall who seek ultimate meaning in the Christian revelation, however much they place faith and culture in dialectical tension.

CONCLUDING REMARKS

I conclude *In Search of a Vital Protestant Center* with a few summary statements. The core of my argument stems from the persisting nature of the great divide at the heart of current US Protestantism, as reflected in its evangelical

---

64. Hall, *Confessing the Faith*, 278.
65. Ibid., 279.
66. Lints, *Fabric of Theology*, 256.

and mainline camps, on whether one starts with the Bible or experience as the primary source of faith in God revealed through Christ. As evident in the mediating theologies of Hall and Lints, this is an enduring dilemma within contemporary US Protestantism theology, biblical study, and religious culture. The divide exists at the congregational level as well as within the fabric of formal theological discourse. It is exemplified by which authors are read or ignored in particular seminary or congregational settings. The result is that a great many Protestant ministers, educated lay persons, and even theologians do not have a substantial understanding of the nature of scriptural exegesis, theological argumentation, or even basic biblical understanding of those whose positions substantially differ from their own within the camp of present-day Protestant discourse. The consequential impact is an all-too-quick resort to stereotypical thinking or downright dismissal of even highly cogent alternative depictions of both Christian scholarship at the seminary level and approaches to worship, preaching, and teaching at the congregational level.

In covering the ground from Packer to Brueggemann, I have sought to imaginatively traverse some of the distance in contemporary Protestantism within a broad-based "generous orthodoxy." The differing emphases on biblical interpretation, culture, and theology within the schools of thought and practice represented by these four theologians need to be placed in critical dialogue for any even imaginative bridging of the great fundamentalist/modernist divide to take hold. The schema of placing Packer, Bloesch, Fackre, and Brueggemann in the sequencing that I have set up is based on a rough ordering, from conservative to liberal, within the context of an overarching Christian orthodoxy in search of a vital Protestant center. My strategy has been to juxtapose core concepts of these authors in a predominantly irenic manner, even as I have raised critical issues with certain aspects of all of these conversation partners. The value of their many reflections is enhanced by the fact that each author has taken a mediating approach in an effort to reconcile a broad swath of theological insight within the given sphere of their respective realms of influence. I have also suggested that the critical insights of these writers on biblical interpretation, the theology of God, and the faith-culture relationship can be fruitfully drawn upon by those whose theological predispositions move in other directions than those of one or more of the identified authors.

Thus, Packer's insights on biblical interpretation, personal piety, his work on illuminating the riches embodied in Puritan thought and practice, and his emphasis on the sovereignty of God can be read with much profit by clergy, laity, and theologians within the mainline denominations. In addition to that of enriching their understanding of the critical areas that Packer addresses, his popular and more technical writings open up to mainline Protestant readers dimensions of serious evangelical theology on its own terms. Such reading does not require acceptance of the entirety of Packer's theology. Rather, it calls for interpretations that are both empathetic and critical, in which discerning dialogue remains central to any effort at broadening one's own theological understanding.

Similarly, there is much within the insights of Brueggemann that can enrich evangelical theology. This includes Brueggemann's emphasis on "faithful imagination"[67] as a critical lever for engaging the Bible and something of the ineffable Spirit underlying the Christian revelation. Brueggemann's extensive commentary on individual Old Testament passages offers much insight for evangelical reflection, as does his analysis of the condition of postmodern life in the US and in the mainline Protestant churches. Such appreciation does not preclude criticism on what may be viewed as the excessive analogizing of the many Old Testament scenarios he draws upon in discussing how life is with us in the current setting. Neither does appreciation of Brueggemann's dialectical theology rule out a critical warrant based on his skepticism of the canonical approaches to scriptural interpretation as depicted in the views of Packer, Fackre, Childs, and Lints.

Throughout this book I have taken the position that any substantial revitalization of a theology rooted in the tradition of the Protestant Reformers within mainline and evangelical theological camps will require a substantial embrace of Barth's biblical turn as the primary theological source for interpreting the culture. To this I add the proviso that apologetics will need to take on a supportive and supplemental role beyond what Barth addressed in his *Church Dogmatics*. Cogent reasons to believe require solid articulation in our secular era. Given the compelling force of other metanarrative construals among large sectors of the contemporary faith community among mainline and evangelical theologians and faithful practitioners, convincing reasons to believe are anything but self-evident.[68]

While a rigorously nuanced apologetics is extremely important work, it is not the focus of this book. Nor is it the most pressing issue in terms of faith identity facing the contemporary Protestant community at this time. In this era of mainline decline and serious evangelical diaspora, the more pressing issue is the onslaught of an engulfing secularization on the impact of *Christian* consciousness.[69] Grappling with this challenge calls for

---

67. Brueggemann, "Biblical Authority," 28.
68. Taylor, *Secular Age*, 473–535; Wells, *No Place for Truth*.
69. See Wells for the impact of secularization in evangelical religious culture. Wells claims that "gone is the possibility that there can be in culture men and women of broad understanding who, standing at the center that God has given in his Word, can

attentiveness that is both culturally discerning and profoundly theological. Such work will require the delineation of a sharply defined, sophisticated, and comprehensible *countercultural* identity based on the core precepts of the Christian kerygma in sharp juxtaposition to the secular metanarrative. Without this, the press of the secular trajectory will likely maintain such a persuasive influence that it can only further engulf any flourishing of a richly informed theological identity within contemporary Protestant thought and congregational life based on the overarching metanarrative claims of the Bible.

The capacity to expand the Barthian project as an ongoing theological work is an issue of the most critical sort given the foundational status of the Bible as the classical Protestant magisterium. The persisting reality of the cultural divide between fundamentalism and modernism permeates, to its core, all sectors of US Protestantism. This split compounds the challenge of embracing Scripture as the primary narrative of faith in its complex relationship to church tradition and the broader cultural matrix. An imaginative coming to terms with the implications of this chasm at the level of theology, ecclesiology, ethics, and personal piety represents a crucial baseline for any viable Protestant renewal. As argued throughout this book, any such reform within Protestantism will not come easily. Notwithstanding the many tensions within contemporary Protestant thought and culture, there is some hopeful basis for enhancement of centrist ground. Such ground is exemplified in the critical dialogue between evangelical and postliberal theology and in the reclamation of the neo-orthodox legacy which has the capacity to speak to searchingly attuned sensibilities underlying confessing Christ movements within the mainline denominations and critically oriented evangelical perspectives.

However problematic the Barthian turn may be, I maintain that the alternative of positing some aspect of culture in the more privileged position than the Bible is even more so. To do so would undercut the potential depth of what a theologically sophisticated and ecumenically grounded faith commitment could come to mean for a contemporary Protestant identity that seeks to be faithful to the core kerygma in a manner that *also* has the capacity to be profoundly culturally relevant. I view this latter objective as a critically important secondary concern.

---

understand life's diversity in the light of its unity, can see its multiplicity in light of the overarching themes that are common to all of it. This unity is lost. The diversity of culture, religions, professions, and personal circumstances is triumphant. More than this, this diversity is all we have. And, as the center has collapsed, our psyches have become more and more strained, even fractured." *No Place for Truth*, 8.

I make the comparable argument that dialectics needs to be incorporated within dogmatics and cannot stand as the final arbiter of faith. To make it such would be to situate paradox and doubt as positive theological values in their own right rather than essential experiences along the pathway of faith in "work[ing] out...[our] salvation in fear and trembling" (Phil 2:12). I contend that, in all periods and situations, radical belief (Jas 1:6) in the sovereignty of God, the incarnation of Jesus Christ, and the power of the Holy Spirit to shape lives in a godly direction is the biblical norm, even in the acknowledgment that our knowledge is partial and doubt is an inevitable aspect of the human condition.

Such a faith—in its ecumenical and kegymatic fullness—is a radical rejoinder to the most fundamental precepts of the secular paradigm. It is a faith stance that needs to be embraced with humility and boldness within the contemporary Protestant sector for any plausible effort to overcome of some of the idolatrous forces of the secular era. The case may be overstated in that the relationship between the Bible and the culture in any given context, including the current one, is infinitely more complex than one can hope to describe through the symbolism of words. Yet, the matter of ultimate identification remains inescapable.

The critical issue for contemporary Protestant life and identity formation remains the basic one about whether the culture, in all that that implies, becomes the source for interpreting the Bible or whether Scripture, in all that that implies, becomes the basis for interpreting the culture. This is a matter that has attendant implications for theology, congregational life, ethics, and personal piety. For all of the complexity and nuance in the relationship between contemporary culture and theological discourse, what cannot be avoided is that of prioritizing centers of value. It is this realization—and the identification of radical monotheism as the ultimate center of value underpinning all of creation as an uncompromising ontological assumption—that requires sustaining epistemological assent in the embrace in faith of whatever grace is given. It is this assumption that opens the biblical text as the most singular viable entry point to the strange new world of God's revelation in Jesus Christ, who in faith, is "the exact representation of his [God's] being" (Heb 1:3).

On the substance of this incarnational epiphany, I contend that the very identity of Christianity stands or falls in this era and in every age. It is this faith claim about the nature of reality that grounds the search for a continuously greater understanding of its many manifestations within and through its various embodiments in the time in which we live. We live in a time of unaccustomed diaspora, in all that that implies for Protestant identity reconstruction. In the more fundamental sense, our residence is between the first and final coming of Christ's appearance, in all that that implies for grappling with the ineradicable tension between that which we are called to believe and that which we can know by sight. Faith is the substance that mediates the difference.

Bibliography

Aichele, George, et al. *The Postmodern Bible: The Bible and Culture Collective*. New Haven: Yale University Press, 1995.

Aulen, Gustaf. *Christus Victor: An Historical Study of Three Main Types of the Idea of the Atonement*. Eugene, OR: Wipf & Stock, 2003.

Barth, Karl. "The Barmen Declaration." In Green, *Karl Barth: Theologian of Freedom*, 148–51.

———. *The Call to Discipleship*. Minneapolis: Fortress, 2003.

———. *The Doctrine of Reconciliation*. New York: Continuum, 2004.

———. *Dogmatics in Outline*. New York: Harper Torchbooks, 1959.

———. *The Epistle to the Romans*. 6th ed. Translated by Edwin Hoskyns. London. Oxford University Press, 1968.

Bellah, Robert N. "Civil Religion in America." *Daedalus, Journal of the American Academy of Arts and Sciences* 96 (1967) 1–21. http://hirr.hartsem.edu/Bellah/articles_5.htm.

Bercovitch, Sacvan. *The American Jeremiad*. Madison: University of Wisconsin Press, 1978.

———. *The Puritan Origins of the American Self*. New Haven: Yale, 2011.

———. *The Rites of Assent: Transformations in the Symbolic Constructions of America*. New York: Routledge, 1992.

Berger, Peter L. *The Sacred Canopy: Elements of a Sociological Theory of Religion*. New York: Anchor, 1967.

Berger, Peter L., and Richard John Neuhaus, eds. *Against the World for the World: The Hartford Appeal and the Future of American Religion*. New York: Seabury, 1976.

Bernstein, Richard. *The Pragmatic Turn*. Malden, MA: Polity, 2010.

Bird, Jennifer. Review of *The Power of the Word: Scripture and Rhetoric of Empire*, by Elizabeth Schüssler Fiorenza. *Bible and Critical Theory* 4 (2008) 51.1–51.3.

Bloesch, Donald G. "Donald Bloesch Responds." In Colyer, *Evangelical Theology in Transition*, 183–208.

———. *The Essentials of Theology*. Two volumes in one. Peabody, MA: Hendrickson, 2006.

———. *God the Almighty: Power, Wisdom, Holiness, Love*. Downers Grove: InterVarsity, 1995.

———. *Holy Scripture: Revelation, Inspiration and Interpretation*. Downers Grove: InterVarsity, 1994.

———. *Jesus Christ: Savior and Lord*. Downers Grove: InterVarsity, 1995.

———. *The Last Things: Resurrection, Judgment, Glory.* Downers Grove: InterVarsity, 2004.

———. *A Theology of Word and Spirit.* Downers Grove: InterVarsity, 1992.

Bonhoeffer, Dietrich. *The Cost of Discipleship.* Rev. ed. New York: Macmillan, 1963.

———. *Ethics.* New York: Simon & Schuster, 1995.

———. *Letters and Papers from Prison.* Enlarged ed. Edited by Eberhard Bethge. New York: Touchstone, 1997.

Brueggemann, Walter. "Against the Stream: Brevard Childs's Biblical Theology." In *The Book That Breathes New Life*, 165–70.

———. "Biblical Authority: A Personal Reflection." In *The Book That Breathes New Life*, 20–36.

———. "Biblical Authority and the Church's Task of Interpretation." In *The Book That Breathes New Life*, 37–59.

———. "Biblical Authority in the Postcritical Period." In *The Book That Breathes New Life*, 3–19.

———. "Biblical Theology Appropriately Postmodern." In *The Book That Breathes New Life*, 131–40.

———. *The Book That Breathes New Life: Scriptural Authority and Biblical Theology.* Minneapolis: Fortress, 2005.

———. "Canonization and Contextualization." In *Interpretation and Obedience*, 119–42.

———. "Contemporary Old Testament Theology." In *The Book That Breathes New Life*, 117–30.

———. *David's Truth in Israel's Imagination and Memory.* Minneapolis: Fortress, 1985.

———. "Gospel vs. Scripture? Biblical Theology and the Debate about Rites of Blessing." Interview with Walter Brueggemann by Julie A. Wortman. *Witness*, November 2002. http://www.thewitness.org/archive/nov2002/brueggemann.html.

———. *Hope within History.* Atlanta: John Knox, 1987.

———. *Hopeful Imagination: Prophetic Voices in Exile.* Philadelphia: Fortress, 1986.

———. *Interpretation and Obedience: From Faithful Reading to Faithful Living.* Minneapolis: Fortress, 1991.

———. "Interpretation as an Act of Obedience." In *Interpretation and Obedience*, 9–27.

———. *An Introduction to the Old Testament: The Canon and Christian Imagination.* Louisville: Westminster John Knox, 2003.

———. "The Legitimacy of a Sectarian Hermeneutic." In *Interpretation and Obedience*, 41–68.

———. "The Loss and Recovery of Creation in Old Testament Theology." In *The Book That Breathes New Life*, 83–96.

———. *Old Testament Theology: Essays on Structure, Theme, and Text.* Edited by Patrick Miller. Minneapolis: Fortress, 1992.

———. "Proclamatory Confrontations." In *The Word That Redescribes the World*, edited by Patrick D. Miller, 120–44. Minneapolis: Fortress, 2006.

———. "A Shape for Old Testament Theology I: Structure Legitimation." In *Old Testament Theology*, 1–21.

———. "A Shattered Transcendence? Exile and Restoration." In *Old Testament Theology*, 183–203.

———. *A Social Reading of the Old Testament: Prophetic Approaches to Israel's Communal Life.* Minneapolis: Fortress, 1994.

———. *Texts under Negotiation: The Bible and Postmodern Imagination.* Fortress: Minneapolis, 1993.
———. *Theology of the Old Testament: Testimony, Dispute, Advocacy.* Minneapolis: Fortress, 1997.
———. "The Third World of Evangelical Imagination." In *Interpretation and Obedience*, 9–27.
Buchler, Justus, ed. *Philosophical Writings of Peirce.* New York: Dover, 1955.
Bultmann, Rudolf. "Jesus Christ and Mythology." In *Rudolf Bultmann: Interpreting Faith for the Modern Era*, edited by Roger A. Johnson, 288–328. Minneapolis: Fortress, 1991.
———. "New Testament and Mythology: The Problem of Demythologizing the New Testament Proclamation." In *New Testament and Other Mythology and Other Basic Writings*, edited and translated by M. Ogden Shubert, 1–44. Philadelphia: Fortress, 1984.
Carson, D. A. *Christ and Culture Revisited.* Grand Rapids: Eerdmans, 2008.
———. *The Gagging of God: Christianity Confronts Pluralism.* Grand Rapids: Zondervan, 1996.
Chalke, Steve, et al. *The Atonement Debate: Papers from the London Symposium on the Theology of the Atonement.* Grand Rapids: Zondervan, 2008.
Childs, Brevard. *Biblical Theology of the Old and New Testaments: Theological Reflection on the Christian Bible.* Minneapolis: Fortress, 1992.
Colyer, Elmer M. "Donald Bloesch and His Career." In *Evangelical Theology in Transition*, 11–17.
———, ed. *Evangelical Theology in Transition: Theologians in Dialogue with Donald Bloesch.* Downers Grove: InterVarsity, 1999.
———. "A Theology of Word and Spirit: Donald Bloesch's Theological Method." *Journal for Christian Theological Research* 1 (1996) paragraphs 1–88. http://www.luthersem.edu/ctrf/JCTR/Vol01/Colyer.htm.
Cox, Harvey G. *The Secular City: Secularization and Urbanization in Theological Perspective.* New York: Macmillan, 1965.
Culp, John. "Panentheism." In *Stanford Encyclopedia of Philosophy.* Published December 2008, revised February 2013. http://plato.stanford.edu/entries/panentheism.
Daly, Mary. "After the Death of God the Father: Women's Liberation and the Transformation of Christian Consciousness." http://scriptorium.lib.duke.edu/wlm/after. Originally published in *Commonweal*, March 12, 1971.
———. *Beyond God the Father: Toward a Philosophy of Women's Liberation.* Original reintroduction by the author. Boston: Beacon, 1985.
———. *Gyn/Ecology: The Metaethics of Radical Feminism.* Boston: Beacon, 1978.
Demetrion, George. "Born Again." *TheoTalk.* http://www.ctconfucc.org/resources/theology/Demetrion2.html.
———. "Re-Inventing the Self: Passages into History, Business, and Adult Literacy—An American Historian in Search of a Calling." *Theotalk,* http://www.ctconfucc.org/resources/theology/Demetrion3.html.
———. "A Seekers Journey." *TheoTalk.* http://www.ctconfucc.org/resources/theology/Demetrion1.html.
———. "The Small Still Prompting of the Shadow Voice of Secular Modernity." *TheoTalk.* http://www.ctconfucc.org/resources/theology/smallstillprompting.pdf.

———. "This is My Story." *TheoTalk*. http://www.ctconfucc.org/resources/theology/thisismystory.pdf.

Dewey, John. *Experience and Nature*. Rev. ed. New York: Dover, 1958.

Dilley, Andrea Palpant. "The World the Missionaries Made." *Christianity Today*, January 8, 2014.

The Dogmatic Constitution on Divine Revelation of Vatican II. Promulgated by Pope Paul VI, November 18, 1965. Commentary and translation by George H. Tavard. London: Darton, Longman & Todd, 1966.

Dorrien, Gary. *The Barthian Revolt in Modern Theology*. Louisville: Westminster John Knox, 2000.

———. *The Remaking of Evangelical Theology*. Louisville: Westminster John Knox, 1998.

———. *Soul in Society: The Making and Remaking of Social Christianity*. Minneapolis: Fortress, 1995.

———. *The Word as True Myth: Interpreting Modern Theology*. Louisville: Westminster John Knox, 1997.

Drucker, Peter. *The Practice of Management*. New York: Harper & Row, 1986.

Dulles, Avery. *The Assurance of Things Hoped For: A Theology of Christian Faith*. New York: Oxford University Press, 1994.

———. *Modes of Revelation*. Maryknoll: Orbis 1984.

———. "Symbol, Myth, and the Biblical Revelation." http://www.ts.mu.edu/readers/content/pdf/27/27.1/27.1.1.pdf. Originally published in *New Theology*, vol. 4, edited by Martin E. Marty and Dean Peerman, 39–68. New York: Macmillan, 1967.

Erickson, Millard J. *Christian Theology*. 3 vols. Grand Rapids: Baker, 1983–1985.

———. "Donald Bloesch's Doctrine of Scripture." In Colyer, *Evangelical Theology in Transition*, 77–97.

Fackre, Gabriel. "An Alter Call for Evangelicals." In *Restoring the Center*, 112–18.

———. *The Christian Story: A Pastoral Systematics*. Vol. 1, *A Narrative Interpretation of Basic Christian Doctrine*. 3rd ed. Grand Rapids: Eerdmans, 1996.

———. *The Christian Story: A Pastoral Systematics*. Vol. 2, *Authority: Scripture in the Church for the World*. Grand Rapids: Eerdmans, 1987.

———. *The Christian Story: A Pastoral Systematics*. Vol. 4, *Christology in Context*. Grand Rapids: Eerdmans, 2006.

———. *The Christian Story: A Pastoral Systematics*. Vol. 5, *The Church: Signs of the Spirit and Signs of the Times*. Grand Rapids: Eerdmans, 2005.

———. *The Doctrine of Revelation: A Narrative Interpretation*. Grand Rapids: Eerdmans, 1997.

———. *Ecumenical Faith in Evangelical Perspective*. Grand Rapids: Eerdmans, 1993.

———. "The New Ecumenism: Mutual Affirmation & Admonition." In *Restoring the Center*, 123–32.

———. "Jesus Christ in Bloesch's Theology." In Colyer, *Evangelical Theology in Transition*, 98–118.

———. *Restoring the Center: Essays Evangelical and Ecumenical*. Downers Grove: InterVarsity, 1998.

———. "Seminary Cultures—Evangelical and Mainline." In *Restoring the Center*, 161–69.

———. "Wither Evangelicalism?" In *Restoring the Center*, 119–22.

Fackre, Gabriel, and Michael Root. *Affirmations and Admonitions*. Grand Rapids: Eerdmans, 1998.
Farrer, Austin. *The Glass of Vision*. London: Dacre, 1966.
Fosdick, Harry E. "Shall the Fundamentalists Win? Defending Liberal Protestantism in the 1920s." *Christian Work* 102 (1922) 716–22. http://historymatters.gmu.edu/d/5070.
Foucault, Michel. *The Archeology of Knowledge and the Discourse on Language*. New York: Pantheon, 1972.
Frame, John. Review of *On Theology*, by Schubert M. Ogden. http://www.framepoythress.org/review-of-ogdens-on-theology. Originally published in *Westminster Theological Journal* 50 (1988) 157–65.
Frei, Hans W. *Eclipse of Bible Narrative: Studies in Eighteenth and Nineteenth Century Hermeneutics*. New Haven: Yale University Press, 1980.
Geertz, Clifford. *The Interpretation of Cultures*. New York: Basic, 1977.
George, Timothy. *J. I. Packer and the Evangelical Future: The Impact of His Life and Thought*. Grand Rapids: Baker, 2009.
Giddens, Anthony. *Modernity and Self-Identity: Self and Society in the Late Modern Age*. Stanford: Stanford University Press, 1991.
Gleghorn, Michael. "Karl Barth's Early Hermeneutics." Michael Gleghorn's website. http://michaelgleghorn.com/documents/BarthsEarlyHermeneutics.pdf.
Gottwald, Norman. *The Tribes of Yahweh*. Maryknoll: Orbis, 1979.
Green, Clifford, ed. *Karl Barth: Theologian of Freedom*. London: Collins, 1989.
Grenz, Stanley J. "'Fideistic Revelationism': Donald Bloesch's Antirationalist Theological Method." In Colyer, *Evangelical Theology in Transition*, 36–60.
———. *Renewing the Center: Evangelical Theology in a Post-Theological Era*. Grand Rapids: Baker, 2000.
Grenz Stanley J., and Roger E. Olson. *20th Century Theology: God and the World in a Transitional Age*. Downers Grove: InterVarsity, 1992.
Grudem, Wayne. *Bible Doctrine: Essential Teachings of the Christian Faith*. Edited by Jeff Purswell. Grand Rapids: Zondervan, 1999.
Guenther, Bruce L. "The 'Enduring Problem' of Christ and Culture." *Direction: A Mennonite Brethren Forum* 34 (2005) 215–17. http://www.directionjournal.org/article/?1401.
Guiness, Os. *The Dust of Death*. Downers Grove: InterVarsity, 1973.
Habermas, Jürgen. *Moral Consciousness and Communicative Action*. Cambridge: MIT Press, 1996.
Hall, Douglas John. *Confessing the Faith: Christian Theology in a North American Context*. Minneapolis: Fortress, 1998.
———. *Professing the Faith: Christian Theology in a North American Context*. Minneapolis: Fortress, 1996.
———. *Remembered Voices: Reclaiming the Legacy of "Neo-Orthodoxy."* Louisville: Westminster John Knox, 1998.
———. *The Steward: A Biblical Symbol Comes of Age*. Grand Rapids: Eerdmans, 1990.
———. *Thinking the Faith: Christian Theology in a North American Context*. Minneapolis: Fortress, 1991.
Hart, David B. *The Beauty of the Infinite: The Aesthetics of Christian Truth*. Grand Rapids: Eerdmans, 2003.
Hartz, Louis. *The Liberal Tradition in America*. New York: Harcourt, Brace, 1955.

Heidegger, Martin. *Being and Time*. Translated by John Macquarrie and Edward Robinson. New York: Harper & Row, 1962.

Henry, Carl. *God, Revelation and Authority: God Who Speaks and Shows*. Vol. 4. Waco, TX: Word, 1979.

———. "An Evangelical-Ecumenical Dialogue." In *Story Line: Chapters on Thought, Word, and Deed for Gabriel Fackre*, edited by Skye Fackre Gibson, 9–44. Grand Rapids: Eerdmans, 2002.

Herberg, Will. *Protestant-Catholic-Jew: An Essay in Religious in Religious Sociology*. Chicago: University of Chicago Press, 1983.

Hinkle, Mary E. "American Protestant Preaching: A Twentieth-Century Perspective." *Word & World* 20 (2000) 96–109. http://wordandworld.luthersem.edu/content/pdfs/20-1_20th_Century/20-1_Hinkle.pdf.

Hofstadter, Richard R. *The Age of Reform: From Bryant to F.D.R.* New York: Alfred A. Knopf, 1963.

———. *The American Political Tradition and the Men Who Made It*. New York: Vintage, 1948.

Holly, Marilyn. Review of *Religion and Rationality: Essays on Reason, God, and Modernity*, by Jürgen Habermas. *Essays in Philosophy* 5 (2004). http://commons.pacificu.edu/cgi/viewcontent.cgi?article=1115&context=eip.

Hunsinger, George. *How to Read Karl Barth: The Shape of His Theology*. New York: Oxford University Press, 1991.

———. "What Can Evangelicals and Postliberals Learn from Each Other: The Carl Henry-Hans Frei Exchange Reconsidered." In Phillips and Okholm, *The Nature of Confession*, 134–50.

Hunt, Mary E., and Diann L. Neu. *New Feminist Christianity: Many Voices, Many Views*. Woodstock, VT: Skylight Paths, 2010.

Hutchison, William. *The Modernist Impulse in American Protestantism*. Durham, NC: Duke University Press 1992.

Johnson, Robert A., ed. *Rudolf Bultmann: Interpreting Faith for the Modern Age*. Minneapolis: Fortress, 1991.

Kegan, Robert. *In Over Our Heads: The Mental Demands of Modern Life*. Cambridge: Harvard University Press, 1994.

Kelly, Geoffrey B., ed. *Karl Rahner: Theologian of the Graced Search for Meaning*. Minneapolis: Fortress, 1992.

La Montagne, D. Paul. *Barth and Rationality: Critical Realism in Theology*. Eugene, OR: Wipf & Stock, 2012.

Lawrence, Joel. *Bonhoeffer: A Guide for the Perplexed*. London: T. & T. Clark, 2010.

Lawson, J. Mark. *Cracking the Book: How to Start Reading the Bible*. Enumclaw, WA: WinePress, 2011.

Lewis, C. S. *Mere Christianity*. London: HarperCollins, 1996.

Linafelt, Tod, and Timothy K. Beal, eds. *God in the Fray: A Tribute to Walter Brueggemann*. Minneapolis: Fortress, 1998.

Lindbeck, George A. *The Nature of Doctrine: Religion and Theology in a Postliberal Age*. Louisville: Westminster John Knox, 1984.

Lints, Richard. *The Fabric of Theology: A Prolegomenon to Evangelical Theology*. Grand Rapids: Eerdmans, 1993.

Lovin, Robin A. *Reinhold Niebuhr and Christian Realism*. New York: Cambridge University Press, 1995.

Lyotard, Frances. *The Post-Modern Condition: A Report on Knowledge.* Minneapolis: University of Minnesota Press, 1984.
Machem, Gresham. *Christianity and Liberalism.* Grand Rapids: Eerdmans, 2009.
Marsden, George. "Christianity and Cultures: Transforming Niebuhr's Categories." *Insights: The Faculty Journal of Austin Seminary* 115 (1999) 4–15. Republished on Religion-Online. http://www.religion-online.org/showarticle.asp?title=517.
———. *Fundamentalism and American Culture.* 2nd ed. New York: Oxford, 2006.
———. *Reforming Fundamentalism: Fuller Seminary and the New Evangelicalism.* Grand Rapids: Eerdmans, 1987.
———. *The Soul of the American University: From Protestant Establishment to Established Nonbelief.* New York: Oxford University Press, 1996.
———. *Understanding Fundamentalism and Evangelicalism.* Grand Rapids: Eerdmans, 1991.
McConnel, Tim. "The Old Princeton Apologetics: Common Sense or Reformed?" *JETS* 46 (2003) 647–72. http://www.etsjets.org/files/JETS-PDFs/46/46-4/46-4-pp647-672_JETS.pdf.
McDowell, Josh. *Evidence That Demands a Verdict: Historical Evidences for the Christian Faith.* Vol. 1. Nashville: Nelson, 1992.
McFague, Sallie. *Metaphorical Theology: Models of God in Religious Language.* Minneapolis: Fortress, 1993.
McGrath, Alister. "An Evangelical Evaluation of Postliberalism." In Phillips and Okholm, *The Nature of Confession,* 23–34.
———. *J. I. Packer: A Biography.* Grand Rapids: Baker, 1997.
McLaren, Brian. *A Generous Orthodoxy: Why I Am a Missional, Evangelical, Post/Protestant, Liberal/Conservative. . . .* Grand Rapids: Zondervan, 2004.
Metaxas, Eric. *Bonhoeffer: Pastor, Martyr, Prophet, Spy.* Nashville: Nelson, 2010.
Metzger, Paul L. *The Word of Christ and the World of Culture: Sacred and Secular through the Theology of Karl Barth.* Eugene, OR: Wipf & Stock, 2005.
Miller, Perry. *Errand into the Wilderness.* Cambridge: Harvard University Press, 1956.
———. *The Life of the Mind in America: From the Revolution to the Civil War.* New York: Harcourt, Brace & World, 1965.
———. *The New England Mind: The Seventeenth Century.* Cambridge: Harvard University Press, 1983.
Moltmann, Jürgen. *The Crucified God: The Cross of Christ as the Foundation and Criticism of Christian Theology.* Minneapolis: Fortress, 1993.
———. *Experiences in Theology: Ways and Forms of Christian Theology.* Fortress: Minneapolis, 2000.
———. *God in Creation: A New Theology of Creation and the Spirit of God.* Fortress: Minneapolis, 1993.
———. *Theology of Hope.* New York: Harper & Row, 1967.
———. *The Trinity and the Kingdom of God: The Doctrine of God.* Minneapolis: Fortress, 1993.
Morrison, John D. "Scripture as Word of God: Evangelical Assumption or Evangelical Question?" *Trinity Journal* 20 (1999) 165–90. http://www.biblicalstudies.org.uk/article_scripture_morrison.html.
Murphy, Nancey C. *Beyond Liberalism and Fundamentalism: How Modern and Postmodern Philosophy Set the Theological Agenda.* Harrisburg, PA: Trinity, 2007.
Newbigin, Lesslie. *The Gospel in a Pluralistic Society.* Grand Rapids: Eerdmans, 1989.

Niebuhr, H. Richard. "Centers of Value." In *Radical Monotheism and Western Culture*, 100–13.

———. *Christ and Culture*. New York: Harper & Row, 1951.

———. *Radical Monotheism and Western Culture: With Supplementary Essays*. Louisville: Westminster John Knox, 1960.

———. "Theology in the University." In *Radical Monotheism and Western Culture*, 93–99.

Niebuhr, Reinhold. *Beyond Tragedy: Essays on the Christian Interpretation of History*. New York: Scribner, 1937.

———. *An Interpretation of Christian Ethic*. San Francisco: HarperSanFrancisco, 1963.

———. *The Irony of American History*. New York: Scribner, 1952.

———. *Moral Man and Immoral Society*. New York: Scribner, 1937.

———. *The Nature and Destiny of Man*. 2 vols. New York: Scribner, 1941–1943.

Noll, Mark. *The Civil War as a Theological Crisis*. Raleigh: University of North Carolina Press, 2006.

O'Connor, Alice. *Poverty Knowledge: Social Science, Social Policy, and the Poor in Twentieth-Century U.S. History*. Princeton: Princeton University Press, 2001.

Ogden, Schubert M. *On Theology*. Valley Forge, PA: Trinity, 1996.

Olson, Roger. "Locating Donald G. Bloesch in the Evangelical Landscape." In Colyer, *Evangelical Theology in Transition*, 18–34.

Otto, Rudolf. *The Idea of the Holy*. 2nd ed. New York: Oxford University Press, 1958.

Packer, J. I. "The Adequacy of Human Language." In *Engaging the Written Word of God*, 19–42.

———. *Concise Theology: A Guide to Historic Christian Beliefs*. Wheaton, IL: Tyndale Publishers.

———. "Contemporary Views of Revelation." In *Engaging the Word of God*, 57–71.

———. "Encountering Present-Day Views of Scripture." In *Engaging the Written Word of God*, 3–18.

———. *Engaging the Written Word of God*. Peabody, MA: Hendrickson, 1999.

———. *Fundamentalism and the Word of God*. Grand Rapids: Eerdmans: 1958.

———. "Inerrancy and the Divinity and Humanity of the Bible." In *Engaging the Written Word of God*, 151–59.

———. "Infallible Scripture and the Role of Hermeneutics." In *Scripture and Truth*, edited by D. A. Carson and John D. Woodbridge, 325–56. Grand Rapids: Baker, 1992.

———. "An Introduction to Systematic Spirituality." In *The J. I. Packer Collection*, 197–209.

———. "Is Christianity Credible?" In *The Packer Collection*, 174–81.

———. *The J. I. Packer Collection*. Selected and introduced by Alister McGrath. Downers Grove: InterVarsity, 1999.

———. "Jesus Christ the Lord." In *The J. I. Packer Collection*, 150–72.

———. *Knowing God*. Downers Grove: InterVarsity, 1993.

———. "On from Orr: The Cultural Crisis, Rational Realism and Incarnational Ontology." In *The J. I. Packer Collection*, 246–68.

———. *A Passion for Holiness*. Cambridge, UK: Crossway, 1992.

———. *A Quest for Godliness: The Puritan Vision of the Christian Life*. Wheaton, IL: Crossway, 1990.

———. *Taking God Seriously: Vital Things We Need to Know*. Wheaton, IL: Crossway, 2013.

———. *Truth and Power: The Place of Scripture in the Christian Life*. Wheaton, IL: InterVarsity, 1996.

———. "What Did the Cross Achieve: The Logic of Penal Substitution." In *The J. I. Packer Collection*, 98–136.

Payne, Donald J. "J. I. Packer's Theological Method." In *J. I. Packer and the Evangelical Future*, edited by Timothy George, 55–68. Grand Rapids: Baker, 2009.

———. *The Theology of the Christian Life in J. I. Packer's Thought*. Milton Keynes, UK: Paternoster, 2006.

Peirce, Charles. "The Fixation of Belief." In Buchler, *Philosophical Writings of Peirce*, 1–22.

———. "How to Make Our Ideas Clear." In Buchler, *Philosophical Writings of Peirce*, 23–41.

———. "The Scientific Attitude and Fallibilism." In Buchler, *Philosophical Writings of Peirce*, 42–59.

Pelikan, Jaroslav. *The Emergence of the Catholic Tradition (100–600)*. Vol. 1 of *The Christian Tradition: A History of the Development of Doctrine*. Chicago: University of Chicago Press, 1973.

Perdue, Leo G. "Adhering to Israel's God." Review of *Theology of the Old Testament*, by Walter Brueggemann. *Christian Century*, May 20–27, 1998, 524–531. http://www.religion-online.org/showarticle.asp?title=27.

———. *Reconstructing Old Testament Theology: After the Collapse of History*. Minneapolis: Fortress, 1994.

Phillips, Timothy R., and Dennis L. Okholm, eds. *The Nature of Confession: Evangelicals and Postliberals in Conversation*. Downers Grove: InterVarsity, 1993.

Pinnock, Clark. "The Holy Spirit in the Theology of Donald G. Bloesch." In Colyer, *Evangelical Theology in Transition*, 119–35.

Placher, William C. *Unapologetic Theology: A Christian View in a Pluralistic Conversation*. Louisville: Westminster John Knox, 1989.

Popper, Karl. *Conjectures and Refutations*. New York: Routledge, 1963.

———. *Objective Knowledge: An Evolutionary Approach*. Rev. ed. Oxford: Oxford University Press, 1979.

———. "Truth, Rationality and the Growth of Scientific Knowledge." In *Conjectures and Refutations*, 291–338.

Ramm, Bernard. *After Fundamentalism: The Future of Evangelical Theology*. San Francisco: Harper & Row, 1983.

Rasmussen, Larry, ed. *Reinhold Niebuhr: Theologian of Public Life*. Minneapolis: Fortress, 1991.

Rice, Daniel F. *Reinhold Niebuhr and John Dewey: An American Odyssey*. Albany: State University of New York, 1993.

Robinson, Anthony B. *Transforming Congregational Culture*. Grand Rapids: Eerdmans, 2003.

Robinson, John A. T. *Honest to God*. London: SCM, 1963.

Rorty, Richard. *Consequences of Pragmatism*. Minneapolis: University of Minnesota Press, 1982.

Ruether, Rosemary Radford. *Sexism and God Talk: Toward a Feminist Theology*. Boston: Beacon, 1983.

Schaeffer, Francis A. *The God Who Is There*. In *The Francis A. Schaeffer Trilogy: The Three Essential Books in One Volume*, 5–202 Wheaton, IL: Crossway, 1990.
Scheffczyk, Leo. "God: The Divine." In *Encyclopedia of Theology: The Concise Sacramentum Mundi*, edited by Karl Rahner. New York: Seabury, 1975.
Schnelle, Udo. *Apostle Paul: His Life and Theology*. Grand Rapids: Baker Academic, 2003.
Schüssler Fiorenza, Elizabeth. "Christian Feminist Biblical Studies." In Hunt and Neu, *New Feminist Christianity*, 86–96.
———. *The Power of the Word: Scripture and the Rhetoric of Power*. Fortress: Minneapolis, 2007.
Sharp, Carolyn J. "The Trope of 'Exile' and the Displacement of Old Testament Theology." *Perspectives in Religious Studies* 31 (2004) 153–69. http://www.yale.edu/divinity/faculty/personal/Sharp/Trope%20of%20'Exile.'pdf.
Shriver, Donald W., Jr. *H. Richard Niebuhr*. Nashville: Abingdon, 2009.
Spong, John Shelby. *A New Christianity for a New World: Why Traditional Faith Is Dying and How a New Faith Is Being Born*. San Francisco: Harper, 2001.
Steiner, George. *Real Presences: Is There Anything in What We Say?* London: Farber & Farber, 1989.
Stott, John. *Basic Christianity*. Grand Rapids: Baker, 1971.
Strong, James. *The New Strong's Exhaustive Concordance of the Bible*. Nashville: Nelson, 2003.
Taylor, Charles. *A Secular Age*. Cambridge: Belknap Press of Harvard University Press, 2007.
Taylor, Mark. *Erring: A Postmodern A/Theology*. Chicago: University of Chicago Press, 1987.
TheoTalk. Writings by members of the Connecticut Conference (United Church of Christ) churches on matters of faith. http://www.ctconfucc.org/resources/theology.
Tillich, Paul. *Dynamics of Faith*. New York: Harper Colophon, 1957.
———. *The Eternal Now*. New York: Scribner, 1963.
———. *The Shaking of the Foundations*. Eugene, OR: Wipf & Stock, 2012.
———. *Systematic Theology*. Vol. 1, *Reason and Revelation: Being and God*. Chicago: University of Chicago Press, 1951.
———. *Systematic Theology*. Vol. 2, *Existence and the Christ*. Chicago: University of Chicago Press, 1957.
———. "What Is Wrong With the 'Dialectic' Theology?" In *Paul Tillich: Theologian of the Boundaries*, edited by Mark Taylor, 104–16. Minneapolis: Fortress, 1991.
Torrance, Thomas F. "Bloesch's Doctrine of God." In Colyer, *Evangelical Theology in Transition*, 136–48.
———. *The Doctrine of Grace in the Apostolic Fathers*. Philadelphia: Westminster, 1974.
Turner, James C. *Without God, Without Creed: The Origins of Unbelief in America*. Baltimore: John Hopkins University Press, 1985.
"Twenty Seven Years of Craigville Colloquies." *CraigvilleColloquy.com*. http://craigvillecolloquy.com/_Archive/General/historytitles.html.
Urban, William. *Language and Reality*. New York: Macmillan, 1939.
Vlach, Michael. "Defining Supersessionism." *Theological Studies*. http://www.theologicalstudies.org/resource-library/supersessionism/324-defining-supersessionism.

Volf, Miroslav. "Theology, Meaning, and Power: A Conversation with George Lindbeck on Theology and the Nature of Christian Difference." In Phillips and Okholm, *The Nature of Confession*, 45–66.

Wells, David F. *God in the Wasteland: The Reality of Truth in a World of Fading Dreams.* Grand Rapids: Eerdmans, 1994.

———. *No Place for Truth: or, Whatever Happened to Evangelical Theology.* Grand Rapids: Eerdmans, 1993.

Williams, Michael. "Systematic Theology as a Biblical Discipline." In *All for Jesus: A Celebration of the 50th Anniversary of Covenant Theology*, edited by Robert A. Patterson and Sean M. Lucas, 197–233. Tain, Scotland: Mentor, 2005. http://www.biblicaltheology.ca/blue_files/Systematic%20Theology.pdf.

Author Index

Augustine, 81, 85, 263
Aulen, Gustaf, 76

Barth, Karl, 3, 12, 13, 16, 30, 52, 83, 85, 93, 95, 135, 142, 144, 145, 146–53, 169, 213, 219, 222, 225, 226–40, 241, 243, 250, 254, 267, 286
Baxter, Richard, 73
Beal, Timothy K., 4
Bellah, Robert, 30
Bercovitch, Sacvan, 35
Berger, Peter, 21
Bloesch, Donald, 3, 4, 8–10, 15, 53, 56, 58, 81–114, 116–17, 122, 163, 169, 225, 278, 288
Bonhoeffer, Dietrich, 13, 14, 31, 56, 224, 240–247, 250, 267
Bunyan, John, 73
Brueggemann, Walter, 4, 5, 6, 7, 8, 53, 113, 163, 167–218, 225, 287, 288
Bruner, Emil, 83, 84, 85
Bushnell, Horace, 243
Bultmann, Rudolph, 12, 13, 31, 145, 223, 226–30

Calvin, John, 16, 85, 135
Carson, Don, 20, 258
Childs, Brevard, 170–71, 181, 191–93, 216, 288
Clapp, Rodney, 86
Clement of Alexandria, 261
Colyer, Elmer, M., 88, 92. 99
Cone, James, 34
Cox, Harvey, 31, 214, 260

Daly, Mary, 20, 39, 41
David, 205
de Dietrich, Suzanne, 224
Derrida, Jacques, 196
Dewey, John, 209, 232, 249, 253, 254
Dorrien, Gary, 14, 38, 39, 41, 53, 56, 85–86, 91, 112, 113, 224, 225
Dostoevsky, Fyodor, 229
Dulles, Avery, 24, 96, 99

Edwards, John, 73
Erickson, Millard, J., 89, 90, 99, 102, 278
Einstein, Albert, 173

Fackre, Gabriel, 2, 4, 8, 10–12, 53, 56, 58, 115–66, 168–71, 225, 226, 281, 288
Farrer, Austin, 156
Forsyth, Peter, 85
Fosdick, Harry., 28, 45
Frame, John, 20
Frei, Hans, 253
Freud, Sigmund, 196

Geertz, Clifford, 181
Gilkey, Langdon, 31
Gleghom, Michael, 3
Goldwater, Barry, 36
Gottwald, Norman, 181, 205
Graham, Billy, 30
Grenz, Stanley, 38, 53, 86, 89, 90, 91, 99
Grudem, Wayne, 20, 278
Guiness, Os, 89, 274

Author Index

Habermas, Jürgen, 126–27
Hall, Douglas, J., 12, 15, 16, 53, 56, 58, 224, 225, 269, 270–275, 276, 281–82, 283, 284, 285, 286
Hart, David, 19
Hartz, Louis, 30
Hegel, Georg, 229
Heidegger, Martin, 159, 232
Henry, Carl, 102, 122, 142, 153–58
Herberg, Will, 30
Hodge, Charles, 83, 125
Hofstader, Richard, 30
Hume, David, 124
Hunsinger, George, 4, 231
Hutchison, William, 28

Kant, Immanuel, 229
Kierkegaard, Soren, 229
King, Martin Luther, Jr., 33–35, 136

La Montangne, 50
Lawson, Mark, J., 43, 46
Lewis, C.S., 56
Linafelt, Todd, 4
Lindbeck, George, A., 23, 253
Lints, Richard, 15, 16, 225, 269, 275–80, 283–85, 288
Luther, Martin, 16, 85, 261–62, 85, 135, 263

Machem, Gresham, 28, 83
Marsden, George, 27, 28, 129, 154, 225, 264–65, 266
Marx, Karl, 196
Maurice, F. D., 263
McConnel, Tim, 125
McDowell, Josh, 79
McFague, Sallie, 39–40, 224
McGrath, Alister, 4, 57
McLaren, Brian, 23
Metzger, Paul, 227
Miller, Perry, 35
Moltmann, Jürgen, 16, 136
Morrison, John, D., 87–88
Moses, 200
Murphy, Nancey, 53

Newbigin, Lesslie, 5, 43, 45, 46–50, 52

Niebuhr, H. R., 14, 21, 44, 45 111, 129, 136, 187, 214, 224, 254–65, 267
Niebuhr, Reinhold, 14, 30, 45, 56, 111, 187, 224, 247–54, 262, 267
Noll, Mark, 225, 274

Oden, Thomas, 84
Ogden, Shubert, 4, 20, 53
Okholm, Dennis, L., 53
Olson, Roger, 38, 86, 90, 91
Otto, Rudolph, 139
Owen, John, 73

Packer, J. I., 4, 6, 7, 53, 54–80, 82–83, 102, 163,169, 286, 287
Payne, Don, 4
Pannenberg, Wolfhart, 137, 147
Peirce, Charles, S. 49
Perdue, Leo, 5, 178
Pelikan, Jeroslav, 106, 108
Phillips, Timothy, R., 4, 53
Pinnock, Clark, 91, 99
Plato, 229
Popper, Karl, 24, 49

Rahner, Karl, 142, 159–61
Ramm, Bernard, 225
Rasmussen, Larry, 247
Rauschenbusch, Walter, 45
Reid, Thomas, 124
Ritschl. Albert, 259
Ruether, Rosemary, 48

Sanders, E. P., 167
Saul, 205
Schüssler Fiorenza, Elizabeth, 41–42
Solomon, 205
Spong, John S., 6, 20, 51
Spurgeon, Charles, 73
Stott, John, 56, 225, 274

Taylor, Charles, 19
Taylor, Mark, 276
Taylor, Nathaniel, 125
Tertullian, 259
Thiemann, Ronald, 147
Tillich, Paul, 13, 16, 31, 112, 142, 144–46, 159, 161, 223, 233–37, 286

Tolstoy, Leo, 259
Torrance, Thomas, F., 101, 105, 109

Volf, Miroslav, 4, 222
Von Rad, Gerhard, 95

Wallis, Jim, 31
Warfield, Benjamin, B., 83
Wells, David, 20, 225, 274

Yoder, John H., 265

Subject Index

Abolitionism/abolition movement, 114, 243–44
Abrahamic, 279
Acts of the Apostles, 158
Actualism/actualist, 82, 89, 148, 150, 151, 152
Against the Marauding Hordes of Peasants, 262
American Jeremiad, The, 35
Andover Newton Theological School, 114, 128
Afro-centrist theology, 29–33
Age of Reform, 30
American Baptist Churches, 2, 208
American exceptionalism, 35, 214, 266, 270, 271
American Political Tradition, 30
Analogy of scripture, 68, 69, 122
Apologetics, 128, 171–76, 230, 288
Arian/Arianism, 107
Assemblies of God, 2
Atonement, 3, 8, 75, 76, 95, 148, 260, 266, 278, 280
    Penal substitution model, 68, 75–77

Baconian ideal, 28, 155
Barmen Declaration, The, 135, 136, 150, 235
Barth/Bultmann debate, 12–13, 226–33
Basic Christianity, 56
Battles for the Bible, 55, 222
Bethel Seminary, 128
Being and Time, 232
Beyond God the Father, 39

Beyond Liberalism and Fundamentalism, 53
Bible Doctrine, 278
Biblical Theology Movement, 29, 82
Biblical Theology of the Old and New Testament, 193
Biblical Witness Fellowship, 8
Bipolar, 169, 176–85, 203, 210
Black power, 33

Calvinism/Calvinist Theology, 27, 112, 125, 243, 286
Canon/canonical, 3, 4, 8, 9, 11, 24, 26, 42, 43, 50, 52, 56, 64–65, 67, 68, 78, 95, 96, 117, 121, 133, 134, 137, 141, 165, 167, 168, 169, 170, 181, 188, 192, 204, 216, 217, 218, 239, 257, 265, 278, 279–80, 283, 286, 288
Canonical sense, 130–32
Categorical revelation, 160–61
Catholic, 8, 10, 64, 110, 162, 199
Centers of value, 21, 24, 254, 256, 267
Christ and Culture, 14, 44, 214, 225, 257–65
Christian Foundation series, 8, 79–80, 112
Christian Story series, 118, 165
Christian Story, The, Vol. 2, Authority, 120–38
Christian Story, The, Vol. 5, The Church, 159
Christian Theology, 278
Christianity and Liberalism, 28

Christology/Christological, 8, 12, 22, 37, 73, 77, 110, 135, 145, 148, 215, 224, 249
Christus Victor, 76
Church Dogmatics, 150, 219, 227, 229 232, 288
Civil religion, 30, 270
Civil Rights Act of 1965, 33
Civil Rights era/movement, 34
Civil War, 244
Common sense, 124–27
Common Sense Scottish Realism, 90, 124–25, 155
Concise Theology, 70, 71
Confessing Christ Movement/Listserv, 2, 12, 165
Confessing the Faith, 225, 285
Consensus history, 30, 33
Constantinian/post-Constantinian, 15, 226, 270
Cost of Discipleship, 241
Craigville Colloquies, 165
Critical sense, 127–30
Critic-in-residence, 123
Cross/crucifixion, 15, 18, 31, 71, 72, 74–76, 81, 98, 103, 104, 110, 177, 185, 188, 220, 251, 252
Crucified God, The, 136

Dallas Theological Seminary, 128
Darwinism, 27, 28, 173
Davidic Kingdom, 184, 279
Death of God Theology, 31, 32, 136, 176
Decalogue, 194
Declaration of Independence, 33
Dialectical/dialectic/dialectical theology, 15, 17, 112, 187, 207, 210, 228, 233, 236, 267, 269, 275, 282, 288, 290
The Doctrine of Revelation, 11, 121, 145, 147, 159, 162
The Dust of Death, 90

Eastern Orthodox, 8, 10, 64, 110, 199
Ecclesiastics, 200
Ecumenical Faith in Evangelistic Perspective, 3, 53, 77, 78

Embrace of pain, 172, 176, 179–83, 187
Engaging the Written Word of God, 78, 83
Enlightenment, 57, 58, 87, 128, 187
Epistemological/epistemology, 17, 25, 48, 52, 57, 84, 90, 124, 128, 138, 147, 151, 187, 191, 193, 216, 217, 256
Epistle to the Romans (Barth), 227, 232
Errand into the Wilderness, 35
Erring, 276
Essentials of Evangelical Theology, 112, 278
Eternal Now, The, 234
Ethics, 241, 242, 244, 247
Evangelical/evangelical theology/tradition, 10, 15, 16, 20, 23, 27, 55, 59, 69, 77, 79, 113, 211, 212, 217, 225, 246, 274, 275, 277, 286, 289
Evangelical Theology in Transition, 88, 113
Exile/Babylonian Captivity, 176, 177, 178, 182–85, 188, 189, 196, 198, 202, 203, 280, 200
Exodus, 38, 96, 133, 177, 178, 179, 182, 188, 195, 280
Experience and Nature, 232
Ezekiel, 172, 189

Fabric of Theology, The, 279
Feminist theology, 38–43, 117
Fideistic revelationism, 82, 85
Fuller Theological Seminary, 30, 128
Fundamentalism/fundamentalist, 19, 21, 25, 27, 28, 59, 60, 101, 222, 226, 250, 259, 269, 282, 289
Fundamentalism and American Culture, 28
"Fundamentalism" and the Word of God, 55, 59

Genesis, 96, 143
Gnostic/Gnosticism, 41, 107
God the Almighty, 99, 10
God Here and Now, 227, 235
"God hypothesis," 78, 82, 130, 140

Gordon-Cornwell Theological Seminary, 128
Gospel in a Pluralistic Age, The, 5, 26, 43–53
Grand Narrative, 11, 117, 130, 131, 152, 153, 156, 158, 159, 162, 163, 177
Great Depression, 173, 253
Great Tradition, 3, 113

Henotheistic, 255, 256
Hermeneutics/hermeneutical, 11, 78, 82, 83, 98, 130, 157, 174, 188, 204, 207, 213, 226, 271
  hermeneutics of suspicion, 41, 116, 117, 165, 169, 181, 278
  combinationist hermeneutics, 10
  contextual hermeneutics, 11, 123
  evangelical hermeneutics, 16
  external hermeneutics, 11, 132–33
  feminist hermeneutics, 199
  internal hermeneutics, 11, 124–32
Higher biblical criticism, 28, 127
Historical Jesus, 27, 228
Historicism/historicist, 11, 25, 126, 174, 230, 250, 283
Holy Scripture (Bloesch), 95, 99
Hope within History, 172
Hopeful Imagination, 172
Hosea, 199
How to Read Karl Barth, 150, 153

Identity politics, 32, 33, 173
"I Have a Dream Speech," 33, 35
Incarnation/incarnational, 3, 8, 10, 22, 25, 68, 73, 75, 95, 105, 106, 109, 135, 137, 152, 162, 290
Inerrant/inerrancy, 9, 56, 60–61, 77, 83, 85, 125, 154, 155, 217
Infallibility/infallible, 56, 60–61, 65
Inscripurated/inscripturation, 87, 155
Isaiah, 132, 172, 183, 184, 189, 202
Israel's core testimony, 190–96, 201
Israel's counterestimony, 196–203

Jeremiah, 96, 132, 172, 183, 189–90, 199, 200
Job, 182, 199, 200

Justification by Faith, 117, 135, 286

Kairos, 172, 176, 214, 220, 221, 234, 235, 241, 272
Kerygma/kerygmatic, 76, 192, 221, 228, 257, 289, 290
Knowing God, 55, 70, 71

Letters and Papers from Prison, 241
Liberal Tradition in America, The, 30
Liberalism, liberal theology, 27, 28, 51, 65, 74, 80, 82, 100, 113, 116, 246, 247, 266
Liberation Theology, 117, 136, 149, 168, 173, 253, 272
Life of the Mind in America, The, 35

Mere Christianity, 56
Modernist/fundamental split/great divide, 5, 19–20, 23, 27–30, 43, 53, 222, 226, 269, 286, 289
Monotheism, 254–57, 261, 267, 290
Mosaic tradition, 172, 200, 279,
Munus triplex, 135
Myth/mythopoeic, 96-98

Narrative theology, 6, 80, 130, 138–62, 168–71, 204, 267, 269, 280
The Nature of Confession, 4, 53
Nazi/Nazism, 14, 135, 235, 244, 247
New Feminist Christianity, 42
Neo-orthodoxy, 4, 8, 12, 17, 29, 30, 53, 56, 80, 82, 84, 152, 219–67, 271, 289
Noachic Covenant, 11, 141, 143–44, 151

Objective/objectivity, 174
Objectivism/objectivist, 148, 150, 151
Occasionalism, 92, 93
Old Testament Theology, 179, 192
On Theology, 20
Ontology/ontological, 87, 138, 151, 174, 193, 216, 217, 228, 246, 290

Patriarchy/patriarchal, 40, 43
Princeton Seminary, 27
Princetonian Theology, 250

Post-Christendom, 19, 215
Postconservative, 85, 86, 90, 94
Post-critical, 253
Post-exilic, 200, 201, 205
Post-industrial, 19, 112
Postliberal theology, 6, 10, 15, 17, 19, 23, 56, 80, 128, 168, 269, 274, 289
Postmodern/postmodernity, 2, 3, 15, 19, 21, 22, 26, 44, 58, 84, 86, 89, 112, 119, 130, 164, 169, 170, 171, 172, 173, 174, 176, 178, 186, 187, 190, 207, 209, 210, 212, 213, 214, 226, 238, 256, 269, 288
Postmodern Theology, 270, 275–77
Power of the Word, The, 42
Process theology, 31, 100
Professing the Faith, 285
Protestant liberalism/liberal theology/religious culture, 21, 25, 27, 56, 59
Protestant mainline/mainline, 14, 16, 20, 25, 31, 32, 34, 37, 110, 112, 117, 165, 208, 211, 212, 213, 214, 225, 226, 269, 271, 272, 289
Protestant mainline diaspora/disestablishment, 15, 16, 207, 225, 226, 252, 254, 269, 270–275
Psalms, 200
Puritan Origins of the American Self, 35
Puritans, 69, 83
  English, 135
  New England, 35, 270

Radical Monotheism and Western Culture, 14, 44, 225, 256, 258
Redemptive-historical theology, 267, 275, 283
Reformation, 3, 8, 90, 117, 124, 135, 173, 225, 228, 242, 273
Reformation tradition/tradition of the Reformers/Protestant Reformers, 3, 8, 12, 25, 84, 117, 148, 152, 192, 226, 229, 246, 265, 266, 269, 271, 273, 284, 286, 288
Reformed/Reformed Theology, 10, 58, 59, 69, 71, 222

Remaking of Evangelical Theology, The, 85, 282
Remembered Voices, 12
Restoring the Center, 53
Resurrection, 8, 50, 70, 74, 76, 95, 97, 98, 107, 136, 185, 265
Revelation of Jesus Christ, The, 158
Rites of Assent, The, 35

Sabbath, 195
Sabellian, 107
Saga, 9, 95, 96, 143
Scopes Trial, 3, 28
Scottish Enlightenment, 124
Secular City, The, 31–32, 260
Secularism, 187, 210, 243, 252, 266, 288
Sermon on the Mount, 220
Shaking of the Foundations, The, 234
"Shall the Fundamentalists Win?," 28
Slavery, 35, 243–44
Social Gospel, 27, 272
Sojourners, 31
Soul in Society, 34–35
"Strange new world within the Bible, The," 17, 22, 213, 223
Strong's Exhaustive Concordance of the Bible, 127
Structure legimation, 179–83, 179–83, 187
Suffering Servant, 37, 98 132, 183, 202
Supersessionism/supersessionist, 132, 191, 215
Systematic Theology, Vol. 1, 143

Texts Under Negotiation, 171–76
Theoalk, 2
Theology of God
  Bloesch, 99–104
  Brueggemann, 188–207
  Fackre, 138–62
  Packer, 69–73
Theology of the Old Testament, 189, 193, 200
Theology of Word and Spirit, 85
Thinking the Faith, 281, 285
Torah, 180, 186, 189, 196, 198, 200, 205, 206

Treatise on Christian Liberty, 262
Trinitarian, 28, 37, 40, 106, 108, 110, 117, 140, 213, 216, 237
Trinity, 3, 68, 73, 75, 104–11, 135, 260, 266
  economic Trinity, 108, 109, 140
  imminent Trinity, 108, 109, 139, 143
Truth and Power, 57
20th Century Theology, 44, 46

Unapologetic Theology, 53
Union Theological Seminary, 114, 247, 249
United Church of Christ, 2, 25, 26, 117, 165, 208
United Church of Christ in Bayberry, 44

United Methodist Church, 2, 25, 26

Vatican II/Second Vatican Council, 136, 160
Verisimilitude, 24
Vietnam War, 30, 33, 253

West/Western, 6, 19, 40, 48, 58, 124, 142, 173, 212, 256, 258, 276
Word of Christ and Word of Culture, 227
World War I, 173, 271
World War II/Second World War, 135, 253

Yale Seminary, 27, 114, 124

www.ingramcontent.com/pod-product-compliance
Lightning Source LLC
Chambersburg PA
CBHW050619300426
44112CB00012B/1569